4500

Cognition and Perception

Cognition and Perception

How Do Psychology and Neural Science Inform Philosophy?

Athanassios Raftopoulos

A Bradford Book
The MIT Press
Cambridge, Massachusetts
London, England

MIT Press books may be purchased at special quantity discounts for business or sales promotional use. For information, email specialsales@mitpress.mit.edu or write to Special Sales Department, MIT Press, 55 Hayward Street, Cambridge, MA 02142.

Set Stone Sans and Stone Serif by SNP Best-set Typesetter Ltd., Hong Kong. Printed and bound in the United States of America.

Library of Congress Cataloging-in-Publication Data

Raftopoulos, Athanassios.
Cognition and perception : how do psychology and neural science inform philosophy? / Athanassios Raftopoulos.
p.   cm.
Includes bibliographical references and index.
ISBN 978-0-262-01321-5 (hardcover : alk. paper)
1. Cognition. 2. Perception. 3. Philosophy. I. Title.
BF311.R25   2009
121'.34—dc22

                                                          2009000716

10 9 8 7 6 5 4 3 2 1

This book is for Ali, Thomas, and Zogia.

Contents

II Philosophy

Foreword

When I was growing up philosophically, Wittgenstein held broad and deep influence, and a part of the accepted dogma was that philosophy and science were deeply different disciplines that pursued radically different goals by even more radically different methods. This unfathomable demarcation left many of us who were interested in science, history of science, *and* philosophy deeply discomforted intellectually and outsiders socially. The discomfort and the resulting paradoxical attitudes are well illustrated by one of the first real historians *and* philosophers of science, Norwood Russell (Russ) Hanson. Consider these two notes in Hanson's 1958 book *Patterns of Discovery* (Cambridge University Press):

References to psychology should not be misunderstood; but as one's acquaintance with the psychology of perception deepens, the character of the conceptual problems one regards as significant will deepen accordingly. Cf. Wittgenstein, *Phil. Inv.* ... p. 193. 'Its causes are of interest to psychologists. We are interested in the concept and its place among the concepts of experience.' (p. 11, n. 2)

'Philosophy has no concern with fact, only with conceptual matters' (Wittgenstein, *Tractatus*, 4.11); but discussions of perception could not but be improved by the reading of these twenty papers [Hanson had listed 20 papers with references to Gestalt and other psychologists]. (p. 13, n. 2).

Hanson, at least, was a philosopher who worried about real science and its history and spent considerable time examining issues of perception and how they related to issues to evidence, causation, and scientific theorizing. The imposition of the philosophy/science dichotomy has many roots and many predecessors (e.g. romanticism), but I believe the most immediate cause of its modern analytic form was G. E. Moore and the changes in Cambridge philosophy that followed from his and Bertrand Russell's influence early in the twentieth century. The breakdown of this dichotomy is often attributed to W. V. O. Quine's "Epistemology Naturalized" (lecture delivered in 1968; published in 1969 in *Ontological Relativity and Other Essays*, Columbia University Press). But such attribution is mostly hindsight, for the dogma of difference held on for some time and indeed is still with us in many ways today.

But what has all this history to do with Athanassios Raftopoulos's book? Well, the book's subtitle is "How Do Psychology and Neural Science Inform Philosophy?" Until the last few decades, such a question would not have been acceptable. Such informing would be taken to be impossible both by those who believe that philosophy is *sui generis* and by those who believe that the only real questions are those that can be answered by science, through eliminativist reduction. Now, Raftopoulos is not the first to propose robust relations between psychology, neuroscience, and philosophy. But he does it in new and concretely novel ways. You may disagree with his interpretation of the science on which he reports, or you may disagree with how he makes connections between visual neuroscience and cognition, or you may hold out for some extra-physical sense of representational warrant, but even if you would pursue any of these options, you must confront and confute the evidence he brings to bear on the questions of noncognitive content, theory-ladenness, and realism.

Some putative counter-instances to Raftopoulos's claims could be based on anticipatory firings in the nervous system, in the retina, in the thalamus, in the hypothalamus, and in various cortical regions, with regard to expectancies and rewards regarding future events. But such data about expectancies do not vitiate Raftopoulos's claim that these, as well as low-level perception, could be noncognitive. What is in question is what mechanisms are subject to cognitive influence, not what may influence whatever anticipatory or attentional mechanisms may be operative. So it all comes down to what counts as cognition. For example, Raftopoulos claims that object individuation precedes object identification, and correlatively that object individuation is noncognitive. Now, many philosophers and psychologists have talked about object individuation in terms of object discrimination, and have held that discriminatory acts or behaviors are not cognitive in some sense. Yet the real question here is "What difference such a distinction makes?" or "What is the distinction used to support?" In this book, Raftopoulos ties these questions to a defense of realism and anti-constructivism. That is, he ties noncognitive perception to a philosophical position in which perceivers really are "directly" aware of some aspects of the world, albeit in a sense limited to spatiotemporal information about objects. Such a conception of objectivity is a most noble philosophical goal, and, given today's rampant tendencies toward relativism, it deserves a good hearing. And, Raftopoulos argues, that allowing for a noncognitive perception need not commit us to the heinous Sellarsian crime of re-introducing the myth of the given.

This is a most carefully written book. It is one of the first philosophical works to pay explicit attention to the timing of neural processes, which are being seen as more important each day in the writing of neuroscientists. Raftopoulos makes excellent use of the science at his disposal. So read the book carefully, and draw up what arguments you may. It is certain that future accounts of perception will have to deal with the positions defended herein. What more could one ask from a book?

Peter Machamer
Professor of the History and Philosophy of Science
University of Pittsburgh

Preface

The theory regarding the issue of the cognitive penetrability of perception and its philosophical ramifications presented in this book has been gradually evolving over about nine years. Being a member of the Fuzzy Guys Club (a term that Peter Achinstein, my professor at The Johns Hopkins University, reserved for those among us who subscribed to Hanson's, Kuhn's, and Feyerabend's view that perception is theory-laden), and also being very much impressed by Paul Churchland's arguments to the same effect based on neuroscientific findings, I decided to use my strong background in psychology and show once and for all that Churchland is right. Recent neuroscientific findings prove beyond any reasonable doubt that higher cognitive centers in the brain send information in a top-down manner, through reentrant neuronal connections, to the lower or more peripheral levels of the brain and, hence, modulate perceptual processing. Since these cognitive centers are the loci of our theories and conceptual frameworks, perception is theory-laden and/or cognitively penetrable. My conviction that Churchland's views will triumph was further reinforced by the fact that the theory of Churchland's main rival, namely Jerry Fodor's modularity theory of perception, seemed to be contradicted to some extent by empirical findings about, say, perceptual learning and the relative plasticity of the brain. All the scientific evidence pointed to the likelihood that Fodorian modules exist only in Fodor's mind and certainly not in the brain.

I spent three full years studying the relevant psychological and neuroscientific evidence with a view both to establishing the truth of Churchland's views and to shedding further light on the mechanisms that allow the cognitive penetration of perception. To my dismay, I discovered that I was very wrong. Although Churchland was right that what we see (that is, the final product of vision) depends on our conceptual frameworks, there is a substantial part of visual processing that is cognitively impenetrable. So I decided to change camps. If there is a part of vision that is cognitively impenetrable, I have to tell the world (or, rather, the philosophers) about it. Of course, I had not discovered the wheel; many psychologists, most notably Zenon Pylyshyn, have been arguing all along for the same thing, to wit that there is a cognitively impenetrable part of visual processing (Pylyshyn has called it "early vision").

Fortunately for my publishing plans, Pylyshyn had demolished the thesis of the continuity of perception and cognition, another term for the cognitive penetrability of perception, on psychological and methodological grounds. In my mind I had undermined the continuity of perception and cognition on neuroscientific grounds, and more specifically using evidence based on brain scanning techniques. This is not to say, of course, that no researchers had used such techniques from various research perspectives to raise the point that what we perceive does not depend on our conceptual frameworks. But philosophers are supposed to put all things together, and I hoped (and still hope) that I had synthesized the vast amount of evidence under the same roof. Furthermore, Pylyshyn and the other similarly minded psychologists and neuroscientists did not use their findings to attack or discuss philosophical problems. This is where philosophers are supposed to step in, and so I decided to do just that. I thought that traditional philosophical issues, including problems related to nonconceptual and phenomenal content, reference, and realism, could benefit from the views that I had formed while examining the issue of the cognitive penetrability of perception.

The first products of my research were two papers on the theory-ladenness of perception and on the Churchland-Fodor debate that were published in the journals *Cognitive Science* and *Philosophy of Science* in 2001. A short version of the second paper was presented by the chairperson of the relevant session, for I was not able to attend the conference, at the biannual conference of the Philosophy of Science Association in Vancouver in November 2000. I was informed by the reader that all the big names were present when my paper was read, and that a lively discussion followed the presentation of the paper. William Bechtel, one of the attendants, commented that the important term in unraveling the mysteries of the interface between perception and cognition was 'attention'. I took him very seriously and spent two more years trying to understand the role of attention in mediating the interaction between perception and cognition. The results include, in addition to this book, a book that I edited in 2005 (*Cognitive Penetrability of Perception: Attention, Action, Planning, and Bottom-Up Constraints*), a series of publications in various conference proceedings, and papers published in *Behavioral and Brain Science* in 2004 and in *Philosophical Psychology, Mind and Language,* and *Philosophy and Phenomenological Research* in 2006. I collaborated on the last two papers with my good friend and old colleague Vincent Muller, whose knowledge of the philosophy of language proved invaluable.

Although the present book relies on the ideas developed in the aforementioned publications, it goes much beyond them both with respect to the empirical evidence adduced and discussed and with respect to the ideas elaborated, the theses expounded, and the issues examined. There are, in addition, some modifications of earlier arguments—a good thing, because, notwithstanding their validity, they were based on wrong premises.

It is time now to acknowledge the contribution of all those who helped me see this book through. First, I would like to thank the Department of Psychology, the School of Social Sciences and Sciences of Education, and the Rector's Council of the University of Cyprus for granting me a sabbatical for the spring semester of 2005–06, which I desperately needed to finish the manuscript. At the same time, I was honored by the Center for Philosophy of Science at the University of Pittsburgh to be elected as a visiting fellow. That gave me the opportunity to spend the spring semester ('spring' being a euphemism for the bitter cold weather in Pittsburgh during that time) at the Center. I do not exaggerate when I say that I cannot think of a better and more stimulating academic environment for philosophers of science than that provided by the Center. Therefore, I wish to express my gratitude to the members of the committee who elected me as a Fellow; to the Chairperson of the Center, Professor John Norton, for being largely responsible for the excellent academic environment that prevailed at the Center; and to all the staff there, especially Karen, for making me feel comfortable and welcome. Special thanks to the other fellows during the spring semester of 2005–06, who, with their helpful comments during our weekly meetings, helped me to better my ideas on various topics and made very helpful suggestions regarding some of my papers: Gabriele de Anna, Carla Fehr, Malcolm Forster, Lilly Gurova, Nikolay Milkov, and Wang Wei.

Special mention should be made of Professor Peter Machamer, who spent many hours with me discussing the first draft of the book and helping me to improve it. I would also like to thank Peter for giving me the opportunity to present some of the topics of the book in his graduate seminar in the Department of Philosophy and History of Science at the University of Pittsburgh, and, most important, for his constant and enthusiastic support during the five years I have known him.

I would also like to thank Vincent Muller for collaborating with me on two papers, and the audiences at the various conferences at which I presented papers. Marios Avramides, a colleague in the Department of Psychology at the University of Cyprus who specializes in visual attention and spatial representations, read drafts of the first and second chapters of this book. His enthusiastic reaction was a great motive for me to continue writing the book, and so special thanks are due to him.

Finally, I would like to thank the publishers and editors of the journals in which I published the papers parts of which are included in this book for allowing me to reproduce material. The original publications are listed here.

A. Raftopoulos, "Is perception informationally encapsulated? The issue of the theory-ladenness of perception," *Cognitive Science* 25 (2001): 423–451, published by the Cognitive Science Society

A. Raftopoulos, "Reentrant pathways and the theory-ladenness of observation," *Philosophy of Science* 68 (2001): 187–200, published by the University of Chicago Press.

A. Raftopoulos, "Two types of object representations in the brain, one nondescriptive process of reference fixing," *Behavioral and Brain Science* 27 (2004), no. 1: 47–48, published by the Cambridge University Press

A. Raftopoulos, "Defending realism on the proper ground," *Philosophical Psychology* 19 (2006), no. 1: 1–31, published by Routledge

A. Raftopoulos and V. Muller, "The nonconceptual content of experience," *Mind and Language* 27 (2006), no. 2: 187–219, published by Blackwell

A. Raftopoulos and V. Muller, "Nonconceptual Reference Fixing," *Philosophical and Phenomenological Research* 72 (2006), no. 2: 251–285, published by the International Phenomenological Society

A. Raftopoulos, "Perceptual Systems and Realism," *Synthese* 164 (2008), no. 1: 61–91, published by Springer

None of these things would have mattered had I not had permission from my wife Ali and my cats Thomas and Zogia to be away from home for so long during my sabbatical and to be traveling around the world presenting my work, and their continuous support. This book is for them, with my everlasting gratitude.

Introduction

In this book, I discuss the issue of the cognitive penetrability of perception and claim that there is a part of visual processes that results in representational states with nonconceptual content—that is, a part that retrieves information from visual scenes in conceptually unmediated and thus theory-neutral ways. Using the thesis that there exists a conceptually unmediated or cognitively impenetrable part of vision, I first address problems in the philosophy of science, in the philosophy of mind, and in epistemology related to the theory-ladenness or cognitive penetrability of perception. Second, I examine how we access the external world through our perception and what we can know of this world.

Philosophical discussions of realism note that the intervention of perception in our dealings with the world poses a serious problem for our accounts of the world, because perception is deemed to be influenced by our theoretical standings and our cognitive stances. Thus, what we perceive is a blend of what is out there and what we think, believe, and so on. Perception is theory-laden, and thus there is no nonconceptual content in experience on the basis of which one could mount a search for what is really out there and exists independently of our minds. If one holds the above position, then there are two options: either one has to abandon any form of realism, or to salvage realism one has to argue that despite the conceptual character of our experiential content the world is the content of our perceptual states and thus we access it directly. I think the second choice is untenable and deeply problematic: perceptual states are representational states, and thus their content cannot be worldly states of affairs themselves but must consist of representations or presentations of the way worldly states of affairs are. Thus, if no part of this content can be nonconceptual, any attempt to vindicate not only scientific realism but also common-sense realism is hopeless.

The "New Look" theory of psychology (see Gregory 1974 for an overview) in combination with the Gestalt theories of organization of perception left a profound impact on the philosophy of science, mostly through the works of Hanson (1958), Kuhn (1962), and Feyerabend (1962). The older thesis that no observational data are uninterpreted theory-neutral descriptions of events and that every description is made within the framework of a theory (Duhem 1914) was pushed to its full epistemological and ontological consequences. Not only are observational reports embedded in a theory; what we see is already an interpretation of the incoming information based on the theoretical commitments of the perceiver. This being the case, if one does not fear to see the argument through, what sense does it make to talk of a rational choice among theories based on experimental outcome? If what one sees depends on what one believes, and therefore people with different commitments see different worlds, and if there is no neutral basis on which matters of meaning could be resolved, how could people with different commitments communicate? Furthermore, in what sense could one talk of their seeing in different ways the same world?

The undermining of the possibility of theory-neutral perception has led to the abolition of the distinction between *seeing* and *seeing as* (Brown 1987; Churchland 1988; Feyerabend 1962; Hanson 1958; Kuhn 1962), clearing the way for the relativistic theories of science and meaning, since what one sees depends on one's expectations, beliefs, and so forth. Hence, the existence of a theory-neutral basis, on which a rational choice among alternative theories could be based, is rejected, and scientific theories become incommensurable. There can be no communication between scientists who belong to different scientific paradigms, because there is not a theory-neutral perceptual basis that could resolve matters of meaning. Instead, perceptions become parts of a paradigm, modulated by its theoretical commitments, and proponents of different paradigms perceive different worlds. Perception becomes theory-laden. Finally, borrowing the argument from Quine's (1960) discussion of the radical indeterminacy of translation, and borrowing Quine's conclusion that there is not, as a matter of fact, a content that is being translated differently, one can argue that there is no world that is being perceived differently by perceivers with different theoretical commitments. The aforementioned views led to the birth of constructivism in philosophy and to the movement called *conceptual relativism*. Constructivism denies the realist's claims that scientific theories relate mind-independent objects and us. Kitcher (2001) defines two types of constructivism. *Epistemological constructivism* argues that our experience of the world is mediated by concepts, and that there is no direct way to examine which aspects of objects belong to them independently of our conceptualizations. Perception is cognitively penetrable and theory-laden. There is no Archimedean metaphysical point from which one could compare our representations of objects and the mind-independent objects we represent and then identify in what respects and to what extent those objects are as we represent them to be. In other words, we cannot ascertain whether the properties we perceive the objects as having are really properties of the objects in the world. *Semantic constructivism* attacks realism on the ground that there is no direct way to set up the relation between terms and the entities to which they purportedly refer. That relation can only be indirect mediated through the causal relations between these entities and our behavior; it can only be interest-dependent. Since these relations ground terms in the entities to which they refer by fixing their referents, reference becomes theory-dependent.

Constructivism (or Relativism, as it is also known) clearly constituted a coup against the constitutional order for the majority of philosophers of science, who saw the very foundation of their most trusted beliefs crumbling. Being philosophers of science and not epistemologists or metaphysicians, they perceived as the most threatening thesis of the new dogma the claim that all those who live within one paradigm cannot really communicate with those who live in another—that is, the thesis of incommensurability of scientific theories. Accordingly, their efforts were concerted on rebutting this most dreadful consequence of conceptual relativism. I think it is fair to say that these attempts have been mostly successful. Almost no one thinks anymore that there are no communication channels between differing paradigms. The roots of constructivism, however, were left untouched until Fodor (1983) challenged the theory of perception underlying the "New Look" psychological theories. His claim that perception is effected through cognitively impenetrable modules was meant to satisfy Fodor's thirst for restoring order at the level at which it mattered most: that of the status of perception. Fodor saw that the only way to deal effectively with constructivism was to undermine its main tenet, to wit, the theory-ladenness of perception.

Churchland (1988) picked up the glove thrown by Fodor and defended the cognitive penetrability of perception at the level at which Fodor sought to attack it. He defended it by adducing arguments drawn from such diverse areas as cognitive neuroscience, connectionism, and vision. Churchland's strongest points proved to be (a) the claim that the existence of abundant top-down neural pathways from higher cognitive centers to the circuits of low-level vision could be explained only if one assumed that these pathways allowed top-down transfer of information from cognitive areas in the brain to perceptual processing sites and (b) the claim that the indisputable perceptual plasticity of the brain in general, and of the areas devoted to perceptual processing in particular, proves that perception is not effected by Fodorian modules.

Forty years or so after Hanson's and Kuhn's work, not many philosophers of science take the incommensurability theory seriously; most feel that the history of sciences proves that communication across paradigms is possible. Thus, it may seem that there is not much of a point in trying to prove that communication across paradigms is possible. However, to *feel* that Kuhn and Hanson were wrong because scientific practice does not work the way they suggested is one thing. To *show* that Kuhn and Hanson were wrong, one must undermine the "New Look" theory of vision on which their work was based. To do that, one needs a theory of perception, and that is the first aim of this book.

Before I proceed, I should discuss some terminological issues, lest my account be distorted by attaching unattended meanings to the terms I employ. I use the expressions "cognitive penetrability of perception," "theory-ladenness of perception," "conceptual effects on perception," and "top-down effects on perception" roughly interchangeably, the differences being more in emphasis than in substance. Since these terms are not necessarily coextensive, I have to justify my use.

I take "cognitive penetrability of perception" and "conceptual effects on perception" to be synonymous, provided that one takes cognitive penetrability to signify the effects of cognition on the contents of perception and not only on the vehicles of perceptual states (the sub-personal mechanisms and processes that constitute perception). In other words, one is interested not only in whether the perceptual neural pathways receive signals from higher cognitive circuits, but also in whether perceptual content is modulated by cognitive states. Given this, if cognition informs perception, the cognitive states bear on perception, and thus conceptual frameworks influence perception. This is evidenced by the fact that in the literature the thesis of the cognitive penetrability of perception has given rise to the widespread thesis that perception presupposes the application of sortal concepts (Brewer 1999; McDowell 1994).

However, "cognitive penetrability of perception" and "top-down effects on perception" are not coextensive. The reason is that there are top-down and horizontal interactions *within* the various visual modules (Felleman et al. 1997; Lamme and Spekreijse 2000). Thus, top-down flow of information is compatible with a cognitively impenetrable perception. (This is one of the main theses advanced in the present book; being within the visual modules, these channels of information flow do not threaten the cognitive encapsulation of early vision.) Thus, "top-down effects on perception" is not synonymous with "cognitive penetrability of perception." However, in the literature, and most notably in the work of Churchland (one of the most prominent epistemological constructivists), the term "top-down effects on perception" has been used to signify the top-down modulation of perception by cognition. To be consistent with the existing terminology, I take "top-down effects on perception" to mean "cognitive top-down effects on perception" and thus "cognitive penetrability of perception."

Things are a bit more complicated with the expressions "cognitive penetrability of perception" and "theory-ladenness of perception." Though in the literature they are almost unequivocally taken to be synonymous, this is not a trivial thesis. On some occasions, the former term is used to express the effects of cognitive mechanisms and processes on the mechanisms and processes of perception, in which case one is situated at the level of the vehicles of perceptual states, whereas the latter is taken to apply to the contents of perceptual states. However, I am not so much interested in whether the perceptual neural pathways receive signals from higher cognitive circuits as in whether perceptual content is modulated by the content of cognitive states. Thus, "cognitive penetrability of perception" signifies the effects of cognitive states on the content of perceptual states. (This way, one secures oneself from the trap of the usual vehicle-content confusion.) I have also explained why "cognitive penetrability of perception" and "conceptual effects on perception" are treated here as coextensive. Now, conceptual frameworks constitute theories (in a broad sense of the term, not necessarily in a strict scientific sense); thus, "cognitive penetrability of perception," by implicating the conceptual apparatus in perceptual modulation, also signifies "theory-ladenness of perception."

The book consists of two parts, the first "scientific" and the second "philosophical." Part I comprises chapters 1–3; part II comprises chapters 4–8. In the first part, I defend the thesis that there is a part of experience, which I call "perception," that is not theory-laden and whose content is nonconceptual and thus theory-neutral. To show that there is a theory-neutral part of experience, I take recourse to cognitive science. In chapter 1, I discuss the current theories of attention and visual processing and argue that visual processing consists of two phases, one pre-attentional and the other attentional. In the pre-attentional early visual phase, information is retrieved bottom-up (that is, without any cognitive modulation) from a visual scene and is bound up to a certain extent to form the proto-objects, which roughly correspond to structural descriptions of the objects in the scene. At this level there is only a form of awareness that is called *phenomenal awareness*. Attention intervenes later, and characteristics of objects are bound further and behaviorally relevant objects are selected for further processing. The objects that are selected eventually become the contents of our ordinary experience. We have cognitive access to these contents, and thus we have report awareness or access awareness of them.

In chapter 2, I examine the time course of visual processing and attention to delineate the issue of the time course of attentional effects. I argue that object-based attention intervenes relatively late, after the proto-objects have been retrieved from the scene. Thus, the fact that object-based attention may be cognitively driven does not undermine the claim that early visual processing is retrieved from the scene in a cognitively unmediated way. However, spatial attention is a different matter. Its effects are registered at latencies of 70 milliseconds after stimulus onset, which places them well within the time window of early visual processing. Spatial attention is controlled by a mixture of bottom-up and top-down cognitive mechanisms, and therefore this is *prima facie* evidence for the cognitive penetrability of early visual processing. Against that, I argue that the experimental evidence suggests that, although cognitive states may determine where to focus spatial attention, they do not modulate perceptual processing of the incoming information from the focused location; such processing is stimulus driven. In other words, cognition determines where to look but not what one perceives at that location. This is an indirect form of cognitive influence on perception; its repercussions for philosophy will be fully explored in the second part of the book.

In chapter 3, which closes the book's first part, I concentrate on the visual processes that parse objects in a scene and discuss the kind of information that these processes use and deliver. After drawing a distinction between object individuation and indexing (on the one hand) and object identification (on the other), I claim that object individuation precedes object identification, and that object individuation (unlike object identification) is a cognitively encapsulated process. To support this claim, I discuss the kind of information on which object individuation relies and argue that this information is the information retrieved in early visual processing—i.e., information that is retrieved in a purely bottom-up way from a visual scene. The processes of object individuation and indexing are very important for the project in the book, since it is on the basis of these processes that I will develop (in chapter 6) a purely causal theory of reference.

Between the two parts, I recapitulate the main findings regarding visual processing in the first part; I also address some methodological concerns regarding the exegetical reliability of the findings of various brain-scanning techniques, such as PET and ERP, in shedding light on the cognitive mechanisms that underlie the function of the brain/mind.

In chapter 4 (the first chapter in part II), I use the theory of perceptual processing expounded in part I to present a new way of looking at the famed nonconceptual content of experience. The findings presented in part I, particularly the conclusion drawn there that perception's product is not influenced by any top-down cognitive effects, make plausible the existence of nonconceptual content as the content of perceptual states that are representations (i.e., that have representational content). Having argued that nonconceptual content is plausible, I examine the nature of the nonconceptual content, relying mainly on the cognitive sciences and on some limited philosophical analysis. I claim that this content consists in the content of states of which one has no awareness whatsoever—Bermudez (1995) characterizes this as content of the sub-personal information-processing computational states)—and in the content of states of which we have phenomenal awareness in the sense defined in chapter 2. The latter is the phenomenal content of experience. I fully develop the kinds of contents that belong to nonconceptual content and are philosophically interesting. Finally, I show that the nonconceptual content, as determined by the theory of visual processing developed in part I of the book, satisfies most of the constraints imposed on nonconceptual content by philosophers and is representational.

Chapter 5, deals almost exclusively with the notion of phenomenal content. In the first section of this chapter, I specify the phenomenal content by examining the output of the bottom-up processes that make up perception. I discuss the representational nature of phenomenal content. I also relate the present construal of phenomenal content to other accounts of phenomenal (or nonconceptual in general) content, addressing some problems besetting these accounts. In the second section, I answer the criticism against nonconceptual content in general that introducing non-conceptual content revives the "Myth of the Given" (where "the Given" is construed as the unstructured raw sensation or impression, which is the purely sensory result of the world's causal impact on our senses).

In chapter 6, I employ the notion of object individuation and index-ing and develop the theory of perceptual demonstratives of Garcia-Carpintero's (2000) and Pylyshyn's (1994, 2001) notion of object indexing to argue that through acts of demonstration we open "object-files" that individuate and index some of the objects in a scene. The content of these files is information retrieved from the scene in conceptually unmediated ways. The nonconceptual information, however, does not allow the identification or recognition of an object as satisfying a certain description, only its individuation as a discrete persistent object with certain spatiotemporal and other featural properties. In other words, I claim that the reference of perceptual demonstratives is fixed in a purely causal way, and I try to defend the causal account of reference fixing presented in the book against some attacks in the literature.

In chapter 7, I deal with the Fodor-Churchland debate about the theory-ladenness of perception, which regenerated interest in the cognitive penetrability of perception. I examine the arguments in light of the discussion regarding visual processing in the first part, and argue that Churchland is wrong to think that perception is theory-laden and, also, that a kind of semi-Fodorian module can be defended. I also propose a theory purporting to examine, from a representationalist nonconceptual vantage point, the thorny issue of ambiguous or bi-stable figures.

Finally, in chapter 8, I discuss the repercussions of my thesis with respect to problems pertaining to the philosophy of science, more specifically with respect to problems related to the theory-ladenness of perception, and realism. The problem with respect to realism is that if perception is theory-laden then it is not clear in what sense one could talk of seeing and knowing an independently existing world. My claim is that there is a minimal form of realism that is defensible. This minimal realism holds that objects, their spatiotemporal properties, and some of their observable features, all of which can be retrieved directly from a visual scene, are real—that is, mind-independent—entities and properties in the world.

Cognition and Perception

I Visual Processing and Attention

1 The Role of Attention in Visual Processing

As I stated in the introduction, this book aims to examine whether non-conceptual content is possible given our perceptual makeup, to delineate the nature of nonconceptual content, should such a content exist, and to propose a causal theory of reference based on the nonconceptual content of our perceptual states. The success of the endeavor depends on whether we are equipped with perceptual mechanisms that allow the retrieval of information from the environment in a purely bottom-up way (that is, in a way that is immune to top-down conceptual interference) and on whether the information thus retrieved is epistemologically interesting (that is, whether it can be used to promote epistemological issues). Should our conceptual framework intervene at all stages of perception, the contents of perceptual states would be irrevocably conceptually contaminated and any further discussion about whether perceptual content is conceptual or nonconceptual would be moot. Attention and its mechanisms are important in such a discussion. There seems to be ample evidence that spatial attention modulates perceptual processing from its very early stages, and since attention can be cognitively driven (endogenous attention) a strong argument could be made that, through attentional effects on perception, cognition and thus our conceptual schemes modulate all perceptual processing, or at least the part that delivers states with epistemologically interesting content.

In the present chapter, I discuss attention and its role in visual processing. The aims of the discussion are (1) to draw a picture of visual processing and of its stages and (2) to delineate the role of attention (and cognition) in perceptual processing. Since I do not intend to keep the reader in suspense, I will reveal the outcome of the investigation on attention and perception here: There is a part of visual processing—which I will call perception, and which corresponds, to a certain extent, to Pylyshyn's (2003, 2007) early vision—that is cognitively encapsulated and thus retrieves information from visual scenes in a purely bottom-up manner. The qualification is needed because perception the way I construe it is a part of early vision, the other part being sensation. The difference between perception and sensation, we shall see, lies in the kind of information that is processed.

In section 1.1, I discuss various models of attention with a view to shedding light on the way it functions and on its role in visual processing. In section 1.2, I address the matter of the representations involved in visual processing and whether and to what extent they are stored in memory, allowing us to have a coherent view of the world across visual scenes. In section 1.3, I bring forth the issue of the top-down constraints in visual processing, as they are mediated by attention. I analyze these constraints and discuss the predominant role of spatial attention in realizing these constraints

1.1   Attention

Attention is a selection process in which some inputs are processed faster, better, or deeper than some other inputs, so that they have a better chance of producing or influencing a behavioral response, although a bodily response is not necessary; attention limits processing to items that are behaviorally relevant. Attentional mechanisms are needed because a typical visual scene contains more information than the visual system can process at any given time; in other words, the visual system can select only one or a few objects for more thorough processing, as cases of inattentional blindness that I discuss later reveal. Since the visual system does not have the capacity to process simultaneously all inputs in the retina, attention intervenes to select some inputs and to filter some others; attention favors the processing of some inputs by enhancing the responses of neurons that represent the behaviorally relevant stimuli and thereby biasing the competitive interactions among the stimuli.

Attention induces increased (Desimone and Duncan 1995) and synchronous (Fries et al. 2001) neuronal activity of the neurons processing the attended stimuli. The increased neural activity suffices to explain why the associated stimuli are processed faster and deeper. Attention may enhance the output of the salient feature detectors by lowering firing thresholds (Egeth et al. 1984; Kahneman et al. 1992). It can also increase the activity of neuronal systems that process the salient type of information (Ungerleider and Haxby 1994). Spatial attention, more specifically, results in accurate detection and discrimination of stimuli at the attended location

(LaBerge 1995); it does so by increasing the magnitude of stimulus-evoked neural activity for stimuli at the attended location. In other words, it acts like a gain-control mechanism that most likely serves to improve the signal-to-noise ratio of inputs at the attended location so that more relevant information for the task at hand can be extracted from them (Hillyard et al. 1998). The effect of attending to some stimuli on the firing rates of cells in the visual cortex is widely accepted as the neural correlate of attention (Desimone and Duncan 1995).

Stimuli can be behaviorally relevant in two senses: either they are located at behaviorally relevant locations, or they involve objects or have features that are relevant to current behavior. In either case, attention reflects a top-down expectation. The subject actively searches either for a specified feature or object, or for a specified location, depending on which information is available to the subject—that is, depending on whether the subject has information about some feature or object or about the location of the behaviorally relevant feature or object that she seeks. As will become evident below, another function of attention is to solve the binding problem and provide a coherent object representation.

Attentional selection is historically related to "spotlight of attention" models, according to which attention serves to limit processing to a single location in the visual field (Desimone 1999). When one searches for a behaviorally relevant object in a scene, one is essentially engaged in a serial process during which one shifts the spotlight of attention from one object in a scene to the next until the target object is found. Attention serves to enhance neuronal responses to a stimulus at that specific spatial location in the visual field. This response is observed at the extrastriate cortex, and there is also evidence that it is found in striate cortex. According to these models of attention, all visual attention is inherently spatial; objects are selected by attention being directed to their spatial locations (Posner 1980; Treisman 1988). Even objects defined by features (shape, color, etc.) must be found by examining the objects in a scene by this spotlight that serially scans locations.

As an example of an inherently spatial model of attention, consider Treisman's (1993) Feature Integration Theory (FIT), which posits that objects are retrieved from scenes by means of selective spatial attention that picks out objects' features, forms feature maps, and integrates those features that are found at the same location into forming objects. Treisman's theory presupposes the spotlight model of attention, according to which attention acts serially to conjoin elements of a scene on the basis of their common location; the elements themselves are searched in parallel. FIT belongs to the family of theories that hold that when one attends to an object one automatically encodes all of its features in visual working memory and has them available for further processing (Duncan and Nimmo-Smith 1996; O'Craven, Downing, and Kanwisher 1999).

However, Jonides (1980, 1983) proposed, on the basis of experiments using spatial cues, that attention might function in two distinct modes: a focal mode and a spread mode. The former, used when spatial information about a target is available, involves a serial search of locations in the visual field; thus selection operates in the space dimension. The latter can spread in parallel over the visual field and focuses on features of objects rather than on spatial locations.

In general, research on visual selective attention suggests two theoretical accounts for selection (Vecera 2000). The attention that focuses on the spatial dimension is known as "spatial-attention" or "space-based attention"; stimuli are selected on the basis of spatial location by a spotlight, a zoom lens, or a spatial gradient, depending on the specific theory. The function of spatial attention is evidenced by experiments showing that targets appearing at cued locations are processed more efficiently than targets appearing at uncued locations. The attention that focuses on features of objects or objects is known as "object-centered" or "object-based" attention.[1] In this case, stimuli are not selected for their location but either on the basis of some feature or as whole organized objects or shapes. Vecera and Farah (1994) and Egeth and Yantis (1997) argue that either attentional mode can be obtained, depending on the characteristics of the task at hand.

Posner and Rothbart (1992) and Posner and Raichle (1994) also argue for the existence of two separate attentional circuits. The first is a posterior attention network responsible for orienting attention. It involves the parietal lobe (for releasing attention from its current focus), the midbrain (for moving attention from its current location to the new location of a cue), and the thalamus (for selecting and enhancing the contents of the attended area). The second is an anterior attention network (the executive attention network) that mediates awareness of attended objects. The latter circuit intervenes once attention has shifted to a certain location by means of the former and the visual contents there have been transmitted forward in the visual areas of the brain. It activates the anterior cingulate gyrus in conjunction with other frontal areas, such as lateral areas of the upper prefrontal cortex (Posner and Raichle 1994). It is plausible that the distinction between the posterior network for orienting attention and the anterior network that mediates awareness of objects can be mapped onto the distinction between the dorsal and the ventral pathways of the visual processing system. Interesting as this mapping may be, I will not pursue it further here. Alternatively, it may be that the former circuit may be responsible for spatial attention, whereas the latter is responsible for object-centered attention.

An alternative to Treisman's serial space-based spotlight theory of attention is Duncan and Humphreys's (1989, 1992) Attentional Engagement Theory (AET), according to which there is an initial pre-attentive parallel phase of perceptual segmentation and analysis that encompasses all of the visual items present in a scene. At this phase, descriptions of the objects in a visual scene are generated at a number of scales, and grouping principles organize the visual input into structural units; the outcome of this parallel phase is a multiple-spatial-scale structured representation. Selective attention intervenes after this stage to select information that will be entered into visual short-term memory. This is a serial stage that allows conscious processing of the items in the visual field. The task's requirements may be translated to a target template—an object that one expects, as a result of a preceding cue, to appear somewhere in one's visual field among other distractor objects, for instance. The visual input is matched to the internal stored templates; thus, visual items that match the task's requirements are most likely to be selected for visual short-term memory (see also Hollingworth and Henderson 2002, 2004). The target template exercises a top-down influence in visual processing, in that it activates a neuronal assembly in memory which sends top-down signals to the visual cortex that enhance the activation of the neuronal assembly that represents the target object. Duncan and Humphreys's theory posits both a parallel stage (in which items in the visual field—both the target object and distractors—activate neuronal assemblies in the brain) and a competition stage (in which these items compete until only one object is selected). AET, unlike FIT, does not require an attentional spotlight serially searching locations in the visual field and binding into objects features that are located at the same location. Furthermore, the selection need not rely exclusively on spatial information but may rely on featural information.

Humphreys (1999) elaborates further on the way objects are represented in space. He proposes the existence of two forms of spatial representations of objects, by which he means representations of objects in space: within-objects representations, in which elements are coded as parts of objects, and between-objects representations, in which elements are coded as distinct independent objects. Both kinds of representation are realized in parallel in the visual system. The former are mainly used for object recognition, and thus are formed in the ventral system; the latter are used for navigation in the environment and action, and thus are formed in the dorsal system. Dorsal processing areas and the representations they sub-serve are recruited by the visual system when attention focuses from one part of an object to another, or when the spatial relations between parts are important for the identification of the object. Against Treisman's Feature Integration Theory, which posits spatial attention as a necessary condition for detection of objects, Humphreys argues that visual elements are encoded and bound together in an initial parallel phase without focal attention, and that attention serves to select among the objects that result from this initial grouping.

The coding of space devoid of objects is extremely limited, if it exists at all. The memory of locations across fixations depends on coding the relative positions of objects. Although forms of grouping depend on the proximity of the elements and although distance effects modulate selec-tion of objects, which seems to suggest that elements are represented in terms of their position in space, Humphreys (1999) argues that the coding of distance itself is modulated by grouping between stimuli and adduces evidence that representations of space itself involve the relations between objects and are modulated by grouping between parts.

An initial parallel bottom-up phase during which all input is processed in parallel without an attentional bottleneck is also posited in "biased-competition account of visual processing" (Desimone and Duncan 1995; Reynolds and Desimone 2001). In this account, attention acts to bias the competition between neuronal populations that encode environmental stimuli. All the stimuli in a visual scene are initially processed in parallel and activate neuronal assemblies that represent them. These assemblies eventually engage in competitive interactions, either because they project onto cells in topographically organized cortical areas in which neurons have restricted receptive fields and thus cannot process all stimuli or because some behaviorally relevant feature or object must be selected among all present stimuli. Thus, in the biased-competition model of atten-tion, multiple representations of objects (or, as we shall later see, proto-objects) are active and compete to be selected to drive a motor output (pressing a button, reaching to grasp an object, or some other motor behavior).

There are two sources of attentional control in visual searches. First, there are bottom-up influences on processing that arise from environmental stimuli; the scene in the visual field, which constitutes the visual input, provides the bottom-up information that will be searched through and which indicates the locations of objects and the kinds of features present in each location. Second, there are top-down influences that derive from the current behavioral goals of the perceiver, as they are determined by an experimenters' instructions, by goal-oriented plans, and/or by contextual constraints. The sources of the top-down effects lie in the inferotemporal (IT) cortex. Attending to a stimulus at a particular behaviorally relevant location or with a particular behaviorally relevant feature biases the competition in favor of neurons that respond or (equivalently) are tuned to the location or the feature of the attended stimulus. As a result, the activation of the cells that represent the behaviorally relevant stimuli are enhanced, and these cells win the competition for further processing, suppressing at the same time cells representing distracting stimuli. These stimuli are thus attended. Shipp (2004, p. 227) synopsizes the essence of the bias-competition models as follows: "Activity within feature maps depends on a combination of visual input and the top-down bias signal, and the feature maps' output signals are pooled within a topographic, modality-free element labeled 'posterior parietal' (PP). The latter acts something like a salience map." The salience map is a source of top-down bias on visual search.

The biased-competition model has been expanded to include object-based attention (Desimone 1999; Vecera 2000). According to Desimone (1999, p. 13), the class of theories that view attention as the result of a biased competition among neuronal assemblies suggests that any enhancement of neuronal responses in the extrastriate cortex due to attention is better understood "in the context of competitive interactions among neurons representing all of the stimuli present in the visual field." Desimone continues: "These interactions can be biased in favor of behaviorally relevant stimuli as a result of many different processes, both spatial and nonspatial and both bottom-up and top-down" (ibid., p. 13). Top-down influences are derived mostly from working memory. As a result of the biased interaction, behaviorally irrelevant stimuli are suppressed. In this framework, attentional selection is better understood not so much as the enhancement of neuronal responses but more as the modulation of the competitive interaction of the stimuli in the visual field, and attention is better viewed as a dynamic property of the system than as a separate mechanism.

Notice that the biases that feed back to extrastriate cortex (where attentional effects are mostly observed) form higher neuronal assemblies in the brain (working memory circuits in the prefrontal cortex, for instance) are not limited to the cells with receptive fields at a single locus in the visual field; that is, the bias is not necessarily spatial. The processing can be biased by object features (color, shape, etc.), in which case searching for such an object does not require serial scanning of locations, as it does in space-based models of attention in the focal mode. In fact, all stimuli present in a scene are initially processed in parallel. This leaves open the issue of search for conjunctive features, for which it was thought that serial searching of the scene was required. The binding of some features (e.g., the color and shape of an object) seems to require attention, whereas feature combinations (such as shape and location) and other feature conjunctions that lead to segregations are detected pre-attentively (Lamme 2003; Roelfsema 2005). When attention is needed, it is commonly thought that the search for such a conjunction is serial, as in the case of color and shape (Treisman 1988, 1993).

More specifically, there is quite an extensive body of evidence suggesting that searching for particular conjunctions of features does not produce steeply sloped response-time functions by set size (McLeod et al. 1988; Nakayama and Silverman 1986). In searching for the conjunction of form and motion (McLeod et al. 1988), for instance, the search seems to be effectuated in parallel. Eckstein (1998) and Palmer et al. (2000) argue that even when the evidence shows steep slopes in response times, the underlying mechanism may not be a serial search but a parallel search and the plot of response times with respect to set size can be predicted by probabilistic models based on signal-to-noise ratios. In view of the accumulated evidence that undermines the classical view of two different search modes, one serial and the other parallel, it is suggested that the different ranges of response times by set size slopes emerge from a single process, probably parallel in nature, the outcome of which is determined by the relative salience of the target and the distractors (Duncan and Humphreys 1989; Eckstein 1998; Mounts and Tomaselli 2005; Palmer et al. 2000; Spivey 2007; Wolfe 1998).

Suppose that a cue (say, a certain feature) is presented to a subject who, after a delay, is asked to perform a task involving the selection of an object (the target object) with that cued feature among other objects that do not have the specific feature (distractors). After the cue has been presented, the neuronal assemblies in the prefrontal cortex that represent that cue are activated and remain activated for the duration of the task. The description of the target provided by the demands of the task creates a "template" (Duncan and Humphreys 1989) that is stored in visual working memory for the duration of the task (otherwise put, the subject keeps the cue in her working memory to use it in the selection process). The activation of this assembly is fed back to the extrastriate inferior temporal cortex, thereby activating only the neurons that respond to the cued feature. Thus, the features of the cue are temporarily stored in working memory, even when the stimulus has been withdrawn (Miller and Cohen 2001; Rainer et al. 1998; Schall and Hanes 1993; Super et al. 2001b). Working memory biases activity in favor of cells that select the cued feature. When the choice array is presented and the subject has to select the target object, all cells in the IT cortex that respond to any feature in the visual field are initially activated and compete to be further processed. Thus, cells representing different stimuli engage in mutually suppressive interactions, which are biased in favor of the cells that represent the cued feature. The bias is due to the top-down activation of the cells from the signals that originate in working memory. When the subject makes her choice, the activation of cells responding to nontarget stimuli has been suppressed.

A similar account of the mechanism at work when an item in a scene is selected amongst competitors is provided by Findlay and Gilchrist (2003, chapter 6), who propose that the visual display is monitored in parallel with increasing weighting for proximity to the fovea. This last assumption allows this model to take into account the fact that many visual functions show gradually declining ability as the stimuli are placed more eccentrically (that is, as the stimuli are removed from the fovea), although there are some notable exceptions, such as the monitoring for change in the environment that is considered to be mainly a function of peripheral vision. The salience map in this account is a representation in which information originating from the retinal image is represented in a two-dimensional spatial way. This map can be seen as the pattern of the activations of the units in a two-dimensional neural network in which the visual field is being mapped in a retinotopic way. The level of neural activity at each point of the neural network (and, therefore, at each point of the two-dimensional representation of the visual field) encodes the salience. "It is assumed," Findlay and Gilchrist write (2003, p. 115), "that information feeds into this salience map so that the level of activity corresponds to the level of the evidence that the target is present at any location. As a result, items sharing a feature with the target will generate a higher level of activation than items sharing no target feature. Proximity to fixation also increases an item's salience. Within this framework, the saccade is made to the location of highest activity on the salience map."

Furthermore, the saccade to the location in space where the eyes will be directed once the target has been spotted is explained by an account of what transpires at the superior colliculus (SC). The buildup cells[2] in the intermediate layers in the region of the SC that corresponds to the location in space at which the target is located gradually increase their activity. At the same time, cells in the fixation center show a decrease in activity. At some point, the activity of the latter cells ceases and the burst cells start firing. At that time, the characteristic activity of saccades occurs in the midbrain reticular formation (MRF) and the paramedian pontine reticular formation (PPRF) (Findlay and Gilchrist 2003, chapter 4).

The main characteristic of models that construe attention as a "biased competition" among stimuli is that attention becomes the outcome of a competitive process among neighboring objects of which one or a few victors prevail and survive, rather than the cause of selection of one of these objects. To put it differently, it is the object or objects that win the competition that are said to be attended rather than the case being that some faculty, namely attention, determines or selects the winner. Independent evidence that decisions in simple memory and perceptual tasks (which are traditionally thought to require "focusing of attention" on some object) in fact result from biased competition among stimuli according to the outcome of which the winner is selected and affects behavior comes from neurobiological studies of single neuron firings in such tasks and from mathematical models that model both the behavior of these neurons and the behavioral data from similar psychological studies. The most successful models are the sequential-sampling models that assume that decisions are based on accumulating noisy information about the stimulus. There are two broad classes of such models: the random-walk models and the accumulator models (Smith and Ratcliff 2004). In the random-walk models, the information is accumulated as a single total and eventually one response (for instance, a certain selection out of two or more alternatives in a memory selection task) reaches a response criterion and the subject makes the corresponding selection. In these models, evidence for one response is evidence against the other alternatives. In the accumulator models, information about the two responses accumulates separately and eventually one of the two is the first to reach the response criterion and wins the competition.

When the competitive interaction is biased in favor of some stimulus that is behaviorally relevant because of its location, attention becomes spatially directed (it works on the space dimension). Spatial attention can be controlled by bottom-up signals, such as the raw visual qualities forming feature maps that determine the salience of an object in a scene, making it "pop out" (that is, draw attention to itself). The mechanisms of these signals may be implemented by colliculo-thalamic interactions along the ventral visual pathway. Spatial attention can also be controlled by top-down signals that involve wide cortical areas, including the frontoparietal system and the IT (Shipp 2004). This way, spatial attention involves a feedback bias that modulates the interactive competition between the attended and unattended stimuli in the visual field (Clark and Hillyard 1996; Luck and Hillyard 2000).

Although Desimone and Duncan's (1995) biased-competition account of visual processing posits the existence of a parallel bottom-up stage at which information from the environment is fed toward the visual areas of the brain, it is not clear what kind of information is so processed. Their stimuli include object features, such as color and oriented lines, but they do not explicitly deal with the problem of feature binding that may occur during the parallel stage of processing; that is, they do not specify which features retrieved in the parallel mode may combine during this mode to form a more complex structure. Vecera (2000) concentrates on object-based attention and extends the biased-competition account of visual search to the segregation or segmentation of objects from backgrounds and the selection of these objects by attentional processes. Object segmentation is the set of preattentional visual processes that determine which features combine to form the shapes present in a visual scene (Driver et al. 2001; Scholl 2001; Vecera 2000). These processes segment a shape from the background and segregate it from other shapes that are similarly seg-mented from the background. Vecera defines object-based attention as the visual processes that select a segregated shape from among several segre-gated shapes.

Given that the visual system cannot process all stimuli present in multi-object scenes within the visual field, objects or regions in space compete with one another for processing in two respects. Vecera (2000, pp. 359–360) writes: "First, there is a competition within object-based segregation processes and the segregated regions formed by segregation processes; the outcome of this competition is a perceptual group or figure that is more salient than other groups or figures. Second, there is a competition within object-based attentional processes; the outcome of this competition is the selection of one perceptual figure or group over another."

The competitions are resolved by a bottom-up bias (which arises from image cues or salient information in the environment) and a top-down bias (which arises from task-relevant or goal-relevant information). These two sources of bias operate in parallel and compete or cooperate with one another. Bottom-up information (that is, information contained in the environment and retrieved by bottom-up visual processes) may define perceptual groups and may bias some groups rendering them more easily perceived than others; it biases object segregation. Then, these perceptual groups bias the allocation of visual object-based attention in a bottom-up manner and determine a perceptually salient object. However, a scene may contain more than one perceptually salient objects or regions that are task-relevant or goal-relevant, or it may even contain an object that is perceptually more salient than a behaviorally relevant object. In this case, top-down sources of information are needed to bias the competition in favor of one behaviorally relevant object or in favor of the behaviorally relevant object over the more perceptually salient but goal-irrelevant object.

To implement this process of parallel competitive interactions in figure-ground segmentation, Vecera and colleagues (Vecera 2000; Vecera and Farah 1997; Vecera and O'Reilly 2000) rely on parallel distributed processing (PDP) connectionist models. Their model posits top-down feedback signals from object representations to an earlier process of figure-ground segregation. The latter extracts information from the stimuli in a parallel bottom-up manner (in the way of biased-competition models of visual processing), which consists in simple image features (edges) present in the visual scene. The information is stored in the boundary layers and is fed to the next layer in the network that extracts the surfaces that are "figure" as opposed to ground. The figure layer receives top-down feedback from the object-recognition layer in which familiar shapes are represented and sends feedback signals to the boundary layers. There are two kinds of competitive interactions in this network. The first of these is the overall competition between bottom-up and top-down signals in the figure layer. Thus, the selection of figure is biased both from object representations top-down signals and from bottom-up image cues. Second, there is competition among the boundary layers, as different boundaries shared by regions in the figure-ground display compete (the model presupposes that some regions or boundaries are activated selectively over others) to become foreground figure. This competition is implemented by inhibitory connections among opposing boundary units.

This model envisages a role for competition between top-down and bottom-up biases only if the bottom-up image cues are ambiguous (as in bi-stable or ambiguous figures). The input provided in the simulations by Vecera and colleagues contained no bottom-up cues that would resolve the competition between candidate boundaries. "Because the bottom-up input is insufficient to resolve this competition," Vecera argues (2000, p. 378), "there must be top-down inputs to bias the bottom-up competition. In our model, the top-down inputs came from object representations: One of the two regions in the figure-ground display corresponded to a familiar object that was represented by one of the object units." It seems thus that the presence of unambiguous perceptual cues in a scene suffices to resolve the competition and to segment figure from ground in the initial parallel bottom-up processing step. In addition, bottom-up signals are stronger than top-down signals, the latter acting more as gain enhancers of activity that is already present than as activators of neurons that are otherwise silent (Hupé et al. 1998).

The "competition" models of attention emphasize the competition among structures that are derived from a visual scene during a first stage of perceptual processing in which information is retrieved in a parallel bottom-up way from the visual scene. Different stimuli in a visual scene will activate in parallel neuronal assemblies responding to, and thus encoding, these stimuli. If one feature or object must be selected, and/or if a local region of cortex receives input from these neuronal assemblies, there is a competitive interaction between the stimuli (the competition is the strongest when the two stimuli fall within the same receptive field of neurons in visuotopically organized areas in which neurons have restricted receptive fields). Eventually a structure wins the competition and gets the opportunity to be further processed upward in the visual stream in a second serial stage of visual processing (the stage is serial because of the attentional bottleneck that allows objects to be processed one at a time).

The competition may be biased by various top-down influences that reflect the expectations and goals of the perceiver. To repeat a point made before: Attention is seen as the dynamic cause of the competitive interaction between bottom-up and top-down processes. Attention acts to bias the competition between neuronal populations that encode environmental stimuli. The biases may be either spatial or featural, depending on the task and the kinds of cues (Deco et al. 2002; Vecera and Farah 1994; Usher and Niebur 1996)—that is, they are not limited to cells with receptive fields at a single locus in the visual field; they include biases in favor of behaviorally relevant features. If the biases are spatial, then the selection of a target object in a visual scene requires a serial scanning of locations (of the type posited in FIT, for instance). If the bias is featural (as it is, for example, when the cue concerns a feature of the target object), the selection of a target does not require a serial scanning of the scene; it takes place in a parallel stage in which all stimuli present in the scene are processed until the target object is found.

Usher and Niebur (1996) offer a model of object-centered attention. It consists of a parallel mechanism for selective object-based attention that is complemented under certain conditions with a serial search in the focal mode—that is, with a serial spatial attention. Usher and Niebur study the behavior of cells in the IT cortex. These cells, with their large receptive fields, respond to complex structures, such as specific shapes or faces, irrespective of their position in the visual field. Research (Chelazzi et al. 1993) with tasks in which monkeys have to search for target objects that are characterized by some feature suggests that the response of IT neurons to displays that include two objects has two phases. The first of these is a parallel phase in which the activation of neurons responding to both objects is enhanced (each group of neurons responds to its preferred stimulus). The response does not depend on whether the preferred object is a target, and thus the activation is task independent. In other words, there is a parallel phase in which information is retrieved bottom-up from a scene irrespective of task demands and independent of any top-down expectation-driven feedback. This stage can be construed as "preattentive," in that no selection is involved. In the second phase, the response of the neurons shows expectation-driven top-down modulation of processing. Activation is enhanced only for the neuronal assembly that represents the target, and is suppressed for the other neuronal assembly. The second stage underlies selective object-based attention.

The Usher-Niebur model is based on a neural network with distributed representation, so that cell assemblies that represent similar objects share some cells. The network has three layers of units: the input layer (whose units simulate the neurons in V1 primary visual cortex), the visual sensory memory level (whose units simulate the neuronal assemblies in the IT cortex), and the working memory layer (whose units simulate neurons in prefrontal cortex). The first layer sends input to the second layer, and the third layer has feedback projections to the second layer. To make the system sensitive to input, there are excitatory connections between the cells in each cell assembly and inhibitory connections among assemblies. The excitatory connections between cells in each neuronal assembly in the visual sensory memory are strong enough to generate competition between the objects in the input but not strong enough to make the activation of the cells in the visual sensory memory layer independent of the input.

Each cell assembly in working memory corresponds to a cell assembly in visual sensory memory. The activation of a cell assembly in the working memory layer is stronger than the activation in the corresponding cell assembly in the visual sensory memory, so the response of the former persists even during the delay between the presentation of a cue and the presentation of the test display (that is, during the absence of sensory stimuli). Each working-memory assembly sends a feedback signal to its corresponding cell assembly in the visual sensory memory, strengthening its activation. This means that a cell assembly that responds to an object in the visual field which is already stored in working memory (because it has been designated as a target by a preceding cue) has, eventually, a stronger activation than a cell assembly responding to an object in the visual field but not in working memory (in the way described in Desimone 1999). This is also what it makes the search for a target an expectation-driven search. To simulate the findings of Chelazzi et al. (1993) that suggest an initial parallel stage of bottom-up target-independent extraction of information, the feedback input is weak, so that initially both objects in the visual primary cortex are activated. Eventually, the assembly that receives additional input from working memory wins the competition and suppresses the activation of the other assembly.

The model was designed to simulate the behavioral characteristics of IT cells in delayed match-to-sample tasks and to shed light on the mechanism underlying expectation-driven selective attention for object features. "The function of the described mechanism," Usher and Niebur write (1996, p. 317), "is to 'look for' an expected stimulus among distractors in the display (the expected stimulus being the one that had been shown previously, i.e., the 'cued' one). When such a target stimulus is found, the corresponding assembly is selected for activation, while otherwise (in the absence of a target) no assembly achieves full domination of the system." This is a parallel mechanism in that it does not compare the stored target with the distractors through a serial search on locations in the display until it finds the target; instead, it selects the most likely stimuli to be the target in an expectation-driven process.

The Usher-Niebur model is not limited to a serial processing, as FIT models are. In FIT models, the selective attention that is at work is attention in its focal mode—that is, spatial attention. Spatial attention can search for one spatial position at a time. This means that the distractors present at different locations in the display are serially searched and compared with the mnemonic trace of the target before they are suppressed. In the Usher-Niebur model, on the other hand, the selective mechanism that is driven by top-down expectations searches for one object at a time. In the preattentive stage, neurons responding to the different objects in a scene (whether they be targets or distractors) are activated in parallel. In the selective-attention stage, the neuronal assembly whose activation is enhanced by the top-down feedback input from working memory eventually wins the competition and suppresses the activations of the other

assemblies. This way, attention selects the target object for further processing; it is serial with respect to the number of targets, but not with respect
to the number of distractors.

Spivey (2007) performed a series of simulations purporting to test the
efficiency of the biased-competition account of attention in accounting for
the amassed data on visual search. Spivey used a normalized recurrence
localist network to study whether a model of visual search in which several
objects in a scene are all represented in parallel could explain the various
experimental results on searching for a target amidst distractors, on target-
distractor similarity, and on distractor-distractor similarity. Recall that,
according to the standard account for visual search, when an object is
searched amidst distractors that share only one feature then search is not
affected by the number of the distractors, presumably because the search
is parallel and the target item pops out. However, when the search is conjunctive (that is, when the search involves looking for the conjunction of
features), then, given the standard assumption that searching for conjunctive features involves attention and serial matching of the objects in the
scene with the target's template in memory until a match is found, the
search slope increases steeply as a function of the size of the set. Against
this model, Spivey's simulation provide an existence proof that a biased-
competition model of visual search in which several objects in the scene
are all represented by being partially activated, and by being processed
in parallel while competing simultaneously to dominate processing, can
explain the steep search slopes that are thought to support a serial search
pattern without positing a serial search; all that need be posited is parallel
biased competition among the representations of objects that are all processed in parallel. The parallel competitive architecture mimics the linearly
increasing search function without positing serial matching guided by
attention. This shows, in the words of Spivey (2007, p. 228), that "with
the normalized competition algorithm, conjunction searches (as well as
feature searches) are capable of a wide range of response time by set size
slopes. . . . The past results and current simulations suggest that visual
search phenomena are best described via a continuum of search efficiency
(Duncan and Humphreys 1989), rather than via a discrete distinction
between parallel (sensory) and serial (attentional) processing (Treisman
1988)."

A parallel account of selective attention in search tasks leaves open the
issue of the role, if any, of spatial or focal serial attention in such tasks.
Usher and Niebur (1996) argue that focal serial attention is needed in two
search situations: when spatial information that could help locate the

target is available (when, for example, there is a spatial cue as to the location of the target) and when the parallel selection mechanism reaches its limits (as when the target vs. distractor discrimination is difficult because they share features, or when the search tasks consists in searching for conjunctive stimuli). In these cases, the decision has to be made on the basis of a serial scan of all objects. I would like to a add a third reason why spatial attention may be necessary even for a much more extended range of tasks, including the mundane but fundamental for vision task of dealing with the environment by representing the features and objects in it. In a nutshell: since visual processing does not result in detailed iconic representations being stored in memory, when such detailed information for an object in a scene is needed, one must orient one's eyes to the location of the object to gather the required information. This is the task of spatial attention, which, to succeed, presupposes that the spatial layout of the scene and specific positions of objects are retained in memory. I will elaborate on that in the next section.

1.2 Visual Representations

It has traditionally been assumed that upon viewing a scene we construct rich sensory representations of all, or most, of the objects in the scene, which we then store in a visual buffer (Neisser 1976). This buffer is supposed to integrate the contents of individual eye fixations so that a complete coherent representation of a scene can emerge (Feldman 1985; Trehub 1994). Attention is thought to be the mechanism that integrates visual features into long-lasting representations of objects (Kanwisher and Driver 1992; Treisman 1993). However, either a visual buffer that integrates representations from successive views of a scene does not exist, as is suggested by the work of Rensink and colleagues, or, if it does exist, it does not store rich point-to-point iconic sensory representations of objects (Hollingworth et al. 2001; Hollingworth and Henderson 2002, 2003).

According to Rensink's work, representations of objects in a visual scene do not accumulate as the eyes move from parts of the scene to other parts. Furthermore, objects are represented in detail only for so long as attention is focused on them. If representations of objects are not stored in a visual buffer, and if they persist only so long as attention is focused on them, then, to interact successfully with the environment, one must be able to shift the focus of processing activities effectively and quickly from one location to another and to select to represent briefly those objects that are indispensable to achieving one's goals. In this case, object representations do not accumulate, and are not stored; rather, they are assembled as needed. To know where to look for an object in order to focus on it and gather the required representation, one must retain in memory, among other things, a map of relative locations. Spatial attention then orients the eyes to that location. I will now discuss the relevant evidence and the attentional mechanism required to ensure that capability, concentrating on Rensink's (2000a,b) work.

Rensink discusses research on change blindness (CB) and inattentional blindness (IB). "Change blindness" refers to the phenomenon in which changes in an image of a real-world scene are not detected or become difficult to detect when made during a flicker, a blink, a saccade, a movie cut, or some other short interruption (Rensink et al. 1997, 2000; Simons and Levin 1997). "Inattentional blindness" refers to the phenomenon in which observers attending to a particular object fail to report the appearance of irrelevant or unexpected items (Mack and Rock 1998). Both phenomena, owing to the fact that they can be induced in a large number of ways and to the fact that they occur with real-world scenes, are central to the way we represent the world around us. The explanation of CB is that under normal conditions, changes in the world are accompanied by motion signals in the input that attract attention to their location and render the changes visible. Spatial analysis of shape and spatial relations among objects, and detection of motion, are the most relevant processes on physical properties that form the basis for focused attention (Egeth et al. 1984; McCleod et al. 1991). When these motion signals coincide with and thus are masked by other transients (flickers, saccades, etc.), they cannot draw attention, and CB is induced. The explanation of IB is that the ability to report an event requires attention. If the attention is focused elsewhere, the event may go unnoticed.

The problem CB and IB pose for the view that we store rich and stable representations of visual scenes is that, if we did store such representations, then a simple comparison of the actual scene after the brief interruption with the contents of the buffer (the scene before the interruption), or a simple detection of anomalous structures formed by superimposing the scene before and the scene after the interruption, would suffice to render the changes diaphanous to consciousness and thus reportable. Thus, these phenomena suggest that there is no visual buffer that accumulates and integrates the contents of individual eye fixations, undermining the idea that a detailed representation of a scene is carried across saccades so that the visual system construct a composite perceptual system (Henderson and Hollingworth 1999). If such a buffer does not exist and as a result we do not build complete representations of visual scenes, then the contents of successive representations due to individual eye fixation cannot compared and any change in a scene would be difficult to notice.

Rensink (2000a,b) offers a theory of vision that purports to explain visual mechanisms in a way that is consistent with the empirical findings related to CB and IB. His account consists of two parts: a mechanism for vision and attention (the coherence theory), which deals with the "scrutinizing" aspect of vision, and an account of the nature of representations resulting from this mechanism (virtual representations), which deals with the "seeing" aspect (2000b).

The coherence field theory of attention posits three stages of visual processing of a scene.

First, there is an early preattentive stage consisting of three substages during which properties of stimuli are bottom-up retrieved rapidly (within a few hundred milliseconds) and in parallel from a visual scene. This stage is referred to as *low-level vision*. In the first substage (the transduction stage), the photometric properties of stimuli are retrieved. In the second substage (primary processing stage), image properties are measured by means of various filters. The two first substages perform "quick and clean" measurements at the expense of complexity. The third substage (secondary processing stage) performs "quick and dirty" interpretations at the expense of reliability. The interpretations form structures by binding together features retrieved at the previous substages. These structures are the proto-objects that provide local descriptions of scene structure (e.g., three-dimensional orientation, grouping of related edge fragments) and thus correspond to localized structures in the world.

Though proto-objects can be complex structures, they are coherent only over a small region and over a limited amount of time; they have limited spatial and temporal coherence (where "coherence" means that the structures refer to parts of the same system in space and time; in other words, that their representations in different locations and over different times refer to the same object). Proto-objects are very volatile, in that they are either overwritten by subsequent stimuli or else fade away within a few hundred milliseconds; the volatile representations last about half a second (Rensink 2000b). Each time the eyes move and new light enters them, the older proto-objects fade away and new proto-objects are generated.

The second stage involves attention, which "acts as a hand that grasps a small number of proto-objects from this constantly-regenerating flux. While held, they form a coherence field representing an individuated object with a high degree of coherence over time and space." (Rensink

2000b, p. 1473) This is mid-level vision. Attention has access only to proto-objects, the output of the secondary processing stage, and does not modulate processing in the first two substages. Thus, proto-objects are both the lowest-level operands upon which selective attention can act and the highest-level outputs of low-level vision (the preattentive parallel bottom-up stage of visual processing). Focused attention provides structures that are coherent over an extended region of space and time, and thus it is inextricably involved in object perception—that is, in the perception of objects as they are experienced through our senses. Notice that attention, through the continuity in space and time it provides to objects, is indispensable in perceiving changes in visual scenes, for it allows a new stimulus to be treated as the transformation of an existing object rather as the appearance of a new object (as we shall see later on, this is accomplished by means of the object-files that the visual system opens for the objects it parses in a scene).

For the third stage, Rensink posits a "nexus," the place in which the interaction between attention and proto-objects takes place. Since attention combines proto-objects, the nexus consists in a single structure representing the attended object (for example, its shape, size, color, and orientation). It becomes clear that Rensink's proto-objects may be object parts that, when combined together, constitute a single object or distinct objects that attention combines to form a complex object. Not all properties of the proto-objects can be represented in the nexus; thus, only some among the properties of objects can be represented and perceived at any one time. This is important for perception of change too, since only if the change concerns one of the represented aspects of the object will the change be seen; otherwise, CB results.

When proto-objects are attended, links are established between them (in order to form the attended object) and the nexus. The links are bi-directional, allowing two-way transmission between the nexus and the proto-objects. Bottom-up information allows the nexus to represent selected properties of the proto-objects and allows mapping between the constantly changing retinotopic coordinates of proto-objects and the more stable viewer-centered or object-centered coordinates of the nexus. Top-down information provides stability and coherence to the attended proto-objects. It is the recurrent flow of information between the nexus and the proto-objects made possible by the links between the nexus and the proto-objects that establishes the circuit known as a *coherence field*.

After attention is released, the object dissolves back into its constituent proto-objects, losing its coherence over an extended region of space-time.

There is no attentional aftereffect of the representation of an object; once attention has been withdrawn, the object ceases to be represented (see also Wolfe 1999). This means two things. First, it is wrong to assume that when attention captures objects, they enter a visual working memory where they are stored even when attention is withdrawn. Second, as a corollary of the first point, it is wrong that visual working memory could be identified with the attentional hold, in that attending an object is both a necessary and a sufficient condition for the object to be in visual working memory. Rensink (2000a, p. 26) does not deny that there exists a working memory (which he calls *short-term memory*, abbreviated STM) for objects that have been previously attended, in which traces of object types are stored. But this is different from the standard visual short-term memory (VSTM) or visual buffer, which is supposed to be purely a visual memory that stores representations of object tokens.

Rensink argues that focused attention provides the short-term coherence and stability of one object at a time, although more than one object could be attended at one time if they form a whole new object. The attended object is represented in a short-term buffer as a working representation, but the representation contains a limited amount of information, mainly information about size, shape, color, orientation, location, and motion (Kahneman et al. 1992). This counters earlier claims that attention binds features into a complete representation of an object (Treisman 1993). Once attention is withdrawn, the only memory of the scene that persists is its gross spatial layout and its gist.

Though attention is a necessary condition for seeing change, it is not a sufficient one, since changes to objects may go unnoticed even when the objects are attended to, especially if the changes are unexpected (Simons and Rensink 2005). Simons and Rensink's finding suggests that even when coherent representations of objects are formed through the action of attention, the contents of these representations are usually limited to those that suit the task at hand, and that is why changes in behaviorally irrelevant or unexpected features go undetected even when the object is being attended to. If one considers that information on color, size, motion, location, and orientation is in most cases important to almost any task, one is led to the conclusion that Kahneman et al. 1992 reach: that the information contained in a coherent and stable representation of an object is usually limited to such information.

Accepting that working representations of objects in a scene do exist, Rensink rejects (see the detailed discussion in Simons and Rensink 2005) the strong conclusions occasionally drawn from studies on CB and IB that these two phenomena suggest that the brain forms sparse or no representations at all (O'Regan 1992; O'Regan and Noë 2001). The working representations are fragile and easily overwritten, but they survive long enough to allow successful recognition performance (Mitroff et al. 2004). In fact, not only do we form representations, but we form multiple representations that can be used in multiple tasks. As we have seen, though attention does not bind features into a complete representation of an object, still the working representations are about a distinct object that persists in space and time and contain information about its size, color, shape, orientation, motion, and location.

The role of attention in vision can explain the findings on change blindness and inattentional blindness. If seeing and reporting the change presupposes that attention is being allocated to the points in space and time at which motion change signals occur, the lack of attention renders intelligible why one could fail to report a change in a scene in change blindness or even the appearance of a new object in the scene in IB. Notice that the emphasis is on seeing and reporting a change, not on detecting or perceiving the change. The reason is that, despite the fact that without attention one cannot see and report a change (i.e., that without attention one cannot be made consciously aware of that change), that does not mean that the change is undetected or not perceived; on the contrary, it is detected and may influence the behavior of the perceiver.

This is a clear case of perception without attention and awareness, which Rensink calls "implicit perception." Indeed, studies of change blindness and inattentional blindness and studies of perception in the absence of attention (Driver et al. 2001; Humphreys 1999; Kanwisher 2001; Mack and Rock 1998; Merikle et al. 2001; Moore and Egeth 1998; Treisman and Kanwisher 1998) suggest that even when there is no awareness of stimuli when either space-based or object-based attention is diverted elsewhere, stimuli are nevertheless perceived, and grouping of features into some form of objects takes place along the visual system. The claim that some form of object representations can be constructed in the absence of focal (i.e. serial) attention is further reinforced by studies suggesting that there is a parallel selection of parts within objects, and that thus, focal attention need not apply to each visual element separately.

Priming studies show, for instance, that shape can be implicitly registered (Treisman and Kanwisher 1998). Evans et al. (2000), Han et al. (2000), Heinze et al. (1998), Koivisto and Revonsuo (2004), and Paquet and Merikle (1988) present evidence from priming studies and argue that global and local stimuli are processed in parallel at preconscious processing stages (that is, as early as 100 ms after stimulus onset, which, as we shall see, is roughly the threshold at which some form of awareness enters the picture and preconscious processing ceases) even in the absence of attention, although global stimuli are analyzed at that stage more than local stimuli (which explains in part the global precedence hypothesis of Navon (1997)). Moreover, there is evidence that semantic processing of stimuli takes place when the stimuli are not attended to, and under conditions that preclude awareness of the stimuli (Dehaene et al. 1998; Ladavas et al. 1993; Merikle et al. 2001). Thus, one should not hurry to assert that semantic top-down processing is necessarily accompanied by awareness, a finding that reinforces Kanwisher's (2001) choice to treat perception as independent of any form of awareness and to discuss awareness after perceptual processes have been analyzed.

According to Rensink's coherence field theory, there is no aftereffect of attending an object. Once attention has been withdrawn, there persists no representation of that object token. In view of this, it is natural to ask how could we interact successfully with our environment, given that such interaction presupposes reliable representation of object features in the world. Rensink's answer to that is the idea of a *virtual representation*. Granted that we need to represent various aspects of our environment, it is also true that we never need a detailed representation of all objects and object features in a scene; we need represent only those aspects that are relevant to a task at any time. Thus, instead of forming a detailed representation of all objects in a visual scene, we represent only the object and features needed for the task at hand. The objects in a scene are virtually represented, in that they could be brought forth into the focus of attention and thus represented whenever needed. This presupposes that there is a reliable mechanism that can coordinate attention so that a coherent and detailed representation of an object in a scene could be assembled by picking up relevant information from the environment whenever it is needed. In this case, "the representation of a scene will appear to higher levels as if it is real, that is, as if all objects are represented in great detail simultaneously" (Rensink 2000a, p. 28).

Successful use of virtual representation requires attentional shifts to the appropriate object at the appropriate time. This gives rise to two problems. First, to direct attention to the appropriate object presupposes that the location of the object is known before the allocation of attention. How could this be? Second, and related to the first, supposing that such knowledge is possible, knowing the location of an object in a scene requires a memory of the objects in the scene; but how can there be a memory of the scene, given that attention has no aftereffects and representations are assembled *in situ*? These are problems related to one of the three different aspects of vision: "seeing."

To account for a mechanism that coordinates attention, Rensink (2000a,b) proposes a "triadic architecture" of three largely independent systems. The triadic architecture is based on the notion of "pointers," aspects of structures in the world that are extracted from a scene and serve as pointers to entities in the world. A pointer is a characteristic example of a deictic or indexical representation of objects in the world.

When one views a scene, one might represent the objects in it by forming and storing rich representations, a fact that is disputed by the evidence coming for studies of change blindness and inattentional blindness. Alternatively, one could store in one's memory the location or some characteristic feature of the objects, which, upon needing some information about these objects, would allow one retrieve the required information. The stored location or feature of an object is a representation of that object in that it comes from that object; it acts as a pointer that has indexed the object and allows one to track it and find more about it. This representation is called "indexical" or "deictic" representation for two reasons. As is true of all indexicals (such as 'this' or 'that'), its meaning consists mainly in the fact that it denotes or points to a certain object in the environment. The representation hardly has an internal structure, although it points to structures in the world, which could constitute its meaning; some philosophers go as far as to claim that an indexical does not have a meaning outside its external relation to the object it denotes. Compare the representation of an object by means of a pointer to its location, which if articulated would consist in a simple "there," versus its representation by means of a detailed description of its properties, which if articulated would consist in a set of sentences implementing this description. In the latter case, the representation has a meaning on its own right by virtue of its having an internal structure.[3]

Rensink's triadic architecture consists of the architecture of the coherence field theory that I discussed above in which a third element is added, to wit, a limited-capacity preattentional system that provides a setting that guides the allocation of attention to different parts of a scene and which ensures that attentional shifts be made to the appropriate object location at the appropriate time. The setting system can guide the allocation of attention to the appropriate locations of a scene by representing at least three aspects of a scene's structure.

First, the gist of the scene (whether the scene is a city, a market, or something else) allows attention to be directed to objects that are important in the context of the scene. At first sight, talk about the gist of a scene perceived during early vision seems problematic, insofar as "getting the gist" seems to rely on a mental abstraction and thus seems to require high-level semantic processing. However, the gist seems to be determined within 100–120 ms after stimulus onset, before the onset of attention (Koch 2004; Potter 1993; Rousselet et al. 2002). It precedes the identification of objects in a scene and thus is extracted by means of simple measures of the image or other properties of the proto-objects—that is, during low-level vision. Of course, for the context to influence perception, the context must be available early on if it is to exert any influence on the perceptual processes. The evidence suggests that this is indeed the case. Similarly, Rensink (2000a,b) and Henderson and Hollingworth (1999) review evidence suggesting that the type of the scene can be identified as soon as 45–135 ms after stimulus onset.

Findlay and Gilchrist (2003, p. 138) point to the fact that, since objects not fixated closer than 2° or 3° are not recognized, eye movements are necessary for the identification of objects within scenes. It is known that the eyes perform three or four saccades in a second. However, the gist of the scene can be extracted from a single glimpse of the scene, which means that the scene's abstract schema can be evoked with very little delay. It seems that "a initial rapid pass through the visual hierarchy provides the global framework and gist of the scene and primes competing identities though the features that are detected" (Treisman 2004, p. 541).

In chapter 5, I discuss Petitot's (1995) notion of the "positional content of a scene." The main point of that discussion is that positional content is nonconceptual and conveys information about nonvisual properties, such as causal relations (e.g., X "transfers" something to Y). Suppose that one witnesses a scene in which X gives Z to Y. The semantics of the scene consists of two parts: (i) the semantic lexical content of X, Z, Y and 'give' as a specific action and (ii) the purely positional local content. The latter is the image scheme of the "transfer" type. X, Y, and Z occupy a specific location in the space occupied by the scene (just as they are the arguments in the three-place predicate 'to give'). In the image scheme, X, Y, Z are thus reduced to featureless objects that occupy specific relative locations, and in that sense they can be viewed as pure abstract places. X, Y, and Z, which in a linguistic description of the scene are the semantic roles, "are reduced to pure abstract places, locations that must be filled by 'true' participants." A structured set of such relations constitutes the positional content of a more complex scene, such as "being in a market." It seems, thus, that the nonvisual properties in which the gist of a scene consists could be retrieved directly from a scene in a bottom-up way. This suggests that 'gist' should not be construed as involving an act of mental abstraction, but a perceptual act of retrieving the positional content of the scene, which is abstract in the sense explicated above.

Second, perception of the spatial arrangement of objects in the scene without regard to other features allows attention to be directed to a particular object in a scene. The perception of the layout of the objects, in other words, allows one to know the location in the scene of the object that one seeks. Akin to the gist, the layout of a scene is extracted from the scene by means of low-level vision, and more specifically through the proto-objects at which low-level vision culminates. Recall that proto-objects are construed by Rensink as object-parts, but they can also be objects that are combined to form complex objects. Pylyshyn (2001) thinks of proto-objects as viewer-centered structural descriptions of objects. Be that as it may, the first two aspects involve working representations.

Third, an abstract scene schema that is stored in long-term memory facilitates the perception of both gist and object layout in the scene. At the same time, the gist and the layout facilitate the long-term learning of the characteristics of the particular scene. The scene schema involves the category in which a particular scene belongs and an associated collection of representations, such as an inventory of objects that are likely to be present in the scene and their relative locations.

Rensink's account of attention, although it puts no emphasis on the competition between top-down and bottom-up information but only on the competition between bottom-up signals generating proto-objects, agrees with biased-competition accounts that there exist two main stages of visual processing, one parallel (in which proto-objects are formed) and one serial (in which some object is selected for further processing). The theory of virtual representation leads Rensink to underscore both the spatial role and the object-based role of selective attention. Attention may be focused either on locations or on objects, because, for virtual representation to be effective, objects must be attended on request by effectively allocating attention to various parts of the scene. The allocation of attention may be guided by the layout of the scene (which emphasizes likely locations of objects in a scene) or by the gist and the causal type of the event in Petitot's (1995) sense, (which emphasize those objects that are important in the context of the scene), or perhaps both. Recall that the layout and the gist of a scene are retrieved in early vision before the onset of attention. It is the nature of the task that determines which kind of attention (spatial or object-based) will be deployed, a finding that is reinforced by other studies (Egeth and Yantis 1997; Vecera and Farah 1994; Vecera 2000). Thus, Rensink's work provides a role for spatial attention in addition to those discussed by Usher and Niebur (1996).

As another result of the theory of virtual representation, Rensink goes beyond biased-competition models of visual search in that he posits an explicit mechanism guiding selective attention, whether it be spatial or object-based. This mechanism is lacking from the biased-competition models, since they are specifically concerned with the way objects are selected in a scene, that is, how they win the competition against other candidate objects. The biased-competition models are not concerned with how one has to search a scene to gather information about several objects that may become behaviorally relevant at different times. A reason for that may be that some of the proponents of biased-competition models subscribe to the view that through attention a complete representation of an object is stored in memory and thus one need not constantly search the scene to gather information about objects in it; this information is stored in memory and can be retrieved from there. One could, thus, argue that the biased-competition models are mainly concerned with the "static" role of attention in selecting and perceiving an object at some specific time, whereas Rensink is also interested in the "dynamic" role of attention in providing information about objects on request.

Rensink's non-attentional setting in his triadic architecture has some affinity to Cave and Wolfe's (1994) and Wolfe's (1994) *priority maps* in models of visual search. The Cave-Wolfe model posits a parallel process that guides a focal serial search. Wolfe's (1994) guided search model also posits the existence of a parallel feature-competition stage that guides a subsequent serial visual attention stage. The parallel stage generates a priority map that is used to guide the localized control of the spatial attention mechanism at a serial stage of processing. In other words, the parallel stage forms feature maps whose outputs are pooled into a salience map that guides the attentional focus on salient locations serially from item to item in space in the visual field by representing topographically the relevance of the different parts of a visual scene. In that respect, this system functions the same way Rensink's preattentional system does. The feature-competition stage calculates the order of serial inspection of the visual field, hence the priority map. The priority map is generated after the binding of features, which means that the competition mechanisms are involved after a parallel bottom-up stage in which features are retrieved from the scene and bound to a certain extent, in accordance with the class of biased-competition models (recall that for Rensink the gist of a scene is retrieved about 120 ms after stimulus onset).

Rensink's work on change blindness and inattentional blindness also sheds light on another issue. The fact that without attention one cannot see and report a change (that is, that without attention one cannot be not made consciously aware of that change) does not suggest that the change is undetected or not perceived; on the contrary, it is being detected, and it may influence the behavior of the perceiver. Indeed, there is abundant evidence (Block 2005; Desimone 1999; Desimone and Duncan 1995; Duncan and Humphreys 1989; Fernandez-Duque and Thorton 2000; Fernandez-Duque and Thorton 2003; Kanwisher 2001; Lamme 2003; Merikle et al. 2001; Merikle and Joordens 1997; Rensink 2002; Thorton and Fernandez-Duque 1999; Usher and Niebur 1996; Wolfe et al. 2002) that there is significant processing of information that can affect behavior (for example, cause priming effects, affect semantic decisions, or even enter long-term memory (LTM)) without attention and without consciousness. For this reason, Driver et al. (2001) and Wolfe (1999) think that in change blindness and inattentional blindness it is not the case that change is not perceived; change is perceived but cannot be reported and that is why the phenomena should not be called "change blindness" or "inattentional blindness" but rather "inattentional amnesia." Rensink calls perception without attention and awareness "implicit perception," and associates it with "sensing," one of the three different aspects of vision, the other two being, as we have seen, "seeing" and "scrutinizing" (Rensink 2000b).

Rensink's thesis that once attention is withdrawn from objects the objects lose their constitutional coherence and revert to unstructured collections of object parts is hotly debated. The debate extends to another related thesis of Rensink's, namely that IB and CB phenomena suggest that there is no accumulation of visual information from a series of viewings of a scene into some visual memory buffer. There is evidence (Hollingworth et al. 2001; Hollingworth and Henderson 2002, 2004) that undermines both of Rensink's theses. This evidence suggests that when attention withdraws, information about objects that were previously attended to has been stored in VSTM and/or LTM and can be used for comparisons of scenes or for accumulation of visual information across fixations. Wolfe et al. (2000), for instance, leave open the possibility that representations of objects may be retained in memory for some time once attention has been withdrawn. This has several repercussions regarding the issue of CB and IB that open the road to alternative accounts of the phenomena to those offered by Rensink and his colleagues, but I will not discuss these accounts here.

What is important for the aim of this book is the clarification of the role of attention in visual processing and in the formation of representations of objects in visual scenes. Recall that the "phenomenal" preattentive percept or proto-object consists of tentatively but uniquely bound features that are segmented from visual information. This representation is a short-lived, vulnerable, and not easily reportable form of visual experience. When attention is directed toward the scene, two things happen (Hollingworth et al. 2001; Hollingworth and Henderson 2002, 2004). First, the sensory and perceptual information extracted preattentively from the scene is augmented with a more abstract higher-level visual representation, which consists of abstract visual categories that are formed in more anterior areas (medial and inferior temporal cortex) and which is stored in short-term visual memory (STVM). These higher-level representations are the representations that are functional across saccades and thus contain the content that is accumulated from saccade to saccade (Henderson and Hollingworth 2003). Although the higher-level representations contain information about the visual form of the scene and preserve a great deal of visual information, they are more abstract than the sensory representations in that they do not have the iconic form of the latter—for example, they do not retain the metric of the scene as the iconic perceptual representations do. They also do not encode the perceptual content in all its detail. For example, they do not encode the exact shade or hue of a color but only the class of the color with a rough description of its brightness or the exact texture of an object. Second, the higher-level representations through the VSTM are consolidated in due time into a more stable long-term memory representation (whether the representations in long-term memory are modal or amodal is an interesting question; see Barsalou 1999 for a discussion).[4]

Both lines of research—Rensink's and Henderson and Hollingworth's—recognize that successful visual interaction with the environment would not be possible unless implicit visual memories allowed us to select and retain information across space and time. The difference between the two classes of theories lies in that in Rensink's work what is retained is the gist of the scene and the gross spatial layout of the objects, so that the observer could know where to focus her attention to acquire the required task-related information, whereas for Hollingworth and Henderson the mnemonic traces of previously attended scenes are richer, in that they also contain visual information about the objects in the scene, although the representations of objects stored in memory, whether it be VSTM or LTVM, are more abstract than the sensory representations in that they do not have the iconic form of the latter.

Both accounts could use, for instance, Maljkovic and Nakayama's (1994, 1996) priming of pop-out mechanism of visual memory, which uses traces of previously attended features or locations to help guide attention and eye movements toward task-relevant objects. This mechanism goes beyond Rensink's triadic architecture that ensures the successful use of virtual representation, which requires that attentional shifts be made to the appropriate object at the appropriate time, in that in addition to the spatial layout it may include mnemonic traces of object features to guide the orientation of attention. Contextual cueing (Brockmole et al. 2006; Chung and Jiang 1998, 2003; Jiang et al. 2005) may also be a mechanism of visual memory that fits within both accounts but is better suited for Henderson and Hollingworth's work. This is a mechanism that retains in memory both the spatial layout of a scene and the specific positions of objects and can, therefore, efficiently guide search within scenes (Hollingworth 2005, 2006). Notice that both mechanisms are implicit, in the sense that the observers have no awareness of the information they use to guide spatial attention toward task-relevant aspects of the scene and in the sense that explicit knowledge that a new object will appear does not alter the probability or speed of fixating that object.

The research I have discussed thus far brings forth the role of attention in constructing representations of objects and in rendering subjects conscious of these objects. One might be tempted to construe attention as a necessary and sufficient condition for visual conscious awareness—that is, to think that consciousness requires attention and that attention guarantees consciousness. Rensink is not clear on that, although his account of CB and IB seems to suggest that he thinks attention necessary for awareness, which is closely linked to the ability to report a stimulus, although his account leaves open, if it does not outright suggest, that one can have some form of awareness of the proto-objects. As we shall see next, for Lamme neither the necessity nor the sufficiency conditions hold true.

Further evidence for the role of attention in visual processing and awareness comes from Lamme's (2000, 2003, 2005), Lamme and Roelfsema's (2000), Roelfsema's et al. (2000), and Roelfsema's (2005) studies on perceptual processing and the relation between attention, perception, and awareness. Lamme starts by offering neural definitions of the psychological phenomena of perception, attention and awareness. He argues for two kinds of processing that take place in the brain: the feedforward sweep

(FFS) and recurrent processing (RP). In the FFS, the signal is transmitted only from the lower structures of the brain to the higher or more central ones. There is no feedback, and thus no signal can be transmitted from the higher centers to the lower structures during the FFS, although there is evidence that horizontal or contextual modulation occurs very early and involves even area V1 of the visual cortex. This should not be read to mean that the early visual areas at which the FFS takes place do not receive any signals from higher centers. As we shall see in the next chapter, they do. However, the top-down signals are delayed and thus do not affect the FFS processing that occurs at the same areas. Feedforward connections can extract high-level information, which is sufficient to lead to some initial categorization of the visual scene and to some behavioral responses. In RP, signals flow in both directions.

Lamme (2000, 2003, 2005) offers a detailed account of the processes along the ventral pathway, the pathway along which objects are represented for purposes of identification and categorization. When a visual scene is being presented to the eyes, the feedforward sweep (that is, the feedforward propagation of information from the periphery to the center without any recurrent processing) reaches V1 at a latency of about 40 ms. Multiple stimuli are all represented at this stage. Then this information is fed forward to the extrastriate, parietal, and temporal areas of the brain. By 80 ms after stimulus onset most visual areas are activated, and at about 120 ms activation is found in the motor cortex transmitted through the dorsal pathway. The preattentional feedforward processing culminates within 100 or 120 ms after stimulus onset. The processing in the FFS is unconscious and is capable of generating increasingly complex receptive field-tuning properties and thus extracting high-level information that could lead to categorization. Some groupings are computed at this stage; during the FFS, contours are extracted in early visual areas, and form features and patterns of motion are extracted in higher visual areas (V2 to MT). The initial pattern of neuronal activity that results from the stage of parallel extraction of features in a visual scene by specialized areas of the visual cortex has been called "base representation" (Roelfsema et al. 2000; Roelfsema 2005).

Then the feedforward signal reaches area V4, where recurrent processing enters the picture with a delay of about 100–120 ms. Horizontal and recurrent processing allows interaction between the distributed information along the visual stream and, more specifically, between neurons at that area and neurons that have been activated earlier at lower levels. In other words, recurrent processing enables information that has been processed in higher visual areas to reenter lower-level areas, such as V1 (Lamme and Roelfsema 2000). This first recurrent processing is local in that it is confined to interactions within the visual areas. Lamme (2003; 2005) argues that at this stage visual awareness emerges, and, more specifically, a form of awareness: "phenomenal awareness." The recurrent interactions at this stage functions as the marker of phenomenal awareness (Block 2005, Super 2001). It seems, thus, that when one perceives, in the sense that one is aware of some perceptual content no matter what this content might be, there is not a terminal perceptual area in which when the signals enter awareness emerges. Instead, awareness is the result of the activation of a whole nexus of brain areas through recurrent processing, the same brain areas that are involved in the processing of the visual stimulus in the first place. Studies by Moutoussis and Zeki (2002) suggest that the difference between mere visual processing and awareness in the nexus of brain areas that are involved in both is marked by an elevated level of activity of neurons when awareness occurs.

At this stage an initial coherent perceptual interpretation of the scene is provided, since features bind further. The base representation resulting from the stage of parallel feedforward extraction of visual features leaves many problems unresolved. Owing to the distributed nature of the neuronal representations formed in the base representation, many features of objects (e.g., location and shape) are represented at different visual areas. When there are multiple objects in a scene, the distributed representation creates the binding problem—that is, the problem of which features belong to some object rather than to another. Horizontal and local recurrent processing addresses this problem by providing "base groupings" (Roelfsema et al. 2000)—that is, by creating conjunction detectors that bind features together (Roelfsema 2005).

Thus, feedback and horizontal connections are involved in the integration of information about different parts of the visual field (Hupé et al. 1998). This contributes to solving the object-segmentation problem for those objects that are not segmented in the first FFS pass. Cortical feedback from V5 (a small area of the superior temporal sulcus) and from MT, for instance, improves discrimination between figure and ground by neurons in either striate areas (V1) or extrastriate areas (V2, and V3) by amplifying their responses and focusing their activity, although the effect is more pronounced for the extrastriate areas (Hupé et al. 1998).

Contextual or horizontal modulation and its effects are well documented (Felleman et al. 1997; Gilbert et al. 2000; Kapadia et al. 1999; Lamme 1995; Lamme and Spekreijse 2000; Lamme and Roelfsema 2000; Lamme et al.

2000; Zipser et al. 1996) in most visual areas. The contextual influences are implemented by horizontal connections that link cells with widely separated receptive fields. In V1, horizontal connections connect mainly neurons that have closely spaced receptive fields and whose preferred stimulus is collinear line elements, that is, cells that have similar orientation tuning (Gilbert and Wiesel 1989; Gilbert et al. 2000; Roelfsema et al. 1998; Schall and Bichot 1998).

There is ample evidence (Cavanagh 1988; Livingstone and Hubel 1987; Moutoussis and Zeki 1997; Zeki 1981, 1993) that the early vision module consists of a set of interconnected processes for orientation, shape, color, motion, stereo, and luminance that cooperate within it. These are functionally independent, they process stimuli in parallel, and they provide input both to each other and to other visual areas that bind incoming information and segregate figures from ground. Studies (Moutoussis and Zeki 1997; Zeki 1981, 1993) also show that color, form, and motion are perceived separately and at different times. Color is perceived first, then shape, then motion. It seems, thus, that the brain consists not only of separate processing systems, but of separate perceptual systems that form a perceptual temporal hierarchy in vision. The same studies suggest that when two areas with different specializations (say, color and shape) project to a third area in the brain, information integration or binding does not occur by direct convergence in that third area (that is, the inputs are not integrated in that third area by a converging process that takes place there), but is brought about by the action of neural connections interlinking the two separate areas—in other words, by means of the contextual or horizontal modulation.

Thus, figure-ground segregation could be based on differences in orientation, disparity, color, or luminance; contextual modulation in V1 provides such a segregation for all these cues (Lamme 1995; Zipser et al. 1996). Contextual effects create the "nonclassical" receptive field, that is, the areas to which the cell is responsive through inhibitory and excitatory connections with other cells. Roelfsema et al. (1998) and Gilbert et al. (2000) claim that horizontal connections and the contextual effects they create may be involved in the propagation of attentional modulation in early visual areas.

The feedback and horizontal modulations of cell activity in early vision suggest that the activity of neurons in early visual areas does not depend solely on feedforward inputs but depends also on the activity of other neurons in the same area with which they are linked through horizontal connections, and on the activity of other neurons in higher-order visual areas, is the latter being fed back to earlier areas through the feedback projections. In this sense, the activities of V1 cells, for instance, express different aspects of visual processing depending on the latency. At short latencies they represent local field features, whereas at longer latencies, owing to horizontal and/or feedback connections, they may represent various aspects of perceptual organization. In tasks in which many figures segregated from background were shown (Lamme et al. 1999), it was found that at 55 ms after stimulus onset V1 cells are selective for orientation, at 80 ms they are selective for the figure-ground boundary, and at 100 ms they are selective for the figure-ground relationship of the surface features that cover the receptive field of the cell. Top-down attentional effects are registered at a latency longer than 200 ms, a time by which the enhancement and inhibition of cells correlates with the number of objects present in the scene (Lamme et al. 2000).

Feedback connections can enhance or inhibit activation of neurons in lower processing areas only if the latter are already active. Otherwise the feedback projections cannot by themselves activate or silence neurons; only feedforward connections can play this role (Hupé et al. 1998). Note also that these horizontal and feedback interactions mostly occur within latencies shorter than 100 ms and thus belong at a preattentive stage of visual processing (Lamme 2000); as we shall see, attention is effectuated when full or global RP becomes possible at a latency of about 200 ms, since it involves working memory and learning. Even when the horizontal connections are involved in the propagation of attentional modulation in early visual areas, as Roelfsema et al (1998) argue, this modulation, as we shall see in detail in chapter 2, occurs with such a long delay that places the modulatory effects after the termination of the FFS and local RP.

In its first stages, recurrent processing is limited (by attentional suppression) to early visual areas and there is no feedback from cognitive areas. At these levels there is already some competition between multiple stimuli, especially between close-by stimuli. Not all stimuli can be processed in full by the receptive fields that get larger and larger going upstream in the visual cortical hierarchy. This results in crowding phenomena that render close-by stimuli difficult to process separately. However, the competition at this level is limited, and this renders possible the phenomenal awareness of many perceptual groups. Lamme suggests that visual recurrent processing may be the neural correlate of binding or perceptual organization. Whether at this preattentional stage the binding problem has been solved is not clear. The binding of some features of a particular object (say, its color and its shape) requires attention, while other feature combinations (such as shape and location) and segregations are detected preattentively either in the base representation (i.e., the representation formed during the FFS sweep; see Roelfsema 2005) or by means of binding operators when horizontal and local RP occurs.

At a latency of about 200 ms, recurrent processing may gradually involve higher cognitive centers (e.g., frontal and prefrontal cortex and the mnemonic circuits) in the brain and output areas. In that sense, this kind of RP is global, as opposed to local RP involving only visual areas. Suppose, for instance, that an abstract cue has been presented to a subject in a selection task or in some task that requires that the subject report her experience. In order for the cue to affect selection or allow the subject to report her experience, "parts of the brain that extract the meaning of the cue, and that able to relate this to current needs and goals, must preactivate or otherwise facilitate the appropriate sensory pathways, mostly via corticocortical feedback or subcortical routes" (Lamme 2003, p. 15). The transformation of visual information into motor activity enables a report (or, in general, a behavioral response), which is based on the content of phenomenal experiences.

At this level there is considerable competition, since not many stimuli can interact with the higher levels. Further selection becomes necessary when stimuli reach the brain but only one response is possible; then one stimulus must be selected and processed further so that a response is possible. Attentional selection intervenes at this stage to resolve this competition. The selection results from the combination of the information processing with short-term and long-term memory, which recover the meaning of input and relate it to the subject's current goals.

The work of Lamme and colleagues shows that access awareness arises about 270 ms after stimulus onset, a result that is supported by studies of attentional blink in which the P3 component of event-related potentials (ERPs) is elicited at latencies of about 270–300 ms (Hopfinger et al. 2004) and by studies correlating behavioral visibility ratings and recordings of ERPs (Sergent et al. 2005). The P3 component is generally taken to index explicit detection (of, say, changes in objects in a scene) and, thus, conscious awareness (Evans et al. 2000; Niedeggen et al. 2001). This means that the subject has access to the content of her perceptual states and can therefore report them; hence the use of the term *access awareness* or *report awareness* for this kind of awareness. Access awareness is the characteristic mark of conscious visual experience.

Block (2005a,b) raises the possibility that a "doubter" might argue that the contents formed up to the local RP level are not really objects, not even in the sense of proto-objects, and thus they are not contents but proto-contents; they become contents when and if they are grasped by attention and enter the global workspace that constitutes the basis of consciousness. Against that objection, Block cites work of Super et al. (2001b) which shows that the marker of phenomenal consciousness (that is, recurrent processing) is present in monkeys trained to saccade to a target, independently of whether the monkey accesses the target—that is, independently of whether attention focuses on the target. This shows that phenomenal awareness is activated even in the absence of a subsequent phase at which attention intervenes and transfers contents to the realm of access awareness.

The proposal by Lamme et al. that access awareness or conscious visual experience results from global recurrent processing involving higher areas in the brain, such as frontal and prefrontal areas and mnemonic circuits, finds support in recent work (Dehaene et al. 1998; Dehaene et al. 2003; Dehaene and Changeux 2005; Sergent et al. 2005) that puts forth the hypothesis of the "global neuronal workspace model." According to this hypothesis, the step to conscious visual experience (which Dehaene and colleagues call "conscious perception") consists in the entry of processed visual stimuli into a global brain state that relates distant areas, including parietal, prefrontal, frontal areas, and anterior cingulated nodes. These higher cortical association areas have neurons that are interconnected through long-distance connections and which send top-down signals to sensory areas, mobilizing them in a top-down manner. As a result of this combined bottom-up and top-down activity, a dynamic neural system emerges that is characterized by recurrent processing involving both visual areas and higher cortical areas. The entry of perceptual information into such a dynamic loop renders it reportable by multiple means, and stimuli gain access to consciousness by mobilizing a global workspace. For a stimulus to enter into the global workspace, its duration, and therefore the strength of the bottom-up signal along thalamocortical connections that the stimulus elicits, much exceed a threshold. Thus, there exists a critical stimulus duration beyond which the early visual areas can receive top-down signals from the workspace neurons reverberating their activation.

The same work also supports the thesis that visual processing consists of two stages of stimulus processing: an early stage of parallel unconscious processing that comprises Lamme's FFS and local RR[5] and a later stage, of limited capacity, that imposes a bottleneck on visual processing, and which is responsible for access awareness or conscious visual experience. Dehaene and Changeux write: "Because of its long-distance brain-scale connectivity, the global workspace establishes a central processing bottleneck such that, in the presence of two competing stimuli, processing of the first temporarily blocks high-level processing of the second." (2005, p. 0002) It is at the later stage that stimuli enter the global neuronal workspace. It is important to notice a dimension of this work, not covered much by Lamme, about the fate of those stimuli of the first stage that somehow do not pass the bottleneck of the second stage and thus do not make it into consciousness. The processing of these stimuli is not stopped when they fail to pass to the next stag; it can continue for a long time within the left temporal lobe (Sergent et al. 2005). As a result, conscious and unconscious processing proceed along partially distinct and parallel anatomical pathways, and they may overlap in time (see the discussion on the processing of unconscious stimuli in this chapter).

Lamme and Roelfsema discuss the nature of information that has achieved only local recurrent embedding and therefore has not reached the level of access awareness, and one can only be phenomenally aware of it. The information is situated between feedforward (unconscious or preconscious) and globally recurrent (access conscious) processing. The local recurrent interactions relate features to other features (recall that some binding and the formation of complex stimuli also take place during the FFS sweep), allowing binding and segregation to occur; this results in some form of perceptual organization at that stage, which produces "phenomenal awareness." Marr's $2\frac{1}{2}$D sketches are formed at that stage (thus, we are phenomenally aware of them), and in general this stage delivers a structural representation of an object. In addition, motion and size can be retrieved in the preattentive stage, since these are represented in cortical areas in which the FFS and local RP take place. Color is included in the list of features that can be preattentively extracted from a scene, although binding shape and size seems to require attention (Lamme 2003).

The "phenomenal" preattentive percept consists of tentatively but uniquely bound features that are segmented from visual information and are candidate objects for further processing (Driver et al. 2001; Lamme 2003, 2005; Wolfe et al. 2002). This information is a short-lived, vulnerable, and not easily reportable form of visual experience (Lamme 2003, p. 15). Pylyshyn (2001) calls this kind of object representation (that is, the representation output by early vision) a "proto-object." According to Pylyshyn (ibid., p. 361), the "proto-objects" are classes provided by early vision that are, at a first approximation, classes of viewer-centered shapes expressible in the vocabulary of geometry. Early vision, Pylyshyn argues (1999), delivers a small set of alternative proto-hypotheses, in the form of shape-based perceptual options, from among which focal attention selects an option for further processing. Thus, Pylyshyn's proto-objects are related to those of Rensink (2000a,b), although for Pylyshyn the proto-objects are structural descriptions of objects, whereas for Rensink they should more appropriately viewed as object parts, or objects that are bound together to form more complex objects.

However, these two ways of construing proto-objects need not be taken as contradictory. Recall that according to Humphreys (1999) there are two ways of representing objects in space, both of which exist in parallel in the visual system and which may serve different purposes: within-objects representations (in which elements are coded as parts of objects) and the between-objects representations (in which elements are coded as distinct independent objects). Thus, it may be that Rensink's work emphasizes the former form of representation, whereas Pylyshyn's work focuses on the latter. This is further supported by the fact that Rensink is mainly interested in the way attention selects among the proto-objects to identify objects in a visual scene; between-objects representations are formed in the ventral system, which is implicated in object identification. Hence, Rensink construes proto-objects as object parts that are glued together by attention to form the stable percepts that lead to object identification. Pylyshyn's work, on the other hand, stemmed from his Multiple Object Tracking experiments, in which subjects had to select points on a screen and mentally group them together, and then follow their motions in space amidst other identical points that served as distractors. This task involves apprehension of relative spatial relations among the points, motion in space, and navigation in the environment, tasks that are closely related to the dorsal system, in which the between-objects representations are constructed. Hence Pylyshyn construes proto-objects as individual objects in space. Of course, in most cases these streams interact in vision and thus both representations are formed in parallel and interact with each other (Glover 2004; Goodale and Milner 1992, 2004).

The formation of perceptual content through local RP is essential for the stimuli to reach some form or other of awareness, meaning phenomenal or report awareness. Walsh and Cowey (1998) review work with Transcranial Magnetic Stimulation (TMS), in which magnetic stimulation in the form of a single magnetic pulse or a train of pulses is applied for about 1 millisecond to the scalp. The magnetic stimulation produces functional disruption in the area affected for a short time (10–30 ms), and thus can be used as a lesion technique. TMS was initially applied to the occipital cortex of subjects performing a letter-identification task (Amassian et al.

1989). When the pulse was applied 0–40 ms after stimulus onset, there was no effect on performance. Application of the pulse 60–140 ms after stimulus onset did impair performance. A more pronounced effect, such that the subjects were incapable of detecting any of the letters, was found for applications of the pulse 80–100 ms after stimulus onset. In the framework of Lamme's model of visual processing, these results can be easily explained, and this provides additional support to the model. More specifically, early application of the pulse affects the FFS sweep but because of the short time of the effect enough information reaches the areas in which local RP and later on global RP takes place, and this allows the subjects to identify and report the letters. When the disruptive effect is applied with latencies of 80–100 ms, it coincides with the critical timing at which local RP since it disrupts the local RP that occurs at about 100 ms after stimulus onset. This prevents the representation of the letter form, and thus the performance deteriorates completely.

Attention determines the passage from phenomenal awareness to access awareness. It does so because a conscious report is a motor output and thus involves the motor cortex, and a selection or a decision in some task is situated between the early RP stage and the motor output. Whenever either a motor output or a decision or selection takes place, the meaning of stimuli must be recovered and related to the subject's goals and needs, and this involves higher cognitive areas in the brain. This, in turn, as we have seen, requires selective attention.

To recapitulate: Lamme, first, defines attention as a selection process in which some input is processed faster, better, and/or deeper than other input. Thus, it has a better chance of producing or influencing a behavioral response or of being memorized. Attentional selection modifies sensorimotor processes. Attention selects, according to behavioral needs, some among the proto-objects that are processed by the visual system in parallel and of which we are only phenomenally aware. Those that are thus selected will enter the realm of report awareness or access awareness. However, there are other forms of selection that are non-attentional. These include the processes that prevent many stimuli from reaching awareness, even when attended to. Such stimuli are the high temporal and spatial frequencies, anti-correlated disparity, physical wavelength (instead of color), crowded or masked stimuli, and so forth. Lamme, second, defines awareness as the occurrence of recurrent processing. Without RP there is no awareness whatsoever. The processes in the FFS are necessarily unconscious. When RP occurs, awareness arises. Initially, when RP is limited (e.g. by attentional suppression) to early areas, there is only phenomenal experience, and thus this form of awareness is called "phenomenal awareness." When RP also involves mnemonic and output areas, there is "access awareness." Since the content of this awareness can be typically reported, this form of awareness is also called "report awareness." It is at this point that selective attention intervenes to resolve competition that is caused by the processing bottleneck, allowing only some of the information available at that point to be further processed. Thus, the evolution from phenomenal awareness to access awareness depends on attentional selection mechanisms; only the information available at the local RP that is selected by attention will enter the realm of report awareness.

However, whether neurons engage in recurrent interactions, and thus whether one goes from unconscious to conscious processing, is determined by neural mechanisms independent of attention. The type of information of which one is phenomenally aware is situated between feedforward (unconscious) and globally recurrent (access-conscious) processing. As I have said, the information of which one is phenomenally aware is a short-lived, vulnerable, and not easily reportable form of visual experience (Lamme 2003, p. 3). In contrast, the "access awareness" (that is, the awareness that accompanies our normal experience) is more stable and is easily reportable.

Lamme's account of awareness and attention renders the former independent of the latter. One can have phenomenal awareness without attention and one can have attention without any form of awareness; recall that many of the stimuli never reach beyond the FFS even though they are being attended to. Recurrent processing is all it takes to ensure some form of awareness. Attention, on the other hand, is a selection process that arises for independent reasons and is implemented by different neural circuits; thus, at the neural level attention and awareness can be defined as two fully separate mechanisms. However, attention is related to awareness, since it is when attention intervenes that one goes from phenomenal awareness to access awareness. Attention is the competition between neural inputs for output space. Awareness in general—that is, the passage from unconscious to conscious processing—is the result of recurrent processing, independent of this competition, but its extent and its type depend on this competition.

Kanwisher (2001) reaches more or less the same conclusion. Kanwisher distinguishes perception from awareness: one can be in perceptual states while being unaware that one is in such states. Philosophers call these states "subpersonal," since they are not available to the person's awareness. Perceptual awareness "involves not only activation of the relevant perceptual properties, but the further construction of an organized representation in which these visual properties are attributed to their source in external objects and events" (ibid., p. 90). Thus, perceptual awareness presupposes binding of activated features with a representation that specifies a specific token, as opposed to type, object. This binding requires (ibid., p. 108) "visual attention," which thus becomes crucial for visual awareness, although attention is not, strictly speaking, necessary for awareness, since we can become aware of things that we do not attend to; one can be conscious of an unattended voice although not of the spoken words (Fernandez-Duque et al. 2003; Treisman 2004; Treisman and Kanwisher 1998), since, as we shall see next, there are many ways one can be aware of a stimulus. Kanwisher's "perceptual awareness," insofar as it requires attention, is equivalent to Lamme's and Block's report awareness. However, for Kanwisher various forms of binding occur before the subject becomes aware of a percept.⁶

There are many ways one can be aware of a stimulus. One may be aware of a mere presence (as opposed to absence), or of certain of the features of the stimulus, or of the category of the object present, or of the gist of a complex scene (Kanwisher 2001, p. 97). Thus, one can be visually aware of features or of the presence of an object and one can be also aware of the content of an organized representation. These are different kinds of awareness and only awareness of an organized representation requires visual attention. It is reasonable to argue, therefore, that the distinction between phenomenal awareness and access awareness or report awareness is latent in Kanwisher's work. The distinction between the awareness of the mere presence of an object with some properties and the awareness of the content of an organized representation is Kanwisher's distinction between the perceptual awareness of a type and the perceptual awareness of a token. Notice that the fact that without attention one can be aware only of a type instead of a token does not mean that one is not aware of a specific object. It means, rather, that without attention one cannot be aware of the fact that one has a representation with a specific content; one only perceives the content of a representational state that one has, but one is not aware of the fact that one has an organized representation of an object. To put it differently: One does not relate the features to a source in space and time, in the sense of having a representation of these features as features of that specific object token, although one perceives the features bound to an object. Representing a specific object-token involves a separate mental act that requires attention. Treisman and Kanwisher (1998) remark that although object recognition can occur within 100–200 ms after

stimulus onset, it takes another 100 ms for the required subsequent processes to bring this information into awareness so that the perceiver is
aware of the presence of a token object, which means that the perceiver
has access awareness to the contents of her cognitive states only after the
object has been identified. This fits well with work by Rensink and Lamme,
since in their accounts awareness requires attention, and it is attention
that allows object identification. It is also consistent with Lamme's finding
(which I will discuss in chapter 2) that access awareness or report awareness
arises much later that the onset of spatial attention and that in that
sense awareness is a late development and has a broad dorso-parietal
distribution.

Kanwisher argues further that the *contents* of awareness are being represented in the domain-specific areas of the ventral system, where the activation of a large region, the lateral occipital complex (LOC), shows strong
correlation with awareness (2001, p. 98). Kanwisher speculates that the
identification of an object takes place in the ventral system, a hypothesis
that is also advanced by studies on the distinction between ventral and
dorsal systems (which I will review in chapter 3), although, as she notes,
there are known exceptions to her hypothesis. But the *content-independent
aspects* of perceptual awareness—perhaps what it feels like to be aware of
something —depend on the interaction between the attentional network
in dorso-frontal-parietal areas with the dorsal pathway. Kanwisher's claim
that the content-independent aspects of perceptual awareness may be
correlated with activity along the dorsal system, whereas the contents of
awareness being represented along the ventral system conforms with
Matthen's (2005) view that dorsal processing gives rise to the feeling of
presence of objects in a visual scene, although awareness of the features of
these objects occurs in the ventral system.

Kanwisher's claim that representations of objects that can be formed
without attention (and thus without report awareness) correspond to representations of types of objects rather than to representations of tokens of
objects fits well with both Lamme's account of vision and Rensink's. Recall
that for Kanwisher representation of a type rather than of a token of an
object does not mean that one does not perceive a specific object. One is
aware of the existence of an object; and notoriously we are not aware of
types, only of specific object tokens. For Kanwisher, representation of a
type rather than of a token means, rather, that one is not aware of the fact
that one has a representation with an organized content; one perceives the
content of one's representation that is formed before the onset of attention. This, in turn, implies that the preattentional information about an

object is restricted to what information is retrieved directly from the environment in early vision and cannot benefit from information stored in memory or from information constructed in later stages of vision. As we have seen, in Lamme's and Rensink's accounts, in the absence of attention, it is possible to construct only some fleeting unstable representations of objects that contain sparse information and lack specific details about objects. Thus, these representations correspond to types rather than tokens of objects, types being at a more general level of abstraction and thus containing less information than tokens. This remark will help me elucidate (in chapters 4 and 5) some problems besetting the philosophical discussion pertaining to nonconceptual content, and more specifically the issue of the fine-grained as opposed to coarse-grained nature of the nonconceptual content of experience.

1.3   Top-Down Attentional Influences on Perception

As we have seen, in theories that construe vision as a biased-competition account attention is viewed less as the enhancement of the processing of the attended information than as the result of the biased competition between neuronal populations that encode environmental stimuli. The bias can be either bottom-up or top-down, and usually it is both. Closure and common region, for instance, are properties of the stimulus that bias the competition toward segmenting and selecting objects that have the properties of forming closed or common regions. The goals of the observer, on the other hand, affect these same processes in a top-down way; obviously, we tend to select in a scene those objects that are behaviorally relevant.

According to Vecera (2000) there are at least three sources of top-down information that can bias either object segregation and/or object attention: object-recognition processes, perceptual set processes, and spatial attention processes. It is known that familiar objects have an advantage over unfamiliar objects in object figure-ground segregation (Peterson 1994; Vecera and O'Reilly 2000) and in object attention (Vecera and Farah 1997). Using Desimone's (1999) account of biased competition, one can explain these findings by arguing that familiar objects, which are stored in visual long-term memory, in the appropriate context (that is, when they become task relevant), activate cells in visual working memory that represent the familiar objects' features, thus providing top-down feedback that enhances the activation of neurons in the visual cortex that respond to these objects, giving them an edge in their competition against neuronal assemblies that respond to unfamiliar objects.

The second top-down source of bias on object segmentation and attention is *perceptual set*, which refers to the expectancies or goals held by the observer and which, in the context of an experimental set-up, are usually determined by the experimenter's instructions (Vecera 2000). Neisser and Becklen (1975) and Baylis (1994) have shown, indeed, that perceptual set can influence object-based attention. Folk et al. (1992) uses the term *attentional control settings* to denote all those factors that guide perceptual acts (that is, the perceptual goals held by the observer during the task, such as visual search). Such goals may include either the experimenter's instructions (search for a certain object, or focus at that location) or the subjects' plan of action (search for the book in the library). When it comes to object-based attention, perceptual set corresponds to Duncan and Humphreys's (1989) *template*, that is, the description of a target object, as defined by the experimenter, that the observer must keep active in her working memory for the duration of a task. Being active, this description enhances and thus biases the activations of neuronal assemblies that represent the target object and allows the selection of the target object. In this way, perceptual set influences object-based attention.

The activation of a template or a perceptual set may explain the process by which perceptual set operates with bi-stable stimuli (stimuli that support two perceptual interpretations, such as the Necker cube or the duck/rabbit figure), in which only one stimulus is present and there is not a target object that must be selected amidst other distractors; this is a case of figure-ground segmentation. In this case, the template facilitates one interpretation over another. Peterson and Hochberg's (1983) work with bi-stable stimuli sheds light on the mechanisms that underlie the way perceptual set biases object segmentation, that is, on the visual processes involved in top-down biases. Their findings show that the intention of the observer (i.e., that she is looking for a certain figure) does not affect by itself the organization of the stimulus. Some crucial points of fixation influence the organization of the stimulus, that is, by stimulus bottom-up information. The way a bi-stable stimulus can be perceptually interpreted depends on where the observer fixates her attention, because there are in the figure crucial points fixation on which determines the perceptual interpretation. This means that the mechanism underlying the bias of perceptual set in figure-ground segmentation involves the voluntary control of spatial attention: the instructions of the experimenter, or the attentional setting in general, induces the observers to allocate their attention to a specific region in the stimulus (Peterson and Gibson 1994). This means that the mechanism underlying the bias of perceptual set in figure-ground segmentation involves the voluntary control of spatial attention and not directly the modulation of early perceptual processing. Further evidence that the perception of bi-stable figures is not determined during early visual processing by suppression of monocular cells but in higher visual areas (such as V4 and MT) in which shape is encoded is adduced by Leopold and Logothetis (1996) and Logothetis and Schall (1989). I discuss this evidence in chapter 2.

The third top-down source of bias on object segmentation and attention is spatial attention. In fact, it seems that spatial attention may be the mechanism that underlies perceptual set, in the sense that the effects of perceptual set are mediated by the control of spatial attention. In other words, the cognitive states of the observer induced by perceptual set drive the observer to allocate her attention to a region in space that is behaviorally salient. There is evidence that spatial attention affects figure-ground segregation (Driver and Baylis 1996). Subjects performed a contour-matching task with ambiguous figure-ground displays in which they had to match the contour of one of the regions of the ambiguous display. Before the display, a spatial "pre-cue" appeared that either predicted or did not predict the region that the subjects would have to match. The subjects performed faster only when the cue was predictive of the region to be matched. Since only the pre-cue influenced performance, the study shows that spatial attention influenced the figure-ground matching process and thus object segregation.

As in the studies by Peterson and Gibson (1994), Peterson and Hochberg (1983), and Driver and Baylis (1996), spatial attention seems to be the mechanism that implements the effects of perceptual set by guiding the observer to focus attention on critical points at locations that bias the competition and determine the outcome of the visual process. Now, we have seen that object segmentation takes place at various levels of visual processing both early and late. If the effects of spatial location can be registered with latencies that are within the time course of early perceptual processing, then this seems to be clear evidence for modulation of early perceptual processing by cognition through the effects of endogenous (i.e., cognitively driven) spatial attention. As we shall see in the next chapter, the spatial effects are indeed registered at short latencies (about 70 ms after stimulus onset), and thus there is a *prima facie* case for the cognitive penetrability of perception. However, things will turn out differently, owing to what I will call the indirect character of the manner in which spatial attention influences perception.

This section has shed some light on the role of top-down constraints in object segmentation and identification. A theme emerged clearly from the discussion, namely the predominant role of attention in general and spatial attention in particular in mediating the top-down cognitive influences on perception. Thus, attention becomes crucial in any discussion of the interface between perception and cognition, and therefore in any discussion of the cognitive penetrability of perception.

1.4 Concluding Comments

In the next chapter I will discuss the effects of attention on perceptual processing, emphasizing the role of spatial attention. But here I would like to note some things and recapitulate the main findings of my first chapter.

First, the reader will have noticed that Lamme's phenomenal content is very similar to Pylyshyn's (1999, 2003) proto-hypotheses or proto-objects and to Vecera's and Rensink's proto-objects, in that phenomenal content is retrieved in a bottom-up preattentive stage from the visual scene, and has a shaky existence (in the sense that it has limited spatial and temporal coherence) that differs from the stable percept of which one has access awareness or report awareness and which is delivered at the final stage of visual processing. Furthermore, Lamme and Rensink agree that it is attention that makes the formation of the stable percept possible. The proto-objects are not cognitively accessible and thus one does not have access awareness or report awareness of them, and they are in competition for further processing. However, they are within the realm of phenomenal awareness—Block's (1995) phenomenal consciousness. The proto-objects and their features constitute the content of Lamme's and Block's phenomenal awareness and of Raftopoulos and Muller's (2006a,b) nonconceptual contents of experience. Thus, the locally recurrent processing is the neural correlate of phenomenal experience *per se*, or phenomenal awareness (Block 1995). Lamme's work suggests that even though the output of the ventral system is the content of our ordinary experience of which we are aware, a substantial part of the processing in the ventral system is unconscious; it also suggests that there is information processed in this system that never reaches awareness even when attended to, and information of which we are only phenomenally aware and which we can report only with difficulty, if at all.

Second, note that all the aforementioned models differ from traditional models of selective attention (such as FIT) that also posit that visual processing consists of two stages. FIT distinguishes two stages of visual processing: a preattentive parallel stage at which all information across the visual field is processed and which extracts primitive features from the scene without integrating them, and a serial attentive stage at which only some information is selected for further processing and is integrated to form shapes and eventually objects (Treisman and Gelade 1980). The difference is due to the fact that, in the class of models of attention and of visual processing discussed here, the parallel stage of processing delivers structures that integrate to some extent features in the stimuli. There is, indeed, extensive evidence that in some cases complex information can be extracted in parallel across the visual display (Enns and Rensink 1991; Gilchrist et al. 1997). Some researchers (e.g. Wolfe et al. 2002) argue that the object-segmenting stage (that is, the separation of object-structures from the background) is preattentive, rather than being performed by serial scanning for each likely object location. These structures are the proto-objects (Driver 2001; Pylyshyn 2001; Rensink 2000a,b; Scholl 2001; Vecera 2000).

Thus, the preattentive parallel stage does not consist merely in the extraction of primitive features that are not integrated. As Spekreijse (2000, p. 1179) remarks, "pre-attentive mechanisms transform the visual input rapidly and in parallel, and parse the image into coherent parts. One of these parts may pop out and trigger a behavioral response. However, in many cases pre-attentional mechanisms are not sufficient, and visual attention needs to be invoked." If one substitutes "proto-objects" for "parts" and reads "coherent" bearing in mind the role of attention in the formation of coherent representations out of the more volatile proto-objects, then the above statement fully expresses the thesis defended in the present chapter.

Feature integration, as a process that binds parts of a scene into units, and thus object segmentation or segregation, takes place at many levels of visual processing, some early and some late (Driver et al. 2001; Scholl. 2001). Lamme's (2000; 2003), Lamme and Roelfsema (2000), and Roelfsema's (2005) model of visual processing emphasizes, among other things, that feature binding takes place at many levels of visual processing and that top-down and lateral recurrent interactions between cortical areas are important in feature binding. Though the preattentive stage is naturally related to the feedforward sweep and the recurrent processing is naturally related to attentive grouping, this does not mean that there is no grouping without attention. As we have seen, Lamme argues that grouping and recovery of structure take place both during the FFS sweep and during the stage of local RP—that is, before the onset of attention.

To sum up: The evidence examined in this chapter suggests that during early vision there is a bottom-up (in the sense of a process that is guided

only by the stimuli and not be cognitive influences), preliminary segregation of the sensory data into separate candidate objects, or, rather, proto-
objects. Top-down effects, including familiarity with objects or scenes or
some form of attentional setting, may override this initial segregation in
favor of some other parsing of the scene into objects. The top-down effects
also resolve ambiguities when the bottom-up processes do not suffice to
segment a scene into its objects (Treisman and Kanwisher 1998). However,
these top-down effects occur after early vision has performed its first pass
into parsing the scene into separate objects. Feature integration and object
segregation, thus, is better seen not as a separate stage of visual processing
higher in the brain, but as "an emergent phenomenon due to interactive
activation among the cortical areas" (Deco et al. 2002, p. 2939).

It seems, therefore, that there are various stages within visual processing
that can be summarized in the following distinction among three stages
of visual processing, to wit, sensation, perception, and observation[7]: All
processes that apply to the information contained in the retinal image
fall within the scope of *sensation*. Thus, we have processes that compute
information on light intensity. Sensation includes parts of early vision,
such as those processes that compute changes in light intensity by locating
and coding individual intensity changes. Sensation includes Marr's *raw
primal sketch* that provides information about zero crossings, bars, blobs,
boundaries, edge segments, and so on.[8] The idea is that much of the information about surfaces is encoded in changes in the intensity of reflected
light on the retina. Thus, the task of the very early visual system is to
decode this information by locating, representing, and interpreting both
the intensity changes and the ways in which the intensities are reorganized
at various spatial scales by more abstract properties, such as the alignment
of termination. Sharp changes in intensity, for instance, are interpreted as
surface boundaries. Since, however, this is not a world of uniformly illuminated smooth flat surfaces, the visual system must also represent and
interpret gradual changes in intensity. The properties of stimuli recorded
at this level (high temporal and spatial frequencies, anti-correlated disparity, etc.) never reach awareness. There are non-attentional selection mechanisms involved here that filter out information (Lamme 2003, 2004). In
neuroscientific terms, sensation consists in those processes that belong to
Lamme's feedforward sweep. It may be that they occur before the binding
of features extracted from the retinal image. The "image" resulting from
sensation, which initially is cognitively useless, is gradually transformed
along the visual pathways in increasingly structured representations, via
perception.

The processes that transform sensation to a representation that can be processed by cognition constitute *perception*. The output of these processes is a cognitively impenetrable content that is retrieved from a visual scene in a bottom-up way. A subset of this output—that which can be brought to a kind of awareness called "phenomenal awareness"—is the "phenomenal content." In Lamme's theory, phenomenal awareness requires local recurrent processing. It follows that only content that is formed by means of local RP can be "phenomenal content." Another subset is the content of subpersonal information-processing states. As an example of perception, consider Marr's various grouping procedures applied to the edge fragments formed in the *raw primal sketch*. They yield the *full primal sketch*, in which larger structures with boundaries and regions are recovered. Through the *primal sketch*, contours and textures in an image are captured in a purely bottom-up way, although processing at that level involves lateral and local top-down flow of information, which, however, being within early vision, does not threaten the bottom-up character of the relevant processes. Perception comprises the intermediate-level vision that includes processes (such as the extraction of shape and of spatial relations) that cannot be purely bottom-up but which do not require information from higher cognitive states, since they rely on lateral and local top-down flow of information (Hildreth and Ulmann 1995). Note that since the extraction of shape and of spatial relations require local RP, they are within the scope of phenomenal awareness. Thus, being nonconceptual, perceptual processes are not affected by our knowledge about specific objects and events. In Marr's model, the $2\frac{1}{2}$D sketch is the final product of perception. As we have seen, spatial relations, position, orientation, motion, size, viewer-centered shape, surface properties, and color are all bottom-retrievable by low-level vision processes. It may be that, in Lamme's framework, perception consists in those stages of the FFS that bind features in the image, such as edge fragments, and thus result in states that have a rudimentary structure, and in the stage of vision that involves local recurrent processing. Both sensation and perception constitute Pylyshyn's (2001, 2003, 2007) early vision.

All subsequent visual processes fall within *cognition*, and include both the post-sensory/semantic interface at which the object-recognition units intervene, as well as purely conceptual processes that lead to the identification and recognition of the array (high-level vision). At this level, we have *observation*. In Marr's theory, the culmination of visual processes is the *3-dimensional model* of an object. The recovery of the objects cannot be purely data-driven, since what is regarded as an object depends on the subsequent usage of the information, and thus is cognitively penetrable.

Several theories of vision hold that object identification is based on part decomposition, which is the first stage in forming a structural description of an object and which seems to depend on knowledge of specific objects. Other theorists, including Edelman (1999), propose that objects are identified by template-matching processes. Object recognition requires matching between the internal representation of an object stored in memory and the representation of an object generated from the image. Similarly, template matching relies on knowledge of specific objects and is, consequently, cognitively driven, since the templates result from previous encounters with objects that have been stored in memory.

2 The Timing of Visual Processing and the Effects of Attention

In the preceding chapter I argued that vision could be roughly divided into two parts: an early pre-attentional visual processing stage (in which information is retrieved in parallel and bottom-up fashion from the environment) and a higher attentional visual processing stage.[1] The former stage delivers the proto-objects, whereas the latter eventually delivers the objects of our ordinary experience. In the first section of this chapter, I discuss further the various stages into which vision can be decomposed by taking account the timing of visual processes. As will emerge from the discussion, and this is the main claim of this chapter, there is a part of vision, which I will call *perception*, that is cognitively encapsulated and thus cognitively impenetrable. This is the stage of visual processing that delivers the proto-objects. It consists in pre-attentive processes and processes that are modulated by spatial attention, but in an indirect way that does not entail cognitive penetration.

My argument will be, in a nutshell, that attention can be divided into *object-centered* and *visuo-spatial* attention. Attentional effects due to object-centered attention occur after perception, and therefore the possibility of their being cognitively driven does not undermine the cognitive impenetrability of perception. Visuo-spatial attention may act in two ways. First, it may enhance the base-line activation of the neuronal assemblies tuned to the attended location in specialized extrastriate areas V2, V3, V3a, V4, in parietal regions, and perhaps in striate cortex V1. This phenomenon, referred to as the *attentional modulation of spontaneous activity*, reflects the fact that spontaneous firing rates of neurons in all visual pathways are increased when attention is shifted, by means of a cue, toward the location of an upcoming stimulus *before* the presentation of the stimulus. This is a pre-perceptual effect that does not affect the cognitive penetrability of perception (Pylyshyn 1999; Raftopoulos 2001a,b). Second, spatial attention modulates perceptual processing, and this poses a serious threat to the thesis of cognitive impenetrability of perception, since spatial attention is usually driven both by bottom-up and top-down signals; thus it may be cognitively driven. To defend the cognitive impenetrability of perception, I discuss the way attention (spatial attention in particular) affects perceptual processing. I argue that spatial attention in its second form has an indirect effect that, in the last analysis, does not undermine the thesis of cognitive impenetrability.

2.1   The Time Course and the Modulation of Visual Processing by Attention

Leopold and Logothetis (1996) and Logothetis and Schall (1989) studied in animals the activity of neurons in areas ranging from the primary visual cortex (areas V1 and V2), where retinal signals first enter the brain, to the area V4 and the area called IT, which is the very end of one fork of visual processing. The last two areas are involved in encoding shapes and figure-ground segregation. Their study showed that in the primary cortex only 18 percent of neurons changed their response according to the image perceived by the animal. In areas corresponding to the midway of visual processing 38 percent of the neurons changed their response (in area V4). In the MT area, 43 percent of the neurons showed modulation by the conscious percept of the animal. These findings suggest that most of the neurons in early perceptual stages are tuned to information that can be extracted from the information recorded on the retina and are not influenced by the higher cognitive functions, that is by what the animal perceives the object to be. Other studies of visual perception (Chelazzi et al. 1993; Perrett et al. 1990; Schall and Bichot 1998) also show that cell firing in the temporal cortex is not modulated by what the animal perceives the object to be. This is evidence that early perception may not be modulated by the percept and thus the cognitive states of the observer. To examine in detail the time course of perceptual processing and the extent to which cognitive effects modulate perceptual processing through attentional effects, I will have recourse to brain scanning techniques of subjects that perform various perceptual and cognitive tasks.

Research (Kosslyn et al. 1993; Posner and Petersen 1990; Posner and Carr 1992; Posner and Raichle 1994; Heinze et al. 1994; Ziegler et al. 1997) with positron emission topography (PET) and event-related potential (ERP) provides a spatio-temporal picture (literally) of the brain of subjects while they are performing (a) bottom up processes, such as passive visual tasks (viewing on a screen strings of consonants, words, and pseudo-words), (b) processes that require some top-down influences, such as active attention-driven tasks (searching visual arrays for thickened letters), (c) processes that rely heavily on top-down semantic processing (generating a use in response to a visual word), and (d) processes that are purely top-down, such as imagery. This picture sheds light on the role of top-down pathways. At the same time it supports the principle of modular design and the independence of the lower levels of visual processing from top-down influences.

In studies of passive visual tasks, subjects were asked to fixate their gazes on a point in the middle of a monitor, in which four kinds of complex stimuli were to appear: false fonts, letter strings, pseudo-words, and words. PET scans provided a pictures of the activation of visual areas in the brain during these tasks. The analysis of these pictures relied on the assumption that the visual stimuli consisted of four codes. First, the "words" presented were complex collections of visual features, second, these features were aligned to form the letters of the English alphabet, third, some of the "words" had forms that satisfied the rules of English language, that is, they were English words, and fourth, some of these words had meanings.

The responses observed were responses to some, or all, of the four codes. All four groups produced bilateral responses in multiple areas of the visual system. The subtraction of the PET images when the brain processes the visual features of the array from the PET images in semantic processing shows that only words and pseudo-words produced characteristic responses in the inner surface of the left cerebral hemisphere, an area which is related to semantic processes. This suggests the existence of two levels of analysis in the visual system. The brain initially analyzes the visual features of the stimuli regardless of relationships to letters and words. At a second level, the brain analyzes the visual word forms. I hasten to note here that the fact that the subtraction of the PET images reveals an intense activity in the left hemisphere when semantic processing is taking place does not mean that semantic processing is localized at that area only. The method of subtraction only highlights areas that are activated in the one task but not in the other. It does not reveal the entire area that participates in semantic processing. In fact, we know that areas in both hemispheres are related to semantic activity.

More interesting were the PET images obtained in the active attention-driven visual tasks and in tasks of visual imagery. In the active attention-driven visual tasks, subjects were presented with succession of images on a screen and were asked to react whenever some attributes (color, motion, form) were different from one image to another (focal attention groups).

Thus, in this task the selection involved was due to the object-centered attention. The passive control group was instructed to watch the screen without reacting. The divided attention group were instructed to react to any changes whatsoever in the images.

The PET images of the passive group showed activations of areas traditionally associated with registration of color, motion and form in the extrastriate cortex. The subtraction of the divided attention PET images from the focal attention PET images allows the isolation of the areas that compute the specific features of the focal attention groups. The results were clear. Attention enhances blood flow at the same areas which are activated during the passive tasks. Thus, the same areas that process information in the passive tasks, process information in the active attention tasks, only this time their activation is amplified. The subtraction of the PET images in the passive acts from the PET images in the focal attention tasks allows us to track those areas outside the visual areas that are also activated only during the focal attention tasks and not during the passive tasks. There were found areas in the basal ganglia and the anterior cingulate gyrus (an area at the underside of the frontal lobe). These areas seem to be the sources of the amplification observed when attention is involved and it is likely that they constitute the attentional networks activated in the focal group conditions.

Similar results were obtained with the visual imagery tasks. Evidence (Farah 1984; Jacob and Jeannerod 2003; Ungerleider and Haxby 1994) shows that visual imagery activates the same brain areas as visual perception. Behavioral studies suggest that the processing of imagery and of visual perception share some mental operations. Studies with patients (Kosslyn 1988; Farah 1991) reveal that the mental operations that support visual imagery are highly localized (are carried out in precise locations) and distributed in many different areas in the brain (in both hemispheres). Also, many of the neural systems at which mental images are generated are the same as those that are activated during visual perception. Neuroimaging studies confirm these results. The subtraction of PET images during passive control tasks from the PET images in imagery tasks and from the PET images in visual perceptual tasks shows similar activations in imagery and perception, especially in posterior areas. Specifically, when a subject is mentally imaging faces or objects, the activated areas in her brain are located either at the occipito-temporal junction or in more anterior regions, including the inferotemporal cortex. These areas are also activated during perceptual tasks such as tasks involving recognition and matching of object shapes.

The PET studies were complemented by ERP studies of subjects who view words and consonant strings. These studies provide evidence that certain areas in the brain are activated about 100 ms after the word or the string is presented. Since these areas are activated irrespective of the stimuli, it can be surmised that they are activated by the features that words and consonant strings share, namely, visual physical features. Differences in the responses to words and consonant strings started about 150 ms after the stimuli appear. This means that the brain registers the word form 50 ms later than the visual features. What is important to note is that the ERP study shows that the distinction between words and consonant strings is not fed back by other higher processing areas but arises at the posterior sites of the cortex.

In addition to the studies by the researchers whose work was cited in the beginning of this section, further ERP studies with subjects who view word forms, that is, words and word-like stimuli (e.g. nonwords, pseudo-words, letter strings) also provide evidence for early registration of word forms (Nobre et al. 1994). As with the other studies, recordings from the inferior temporal lobe show that a region of the posterior fusiform gyrus responds equally to words and nonwords and is unaffected by the semantic context in which these word forms are embedded; this region registers the word form. In contrast, in a region of the anterior fusiform gyrus words and pseudo-words are being distinguished. The word form is registered with a latency of about 150 ms and in brain regions that are distinct from those that respond to other types of complex stimuli, such as faces, colored patterns etc. This suggests that these areas form a functionally specialized processing stream within the ventral pathway.

In other ERP studies (see Posner and Raichle 1994 for discussion), subjects were asked to search for a thickened letter in letter strings. This is clearly an attention-driven task, in which one would expect to find some top-down, task-driven processes. Records of the electrical activity during the search show that this top-down activity involves the same processing areas that are involved in computing visual features. But the search for the thickened letter causes activity in these same areas only about 200 ms after stimulus presentation (recall that the activity recorded when these sites register the visual features takes place 100 ms after the stimulus). Thus, the computations involved in the top-down attention driven tasks take place in roughly the same brain areas—the same electrodes are activated, predominately right posterior area—in which the bottom-up registration of visual features occurs, with a time delay of about 100 ms. Finally, studies of subjects performing semantic tasks, such as generation of the use of a noun, showed that word meaning is registered about 250 ms after presentation of the stimuli, and some of the areas activated are the same with those areas activated when visual physical features are processed.

The above discussion draws a first picture of the time course of visual processing and allows us to get a glimpse of the role of attention in this processing. Let us turn now to studying in detail the effects of attention on visual processing. Chelazzi et al. (1993), using cell recordings, studied the IT cells responses of monkeys in tasks in which they had to search for target-objects that are characterized by some feature; that is, tasks which required object-centered attention (which, as I explained in chapter 1, I take to include feature-centered attention). Their results suggest that the response of IT neurons to displays that include two objects consists of two phases. A parallel phase in which the activation of neurons responding to both objects is enhanced (each neuronal group responds to its preferred stimulus). The response does not depend on whether the preferred object is a target or not, which means that the activation is task independent. Therefore, there is a parallel phase in which information is retrieved bottom-up from a scene irrespective of task demands, and thus, independent of any top-down expectation-driven feedback; this stage can be construed as "preattentive," in that there is no selection involved. At the second phase, the response of the neurons shows an expectation-driven top-down modulation of processing. Specifically, about 150–200 ms after stimulus onset and 90–120 ms before the saccade to the target, the responses to the nontargets were suppressed and the dominant responses were those of the neuronal groups selective for the target; activation is enhanced only for the neuronal assembly that represents the target and is suppressed for the other. The enhancement is delayed and thus reflects the effect of re-entrant connections from hierarchically higher visual areas. This reinforces the results with human subjects discussed above that show that attentional effects are delayed in comparison to a first sweep of visual processing in the brain. Chelazzi et al. (1993) studies show that the inferior temporal cortex is involved in the process of selecting the objects to which one attends and foveates, which suggests that IT may be the locus at which memory (in the form of the internal representation of the cue that remains active during the delay period) interacts with object-centered attention. (I discussed the role of biases originating in visual working memory and affecting the competition between competitive neuronal assemblies in the IT cortex in section 1.2.)

Schall and Bichot's 1998 studies draw a similar picture. Recordings of neural activity in the FEF (frontal eye field) of monkeys that make saccades to a target in a pop-out visual search task or scan complex images show that there is an initial phase that lasts for about 100 ms after stimulus onset in which most neurons in FEF do not discriminate between target and distractors in the visual field. Discrimination occurs gradually starting at a latency of about 120 ms and culminating at 200 ms after stimulus onset, before the onset of saccades to the target, which is initiated about 180–220 ms after stimulus onset. The observed latency is an effect of the attentional mechanisms that result from the cueing of the target object and which exert their top-down effect on visual processing. The discrimination process maps the activity of visually responsive cells in the FEF as they start to signal the location of the target in the visual field. Again, this is evidence that attentional effects are delayed in time and affect the same visual areas that participate in non-attentional early visual processing. Note that Schall and Bichot's results agree with those of Chelazzi et al. (1993), in that target/nontarget discrimination takes place well before the initiation of a saccade to the target.

Leopold and Logothetis's (1996) and Logothetis and Schall's (1989) studies with monkeys on the modulation of neurons along the visual path by the conscious percept show dramatically that there is a stage of visual processing during which the neurons in early visual areas are unaffected by what the animal perceives at the end of visual processing. The activity of neurons in areas ranging from the primary visual cortex (areas V1 and V2) to the area V4 and the area MT in animals were studied. The last two areas are involved in encoding shapes and figure-ground segregation. The animals were subjected to the binocular rivalry, that is, the phenomenon of a percept that ensues when dissimilar stimuli are presented to the two eyes. In this case, the subject perceives a percept that alternates between that presented to the left eye and that presented to the right eye. The monkeys were showed two opposite patterns of motion (up and down), one in each eye, and they were rewarded to report the pattern they perceived. As expected the animals reported the two patterns randomly. These studies showed that in the primary cortex only 18 percent of neurons changed their response according to the motion perceived by the animal. In areas corresponding to the midway of visual processing 38 percent of the neurons changed their response (in area V4). In the MT area 43 percent of the neurons showed modulation by the conscious percept of the animal. These findings suggest that most of the neurons in early perceptual stages are tuned to information that can be extracted from the information recorded on the retina and are not influenced by what the animal perceives the pattern of motion to be. Another result that emerges from these studies is that the hypothesis that explains binocular rivalry by positing the suppression of early monocular cells in V1 and V2 areas is rendered unlikely by the experimental findings. Instead, binocular rivalry is better explained by proposing that the rivalry is between alternate stimulus representations (the two patterns of motion) that are encoded in the activity of many neurons in areas such as V4 and MT, in which shape encoding and figure-ground segregation encoding takes place. This result is important because it suggests that one of the alternate patterns of motion, or alternate objects in general, should be suppressed not during early visual processing but at the level at which shape and figure-ground segregation are encoded. Even at those higher areas, however, the majority of the neurons still respond to their preferred stimuli (57 percent). This means that it is likely that both patterns of motion or objects are encoded there and enter into competition. That the two alternate objects start to compete at this stage is evidenced by the fact that only in V4 and MT areas do neurons exist that respond when their preferred stimulus is suppressed. Areas V1 and V2 do not exhibit this phenomenon, which is evidence that it is unlikely that there is early competition between monocular neurons. Logothetis and Schall (1989) argue that the temporal dynamics of the phenomenon make it possible that the perception-related modulation of the neurons in MT area may be a result of feedback from higher centers. As we shall see when we discuss next Lamme's (2003, 2005) model of visual processing, V4 is the area at which recurrent processing emerges along the visual pathway. Thus, it is likely that both objects are being encoded in parallel during the early visual processing and then one of them is selected to be further processed and eventually being perceived. This means that early perceptual processing is not modulated by what the subject sees the object to be, that is, by its cognitive state. Leopold and Logothetis (1996, p. 552) argue that this explanation of binocular rivalry in terms of the rivalry between alternate shapes in higher visual centers might be extended to cover cases of bi-stable stimuli (such as the Necker cube or the duck/rabbit figure) and that "it is therefore possible that a common neural mechanism underlies all these forms of multistable perception."

Thompson and Schall (1999, 2000), using backward masking to affect the detection of a target, recorded from macaque frontal-eye-field (FEF) neurons. They found that these neurons initially (before 100 ms after stimulus onset) respond to the actual presence or not of the target. Later (100–300 ms), the activation of the same neurons corresponds to the monkey's behavioral response. Super and colleagues (2001a, 2003) found similar results recording multi-unit activity in V1 in monkeys performing a figure-ground discrimination task. The multiunit spiking activity in this area was correlated with many electrode sites in the cortex. It was delayed and its strength was partially predictive of whether the animal would report seeing the brief visual stimulus against a noisy background. Thus, there seem to be two phases of activation, one early phase related directly to the stimulus and a later response related to the subjects' behavioral responses. The late-time activity is contributed to feedback mechanisms through which top-down signals reenter the V1 area neurons.

Lamme (2003, 2005) elaborates further on the various phases of visual processing. Lamme and his colleagues argue that recent functional MRI studies combined with electrophysiological recordings, such as EEG/MEG, suggest that one can distinguish three stages in visual processing. The feedforward sweep (FFS), local recurrent processing (RP), and "full" or "global" recurrent processing involving higher cognitive centers. According to Lamme, activation reaches V1 at a latency of about 40 ms. Multiple stimuli are all represented at this stage. Then this information is fed forward to the extrastriate areas, parietal, and temporal areas of the brain. By 80 ms after stimulus onset most visual areas are activated. At this stage there are no attentional effects, a thesis that is further evidenced by findings that the first ERP wave subcomponent C1, which is registered at about 50–60 ms after stimulus onset and which represents the initial stimulus-evoked response in area V1 is unaffected both by spatial and object-centered attention (Hopfinger et al. 2004). This means that the initial FFS, that is, the initial feedforward sweep from LGN to the striate cortex leaves the V1 neurons' responses unaffected by spatial attention. The highest levels of visual cortical processing hierarchy in the ventral stream are reached within 100 ms, and at about 120 ms activation is found in the motor cortex as well, although activation reaches the motor cortex at this latency only through the dorsal system, the activation through the ventral system arriving with a longer latency (Lamme and Roelfsema 2000). At 100–150 ms after stimulus onset the first signs of recurrent processing are found, which however are restricted within early vision and thus exclude top-down signals from either memory of other cognitive centers in the brain. At 200 ms after stimulus onset, recurrent interactions with areas outside the visual stream allow the emergence of access awareness or report awareness, since they render the content of those perceptual states transparent to the person that is in those states.

Lamme and Roelfsema (2005, p. 572) argue that response latencies at any hierarchical level are about 10 ms longer than those at a lower level. "Thus, because 10 ms is in the range of the minimal interspike interval, a typical cortical neuron can fire at most a single spike before the next hier-archical level is activated, leaving no time for lateral connections and no time for feedback connections to exert their effect. Therefore, the ensemble of neurons that participate in the first sweep of activity through the hier-archy of visual areas is primarily determined by the pattern of feedforward connections."

The unconscious processing in the FFS is capable of generating increas-ingly complex receptive field-tuning properties and thus extracting high-level information that could lead to categorization. Thus, the FFS determines the classical receptive field of the neurons and their basic tuning properties. However, Lamme and Roelfsema argue (2005, p. 574), this does not justify the claim made by Oram and Perret (1992) that visual cortical processing is finished with the completion of the FFS, since many aspects of visual processing rely on recurrent processing. The pre-attentive feedforward processing culminates at about 100 ms after stimulus onset and results in some initial feature detection. At about 100–120 ms, local recurrent pro-cessing starts allowing further binding and segregation to occur; this results in some form of perceptual organization of the stimuli.

Since the FFS terminates at about 100–120 ms after stimulus onset, visual tasks (such as visual search for a target) that result in longer delays must involve recurrent processing. Moreover, delays around that time interval indicate the result of lateral effects. These imply that the neurons in early visual pathways involved in such tasks should receive lateral and top-down signals (reentry signals) from other areas in the visual system and other cognitive centers higher in the brain. It is natural to assume that the attentional modulation of the visual pathways takes place through such reentrant connections. Various pieces of evidence substantiate this assumption. Recordings (Roelfsema et al. 1998) from the visual cortex of monkeys who perform a texture segregation task show that V1 cells select for orientation of textures at about 55 ms after stimulus onset. The same cells are selective for the boundary between figure and ground at about 80 ms, and show an enhanced response when their receptive fields cover the figure surface compared to the background surface at about 100 ms. This is clearly an effect of contextual lateral or horizontal processing that originates in area V4.

Roelfsema's et al. (1998) and Lamme and Roelfsema's (2000) neurophysi-ological studies with monkeys that were trained to perform a curve-tracing task in which the target curve started with a marker of a given color that the monkey had been cued before the presentation of the stimulus, show two things regarding the modulation of early visual processes by attention.

First, V1 cells representing the cued color enhance their response 159 ms after stimulus onset, an enhancement caused by a color-selective feedback signal from higher visual areas and reflecting the effect of object-centered (feature-based, to be precise) attention. Second, object-centered attention enhances the responses of V1 cells that respond to the target curve as opposed to the distractor curve 235 ms after stimulus onset. Specifically, Roelfsema et al. (1998) trained macaques to select one of two equally salient curves and then they implanted 40–50 multiunit electrodes to various sites in V1 cortex. Manipulating the experimental conditions they made certain that the enhancement of the neuronal activity in V1 was due to object-centered attention and that it was not a simple sensory effect. However, the finding that the activity of cells in the primary visual cortex is enhanced by object-centered attention, and thus that attentional modulation occurs in the primary visual cortex as well, does not undermine the thesis that attentional effects occur after the FFS and local RP, since the attentional effects enhance the responses of V1 cells 235 ms after stimulus onset, a time by which both the FFS and local RP have terminated.

Dipole studies (Martinez et al. 2001; DiRusso et al. 2003) using high-spatial-resolution fMRI also show a delayed modulation of V1 activity during spatial attention that starts about 130–160 ms after stimulus onset. Combined with evidence, showing that the first effects of spatial attention (as exemplified by the P1 subcomponent wave of ERPs) take place about 70–100 ms after stimulus onset originating from in or near V3/V3a areas in the mid-occipital brain regions, the aforementioned findings makes plausible the hypothesis that selection of stimuli at the attended location first occurs at extrastriate cortical areas and it is a delayed feedback from these areas that modulates in a top-down manner the activity in primary visual cortex V1.

Aine et al. (1995), who used visual evoked magnetic fields, also report that the activity in striate cortex may be modulated by spatial attention. However, this occurs at long latencies (130–160 ms). The long latency indicates, in agreement with the interpretation of the results from the aforementioned dipole studies, that the activity is probably due to the reactivation of striate cortex as a result of recurrent signals from higher centers rather than in the modulation of the initial processing in the striate cortex.

Studies that examine the modulatory effects of task instructions regarding some particular feature or the location that subjects are instructed to attend before stimulus presentation on visual areas from V1 (Haenny and Schiller 1998; Luck et al. 1997) through extrastriate areas V2 and V4

(Connor et al. 1997; Luck et al. 1997), to MT (Treue et al. 1996), suggest that the modulation is more pronounced in areas far removed from V1. Attentional effects on V1 are marginal if at all observed (Clark and Hillyard 1996; Hillyard et al. 1998). Processing in neurons in V4 is modulated by attentional effects, but this modulation is more pronounced at 100–200 ms after stimulus onset, again after the FFS. Thus, the attentional effects are associated with enhanced activity in cells in extrastriate areas, when attention is directed to an image location to which these cells respond, and not with striate areas of the visual cortex (see also Heinze et al. 1994, whose PET studies failed to detect spatial attentional modulation of the striate cortex).

Zipser et al. (1996) argue that a long latency component in the neuronal responses in striate cortex to a texture patch covering the receptive field of the relevant neurons is under certain conditions enhanced, which suggest that the activity of V1 neurons can be modulated by activity that originates from extrastriate visual areas. Again here, the effect has a long latency. Furthermore, the response of V1 cells is enhanced if the texture surrounding the central patch is made perceptually distinct from the central patch because of differences in illumination, orientation, color, or disparity. This means that the effect is stimulus driven by bottom-up spread of activation and it does not reflect top-down attentional modulation but exogenous attention; in this sense it is attributed to a pre-attentive mechanism (Roelfsema et al. 1998). Thus, it falls within the realm of contextual effects occurring within the visual system and as such it is neutral with respect to the issue of the cognitive penetrability of perception. Note that all these results concerning the modulation of V1 area by attention contrast with other research that shows marginal modulation of attentional effects on the primary visual cortex (Haenny and Schiller 1998; Hillyard et al. 1998; Luck et al. 1997; Luck and Hillyard 2000).

Joseph et al. (1997), who used reaction times, found that visual feature search tasks are impaired by a sufficiently demanding attentional load. This result, they argue, suggests that attention modulates the perception of features, such as orientation, which were traditionally thought to be retrieved from visual scenes and be represented in V1 primary visual cortex during a parallel pre-attentive phase of visual processing, of the kind amply discussed in this chapter. This shows that there is no direct route of the pre-attentive features to awareness that overrides the attentional bottleneck. Their conclusion is that "these experiments argue against a direct route from pre-attentive processing to perceptual report. By providing a demonstration of 'preattentive' information that cannot be overly perceived without attention, we challenge the current dichotomous view that assumes the existence of a separate privileged category of preattentive perception" (ibid., p. 807).

Notice, however, that Joseph et al. (ibid.) used reaction times, which presuppose that the subjects react to stimuli of which they have access awareness or report awareness. That is why the conclusion they draw is that attention is needed for "perceptual report." But as we have seen, most studies that posit a pre-attentive stage of visual processing agree that attention is necessary for perceptual report, since it is attention that allows the formation of the stable objects of our experience, constructing them on the basis of a base representation of proto-objects that are formed during a pre-attentive parallel stage of feature extraction and of some initial grouping. It is no wonder, therefore, that attention modulates the report awareness of orientation and other pre-attentive stimuli that Joseph et al. (1997) find in their experiments. However, for exactly the same reason, this finding is not evidence against the extraction of the same information during a pre-attentive stage, provided that this information is not within the realm of report awareness or access awareness. In other words, Joseph et al. (1997) use tasks involving perceptual report, which require attention, and they find that these tasks do indeed involve attention. This says nothing against a pre-attentive perceptual processing stage that takes place well before the onset of access awareness or report awareness.

What is important for present purposes is that the aforementioned modulatory effects on striate cortex are at such long latencies that one can conclude that the processing in the striate cortex is not modulated by spatial attention during the critical first 100–120 ms at which the proto-objects are formed. Furthermore, the effects of object-centered attentional modulation on visual processing are delayed and that this kind of attentional modulation is observed in both striate and extrastriate areas of the visual cortex. Finally, although a full account will have to await the discussion of the modulation of perceptual processing by spatial attention, there is some early modulation (70–100 ms after stimulus onset) of the extrastriate cortex by spatial attention, whereas the modulation of V1 area by spatial attention is more delayed in time.

As we have seen, the FFS and local RP allow, in about 150 ms after stimulus onset, the construction of fairly complex representations of stimuli. The local recurrent interactions relate features to each other allowing further binding and segregation to occur. This results in some form of perceptual organization, which certainly includes information about the presence of discrete objects in a scene (that is the segregation of objects), their orientations, sizes, shapes or forms, motions; these features determine the structural description of objects.

Thorpe et al. (1996) conducted ERP experiments with human subjects who had to decide whether an animal was present in a scene on the basis of a 20-ms presentation of the image. This is a go/no-go categorization task; go for a positive answer and no-go for a negative answer to a trial. It took subjects 382–567 ms to decide, a latency that reflects the motor activity involved in providing the answer. Thorpe et al. (1996) found that in 150 ms after stimulus onset there was a clear differentiation in all frontal electrodes between go and no-go categorizations, which they attribute to neural activity that is generated by no-go trials. This means that at that latency the visual system has constructed a fairly complex representation of the stimuli that eventually differentiates between correct and no-go trials. One should note that the onset of a differential response in a brain area does not necessarily mean that the visual processing that is required for a task has been completed, since the task usually involves processing in other areas too; it only shows that a brain area has played its role in the task. In this case, at 150 ms after stimulus onset the brain has constructed a description of the objects in a visual scene that will allow it later on to perform the task at hand. It may be that the visual system by that time represents the shapes of the objects in a visual scene, an assumption that is compatible with the evidence adduced thus far, which later are compared with stored representations of animals and a decision is made on whether an animal is present is the scene or not.

Treisman (2004) offers an interesting hypothesis for the role of the delayed reverberation of striate cortex neurons. According to Treisman (1996, 2004) and Treisman and Kanwisher (1998), attention is needed for some feature binding, for detailed localization, and for conscious perception. The initial unconscious FFS provides the gist[2] of the scene, the gross spatial layout, rough bindings of features into some form of objects (perhaps the proto-objects that have been proposed in other studies), and primes competing identities through detected features. Treisman (2004) argues that attentional modulation of early visual areas occurs to allow a check of the initial rough bindings through the fine spatial resolution of early visual areas. Lamme and Roelfsema (2000), in a similar vein, suggest that the initial identifications for selected scene elements are checked against the sensory data to form the representations of objects as we consciously experience them. Hochstein and Ahissar (2002) hypothesize that awareness emerges first at higher cortical areas. The top-down signals to early visual areas, the neurons of which have smaller receptive fields and, thus, are better suited to detect featural details, serve the function of collecting fine sensory details. This hypothesis may explain the correlation between conscious detection of target objects and enhanced neuronal activity in early visual areas that was found in the studies we have discussed.

The evidence presented thus far suggests that that top-down cognitively driven object-centered attention modulates the competitive interactions between competing stimuli in early visual areas, exemplifying influences emanating from outside the receptive field of the relevant neurons through recurrent feedback connections. This enhancement occurs with latency longer than 200 ms after stimulus onset, although Chelazzi et al. (1993) report that nontarget suppression starts at 170 ms after stimulus onset. The same evidence also suggests that object-centered attentional effects do not modulate early perceptual processing, since they occur after early perception has output the proto-objects or proto-hypotheses. This vindicates Pylyshyn's (1999, 2001, 2003) and Raftopoulos's (2001a,b) claim that some attentional effects are post-perceptual and thus do not affect perception, construed as the early perceptual stage of visual processing. Attention intervenes to select the proto-objects that will be further processed by the cognitive system. Unfortunately for the proponents of a well-defined perception-attention distinction, things are not as straightforward. There is evidence for visuo-spatial attentional modulation on extrastriate areas before the termination of the FFS and the onset of local RP (LRP), that is, before the time interval 100–150 ms after stimulus onset, provided by studies of spatial attention. Thus, if there is a claim to be made for modulation of early visual processing (the FFS and local RP) by attentional effects, this will be substantiated by studies of spatial attention, which I examine next.

There is also another reason that renders this investigation important to the aim of this book. As has been noted, Peterson and Hochberg (1983) argue for the importance of certain crucial points in selecting one interpretation over another in bi-stable figures, which means that spatial attention, by focusing on those points, determines the interpretation of such a figure. Furthermore, Henderson and Hollingworth (1999) and Vecera (2000) argue that most top-down effects on visual processing are effected through spatial attention. Therefore, understanding the role of spatial attention in modulating visual processing is essential in studying the effects of cognitive states on visual processing.

Studies of the effects of spatial attention on perceptual processing show two kinds of modulation. The first regards the attentional modulation of spontaneous activity (Freiwald and Kanwisher 2004) and refers to the enhancement of the baseline activity of neurons that are tuned to a location that is cued and thus attracts, as it were, attention before the onset of any stimuli. Attending to a location may enhance the base-line activation of the neuronal assemblies tuned to the attended location in specialized extrastriate areas V2, V3, V3a, V4, and in parietal regions (Freiwald and Kanwisher 2004; Heeger and Ress 2004; Hopfinger et al. 2004; Kastner and Ungerleider 2000; Reynolds et al. 2000; Treisman 2004) and perhaps in striate cortex V1 (Kastner et al. 1999). This phenomenon is referred to as the *attentional modulation of spontaneous activity* and reflects the fact that spontaneous firing rates of neurons in all visual pathways are increased when attention is shifted toward the location of an upcoming stimulus before the presentation of the stimulus. This cue-related base response is similar for pattern-present and pattern-absent trials and exhibits the signature of spatial attention; it depends on task difficulty and selects retinotopically, that is, it is evident only in the subregion of visual cortex the neurons of which have receptive fields that fall within the attended location.

In fact, this effect is thought to reflect the effects of the neural processes that occur in response to instructions or cues to orient attention to a specific location before the stimulus appears. As such, it is better described as the effect of attentional control rather than the effect of spatial attention on target processing (Hopfinger et al. 2004). ERP studies (Hopf and Mangun 2000; Hopfinger et al. 2004) reveal the presence of two components in areas contralateral to the attended hemispherical hemifield. An early directing attention negativity (EDAN) registered in posterior parietal areas with an onset of 200–400 ms after the presentation of the cue, and a late directing attention positivity (LDAP) over occipital scalp sites with an onset of 500–700 ms after cue presentation. These studies support the hypothesis that "attention acts to prime sensory processing regions, and that the LDAP reflects a biasing of neural activity that may be responsible for the later selective processing of stimuli occurring at attended locations" (Hopfinger et al. 2004, p. 569), that is, the hypothesis that spatial cues enhance the spontaneous activity of the neurons tuned to the attended locations.

Spatial attention enhances the sensitivity of the neurons tuned to the attended spatial location before stimulus presentation by improving the signal-to-noise ratio of the neurons tuned to the attended location over the neurons with receptive fields outside the attended location that contribute only noise; this is done by elevating baseline activations of the neurons tuned to the attended locations. However, this effect does not determine what subjects perceive in that location because by enhancing the responses of all neurons tuned to the attended location independent of the neurons' preferred stimuli it keeps the differential responses of the neurons' unaltered and thus does not affect what it is perceived at that location. In other words, the relevant neurons' responses increase without affecting neural selectivity. What is perceived, the percept, depends on the relative activity of appropriate assembles of neurons that selectively code the features of the stimulus compared to the activity of assemblies that do not code the features of the stimulus and thus contribute noise. Since the percept depends on the differential response of these assemblies, this very early effect of spatial attention by not evoking differential responses leaves the percept unchanged; it makes detection of the objects and their features in the scene easier but it does not determine what the observer perceives.

The second kind of visuospatial attentional effects is about the modulation of perceptual processing by spatial attention itself and not by attentional control mechanisms of the type discussed above. Clark and Hillyard (1996) using visual evoked potentials (VEP) conducted studies on subjects who were presented with patterned flashes to the left and right visual fields, while the subjects maintained central fixation and attended to one visual field at a time. The flashes to attended locations elicited potentials with enhanced amplitude of the P1 and N1 ERP subcomponents compared with the potentials elicited by unattended stimuli. These components were stable with changes in eye position and thus are insensitive to the position of the eyes; they are only affected by the direction of attention not by the shifts in eye position. Hillyard et al. (1998) report studies using ERP and event-related-magnetic fields (ERF) that show a similar enhancement of the P1 and N1 subcomponents.

The P1 component was elicited at a latency of 80–100 ms by Clark and Hillyard (1996) and at a latency of 75–130 ms by Hillyard et al. (1998), which suggests that attentional selectivity and thus amplification of activation of stimulus information incoming from attended locations in the extrastriate cortex begins at about 80 ms after stimulus onset. Since the enhancement of P1 component is not accompanied by changes in its timing waveform or in its scalp voltage topography, it is likely that attention acts as a sensory gain control mechanism that modulates the flow of information from striate to extrastriate areas by improving the signal-to-noise ratio of the inputs at the attended location. Specifically, attention enhances the gain of neural responses, that is, it modulates neural responses in multiplicative ways. It seems, therefore, to constitute a "gain-control mechanism that enhances the excitability of visual cortical neurons coding the attended regions of space" (Hopfinger et al. 2004, p. 570). The larger ratio means that more relevant information can be extracted from the input (Hillyard et al. 1998). The N1 component was elicited at a latency of 120–200 ms (Clark and Hillyard 1996) or 150–190 ms (Hillyard et al. 1998), which shows that the modulation of processing by spatial attention continues until 200 ms after stimulus onset.

The P1 component of spatial attention reveals itself in studies examining the effects of attention on the pre-conscious analysis of global structure (Han et al. 2000; Heinze et al. 1998; Koivisto and Revonsuo 2004). In chapter 1 we saw that there is evidence that global and local levels of stimuli are processed in parallel at pre-conscious processing stages (that is, as early as the 100 ms after stimulus onset, which as we have seen is roughly the threshold at which phenomenal awareness enters the picture and pre-conscious processing ceases), although global stimuli are analyzed at that stage more than local stimuli. Han et al. (2000) showed that under focused-attention conditions the early P1 component of spatial attention (recall that this component is detected at 70–80 ms after stimulus onset), as well as later components, show shorter latencies for global rather than local targets, which means that the processing of global features has been differentiated from that of local features at an early stage of visual processing. This effect is thought to reflect differential spatial attention to the area containing the global or local stimuli.

Other studies on spatial attention (Luck and Hillyard 2000; Luck et al. 1997) were conducted with subjects who were instructed to attend to the left visual field in some trial blocks and to attend to the right visual field in other trial blocks. The subjects were asked to respond when they detect an infrequent target stimulus among the nontarget stimuli at the attended location. The P1 wave (a component of the ERP waveforms) is larger in amplitude for stimuli presented at the attended location than for stimuli presented at the unattended location. Since the difference is due to the attended location, it is reasonable to assume that the amplitude of the P1 wave is modulated by spatial attention. The effect begins 70–90 ms after stimulus onset, which means that it is clearly an early perceptual and not a postperceptual effect. Spatial selective attention increases the activation of the neural sites tuned to the selected loci. The effect is sensitive to stimulus factors such as contrast and position. It occurs before the identification of the stimuli and is insensitive to the identity of the stimuli. It is independent of the task-relevance of the stimulus, since it is observed for both targets and nontargets. It is also independent of the nature of the task, since it is observed for a variety of tasks ranging from passive viewing to active searching locations (see also Hopfinger et al. 2004). The effect is also insensitive to the cognitive states of the observers (expectations, desires, beliefs etc.) In that sense, P1 is thought to be an exogenous sensory component elicited by the onset of a stimulus at the attended location (Evans et al. 2000).

ERP recordings in general reveal various waveform components that are involved in the modulation of visual processing by attention. The first component that is modulated by attention, the P1 waveform, consists of two components. The initial phase (at 80–100 ms) of P1 originates from areas near or in V3/V3a and the later phase (at 100–130 ms) of P1 originates from V4 or near it. These imply that spatial attention influences first visual processing in extrastriate areas of the visual cortex. The initial sensory processing in the primary visual cortex V1, the C1 component that is elicited about 50 ms after stimulus onset, seems to be unaffected by attention (Luck and Hillyard 2000). Thus, the P1 component may represent the earliest stage of visual processing that is modulated by voluntary spatial attention (Mangun et al. 2000). However, the stage at which attentional selection will intervene depends on the conditions in which processing takes place (Mangun et al. 2000). According to Luck and Hillyard, "the presence or absence of selective attention at a given stage of processing depends on the presence or absence of interference at that stage, which in turn depends on the stimuli and the task" (2000, p. 688). Spatial attention seems to play two roles at the early stages of perceptual processing. It resolves ambiguous neural coding by suppressing competing input sources, and it improves signal-to-noise ratios by enhancing in a multiplicative "gain control" way the activation of neurons encoding attended locations. Indeed, there is evidence that attention selects both by enhancing relevant items (that is, those that are in the attended locations) and inhibiting irrelevant items (those in the unattended locations) (for a discussion, see Treisman 2004).

The N1 component, the second waveform subcomponent of spatial attention to register, arises from multiple generators in posterior parietal areas (an early phase at 140–160 ms) and in ventral occipital-temporal areas (late phase at 160–200 ms). Unlike the P1 that was found suppressed at the unattended locations and thus was considerably larger at the attended locations but did not show an enhancement at the attended locations, the N1 was enhanced at the attended locations but it was not suppressed at the unattended locations. It seems that P1 inhibits information from unattended locations, whereas N1 facilitates information from attended locations (Hopfinger et al. 2004; Treisman 2004). Luck (1995) has proposed that P1 reflects a gain control mechanism that suppresses signals from ignored locations, whereas N1 effects index the addition of a limited-capacity discriminative process at the attended location.

N1 is considered to be an index of the orientation of spatial attention to task-relevant objects, that is, objects that are related to the task at hand and are found at the attended locations (Evans et al. 2000). Task-relevant objects are distinguished from target irrelevant objects at about 140–200 ms after stimulus onset. This agrees with Chelazzi et al. (1993) and Schall and Bichot (1998) findings that target (task-relevant)/nontarget (task-irrelevant) discrimination occurs at about 150–200 and 120–200 respectively after stimulus onset. Moreover, experiments examining the precedence of global over local processing show that under certain conditions (difficult tasks in which the distractors are difficult to dissociate from the targets and attention is not easily allocated), both global and local information are processed in parallel at early stages and the asymmetry in their processing shows at latencies that coincide with the elicitation of N2 (Evans et al. 2000). Whereas P1 is enhanced in both exogenous and endogenous attention, N1 is enhanced only in endogenous or voluntary attention; that is, it is elicited only when subjects view a scene and decide where to attend, not just when they passively view the scene. This reflects the role of N1 in target/nontarget discrimination. However, N1 is insensitive to the type of the target and occurs long before the identification of the target.

The third waveform subcomponent observed in ERPs is the N2 component, which is elicited about 200–300 ms after stimulus onset and whose site is in monkeys (and perhaps in humans) area V4 and the inferotemporal cortex. Research (Chelazzi et al. 1993; Luck 1995; Luck et al. 1997) suggests that N2 reflects the allocation of attention to a location and/or object and is influenced by the type of the target and the density of the distractors. It is also sensitive to stimulus classification and evaluation (Mangun and Hilyard 1995). Its occurrence in tasks of local vs. global processing, for instance, may signify the process by which information is classified as having a global or a local source (Evans et al. 2000). For this reason, N2 is considered to be an endogenous attentional component. The timing of N2 is in line with the evidence discussed thus far suggesting that identification and classification of stimuli starts to take place about 200 ms after stimulus onset.

An important component is the P3 waveform that is elicited about 250–600, or 300–600 ms after stimulus onset and is generated in frontal/central, central/parietal, parietal/occipital areas, the temporal lobe, the temporal/parietal junction, and neighboring parietal and temporal neocortical regions. The generating sites and timing onset show that P3 is associated with cognitive/semantic processing. Such evidence is provided by ERP measurements in the attentional blink tasks. In the attentional blink paradigm, detecting one target leads to a period of approximately 500 ms during which a second target is not detected (that is, it does not register in access consciousness or in report consciousness), but which is otherwise perceived, since the P1 and N1 waveforms are not suppressed when the second target appears. The attentional blink paradigm suggests (Hopfinger et al. 2004) that the failure to detect the second target is caused by the failure to encode the second target in working memory because the consolidation of the first target in memory prevents the second target from being consolidated. In the attentional blink paradigm, P3 was completely eliminated when the second target appeared but was present when the first target appeared. This seems to imply that the P3 wave is associated with working memory encoding and thus indexes high postperceptual cognitive processes. Furthermore, the P3 positive late complex is typically elicited by binary decisions, recognition, and identification judgments, which, obviously, require cognitive/semantic processing. In change blindness experiments, for example, the search of the scene and detection of change is concluded with a P3 (Niedeggen et al. 2001). Recall also that in the tasks involving object-centered attention, the recognition and identification of targets takes place about 300 ms after stimulus presentation, which is the onset time the P3 component is elicited.

The preceding discussion about the modulation of visual processing by spatial attention shows that although the voluntary endogenous control of spatial attention is driven by cognitive demands and task demands, its early effects, to wit P1 and N1, are modulated by the nature of the stimuli and the nature of the stimuli and its relevance to the task respectively and not by the identity and or classificatory type of the stimulus.

One might argue at this point that it is certainly cognitive factors that determine the nature of the task and that, thus, cognition affects through N1 early visual processing. The rejoinder in defense of the cognitive impenetrability of perception is twofold. First, N1's onset (about 150 ms after stimulus presentation) is delayed enough so that it does not affect the FFS. Furthermore, the P1 component that does affect the FFS is clearly an exogenous component that does not index any cognitive top-down transmission of information to early visual stages. Moreover, N1 is elicited after much of LRP has taken place. This means that for about 150 ms perceptual processing is unaffected from any kind of cognitive effects, despite its early modulation by spatial attention. Second, the cognitive factors do not have an immediate effect on early visual processing; it is only by determining the nature of the task that they influence perception. Hence they modulate perception only indirectly. I will claim in section 2.2 and in chapters 7 and 8 that this is evidence that cognitive factors affect perception only in an indirect way through the effects of spatial attention and that this indirect modulation of perception by cognition, even at that relatively late stage, does not validate any claims as to the cognitive penetrability of perception.

Two findings of the aforementioned studies of spatial attention are of particular interest for the purposes of this book.

First, ERP studies of subjects asked to attend to and select stimuli on the basis of nonspatial features (color, shape, orientation, etc.) show that the elicited components are different from P1 and N1, as it was expected given that the early P1 and N1 reflect neuronal modulation by spatial attention and not object-centered attention that is registered much later. Stimuli that matched the expected features elicited a "selection negativity" (SN) with latency of 120–220 ms, which "provides a precise measure of the time at which an attended feature is being discriminated and selectively processed" (Hillyard et al. 1998, p. 204). Hillyard et al. (ibid.) report further studies with subjects that had to select stimuli on the basis of a conjunction of features, which show that separate SN may be isolated, indicating the order and timing of selection of each feature. At early stages (120–200 ms) the SN indices for each feature do not interact, a finding that suggests that at an early phase there is an independent parallel selection of task relevant features (in accordance with findings reported in chapter 1 suggesting that the different features in a scene are initially processed in parallel and independent of each other). At a later stage (200–250 ms) the SN for the particular conjunction of features is enhanced, although on some occasions feature conjunctions may be selected before 150 ms, which means that selection of conjunctive features may occur before the analysis of individual features has ended. These findings are important to us for two reasons. First, they show clearly that attentional selection of features is delayed in time and occurs after the termination of the FFS and of local RP. Second, even when features are selectively attended to, they are initially processed in parallel and independent of each other before their conjunction is being attended to. Bearing in mind that object recognition and identification usually requires use of a conjunction of features, whereas object individuation may rely on one feature only (it suffices that one object is black and the other red to individuate them, but to identify and recognize the first object one usually needs more than the color information), it follows that object individuation based on nonspatial features precedes the feature-based identification of objects (more about that in the next chapter).

The second interesting result concerns the selection of conjunction of features one of which is location. In tasks in which selection was based on both location and a nonspatial feature, say color, the processing of the nonspatial feature was hierarchically contingent upon the prior selection of location, as the comparison between the SN for color and P1/N1 for location components of ERP reveals. Hillyard et al. (1998, p. 204) conclude that selection by location has a special status and may control the further processing of nonspatial features.

Lavie and Driver (1996) also investigated the combined effects of spatial and object-centered attention. The subjects in their experiments viewed two overlapping lines or objects and discriminated features that appeared on the same or different lines or objects. In one of the experiments, a spatial cue appeared that drove the subjects to focus attention to a sub-region of the display that contained features from the different objects. The subjects were as fast to report features on the same object as they were to report features in the subregion of the two different objects. This finding contradicts the single object superiority effect and thus suggests that spatial attention overrides object-centered attention.

However, Vecera (2000) offers a somewhat different account of the experiments arguing that less-predictive spatial pre-cues than those used by Lavie and Driver (1996) may not abolish object-centered attention. Humphreys (1999) also argues that coding of spatial location is modulated by grouping between stimuli and that spatial representations supervene on the relations between objects, since parts can be assembled into objects in a parallel manner, without the need for focal attention. As we saw in chapter 1, attention, according to Humphreys (1999) and others, is not necessary to retrieve information from the environment or to group form elements to construct object descriptions, since both information retrieval and some grouping take place during a parallel pre-attentive stage of visual processing (the early visual processing). Attention is involved in selecting among the several object descriptions (in Humphreys's terminology, "within-object descriptions," in which elements are coded as parts of objects) that are formed during early visual processing for object identification. The supervenience of spatial representations on the relations between objects implies that attention is not usually focused on empty space (which explains experimental results showing poor performances in encoding empty space) but only to occupied locations, although sometimes attention to spatial relations between objects may be required for object identification (Humphreys 1999). It goes without saying that further research is needed to delineate the intricate relation between spatial and object-centered attention, although it is clear that the two accounts need not be mutually exclusive, since it may well be that, all other things being normal, object-based and space-based systems interact with each other, as in the case of the biased-competition account of visual processing and attention discussed in chapter 1. As Humphreys (1999, p. 1666) writes, "features coded during early stages of visual processing may be activated by both directed spatial attention and (top-down) by activated object representations, so that spatial attention affects object selection (biasing selection toward objects in the attended locations) and object properties affect spatial selection (so that spatial attention becomes locked onto objects). Such accounts allow for forms of interaction between 'object' and 'spatial' processing streams, so that coherent behavior results."

Furthermore, the studies of spatial attention show clearly that the modulation of perceptual processing by spatial attention occurs much earlier than the modulation of perceptual processing by object-centered attention is at work. Spatial attention effects were recorded as early as 70 ms after stimulus onset as opposed to 170 ms after stimulus onset (the latency at which suppression of nontarget stimuli begins in the visual search experiments by Chelazzi et al. (1993)) or 200–270 ms after stimulus onset (as reported by others). Desimone (1999, p. 21) argues that this difference in onset times may be due to differences in the nature of the feedback bias in spatial and object-centered attention. In spatial attention, Desimone writes, the feedback bias "may be more accurately targeted to all cells with the same receptive field in a small portion of a visuotopically organized area than to cells that share a common selectivity for shape or colors but which are widely distributed throughout the cortical area."

2.2   The Effects of Attention: Spatial Attention Influences Perception Indirectly

Let us now consider the top-down biases affecting visual perception and more specifically the process of object segregation and object identification, as they pertain to the issue of the cognitive penetrability of perception. The accounts of visual processes and attention reviewed thus far suggest that when viewing a scene the retinal image is translated into a set of visual primitives, which are used for the construction of the structural descriptions (proto-objects) of the objects or parts of objects in a scene.

Next, attention intervenes to select among the proto-objects those that are salient and to transfer the unstable proto-object information into a stable medium, namely visual working memory and eventually long-term memory. The representation built in working memory is matched to representations of objects stored in long-term memory (again, I ignore the ramifications of implicit processing for the role of attention in vision). This results in the identification of the objects in a scene and their categorization as members of a class (for example, the animal I see is a tiger). The processes in this phase are clearly cognitively driven. The problem that emerges for the debate about the cognitive penetrability or impenetrability of perception is whether the cognitive influences extend to the first two stages as well.

Henderson and Hollingworth (1999) state that models of object identification are divided into three groups, depending on the stage of the process of object identification at which the semantic context of the scene (which should be distinguished from the nonsemantic gist of the scene discussed in chapter 1), and the cognitive states it generates are supposed to exert its influence.

The first theory proposes that cognitive influences modulate visual processing in the first two stages. Thus, perception is penetrated by cognition. The second theory suggests that the cognitive influences are to be found at the matching stage, that is, when the structural description constructed by the perceptual system is compared to the contents of long-term memory. According to this theory, the processes leading to the construction of the proto-objects are purely perceptual, in the sense that they are independent of cognitive influences. The third theory, to which Henderson and Hollingworth subscribe, supports the view that neither the first stage nor the matching stage is subject to cognitive influences.

The strongest evidence in favor of the first theory is adduced from studies conducted by Biederman et al. (1982), Boyce et al. (1989), and Boyce et al. (1992) in which the researchers explore the detection advantage (detection sensitivity) that the context of a scene conveys on the search of objects consistent with this context. Their results suggest that scene context facilitates object identification. However, this by itself is not enough to substantiate the claim that the cognitive states generated by scene context modulate early perceptual processing that results in the formation of the proto-objects; it tells only against theories that seek to isolate object identification from cognitive influences. This is so because, according to the second theory, object identification is a cognitive process and thus it comes as no surprise that scene context affects object recognition.

To defeat this second view, one must show that scene context exerts an influence on early perceptual processing. Here we are back to attention, since, as I have said on several occasions, attention is the focal level at which cognition and perception interface and any effects on perceptual processes must be mediated by the modulation of perceptual processes by the cognitively driven attention.

Furthermore, serious concerns have been raised by Hollingworth and Henderson (1998), and especially and more devastatingly by Pylyshyn (1999), against the basic methodological assumptions used in these studies, and more specifically against the use of detection measures. Here I will only summarize these criticisms. First, it is not clear that the signal-detection methodology *did* adequately eliminated response biases from sensitivity measures. This may have resulted in the advantage of the objects that are consistent with the scene context arising not from the influence of scene context but from the deficient control of the response bias. Second, "participants may have searched areas of the scene where the target object was likely to be found. If the spatial positions of semantically consistent objects were more predictable than those of inconsistent objects, detection of the former would have been facilitated compared to the latter, even if there were no differences in the perceptibility of each type of object" (Henderson and Hollingworth 1999, p. 256). Research (Hollingworth and Henderson 1998) does support the view that objects that are consistent with scene context are easier to locate, since memory both for the spatial layout of a scene and for the specific positions of object can efficiently guide search within scenes (Hollingworth 2005, 2006).

In other words, what Henderson and Hollingworth suggest is that the context facilitates the focusing on spatial location and not the perceptibility of objects, in the way suggested by Rensink's limited-capacity pre-attentional system that provides a setting that guides the allocation of attention to different parts of a scene. However, this is an argument against the cognitive penetrability of perception only if focusing upon a salient location before the initiation of the perceptual process is a pre-perceptual effect that does not modulate perceptual processing itself. Studies on the attentional modulation of spontaneous activity, that is, the phenomenon of the enhancement of the spontaneous firing rates of neurons in all visual pathways when attention is shifted, by means of a cue, toward the location of an upcoming stimulus *before the presentation of the stimulus* support this view. However, despite this first victory, things are not as straightforward for the proponents of the cognitive encapsulation of perception, since the evidence on spatial attention reviewed in this chapter shows that some effects of spatial attention are delayed in time and do modulate perceptual processing (recall that the P1 effect of spatial attention on perceptual processing occurs with a latency of about 70 ms, which places it well within the window of early perceptual processing). Thus, to defend the cognitive encapsulation of perception, one needs to address this issue. I will undertake that task next, when I review the results on our excursion on attention.

These criticisms of the evidence in favor of the cognitive penetrability of perception (the first group of theories) coming from studies of the role of scene context in the perception of the objects in the scene are on the negative side. On the positive side, the review of the literature seems to support the second group of theories as well. More specifically, the studies reviewed in the first two chapters show that there are two kinds of attention that intervene in two different stages of the visual process to perform two different functions, although depending on the task some form of attention may be absent. First, through the P1 component, spatial attention intervenes at the early stages of perceptual processing to enhance the processing of information at the attended locations on the salient locations by actively suppressing signals from unattended locations. Second, object-centered attention intervenes to select from among the proto-objects that have been formed in the pre-attentive stage of visual processing those that are salient, to solve the competition problem, and to enable binding of all features to tokens of specific objects to form the objects of our conscious experience (Kanwisher 2001, 2004). The time delays associated with the effects of object-centered attention render clear that object-centered attention intervenes after some of the features retrieved in a bottom-up manner from the scene (size, shape, motion, spatial relations) have fused to deliver the candidate physical form of the proto-objects.

Pylyshyn (1999, 2003) and Raftopoulos (2001a,b) have argued that the interface between cognition and perception occurs through the function of attention and this occurs in two ways. First, object-centered attention selects among the various outputs of perceptual processes those that are relevant to the task at hand. The top-down flow of information is used so that attention might select the "hypothesis" or "proto-object" (or interpretation of the visual array) that fits the context from among the "hypotheses" (or alternative possible interpretations of the visual array) that perception delivers. Attention selects a hypothesis by "enhancing or attenuating the availability of certain perceptual categories . . . this is what Bruner meant by 'perceptual readiness'—the ready availability of categories of perception" (Pylyshyn 2003, p. 89). Folk et al. (1992) use the term *attentional control settings* to denote all those factors that guide perceptual acts, such as visual search, and consist in the perceptual goals held by the observer during the task. Such goals may include either the experimenter's instructions (search for a certain object, or focus at that location) or the subjects' plan of action (search for the book in the library). Duncan and Humphreys's (1989) *template*, that is, the description of a target-object as defined by the experimenter, is among the attentional control settings, as is Vecera's *perceptual set* that I discussed in section 1.2. At this stage, an object is identified and may be categorized. This selection requires recourse to memory and is usually accompanied by judgments pertaining to what is in the scene. Since this is a postperceptual effect, the interface between cognition and perception does not threaten the thesis that perception is cognitively impenetrable. Second, spatial attention intervenes before the onset of the perceptual processes and determines the location at which search will be conducted, in the sense that it enhances the activity of the neurons whose receptive fields fall within the attended location. The phenomenon of the enhancement of the spontaneous firing rates of neurons before the presentation of a stimulus shows that this is indeed one of the effects of spatial attention. Although cognitive factors determine where to orient atten-tion, that is, where to attend to, this is a pre-perceptual effect and does not threaten the cognitive impenetrability of perception.

 Although the research reviewed here does justice to the first part of the claim made by Pylyshyn and Raftopoulos, since it supports the claim that object-centered attention is delayed in time and does not modulate early perceptual processing, the second part of the claim is not fully borne out. This is because spatial attention does affect early perceptual processing, and thus undermines the thesis about the cognitive impenetrability of perception since its effects start at about 70 ms after stimulus onset, well within the time course of early perceptual processing. When one fixates one's gaze at some location before the stimulus onset, through say the instruction of the experimenter or a spatial cue or in general through some attentional control setting, there are effects of spatial attention in addition to the enhancement of spontaneous activity of the relevant neurons that are delayed and thus pervade early perceptual processing that starts after the eyes have focused on some location (recall that the stimulus is presented after attention has focused). In other words, when we focus on some location this focusing seems to modulate through spatial attention the perceptual processing that will follow the appearance of the stimulus. Hence, the argument that the effects of spatial attention are pre-perceptual and therefore the cognitive driven character of spatial attention does not undermine the cognitive impenetrability of perception fails.

I think that the mistake in Pylyshyn's and Raftopoulos's arguments that spatial attention determines the location at which search will be conducted and thus it is a pre-perceptual effect stems from an erroneous construal of spatial attention as a spotlight that focuses our resources on a certain area in space and enhances the processing of information found at that location. In such a framework it makes sense to say that spatial attention focuses first on locations, does what it does, and then perceptual processing begins after the attention has selected the locations at which search will be conducted. However, as I have argued in this book, there is strong evidence that attention should be understood as a competitive process among stimuli that are at first all processed in parallel. In this framework it does not make sense to say that spatial attention focuses on a specific location and then perceptual processing of information at that location begins. The effects of spatial attention occur when and where there is information processing and competition. If the competition arises relatively late and after the processes of early vision or perception, as in the case of object-centered attentional effects, then the attentional effects are post-perceptual and do not pose a threat to the thesis of the cognitive impenetrability of perception. Things are different with spatial attention though. The amplification of activation of stimulus information incoming from attended locations in the extrastriate cortex, by improving the signal-to-noise ratio of the inputs at the attended location, begins at about 70–80 ms after stimulus onset. Thus, competition between information from the attended location and other information coming from other locations within the visual field occurs during perceptual processing and thus spatial attention modulates this processing and is not a pre-perceptual effect.

To assess the ramifications of the early perceptual modulation by spatial attention as they pertain to the issue of the cognitive penetrability or impenetrability of perception, recall the spatial attention studies that show that the P1 effect, which represents the earliest stage of visual processing modulated by voluntary spatial attention, is insensitive to cognitive factors. To delineate this issue I must say a few words about the control of attention. What I will say applies to attention *simpliciter*, and thus, *a fortiori*, to spatial attention, which is the focus here.

Attention can be controlled either in bottom-up or top-down ways. Bottom-up control operates either by triggering shifts of attention (attentional capture) and of gaze control (oculomotor capture) or by guiding attention to particular locations. A sudden motion of an object in a scene, for instance, captures attention and focuses it on the moving object (Girelli and Luck 1997). In general there are various stimuli that capture attention, including the abrupt onset of a new object, provided that the onset is accompanied by strong local luminance transients (Franconeri et al. 2005), a unique shape or color, certain types of motion, luminance based transients, and some types of brightness change (Brockmole and Henderson 2005; Franconeri et al. 2005). In these cases, attention is stimuli-driven.[3] Top-down control of attention is related to the working memory, since sites of that kind of attentional control underlie systems of working memory. The exercise of attention depends on the contents of working memory; when one looks for a spoon, one's working memory informs one that spoons are usually in the kitchen, and one searches the kitchen. Working memory stores information, and performs executive control governing retrieval, encoding, and commands for the expression of attention (Baddeley 1995). These two functions underlie the distinction in the attentional control processes between expectancy of an upcoming event and preparation for that event (Laberge 2000). The expectation of an event is not necessarily accompanied by an attentional preparation for it. Information about the upcoming display of an object may be kept in working memory while selective attention may be directed elsewhere. The top-down attentional control of perception amounts to the attentional expectation for an upcoming event, which may be either a form of Bruner's perceptual readiness for some specific object or class of objects or the enhancement of the activation of neurons that are tuned to a location at which the event is expected to occur.

The template or attentional set is related to the object-centered attention whose effects are delayed in time and do not affect perception itself. For this reason I will examine the spatial component of the aforementioned attentional expectation. The spatial component of the attentional expectation may be exemplified by the late ERP component LDAN that is registered 500–700 ms after cue onset, when subjects are cued to a location before the presentation of the stimulus at that location. LDAN indexes the enhanced activity of neurons that are tuned to the attended location in which the upcoming event is expected to take place. Although the presence of the cue attracts attention in a bottom-up manner, similar enhancing effects occur when cognitive factors determine top-down the location to which attention focuses. When the stimulus, that is the event, is presented the first effects of spatial attention are registered through the P1 and N1 waveforms.

In this theoretical framework, the claim that the effects of spatial attention are insensitive to cognitive factors amounts to the following: First, although the enhancement of spontaneous neuronal activity that occurs before the stimulus onset may be cognitively driven, this effect does not determine what subjects perceive at that location because by enhancing the responses of all neurons tuned to the attended location independent of the neurons' preferred stimuli it keeps the differential responses of the neurons' unaltered. This is so because the percept depends on the relative activity of appropriate assembles of neurons that selectively code the features of the stimulus compared to the activity of assemblies that do not code the features of the stimulus. Since the percept depends on the differential response of these assemblies, this very early effect of spatial attention, by enhancing the responses of all neurons tuned to the attended location, leaves the percept unchanged; it makes detection of the objects and their features in the scene easier but it does not determine what the observer perceives because the neurons' responses increase without affecting neural selectivity. Second, as we have also seen, cognitive factors do not control P1, whose role seems to consist in inhibiting the activity of neurons that are tuned to unattended locations. Thus, P1 along with the enhancement of spontaneous activity that is registered before stimulus onset may reflect the expectation for an event. However, this is not sufficient to ensure attentional preparation for that event. Selective attentional preparation for an event will follow the expectation of that event, if the event is task-relative. This preparation is indexed by N1 (which is not sensitive to the type and identity of the stimulus), and it is elicited long before the stimulus is identified.

Cognitive factors control the expectation of an event by enhancing the spontaneous activity of neurons tuned to the location at which the event is expected to occur. This, as we saw, does not affect the formation of the percept. The expectation for an event is also effected through the inhibition of the activation of neurons tuned to unattended locations, as reflected by P1. This effect is stimulus driven and unaffected by cognitive factors. Then, task-relevant factors "translate" the expectation to attentional preparation for that event. Although the preparation for an event is task-driven, it is not directly determined by these cognitive factors, since N1, which indexes the task-relevance of the stimulus, is insensitive to the type and identity of the stimulus.

It seems, thus, that once spatial attention has selected some loci for focusing, and once it has enhanced the activity of the relevant neuronal sites and inhibited the activity of the other sites, information is registered at that stage of processing irrespective of task demands and cognitive states. In other words, once spatial attention enhances processing of information coming from some specific loci, and once task-relevant stimuli have been distinguished from task-irrelevant stimuli, what one sees at the relevant location depends on what is there, not on the cognitive stances of the viewer. This is a kind of indirect cognitive penetrability of perception; as I explain in chapters 7 and 8, this is what blocks the conclusions of epistemological constructivism. More specifically, although focal attention and thus attentional modulation is cognitively driven insofar as cognitive factors do determine where and what one chooses to attend to and the nature of the task, this does not pose a problem for the claim that perception is cognitively impenetrable. Cognitive factors do not directly modulate perceptual processing itself and do not affect the contents of perception, they only direct attention by orienting covert or overt focusing (Pylyshyn 1999). Using the requirement of enhanced perceptual sensitivity as a criterion for cognitive penetrability of perception, one could say paraphrasing Pylyshyn (ibid., p. 353) that there is not a modifiable physical parameter that results in an increased signal-to-noise ratio for the expected class of signals, which is what we would need to allow the context (cognitive factors) to set parameters so as to select the appropriate signal.

To summarize the main arguments made in this chapter, let us consider a potential threat to the account offered up to this point, to wit the thesis that attention does not modulate early perceptual processing in a way that threatens the cognitive impenetrability of perception. Lamme (2000, 2003) and Lamme and Roelfsema (2000) claim that attention intervenes at the sites of the FFS and affects it, since attentional mechanisms influence both the FFS and RP. This may be taken to mean that top-down effects from cognitive centers modulate FFS processing. Let us dwell upon this issue, because it is important for my discussion of cognitive impenetrability of perception in later chapters. To forestall the discussion there, the problem for a proponent of the cognitive impenetrability of perception thesis is the following. The thesis of cognitive impenetrability of perception means that there exists, at least, some part of visual processing that is immune to cognitive influences. The FFS and local RP stages of visual processing as defined by Lamme suggest themselves as plausible candidates for the cognitively impenetrable part of vision. However, if attentional mechanisms affect the FFS, and since attention may be cognitively driven, there is no part of visual processing that is encapsulated from cognition. In that sense cognition and vision would become continuous (Pylyshyn 1999).

Everything hinges on how one interprets Lamme's suggestion that attentional effects influence the FFS. Lamme has argued (2000, 2003) that attentional effects are delayed in time and that the timing course of the FFS, recall that by 100 ms after stimulus onset the FFS sweep has been completed, does not leave room for feedback connections to exert their effects (Lamme and Roelfsema 2000, p. 572). Given this, in what sense do attentional effects influence the FFS? Some indication is given by Lamme and Roelfsema (ibid., p. 576) in their discussion about the intricacies of relating the FFS with pre-attentive processing. They mention that instruction cues can generate feedback to early visual areas "before the actual stimulus appears, thereby altering the subsequent feedforward sweep." Indeed, Lamme and Roelfsema argue, early instructions cues have been shown to modulate visual responses in parietal areas as well as in the front eye fields (FEF) areas at early latencies (Joseph et al. 1997; Schall and Bichot 1998).

It is very important at this juncture to be explicit about the modes or kinds of attention one considers, that is, whether one refers to spatial-attention or object-centered attention. Lamme and Roelfsema's mention of modulation of activity in early visual areas before stimulus onset means that the attention at issue is spatial attention. In fact, it is very likely that they refer to the evidence we discussed pertaining to the attentional modulation of spontaneous activity, in which spatial attention enhances activity of neurons tuned to the attended location before stimulus presentation. There are two interrelated reasons that claims about the cognitive impenetrability of perception are not threatened by this modulation of the baseline activation of neurons in early visual areas by spatial attention. The first is that this is clearly a pre-perceptual effect and, thus, does not affect the course of perceptual processing itself. The second is that, as we saw above while discussing this spontaneous activity, this enhancement "does not evoke a percept, however, because percepts depend on a differential response, and the attentional boost does not evoke a differential response" (Heeger and Ress 2004, p. 339).

Things differ with respect to the second kind of effects of visuo-spatial attentional modulation on perceptual processing, since these effects occur very early and do affect perceptual processing. But the only effects that occur early enough to be within not only the FFS but also the LRP, are those reflected in the P1 and, at the limit, N1 subcomponent waveforms. As we saw, however, these components are thought to be an exogenous sensory component elicited by the presentation of an object in the visual scene (P1) and a semi-exogenous component that indexes the orientation of attention to a task-relevant object but that otherwise depends on the characteristics of the stimulus (N1). This means that, on the one hand, P1 is not the result of cognitive reentrant signals and that, on the other hand, N1 modulates perception only indirectly through the specification of the task. As I claimed earlier in this section and I will claim again in chapter 7, this indirect modulation of perception by cognition does not threaten the cognitive impenetrability of perception.

Recall, furthermore, the model of object-centered attention as biased competition among competing stimuli discussed in chapter 1. Early instruction cues about object features activate in working memory those cells that respond to the features of the cue. When the visual scene is presented to the subject, bottom-up activation spreads in parallel in the visual stream(s) activating the cells in the visual areas that are selective of the characteristics of all the objects in the visual field. The cells in working memory that have already been activated by the instruction cue enhance in a top-down manner the activation of the cells in the visual stream that are tuned to the features of the cued object, allowing it thus to win the competition for further processing. But this top-down effect of working memory on visual processing, reflecting the effects of object-centered attention, is delayed in time, as Lamme and Roelfsema's own work and work by others suggests, and thus cannot affect FFS and LRP processing. Lamme and Roelfsema (2000) comment on this delay by noting that temporal delays associated with the effects of attention are expected to be more pronounced when the instruction cue and the stimulus array are presented at the same time, as compared with delays that occur when the cue is presented before the stimulus appearance. In other words, should the cue be presented before the stimulus, attentional effects should occur earlier. However, even in the latter case, attentional effects are well delayed in time. The studies reported show that object-centered attention's onset is about 170–300 ms after stimulus onset, which means that object-centered attention does not affect early processing.

Since Lamme and Roelfsema (2000) refer to Schall and Bichot (1998), one may look there to find a clue as to the form of the attentional modulation of perception. We have seen, however, that Schall and Bichot suggest that object-centered attentional effects are delayed in time and occur after an initial processing stage during which all stimuli in a visual scene are processed in FEF irrespective of whether they have been labeled as targets or distractors. At a later stage, attentional effects discriminate between targets and distractors in FEF cells that eventually select the location of the target. Since attention can be driven either exogenously by stimuli features or endogenously by cognition, "FEF may be regarded as a saliency map, a representation of the visual field in which the location of potential targets are registered, tagged by both feature properties and prior knowledge or expectations" (Schall and Bichot 1998, p. 212). Bichot et al. (1996) found evidence that cognitive strategies can modify the selection process in FEF cells. In general, the effects of cognitive strategies, previous experience, expectations etc., are well documented (Gilbert et al. 2000; Henderson and Hollingworth 1999; Vecera 2000). However, all this research adduces evidence that object-centered attentional effects occur with a delayed latency and start after the FFS of Lamme's theory (which terminates at about 100 ms after stimulus onset) and even after the local RP (about 150 ms after stimulus onset).

The overall picture that emerges when subjects perform cognitive tasks that require voluntary endogenously driven attentional search of a visual scene is as follows: When a visual scene is being presented to the eyes, the feedforward sweep reaches V1 at a latency of about 40 ms. Information is fed forward to the extrastriate, parietal, and temporal areas. The first ERP component, C1, is elicited at about 50 ms after stimulus onset and is not affected by attention, be it spatial or object-centered. By 70–80 ms after stimulus onset, most visual areas are activated. The pre-attentional FFS culminates within 100 or 120 ms after stimulus onset. Between 70 and 90 ms after the stimulus onset, spatial attention, by modulating the P1 waveform, enhances visual processing in a voluntary task-driven search at the salient locations. However, P1 is sensitive only to the characteristics of the stimulus. 100 ms after the presentation of the stimuli at those locations, an extensive part of our brain responds to the physical characteristics of the visual array. 150 ms after the stimulus, these features fuse to a single form or structural description of the objects in a visual scene by means of LRP. At 150 ms, the onset of N1 indexes the beginning of the registration of differences between targets and distractors and, in general, differences between task-relevant and task-irrelevant items in the visual scene. About 200–300 ms after stimulus presentation, a voluntary task-driven search is registered in the same areas that process the visual features in the FFS and LRP, enhancing neuronal activation of the salient objects and/or locations. These attentional effects are indexed by the onset of N2, which also signifies the onset of the biasing of processing by object-centered attention. Thus, the top-down effects of attention to features and objects are delayed in time and involve the same anatomical areas as the FFS and LRP, except that attention amplifies the recordings in these areas. Finally, about 250 ms after the stimulus, some of the same areas participate in the cognitive/semantic processing of the input. Global RP takes place, and objects are classified and recognized, a process that is indexed by the onset of P3. In sum, the active attention studies suggest that when top-down processes occur, the activation of some groups of neurons in early perceptual areas is enhanced and the source of this amplification is higher areas in the brain, although which sites are exactly involved in which component of attention is still debatable (LaBerge 2000; Ungerleider and Haxby 1994, but see Treisman 2004).

3 Object-Centered Segmentation Processes and Object Individuation

Traditional models of attention assume that attention restricts various types of information processing to certain selected fields. Thus, attention is supposed to restrict visual processing to certain spatial areas of the visual array.[1] However, as we saw in chapter 1, there is substantial evidence for an object-centered or an object-based attention component to attention. In object-based attention, attentional limitations are characterized in terms of the number of pre-attentively defined discrete objects, or, better, proto-objects that can be processed simultaneously (Lamme 2000, 2003; Olson and Gettner 1996; Pylyshyn 1994, 2001; Scholl and Leslie 1999; Scholl 2001; Spekreijse 2000; Vecera 2000). There are, for example, cases in which objects overlap. In these cases, pre-attentive perceptual grouping criteria that determine the regions of the image that are grouped together to determine proto-objects guide the distribution of visual attention, in the sense that spatially separated proto-objects in the visual field can be pre-attentively individuated and indexed; as a result, the visual system acquires direct access to these objects. These perceptual grouping criteria are implemented in pre-attentive purely perceptual bottom-up segmentation processes (that is, no top-down cognitive effects modulate processing at this stage), which, in a preliminary way, parse a scene into objects. The discussion in the first two chapters suggests that the output of these pre-attentive visual processes consists in viewer-centered shape classes expressible in the vocabulary of geometry, such as the $2\frac{1}{2}$D sketch in Marr's (1982) theory, the size and color of objects, and their motion, orientation, spatial location, and spatial relations.

In this chapter, I examine the segmentation process that parse a scene into objects and the forms of information used by the visual system to segregate objects from ground and from other objects in a scene. In section 3.1, I discuss this process and the types of information used. I present evidence suggesting that the visual system uses primarily spatio-temporal information (that is, information about location or relative position, motion, and continuity in space and time), as well as, if necessary, information about shape, size, and color, to individuate and index the objects in a scene, although binding shape and color seems to require attention and thus shape and color may not be bound together in the pre-attentive stage (Lamme 2003). Since this kind of information can be retrieved bottom-up from a scene, object individuation can be a purely perceptual process encapsulated from cognition. The same evidence suggests that object individuation precedes object identification and categorization, which is as it should be on account of the fact that the former is a perceptual process whereas the latter is a cognitive process and should be delayed in time.

I also argue that the segmentation processes in the visual system are guided by some operational constraints or principles that solve the indeterminacy problems that arise during visual processing. These constraints are hard-wired in the circuitry of the visual system. The discussion of these constraints shows that they concern the shapes, locations, relative positions, and motions of the objects in a scene. This is independent evidence that this kind of information is primarily used for parsing a scene.

As a result of the segmentation process, the visual system individuates objects by means of bottom-up processes and assigns to them indexes that allow their tracking in space and time; in other words (though the reader will have to wait until the end of the book to see this claim fully developed and argued for), the visual system solves the problem of reference to these objects.

In section 3.2, I discuss a possible mechanism of reference to objects through the use of pointers. In section 3.3, I address the forms of representations that are built in the visual system (more specifically, along the ventral and dorsal pathways). My aim in that section is to support further my claims in section 3.1 that spatio-temporal, size, and shape information are primarily used to parse a scene and that object individuation (a perceptual task) precedes object identification and categorization (a cognitive task). To achieve this, I adduce evidence suggesting that representations of objects based on spatio-temporal and size and shape information precede the richer representations of our everyday experience that also encode other featural information, some visual and some nonvisual.

3.1   Object Segmentation

When one perceives a scene, the first thing one usually does is parse it in discrete objects, thereby individuating them. The visual system does that by bundling parts of the visual field together as units. This function, called *object segmentation*, consists in a set of visual processes that determine which features combine to form the objects present in a visual scene. These processes segment a shape from the background and segregate it from other shapes that are similarly segmented from the background.

The pre-attentive perceptual grouping criteria that determine the regions of the image that are grouped together to determine proto-objects guide the distribution of visual attention, in the sense that spatially separated proto-objects in the visual field can be pre-attentively individuated and indexed and, as a result, the visual system acquires direct access to these objects. These perceptual grouping criteria are implemented in pre-attentive purely perceptual bottom-up segmentation processes (which means that no top-down cognitive effects modulate processing at this stage), which, in a preliminary way, parse a scene into objects. In this vein, Vecera (2000) defines object-based attention as the visual processes that select a segregated shape from among several segregated shapes. Object segmentation takes place at many different levels of visual processing, both early and late, and a significant amount of object segmentation occurs in the pre-attentive stage of early vision. Parsing a scene into discrete objects, and thus individuating the objects in it, is the role of a pre-attentive stage of vision (Driver et al. 2001; Pylyshyn 2001; Scholl and Leslie 1999; Scholl 2001; Spekreijse 2000; Vecera 2000).[2]

The pre-attentive segmentation process results in the proto-objects, discussed in length in chapter 1. After objects have been segmented, the visual system assigns indexes to them. This completes the process of object individuation, which according to Pylyshyn (2001, p. 145; 2007) consists of two parts: segmentation of the scene in proto-objects and assignment of indexes to the segmented proto-objects. Object indexes allow the visual system to follow the proto-objects as they move in space and time; it also allows the higher levels of vision, after attention focuses on some of them, to further process the selected proto-objects by applying to them various object-related cognitive processes. The indexing may result in the visual system opening "object-files" for the segmented objects in a scene.

Kahneman and Treisman (1984) and Kahneman et al. (1992) proposed the term 'object-file' to explain conscious seeing. An object-file contains the featural information out of which the representation of an object is constructed. It is a temporary episodic (in the sense that it is constantly updated) representation of a visual object that contains information about the location of the object, its known attributes, and its recent history; it may even include the name of the object. The object-file provides, thus, a description of an object. According to that theory, object-files are created once attention is directed to an object. The object-file links the description of the object to a spatial position in a master map of locations and provides a unified description of the object, which binds the visual features that are associated with the object. Any further information about an object is added to its object-file; this is how the visual system "knows" that this new information is about the specific object. At the same time, any changes in features within the object-file are construed as changes in the specific object; as a result, the visual system sees an object undergoing changes and not a new object appearing. Object-files are maintained in visual short-term memory (VSTM) across saccadic eye movements, providing continuity from one fixation to the next. Thus, the role of object-files is to maintain spatial and temporal continuity of objects across motion and change.

Although Treisman and Kahneman's initial conception of object-files deemed that they are assigned to objects in a visual scene once attention has focused on those objects, the term's usage can be, and has been, extended to the indexes assigned pre-attentively to objects during the object-based segmentation processes. In this case, the object-files are impoverished in that they do not contain semantic information but only purely perceptual information, that is, information retrieved bottom-up from the scene. In other words, the object-files do not encode (encoding is a semantic relation in which the entity encoded is represented *as* having some property or *as* a member of a particular category) the objects they pick out in the world *as* some things or others, nor do they encode any of their properties (including the properties used in object individuation). Furthermore, they are not stored in memory, which means that the continuity they provide to objects lasts only for a given fixation. This means that the object-files in this extended usage, which is also the sense intended in this book, are initially assigned to proto-objects and not to the objects of our ordinary experience.

Object-based attention focuses on pre-attentively defined proto-objects. Once attention grasps some among these proto-objects putting them in the neuronal global workspace of Dehaene et al. (1998), Dehaene et al. (2003), and Dehaene and Changeux (2005), it provides them with an extended spatio-temporal coherence that, as proto-objects, they initially lacked. However, pre-attentive indexing is not restricted to spatially overlapping objects but it is extended to index simultaneously items at multiple spatial locations (Pylyshyn 1989, 1994). In fact there seems to be a shift in the way Pylyshyn views the kind of attention that focuses on the proto-objects. Initially Pylyshyn (1989, 1994) talked about spatial focal attention indexing up to four or five objects at multiple spatial locations, emphasizing thus the fact that properties are detected by means of their locations. In later work, Pylyshyn (2001, 2003) adopted the framework of object-based attention and talked about attention being focused upon individuated objects and not locations. However, as Pylyshyn (2001, pp. 131–132) himself remarks, there need not be an incompatibility between the two ways of describing the indexing process accomplished by early vision. He cites evidence suggesting that the assumption that properties are perceived in terms of their locations amounts to the assumption that what is primary in perceiving properties is the object with which the properties are associated rather than their location. In other words, Pylyshyn reduces detecting properties in terms of their location to detecting the properties by focusing not on their locations but on the object that bears them. This allows him to switch to object-based attention language without having to abandon the evidence based on his earlier work on the role of spatial attention in detecting properties of objects.

Research on object-centered attention (Carey and Xu 2001; Czigler and Balazs 1998; Pylyshyn 2001, 2003; Scholl and Leslie 1999; Scholl 2001) suggests that both adults and infants use initially spatio-temporal information to individuate and track objects in a visual scene. Object individuation based on spatio-temporal criteria (for example, temporal synchrony or continuity and proximity) precedes and even overrides object individuation based on other featural criteria (for example, shape and color). In other words, when a scene could be parsed or objects could be individuated in different ways depending on whether one uses spatio-temporal or other featural information, then the visual system of both adults and infants uses spatio-temporal information first to individuate objects; this is the principle of spatio-temporal priority. Flombaum et al. (2004) observed the same priority with rhesus macaques. Only if spatio-temporal information fails to individuate objects are other features used to individuate objects. This implies that representations of objects based on spatio-temporal information are constructed and used first, before representations that include size, shape, color, and other nonsensory or semantic information, such as the kind of object involved, its function, etc. These representation are used to individuate, index, and track objects in a visual scene, that is, in picking up parts of the scene as things that persist in space and time and following them in space and time. In other words, there is a mechanism in vision that relates parts of visual representations to parts of the visual world.

Think of two identical red squares situated in different locations. Since they are identical in their features, the only way they could be treated as two distinct objects is by considering their spatio-temporal history. This presupposes that there exists a visual mechanism that is sensitive only to spatio-temporal information and not to featural information and that can pick up these objects and allow an organism to treat them as distinct by building two distinct representations of these objects. This mechanism indexes these objects (by opening object-files for some of the objects present is a scene) and allows the organism to follow their paths and transformations while maintaining their identities as two distinct persistent objects and to track multiple objects.

In what follows, I briefly discuss evidence suggesting that spatio-temporal information precedes and often overrides other featural information in object individuation. Xu and Carey (1996) and Carey and Xu (2001) showed that 10-month-old infants can employ spatio-temporal information to infer the existence of occluded objects behind a screen but cannot employ feature information for the same purpose. The objects are individuated by feature-blind indexes. Twelve-month-olds possess the capacity to use both kinds of information. Xu and Carey also showed that spatio-temporal criteria override conflicting feature information. Using two objects differing both in perceptual properties and in categorical kind (a yellow duck and a white truck, for instance), they observed that infants were not surprised (they did not look longer) when the truck disappeared behind a screen and the duck appeared, but were surprised when nothing reappeared after entering the screen. This is evidence that a mechanism tracking the spatio-temporal history of objects is already in place, allowing the infant to individuate and follow the movement of objects, whereas the feature tracking mechanism that identifies objects is overridden by the former mechanism.

Even though the 10-month-olds studied by Carey and Xu (2001) failed to code featural information about segregated objects, other studies (Needham and Baillargeon 2000) show that infants can perceive features and use them to segregate stationary objects and figure/ground from the fourth month. This may happen because in segregation tasks with stationary objects (tasks in which spatio-temporal information is of little help) edge detection is necessary and this detection relies on color and brightness contrast. Thus, there may be two distinct processes: one that tracks segmented objects and relies primarily on spatio-temporal information and one that assigns edges to figures to achieve object segregation. The second process comes into play only if there is not enough spatio-temporal information to differentiate two separate object-files for the objects in the scene. This does not undermine my claim that objects are individuated on the basis of bottom-up visual processes, because edge detection and the perception of brightness and/or color are bottom-up processes. But this evidence contradicts Jacob and Jeannerod's (2003, pp. 192–193) claim that 10-month-olds are restricted in their ability to use information other than spatio-temporal information to individuate objects in a scene, in the sense that they do not exploit featural information alone to individuate objects (although Jacob and Jeannerod acknowledge that these infants are not visual-form agnosics). The evidence discussed shows that spatio-temporal individuation precedes and may override individuation based on other features, not that the latter is beyond the abilities of 10-month-olds.

Spelke et al. (1995) draw similar conclusions and argue that infants can distinguish between featurally identical objects on spatio-temporal information and that spatio-temporal information is used for object individuation and numerical identity. Kahneman et al. (1992) show that features of individuated objects may change while the object is still seen as the same object as before. Studies of apparent motion, finally, show that adults have no difficulty seeing totally different features as states of a single moving object. In conclusion, all these studies underlie the primacy of spatio-temporal information in opening and maintaining object-files.

Once an object-file is opened, features may be bound to it and eventually updated. Yet these features may also be used for object individuation. The features that are overridden in the aforementioned studies include shape and color. Tremoulet and colleagues (2000) show that 12-month-olds use shape and color information to individuate objects. However, this happens only when spatio-temporal information is ambiguous and the segmentation processes fail to assign separate object-files to the objects in the scene. In this sense, featural information may play a role in object individuation; it may be used for such purposes whenever spatio-temporal information is ambiguous (Nakayama et al. 1995).

Wynn (1992) studied infants' knowledge of numerical principles. Infants look longer when arithmetical principles such as $1 + 1 = 2$ or $2 - 1 = 1$ are violated by the experimental condition, but they are not surprised if these principles hold with objects that suddenly change their features during some brief disappearance behind a screen. This shows that infants are perceptually sensitive to the persistence of objects in space and time and they do not expect objects to appear from nowhere or to disappear suddenly. It also shows that they are not surprised by changes in observable features so long as these changes do not threaten the persistence of objects in space and time. In other words, the infants are sensitive to the continuity of objects in space and time. Whether the infants have a "knowledge" of rudimentary numerical principles about cardinality and simple arithmetical operations with small numbers (Wynn 1992), or whether they simply open object-files for the objects in the scene and form a model of the scene and subsequently match the models corresponding to the two scenes (the scenes before and after the appearance of the screen that covers the objects and allows the experimenter to remove, or add an object, or simply change a feature) by applying a one-to-one correspondence process (Carey 1995; Uller et al. 1994) is open to debate. Be that as it may, both accounts presuppose that there exists a visual process that outputs individuated objects, since both presuppose that the infants perceive discrete and persisting objects independent of, and often despite, any featural information—i.e., that they parse a scene using spatio-temporal information.

Flombaum et al. (2004) showed that rhesus macaques exhibit the principle of spatio-temporal priority too. They performed experiments in which subjects watch a lemon rolling down a ramp, coming to rest behind a tunnel, emerging as a kiwi fruit, and becoming occluded at the end of its path behind a screen. When the kiwi fruit emerges from the tunnel at about the time that the lemon should have (that is, when the scene is spatio-temporally continuous), the subjects search for food only behind the screen; which means that they perceive only one object despite the changes in features and kind. However, should a brief interval precede the emergence of the kiwi fruit, in which case the criterion of spatio-temporal continuity is not met, the subjects search for food behind both the screen and the tunnel, which means that they perceived two objects in the scene. In other words, different spatio-temporal criteria lead to two different individuation processes of the objects in the same scene. Furthermore, object individuation based on spatio-temporal information precedes and overrides object individuation based on other featural criteria.

The MOT (Multiple Object Tracking) experiments by Pylyshyn and Storm (1988) point to the same conclusion, this time with adult subjects. In this experiment, subjects must track a number of independently moving identical objects among identical distractors. These objects have been tagged as targets, by means of attentional cues, before they start moving. The subjects can track up to five targets; since targets and distractors are identical and their motions are random, the subjects can succeed only by picking initially the cued targets as objects and then following them as through motion. Thus, success in MOT requires that the subjects attend to spatio-temporal and motion information (relative location and direction of motion) and not to features, such as color and shape, or even the actual location of the objects. Changes in these features, moreover, do not disrupt tracking, as experiments by Pylyshyn (2001) and Scholl et al. (2001) show. One could say that the attentional cues index the targets in parallel by assigning them tags that the subject can follow afterward through motion.

All these studies suggest that spatio-temporal information, size information, shape information, and color information (although the two latter not conjunctively) are primarily used to individuate objects in a scene— that is, to represent objects as individual entities that persist in space and time. Spatio-temporal information is usually the first type of information the visual system seeks to individuate objects; if this information does not suffice for that purpose, the visual system takes recourse to shape, size, and color information. Therefore, it is plausible that spatio-temporal information is computed faster than size and shape information and all these are computed faster than other information in the visual system. This is supported behaviorally by data showing that on-line corrections to changes in spatial attributes of targets are made very quickly (~100 ms). Furthermore, the magnocellular retinocortical pathways, which carry spatio-temporal information and information about shape and size, and which are projected to the superior parietal lobe of the dorsal system and to the inferotemporal cortex of the ventral system, have fast responses. The parvocellular retinocortical pathways that project only to the inferotemporal cortex of the ventral system and carry nonspatial information have slow responses. Neurophysiological and neuropsychological studies using ERP readings also corroborate this (Czigler and Balazs 1998). These studies show that ERPs to the single-object vs. two-objects conditions diverge earlier than the ERP differences between target and nontarget stimuli. This is evidence that the allocation of spatial attention to a particular object precedes even the categorization of the object's features as target-related, non-target-related, or irrelevant.

The discussion above covers evidence from two domains: the development of object individuation and representation in infants and other animals, and the theory of object-centered segmentation processes. The adduced evidence suggests a convergence of the research from the two domains to the extent that the two research traditions find that (a) both infant and adult individuation is based predominantly on spatio-temporal information, (b) both systems have the same size limit on parallel processing (up to four objects can be tracked simultaneously), (c) the representations subserving object individuation survive occlusion in both cases,

(d) in both systems featural information is used for object individuation only if spatio-temporal information is ambiguous, and (e) when other featural information is used, object individuation based on features precedes object identification based on the same features. Thus, there is increasing consensus that the object "representations" initially constructed by infants and the "representations" constructed and supported by object-centered segmentation processes are identical.

It seems, therefore, that infants and adults use the same mechanisms to individuate, index, and track objects. Several theories of mechanisms of object indexing have been proposed. They include Pylyshyn's (1994) FINST theory of visual indexing, Leslie and colleagues' (1998) and Scholl and Leslie's (1999) object-indexing theory, the object-files theory of Kahneman and Treisman (1984), Ballard and colleagues' (1997) theory of deictic codes, and Irwin's (1991, 1992) and Irwin and Andrew's (1996) object-file theory of transsaccadic memory. The common thread of these theories is the claim that there exists a level of visual processing in which objects present in a scene are parsed and tracked as distinct individual objects without being identified as particular objects. Whereas some of these theories consider attentional mechanisms necessary for the assignment of object-files to objects in a visual scene, others accept the existence of pre-attentional segmentation processes that assign object-files to objects before the onset of attention. As I said above, I am going to rely on the latter theories. Object-centered segmentation processes open object-files for the discrete objects parsed in a scene. These files use spatio-temporal information about objects; that is, they are allocated and maintained primarily on the basis of spatio-temporal information. Individuated objects can be parsed and tracked without being identified, and even when an object is misidentified and then correctly recognized, it is deemed to be one and the same object all the time (Scholl 2001). Since I intend to restrict the assignment of object-files to pre-attentional processes, the objects to which the files are assigned are the proto-objects. This imposes restrictions both on the kind of information contained in the object-files (only information that is pre-attentively retrieved from a scene can be included) and on the coherence and stability of the ensuing representations. The proto-objects have limited stability and limited coherence. They do not survive across different fixations, and therefore the object-files are retained only until new incoming information erases the information pre-attentionally retrieved from a scene at an earlier time.

Consider again the two red squares. One may have various representations of these two objects. One can represent them as red squares, but one can also represent them merely as persisting (while the fixation lasts) objects. The former representation involves the identification of an object X. The latter individuates X in the visual field as an object. According to the object-file theory that I elaborate here, the individuation task is accomplished by ascribing object X an object-file—a temporary representation of X that is constantly upgraded as new information about X is acquired, always within the time frame of the same fixation. Suppose that an object for which such an object-file has been opened traverses a path and undergoes some feature changes. The object-file that has indexed the object allows the visual system to follow its trajectory in space-time. The new spatio-temporal state of the object in space-time is compared with that stored in the object-file. Note that the spatio-temporal information in the object-file is not stored in VSTM or in LTM, since it does not last long enough to be consolidated in any form of memory and since the whole process takes place before the onset of any attentional processes (which are required for mnemonic storage). This means that this information cannot be carried along successive fixations (see section 3.3). The spatio-temporal information, or any kind of information contained in the object-file, is probably stored in sensory visual memory within the visual cortex, whose traces have a life span ranging from under 1 second to no more than 2 seconds (versus 10–15 seconds of the VSTM).[3] If the two spatio-temporal states are similar enough, then the system deems that it is the same object that has moved and updates its featural changes accordingly. The whole feat is achieved, in this particular case, with spatio-temporal information, which ensures that the organism perceives a single object moving in space rather than two separate objects in different locations.

I have said that an object can be individuated and indexed either on the basis of spatio-temporal information or, should that prove insufficient, based on other observable features. This should not be read to mean that the information used in the individuation process must be represented in a way that allows the perceiver to have access to this information; of course, since this information is the content of perceptual states, it is represented somewhere in the visual system. One should distinguish between a system that uses information about properties of objects (say, their motion, shape, size, or location) to individuate and index them and a system that encodes these same properties, stores them in memory and, as a result, may have access to these properties. A system may initially use these properties to individuate an object without encoding them. Once it has done so, it perceives the object as an entity that persists in space and time; any featural changes, even if encoded at a subsequent change, cannot be compared with the features of the object at previous times, since the system had not had encoded them. This explains why featural changes in the aforementioned experiments may go unnoticed. Furthermore, if the changes are not behaviorally relevant, as in the MOT experiments in which the subject's task is simply to follow the objects' motions and retain their grouping, they are simply ignored.

The discussion of the MOT experiments gives us a clue to how the uniqueness and individuality of an object is sustained through motion. Variations by Scholl et al. (2001), and Yantis (1995) of the standard MOT experiments, in which the movement of the targets led them to pass behind surfaces or objects that completely occluded them for short time intervals, show that under certain conditions subjects can still successfully track the targets despite the brief occlusions. The conditions under which the subjects are successful are very interesting. Unimpaired performance in these tasks requires that the objects not simply disappear from the scene and appear somewhere else; accretion and deletion cues along fixed contours at the occluding boundaries must be present. Thus, the brief disappearance of an object can be accounted for, so that its object-file may remain open and not eradicated, only if the interruptions of its presence are consistent with occlusion.

Work by Spelke and her colleagues (1990, 1995) on the principles about the behavior of material objects that guide our interactions with them from very early in life may provide an explanation of these results. More specifically, some evidence supports the claim that infants preferentially attend to an object's pattern of motion (Gelman 1990) and that children pay more attention to moving objects than to stationary objects, and that they deal with moving objects more easily. This is a straightforward consequence of Spelke's (1990) views, insofar as motion plays a central role in object perception and in object segmentation. According to Spelke (1990), infants perceive objects by analyzing three-dimensional surface arrays and by following their continuous motion.

Kellman and Spelke (1983) and Kellman (1984) discuss the role of motion in organizing object perception. In their experiment, they habituated 4-month-olds on an object whose top and bottom were visible but whose center was occluded by another object nearer to the observer than the first on (a rod occluded in the center by a box). Kellman and Spelke investigated several habituation displays in which the movements of the rod and the box varied in various ways. Then they showed the infants a test display (consisting of a single rod) or the two pieces of the rod, and monitored the reaction of the infants. The question was whether the infant perceived a single unitary rod or two rod pieces as more different from the habituating event. The results of the experiment were unequivocal. The infants perceived the broken rods as different and the unitary rod as similar to the habituation event only when the test objects had moved, and then only when the ends of the habituation rod had moved in common translation behind the occluding object. This result means that the boundaries of objects are defined by motion. (For further experiments on the same theme, see Kellman, Spelke, and Short 1986; Spelke, Hofsten, and Kestenbaum 1989; Von Hofsten and Spelke 1985.) These views are also confirmed by psychological experiments that show that three-dimensional shapes can be recovered from motion information (Wallach and O'Connell 1953). The way the structure of objects is retrieved from information about their motion is also discussed in length by Kellman (1984). There is also considerable neurophysiological evidence (De Valois et al. 1982; Marr and Ullman 1981) not only for the existence of specialized circuitry for motion processing but also for the existence of specialized motion detection machinery. We know, for instance, that there are cortical neurons sensitive to direction of stimulus movement in both animals and humans (Cynader and Chernenko 1976).

The aforementioned principles about motion detection allow infants, and the subjects in MOT experiments, to infer that under proper movement (the appropriate interruption of its presence) a single object is displaced, despite the fact that this object is occluded by another superimposed object or surface—a fact that could have led them to perceive two separated objects, or to lose track of the target they were following. Therefore, the principles are part and parcel of the segmentation process and allow object individuation and tracking under dynamical conditions.

More generally, studies by Spelke (1990), Spelke et al. (1995), and Karmiloff-Smith (1992) strongly support the assumption that the infant, almost from the beginning of life, is constrained by a number of domain-specific principles about material objects and some of their properties. As Karmiloff-Smith points out (1992, p. 15), these constraints involve "attention biases toward particular inputs and a certain number of principled predispositions constraining the computation of those inputs." Among these predispositions, Spelke asserts, are the conception of object persistence and four basic principles: boundness, cohesion, rigidity, and no action at a distance.

The *cohesion principle* dictates that two surface points lie on the same object only if the points are linked by a path of connected surface points. This entails that if some relative motion alters the adjacency relations among points at their borders, the surfaces lie on distinct objects, and that all points on an object move on connected paths over space and time. When surface points appear at different places and times such that no connected path could unite their appearances, the surface points do not lie on the same object. According to the *boundness principle*, two surface points lie on distinct objects only if no path of connected surface points links them. This principle determines the set of those points that define an object boundary and entails that two distinct objects cannot interpenetrate, because two distinct bodies cannot occupy the same place at the same time. Finally, the *rigidity* and no *action at a distance* principles specify that bodies move rigidly (unless the other mechanisms show that a seemingly unique body is, in fact, a set of two distinct bodies) and that they move independently of one another (unless the mechanisms show that two seemingly separate objects are in fact connected). The force of these principles is such that Gestalt principles are always overridden by the principles underlying the perception of objects in motion. These mechanisms allow, for instance, infants to infer that under proper movement a single object is displaced, despite the fact that this object is center-occluded by another superimposed object, a fact that could have led the infants to perceive two separated objects. But whenever the object remains still, infants perceive two different objects separated by another one. In addition, infants fail to recover the boundary between objects that are adjacent and move together. These principles guide the perception of the motions of objects, of the layout of adjacent objects, of object boundaries, and of object segmentation by both adults and infants, and play a crucial role in the segmentation processes that take place in the visual system upon viewing a scene. Spelke thinks that they constitute part of the innate arsenal of infants, which is necessary to ensure effective learning, and that their role is to facilitate object perception. In this sense, infants have an innate understanding of objects. And habituation experiments bring them into contact with pre-existing innate ideas about objects.

When I say that there are principles guiding the perception of motion, I do not mean to imply that these are rules written in some general data memory and accessed by the visual system whenever the need arises. If that were the case, the system would have access to them in general and would be able to report them. The view that these principles function as premises in arguments is problematic because we cannot do that, and also because that would presuppose the existence of a conceptual arsenal in which these rules could be formulated. But such a sortal arsenal is not required in order to be able to perceive (that is, see in a non-epistemic sense) the world, as opposed to be able to see (in an epistemic sense) the world. As I will explain next, these principles are implemented by being hard-wired in the circuitry of the visual system, allowing it to process information and restricting the range of possible solutions to the various problems of indeterminacy that arise while it attempts to reconstruct the distal cause of the proximal input. For this reason, I will call them "operational constraints" of the visual system.

I also do not share Spelke's sense of strong innateness. However, to avoid unnecessary complications I will side with Karmiloff-Smith's (1992, p. 4) "minimalistic" stand, shared by Clark (1991, 1993), that "it is plausible that a fairly limited amount of innately specified predispositions (which are not strictly modular) would be sufficient to constrain the classes of inputs that the infant mind computes." These predispositions include some maturationally constrained attention biases, and some structures that constrain the way the child processes the input. The former ensure that some part of the input (which is characteristic of a certain domain) will be processed by a mechanism that is suited to do exactly that and that ignores other data; the latter constrain the way these data are processed. The principles guiding perception of objects and their motion fall within the second kind of constraint.

Fortunately, the findings of Spelke and others regarding the way one perceives and understands objects need not be interpreted by appealing to a strong kind of nativism. I am not going to discuss this issue further, except to note that such alternative interpretations are offered by Elman et al. (1996) and by Thelen and Smith (1994). According to these authors, the only kind of innate arsenal lies in the inherent properties of the neural systems, which, one could add, include certain initial predispositions and processing constraints in the form of the structure of cells, their initial synaptic connection weights, and their biases. This picture certainly fits with the framework of the claims made in this book, because such an innate arsenal certainly does not require any conceptual apparatus so that the visual system could deliver perceptions of scenes.

The above discussion certainly does not exhaust the issue of the operational constraints employed by the visual system in its function. The computations leading to the formation of the percepts of objects are determined by the input to the visual system (that is, the optical array), by the physiological mechanisms involved in vision, and by the computations they allow and certain principles that restrict and guide the computation. These principles are constraints that the system must satisfy in processing the input. These constraints are needed because perception is underdetermined by any particular retinal image; the same retinal image could lead to distinct perceptions. Thus, unless the observer makes some assumptions about the physical world that gives rise to the particular retinal image, perception is not feasible. In the following paragraphs, I discuss some among the operational constraints that vision studies suggest constrain the solutions to the problems encountered by the visual system, although the discussion is sketchy and the interested reader is strongly advised to consult the first chapters of Pylyshyn 2003.

Many computational accounts (e.g., Marr 1982 and Ulmann 1979) hold that the aforementioned operational constraints substantiate some very general truths of our world and are not assumptions about specific objects acquired through experience. Instead, they seem to be hard-wired into the system. The formation of the *full primal sketch* in Marr's (1982) theory, for instance, which involves the grouping of the edge fragments formed in the *raw primal sketch*, relies on the principles of "local proximity" (adjacent elements are combined) and of "similarity" (similarly oriented elements are combined). It also relies on the more general principle of "closure" (two edge segments could be joined even though their contrasts differ because of illumination effects) (Bruce and Green 1993, pp. 131–132).

Other assumptions that are brought to bear upon the early visual processing to solve the problem of the underdetermination of perception by the retinal image are those of "continuity" (the shapes of natural objects tend to vary smoothly and usually do not have abrupt discontinuities), "proximity" (since matter is cohesive, adjacent regions usually belong together and remain so even when the object moves), and "similarity" (since the same kind of surface absorbs and reflects light in the same way, the different sub regions of an object are likely to look similar).

The formation of the $2\frac{1}{2}$D sketch is similarly underdetermined, in that there is a great deal of ambiguity in matching features between the two images form in the retinas of the two eyes, since there are usually more than one possible matches. Stereopsis requires a unique matching, which means that the matching processing must be constrained. The formation of the $2\frac{1}{2}$D sketch, therefore, relies upon a different set of operational constraints that guide stereopsis. "A given point on a physical surface has a unique position in space at some time" (Marr 1982, p. 112), and matter is cohesive and surfaces are generally smooth. These operational constraints give rise to the general constraints of "compatibility" (a pair of image elements are matched together if they are physically similar, since they originate from the same point of the surface of an object), "uniqueness" (an item from one image matches with only one item from the other image), and "continuity" (disparities must vary smoothly). Another constraint posited by all models of stereopsis is the "epipolar" constraint (the viewing geometry is known). Mayhew and Frisby's (1981) account of stereopsis posits some additional constraints—most notably the principle of "figural continuity," according to which figural relationships are used to eliminate most of alternative candidate matches between the two images.

As Hildreth and Ulmann remark (1989, pp. 599–600), the physical constraints at work in perception must be reflected in the physiological mechanisms underlying the early stages of vision, since it is these mechanisms that implement them. Indeed, there is ample evidence that the constraints applied to restrict the possible alternative solutions to computational problems of vision are reflected in the physiological mechanisms underlying binocular combination, from cells that function as edge detection to mechanisms implementing the epipolar constraint (Hubel and Wiesel 1968; Ferster 1981; Koch and Poggio 1987; Nielsen and Poggio 1984; Poggio 1984; Poggio and Talbot 1981; Watt and Morgan 1983, 1984).

To repeat in somewhat different terms a point I made a few paragraphs ago regarding the nature of the principles or operational constraints: None of these principles is about specific objects. Instead, they reflect some very general properties of the world, and in this sense the process of early vision is not guided by expectations, by beliefs, or by any "object hypotheses" in general, in a top-down manner. The general assumptions about the physical world probably are built in the perceptual systems and act as constraints that guide perception. These theories provide the body of background knowledge stored in Fodor's (1988) perceptual modules. In some sense, therefore, "perceiving objects may be more akin to thinking about the physical world than to sensing the immediate environment" (Spelke 1988, p. 458). This knowledge, however, is implicit, in the sense that it is available only for a single purpose (Ramachandran 1985, p. 99): the processing of the retinal image. The constraints are implicit, in that they are available only for the processing of the visual image, whereas explicit "theoretical" constraints are available for a wide range of cognitive applications. Implicit constraints cannot be overridden; one cannot decide to substitute another body of constraints, even if one knows that under certain conditions they may lead to errors (visual illusions). This background knowledge foreshadows the way we perceive the world, and it cannot be contradicted. This means that the perceptual modules are informationally encapsulated from higher cognitive states, even though their computations are based on some general assumptions, or theory, about the world.

The operational constraints are implemented by mechanisms in the perceptual system and modulate its processing. As such, they are not available to introspection and function outside the realm of consciousness. One does not "know" or "believe" that an object moves in continuous paths, that it persists in time, or that it is rigid, though one uses this information to index and follow the object. The constraints constitute the *modus operandi* of the perceptual system, and not a set of rules stored in memory used by the perceptual system as premises in perceptual inferences; they are reflected in the functioning of the system.

3.2   Pointers and Deictic Reference

Suppose that one sees object X. One's representation of X may consist in a detailed image of X, or it may consist in some property of X that allows one to seek X successfully whenever one needs more information about X. For instance, one might store in memory X's location or a characteristic feature of it, so that one can attend to that location or seek the feature, when more information about X is needed; the location or the feature act as pointers to X. The location or the feature function as indexicals for two reasons. First, their reference is determined by the external context, i.e., by the relations between the token demonstrative—'that' for the feature, 'there' for the location—and the object itself, should the perceiver wish to point the object to another person, or by the relations between the token internal representation of the location or the feature of the object and the object itself, should the perceiver seek the object on her own. Second, their reference depends also upon a "lexical" convention that determines the way the type of the demonstrative can be used in language. Thus, a token of the type 'there' or 'that' refers to an object "pointed to" by the speaker. In this case there is not a rich representation of X; only an indexical one that refers to the object, which thus becomes indexed.

When the eye fixates at some location in a scene where an object is located, the relevant neurons in the fovea compute information from that location that is behaviorally relevant. This information may be the location of the object or some feature of the object. The object at that location is the referent of the deictic reference, in that the act of fixation assigns to this object a pointer that allows it to be individuated and tracked. This is due to the fact that the fixation of the gaze creates a reference to a point in space and time and to the fact that the properties of the referent can enter computations as a unit.

A theory of deictic pointers that will help us to understand object indexing (and, in addition, to understand the functioning of Rensink's triadic architecture) has been developed by Ballard et al. (1997). To get a picture of the theory, consider their introduction:

At time scales of approximately $\frac{1}{3}$ of a second, orienting movements of the body play a crucial role in cognition and form a useful computational level. . . . At this "embodiment level," the constrains of the physical system determine the nature of cognitive operations. The key synergy is that at time scales of about $\frac{1}{3}$ of a second, the natural sequentiality of body movements can be matched to the natural computational economies of sequential decision systems through a system of implicit reference called deictic in which pointing movements are used to bind objects in the world to cognitive programs. (ibid., p. 723)

The shortest time at which bodily actions and movements (such as eye movements, hand movements, or spoken words) can be observed is the $\frac{1}{3}$-second time scale. Ballard calls this "the embodiment level" and contends that computations at this level govern the deployment of the body's sensors and effectors. The mechanisms that relate conceptual content to the world through the bodily actions of an organism must be sought at this embodiment level. Suppose that one looks at a scene and, through eye focusing, selects a part of it for further processing. The brain's ensuing internal representation is about, or refers to, that specific part of the scene. Acts such as the eye focusing are called "deictic strategies" (from the Greek word *deixis*, meaning pointing or showing). Accordingly, fixation and grasping are mechanical pointing devices, and localization by attention is a neural deictic device (Tsotsos et al. 1995). When one's internal representation refers to an object through such a deictic representation, Ballard et al. call this a "deictic reference." Thus, when fixating a location, the neurons that are linked to the fovea refer to information computed from that location.

Eye fixation exemplifies the role of deictic mechanisms, or pointers, as binding devices—that is, as devices that bind objects in the world with internal representations and cognitive programs, through deictic reference. This binding is implemented by two functional routines in the visual system. When a scene is perceived, the eye movements perform two main functions: they extract properties of pointer locations (which amounts to object identification) and they point to aspects of the environment (object localization). The second function is that of object indexing.

Suppose that the eye fixates at some location in a scene and, as a result, the relevant neurons in the fovea compute information from that location.

Suppose further that an object is present at that location; this object is the referent of the deictic reference. The act of fixation assigns to this object a pointer that allows object individuation and tracking; this is due to the fact that the fixation of the gaze creates a reference to a point in space and time and the properties of the referent can enter computations as a unit.

If using one or two pointers can solve a task, then the pointing act itself is enough for the necessary computations, since it can provide all necessary information for the objects involved. If, however, the task requires additional pointers, working memory comes into play. Since the momentary references created by pointers are maintained as variables in working memory, the items stored in working memory correspond to the referents of computational pointers. If the demands of the task exceed the information provided by the pointers themselves, then information about additional referents stored as variables in working memory are retrieved and used (in this sense, the physical acts of pointing strategies load or bind together items in working memory).

Ballard's pointers participate in a cognitive top-down program, in the sense that "when performing natural tasks subjects make moment-by-moment trade-offs between the visual information maintained in working memory and that acquired by eye fixations" (Ballard et al. 1997, p. 739). Apparently Ballard takes the information maintained in working memory and used in the task as the top-down ingredient of the strategy, which supplements the bottom-up visual information. Though no one would object to the existence of such a trade-off, one need not ascribe to Ballard's view that this top-down ingredient undermines the claim that spatio-temporal information is retrieved in a bottom-up way. This would be the case if such top-down information were used in determining the outcome of the visual routines retrieving this information by influencing the processing in the visual routines (in this sense, Ballard sides with those who claim that no part of vision is cognitively impenetrable). But this need not be the case. First, abundant top-down (and lateral) flow of information takes place within the visual module itself. Second, the top-down information may influence the bottom-up processing in early vision in indirect ways (of the type I alluded to in chapter 2 and which I will discuss in chapters 7 and 8). That is, top-down information may determine attentional focus, or may select one among different interpretations proposed by the bottom-up processes. In the latter case the top-down information modulates visual processing after the routines of early vision have output their processing product. (Fodor 1983; Pylyshyn 1999; Raftopoulos 2001a,b).

It seems clear that one's conceptual system can have a top-down influence on object individuation—think of the different possible answers to the question "How many objects can you see here?" depending on what one counts as an object. It is clear from the psychological literature also that object individuation is not necessarily pre-conceptual; it can also be conceptually or cognitively driven, as when one uses information about kind to individuate an object or establish its numerical identity. In these cases, one uses property changes to individuate objects whenever spatio-temporal information is of little help or when property changes tell against spatio-temporal information (as when one judges that a dead person ceases to be a person even though there spatio-temporal continuity of his body). What property changes are relevant to the task is kind-relative, that is, it depends on the kind the object is deemed to belong to, as Xu and Carey (1996) argue.

The use of pointers has these advantages for an organism, both computational and representational:

• The employment of pointers facilitates spatio-temporal reference by taking advantage of the body's ability to orient, as when the eye fixates on a target and simplifies manipulation strategies.

• Since pointers can fixate at different targets, the employment of pointers leaves a great deal of information out in the world to be used when needed according to task demands. This use of "just-in-time" representation greatly lessens the representational load on working memory making computations less taxing cognitively speaking. In that sense, the theory of pointers falls within the wider context of theories of animate or active vision[4] that take advantage of the cognizers' actions and bodily movements to minimize the demand for built-in representations.

• It follows that pointers simplify sensorimotor routines, since representational products are computed only if they are needed for the current cognitive program.

3.3 Representation of Objects in the Dorsal and Ventral Pathways; Object Individuation and Object Identification

I have presented evidence that supports the existence of a "weak" kind of object representation based on spatio-temporal, size, orientation, motion, and viewer-centered shape information, which is retrievable bottom-up from a scene, allows object individuation, and precedes a representation of the same object that makes possible object identification. In this section,

I argue that this representation is the only representation formed in the dorsal visual pathway, and that it is also the representation that is formed first along the ventral system, although cast in a different frame of reference than in the dorsal system. However, in the ventral system a stronger semantic representation (in the sense of carrying information that exceeds the information that can be extracted perceptually from a scene) eventually emerges. Strictly speaking, since the weak object representation is built on information retrieved from a scene in a pre-attentional stage, the objects involved are the proto-objects of chapter 1 and not the usual objects of our experience. However, I will keep referring to them as objects, since this is how they are used in some of the evidence that I will review in this chapter. The reader, however, should bear the distinction in mind.

There is a consensus nowadays that there are two (Goodale and Milner 1992, 2004; Norman 2002) or three (Glover 2003) visual streams in the cortex, which serve roughly two different functions. The dorsal system utilizes visual information for guidance of action in one's environment. For that purpose, it needs to have information about the dimensions of objects in body-centered terms, that is, in an absolute frame of reference. Thus, the information in the dorsal stream is transformed into a body-centered frame of reference and, thus, is processed in egocentric coordinates, and uses viewer-centered structured representations of the surfaces of objects. The dorsal system interfaces directly with the motor cortex and receives input both form the primary visual cortex (V1) and other subcortical circuits. The ventral system uses visual information for knowing one's environment, that is, for identifying objects in it, for recognizing objects by comparing them with stored representations, and for storing new information in memory. The information is represented in a relational frame of reference in which objects are located and are measured with respect to other objects in a scene and not with respect to the body of the perceiver. The ventral system receives input only from V1 and has no direct links to motor systems, but unlike the dorsal system it interfaces with cortical cognitive structures. It is along this system that awareness arises. Notice that this distinction between the role of dorsal and ventral processing does not coincide with the older distinction (Ungerleider and Mishkin 1984; Ungerleider and Haxby 1994), according to which the dorsal system is a "where" system designed to represent the location of objects, whereas the ventral system is a "what system" designed to represent the features of the objects that allow their identification, and as a result, the two systems process different kinds of information; in the dorsal system spatial information is being processed and in the ventral system featural information is being processed. Recent evidence suggests that both systems process the same kind of information (but it is likely that color is not processed along the dorsal system), although the information in each system is represented in different coordinate systems. Finally, processing along the dorsal system or visuomotor processing is faster than that along the ventral system or perceptual processing. Subjects can correct the trajectory of their hand movement directed to a moving object 300 ms before they become conscious of the object's change of location (Castiello et al. 1991; Goodale and Milner 2004).

The dorsal system processes visual spatial information (that is, information about the location of an object in space and of its relative position with respect to other objects always in an egocentric or body-centered frame of reference), motion information, featural information about size, shape, orientation, and surface properties, and information about the affordances of objects in a body-centered frame of reference. It is disputable whether color information is being processed along the dorsal system (Jacob and Jeannerod 2003). More specifically, all featural information in the dorsal system is computed within an absolute, body-centered frame of reference, in which features are computed with respect to the body of the perceiver (first her retina, then the center of the distance between the eyes, or the center of gravity of her body depending on the goals of the perceiver). Size, for instance, is computed in an absolute metric, that is, with respect to the perceiver, and not relationally with respect to the sizes of other objects in the scene. To see why this has to be so, recall that the dorsal system subserves an organism's on-line interaction with the environment. Successful action requires that, say, the size of a body be perceived and acted upon in an absolute metric and not in a metric that relates it to other objects in the scene. To grasp successfully an object, one need perceive its real or absolute size, so that the aperture of the handgrip fits the real size of the object and not its relational size. This information is retrieved from the scene directly by the low-level vision, without recourse to any central higher processing (Glover 2003; Goodale and Milner 1992; Norman 2002). Glover (2003) argues that the weak representation is stored in the Superior Parietal Lobe (SPL), since lesions of the SPL in either hemisphere are accompanied by visuomotor impairments (Jacob and Jeannerod 2003; Goodale and Milner 2004). The information is fed into the dorsal system through the magnocellular retinocortical pathways that carry spatio-temporal information, including motion information, and information about size and shape. The information in the dorsal system allows a weak form of object representation. The representations of objects in the dorsal system do not last more than a few minutes.

Top-down semantic influences from cognitive centers, do not affect these processes and they do not affect the on-line control of action, which according to Glover (2003) is the function served by the dorsal system. Most of the mechanisms involved in the processing in the dorsal system operate outside of conscious awareness. Hence, the representations of objects in the dorsal system are not in general available to conscious awareness (for exceptions see Norman 2002, pp. 89–90) unless the activities served by the dorsal system lead for some reason or other to some type of judgmental, comparative response or verbal report. In this case, the ventral system intervenes and awareness eventually enters the picture.

The representations formed during ventral processing are more variegated. As we have seen, along the ventral system, information that is bottom-up retrieved from the environment is first stored in the object-files that are originally assigned to the proto-objects that are parsed in a visual scene. The ventral system receives its information from the primary visual cortex through both the magnocellular retinocortical pathways and the parvocellular retinocortical pathways. This information consists, as in the dorsal system, in visual spatial information (that is, information about the location of an object in space and of its relative position with respect to other objects), motion information, and featural information about size, shape, orientation, and surface properties. Colors are also represented along the ventral system. In contrast with the dorsal system, though, all featural information in the ventral system is computed within a relative or relational frame of reference, in which features are computed with respect to the other objects in the scene. Size, for instance, is computed in a relational metric and not in an absolute metric, that is, with respect to the sizes of other objects in the scene and not with respect to the size of the perceiver.[5] The contents of the object-files that are initially formed constitute weak representations of the objects in the scene. Like their cousins in the dorsal system, they have a limited spatio-temporal coherence.

In contrast to the sparse information stored in weak representations of proto-objects in the dorsal and ventral system, representations of objects that are far richer than the weak representations eventually arise in the ventral system due to the role of object-centered attention and of top-down semantic processing. These "strong" representations contain semantic information, that is, information that requires top-down semantic influences deriving from knowledge of specific objects stored in mnemonic circuits (information about fragility, temperature, function, color, weight, usage, functions, etc.) This requires reference to stored memories, and thus, relies on previously stored knowledge about specific objects. This representation is conceptually contaminated, since it is influenced by top-down conceptual inferences. Thus, the processes of the ventral system are influenced by a large array of visual and cognitive give and take.[6] The representation that is used by the ventral system may be stored in the Inferior Parietal Lobe (IPL). There is evidence that the right side of IPL may be involved in the high-level intentional planning of complex actions involving the retrieval of complex information stored in the left side of IPL (Glover 2003). Furthermore, it seems that the right IPL is required for coding spatial relations among objects in the relational frame of reference in which objects are cast in the ventral system, since lesions on the right side of IPL produce disorders in the perception of spatial relations among objects.

Now that I have discussed the differences between the weak nonsemantic (in the sense of the term explained above)[7] representations of proto-objects from the strong semantic representations of objects, I can elaborate further on the notions of object individuation and object identification that I touched upon in sections 3.1 and 3.2. "Object identification" attempts to convey the notion of an object, which is represented *as* being such and such, that is, as falling under a certain description (in other words, it is deemed to be a member of a category). This notion involves a strong conceptual component, in that the object represented has been compared with other objects in some knowledge basis in memory and identified as being such and such. It is clear that object identification presupposes the existence of a concept associated with that object. Thus, the object thus identified can enter as a constituent in thought ascriptions.

The term *object individuation* involves a weaker kind of representation. It purports to convey the sense that an object-file has been opened for that specific object, that the object has been "catalogued" or "indexed" as something that exists and persists separately of other objects with its own continuous spatio-temporal history. In other words, "object individuation" purports to convey the perception of the "objecthood" of objects (here 'perception' is meant to convey that there is no conceptual involvement in object individuation and, thus, that the subject does not apply the concept "objecthood"). The perception of "objecthood" relies mainly on spatio-temporal information (that is, information pertaining to location, relative position, motion, and spatio-temporal continuity), although, as we have seen, if spatio-temporal information does not suffice to parse an object in a visual scene, other featural information may be used. This initial representation allows access to the object for further investigation, and although spatio-temporal information and perhaps other featural information is used for the opening of the relevant object-file, this information is not encoded, that is, it is not stored in any kind of memory other than the visual sensory memory, cannot be used for subsequent identification, and does not provide any kind of semantic description of the object; that is, the object is not represented *as* having a set of properties and *as* being a member of a particular category. Then, information about shape, size, orientation, color, and surface properties is included to complete the non-conceptual object-file for the object. There is no semantic information involved (information about fragility, temperature, weight, usage, functions, etc.), and that is why it constitutes a weaker sense of representation. The object-file thus construed does not require the possession or application of concepts associated with that object, insofar as the relevant information is retrieved from a scene bottom-up. The spatio-temporal and featural information involved in indexing an object is not conceptualized, since it is retrievable from a scene in a bottom-up manner. One does not "know" or "believe" that an object moves in continuous paths, that it persists in time, or that it is rigid, though one uses this information to index and follow the object. Object indexing may eventually result in the belief that an object is here or there, or that two objects must be behind the screen, but this indexing does not appeal to any kind of stored in any knowledge.

3.4 Concluding Remarks

The research on object-centered segmentation and attention that I reviewed in section 3.1 suggests that the weak representation of proto-objects as discrete entities that persist in space and time that are based primarily on spatio-temporal information precede the weak representation of the same proto-objects based on featural information that is retrieved bottom-up from a scene. The weak representations allow object individuation and both precede the strong representation based on semantic information that allows object identification. In view of this, I beg to differ with Jacob and Jeannerod's (2003, pp. 191–192) conclusion, which they trace back to Leslie et al. (1998), that the psychological evidence I discussed in section 3.1 suggests that there are two distinct indexing mechanisms, object individuation that relies on locational information and maps on Ungerleider and Mishkin's (1984) "where" system, and object identification that relies on other featural information (such as shape, color, texture, and orientation) and maps on Ungerleider and Mishkin's (1984) "what" system. The reason for my disagreement is twofold.

First, the experimental evidence I discussed in section 3.1, in conjunction with the conclusions of the first two chapters that shape, color, orientation, and texture information is retrieved bottom-up, that is, non-conceptually, from the visual scene (a thesis that Jacob and Jeannerod (2003, Part 1) also share), suggest (a) that object individuation can take place by means of both spatio-temporal and other featural information and (b) that object individuation, no matter whether it is based on spatio-temporal or other featural information, does not involve any conceptual knowledge. If (a) and (b) are true, object individuation takes place before the application of any sortal concepts. This, in turn, means that object individuation precedes object identification, since the latter presupposes the application of sortals. Thus, object individuation based either on spatio-temporal or other featural information precedes object identification. This does not preclude, of course, the possibility of individuating objects after these objects have been identified. It only shows that individuation can and does usually occur before object identification. The above discussion has another result as well. Object indexing, whether it is based on spatio-temporal or other featural information, takes place before object identification. The source of my disagreement with Jacob and Jeannerod is to be found in those authors' view that object individuation cannot occur through feature detection and that once the features of an object are used then the object is identified. However, against this view, the evidence that we have examined suggests that object features can be used to individuate and not identify an object.

Second, as Jacob and Jeannerod (2003, p. 192) themselves acknowledge, the visual "module" that indexes objects on the basis of spatio-temporal information cannot be mapped to the "where" system of Ungerleider and Mishkin (1984), since object individuation takes place in the ventral system as well and, thus, the spatial "module" must allow the perception of spatial relationships in the ventral system, whereas Ungerleider and Mishkin's (ibid.) "where" system is located in the dorsal visual pathway. Similarly, object individuation based on featural information (with the probable exception of color) may occur at the dorsal system, which means that the visual "modules" that extract featural information cannot be mapped on to the ventral system only.

The discussion of object individuation and object identification allows us to shed light on another issue that is taken up by Jacob and Jeannerod

(2003, pp. 193–198) and is immediately related to some of the topics of this book, namely the constraint of contrastive identification, recognition, or re-identification. According to this constraint "identification, recognition or re-identification of property F . . . requires the ability to contrast and compare different instantiations of property F, either by different objects or items at the same time or by the same object at different times" (ibid., p. 193). Jacob and Jeannerod (ibid., p. 193) claim that this constraint applies to the nonconceptual content (NCC) of visual experiences and proceed to show that the representations in the ventral system do satisfy that constraint, whereas those in the dorsal system do not. If they were correct, Jacob and Jeannerod's claim would entail the thesis that objects can be identified and recognized solely on the basis of the NCC of the relevant perceptual representations of those objects. That thesis is wrong and that is why Jacob and Jeannerod's claim that the constraint of contrastive identification, recognition or re-identification applies to NCC does not stand to scrutiny. Here is why.

To identify an object it means to say that to one can describe that object *as* being a member of some class (that the object I see in front of me is a cat, for instance). This requires that the object be represented under a certain description, which means that the representation of the object is propositional or can be rendered in propositional form without loss of information; this implies that concepts are necessary for object identification. NCC is, by definition, nonconceptual, and hence it cannot support object identification but only object individuation.

Moreover, to recognize or re-identify an object requires the ability to contrast and compare different instantiations of property F, either by different objects or items at the same time or by the same object at different times. This ability presupposes that the first instantiation of property F has been stored in VSTM or LTM and when the same property is instantiated by another object or the same object at some other time one can compare the mnemonic trace with the current percept and judge that it is the same property that is instantiated. There are two things to note at this point, and both point to the conclusion that the contrastive criterion does not and cannot apply to NCC. First, this comparative process involves memory storage and thus imposes a limitation on the kinds of properties that can be so compared. Psychological evidence (Hollingworth 2006; Hollingworth and Henderson 1998; Hollingworth and Henderson 2002; Hollingworth, Williams, and Henderson 2001) supports the hypothesis that the representation of an object in a scene stored in memory is not a point-by-point sensory image, but an abstract and thus impoverished version of it.

Specifically, the representations of objects that are stored in memory are high-level visual representations that are abstracted away from low-level sensory properties (shading, texture, color, etc). They code detailed information about the visual form and orientation of the object and abstract visual categories. This means that the representations stored in memory do not contain information about, say, the specific hue or shade of a color, only information about the category of the color (say, bright red). Bearing in mind that the former information is one of the hallmarks of the phenomenal NCC of the experience of a color, the above shows that there can be no recognition or re-identification of the NCC of experiences, since the richness of the sensory representation is lost in the representations stored in memory.

Block (2007) makes a similar point. He thinks that phenomenal persistence overflows cognitive accessibility, which means that much of the perceptual content slips away before one can grab hold of cognitively. Tye (2000, p. 11) expresses this nicely:

I possess the concept *red*, of course, and I exercise it when I recognize something as red, but I lack the concepts for determinate hues. . . . Human memory simply isn't up to the task of capturing the wealth of detail found in the experiences. Beliefs or judgments abstract from the details and impose more general categories.

If the shade of the color of an object could be stored in memory, then the perceiver could recognize another instance of that same shade that occurs in a different visual scene as being the same shade as the shade that she had experienced in the past. But we fail to do that (Dokic and Pacherie, 2001), although we can recognize the new instance as being of the same kind of color as before. This means that we can store the latter information but not the former. Bearing in mind that shades is one of the hallmarks of the phenomenal NCC of the experience of colors; the above suggests that NCC cannot be stored in visual memory. Thus, the contrastive criterion does not apply to NCC.

Second, storing the representation of an object in memory presupposes that the object is being attended to. But, as we saw in chapters 1 and 2, object-centered attention brings with it the modulation of perceptual processing by cognitive or conceptual information, which means that NCC cannot be stored in memory because if it did it would have ceased to be nonconceptual.

The discussion in the previous paragraphs is not a mere comment on Jacob and Jeannerod's view of the criterion of contrastive identification and recognition. In chapter 6, we shall see that the same theme recurs in a slightly different guise, to wit as the criterion of the re-identification condition (Kelly 2001, p. 403) and more specifically as the "re-identification condition on demonstrative concept possession." This is the condition that subject S must satisfy if it is correct to say that she possess the demonstrative concept for X: "in order to possess a demonstrative concept for X, a subject must be able consistently to re-identify a given object or property as falling under the concept if it does." The point there will be that NCC does not satisfy the re-identification condition, for the same reasons that it fails to satisfy the criterion of contrastive identification and recognition.

The work by Ballard et al. on deictic strategies emphasizes, in the tradition of the active vision research program, that the brain does not need, and does not construct unless they are needed, complex internal representations of objects in a visual scene. Cognitive representations are computed as late as possible before the initiation of action, and they contain only information that is required for the successful execution of the planned action. (See also the account of Rensink's work in chapter 1, according to which what is retained in memory is only the gist of the scene and the locations in the scene in which information about the objects in the scene could be obtained if, and only when, needed.) This is a "just-in-time" strategy that minimizes both computational loads and valuable storage space in memory. Note that the most of our actions are usually planned actions that require the synergy of representations in both dorsal and ventral systems. This means that the above remark applies to representations constructed in both visual pathways. The claim made in this chapter to the effect that the weak representations that support object individuation precede the strong representations that subserve object identification fits the "just-in-time" strategy well. Initiating action toward some object in the scene requires object individuation and tracking. Thus, the object-file that constitutes the weak representation of the object must be constructed very early. Other information will be sought and included only if it is necessary for the action's success, and eventually a strong representation of the object is formed.[8]

Interlude

Terminological Issues

Before philosophical issues are addressed, it is wise to clear the way from terminological obstacles. Let me start by discussing some terminological issues, lest my account be distorted by attaching unattended meanings to the terms I employ.

In this book, I use "cognitive penetrability of perception," "theory-ladenness of perception," "conceptual effects on perception," and "top-down effects on perception" roughly interchangeably, the differences being a matter of emphasis rather than of substance. Since these terms are not necessarily coextensive, I should justify my use of them.

First, I take "cognitive penetrability of perception" and "conceptual effects on perception" to be synonymous, provided that one takes cognitive penetrability to signify the effects of cognition on the contents of perception and not only on the vehicles of perceptual states (the subpersonal mechanisms and processes that constitute perception)—in other words, provided that one is interested not only in whether the perceptual neural pathways receive signals from higher cognitive circuits, but also in whether perceptual content is modulated by cognitive states. Given this, if cognition informs perception, the cognitive states bear on perception, and thus conceptual frameworks influence perception. This is evidenced by the fact that in the relevant literature the thesis of the cognitive penetrability of perception has given rise to the widespread thesis that perception presupposes the application of sortal concepts.

"Cognitive penetrability of perception" and "top-down effects on perception," however, are not coextensive. The reason for this is that there are top-down and horizontal interactions *within* the various visual modules (Felleman et al. 1997; Lamme and Spekreijse 2000). Thus, top-down flow of information is compatible with a cognitively impenetrable perception.

(In fact, this is one of the main theses advanced in this book; being within the visual modules, these channels of information flow do not threaten the cognitive encapsulation of early vision). Thus, "top-down effects on perception" is not synonymous with "cognitive penetrability of perception." However, in the relevant literature, and most notably in the work of Churchland (one of the most prominent epistemological constructivists), "top-down effects on perception" has been used to signify the top-down modulation of perception by cognition. In view of that, I take "top-down effects on perception" to mean "cognitive top-down effects on perception" and thus "cognitive penetrability of perception."

Things are a bit more complicated with the expressions "cognitive penetrability of perception" and "theory-ladenness of perception." Though in the literature they are almost invariably taken to be synonymous, this is not trivially so. On some occasions, the former term is used to express the effects of cognitive mechanisms and processes on the mechanisms and processes of perception, in which case the problem is about the vehicles of perceptual states, whereas the latter is taken to apply to the contents of perceptual states. However, I am not so much interested in whether the perceptual neural pathways receive signals from higher cognitive circuits, but mainly in whether perceptual content is modulated by the content of cognitive states. Thus, "cognitive penetrability of perception" signifies the effects of cognitive states on the content of perceptual states (this way, the trap of the usual vehicle-content confusion is avoided). I have also explained why "cognitive penetrability of perception" and "conceptual effects on perception" are treated as coextensive. Now, conceptual frameworks constitute theories (in a broad sense of the term and not necessarily in a strict scientific sense), and thus "cognitive penetrability of perception," by implicating the conceptual apparatus in perceptual modulation, also signifies "theory-ladenness of perception."

A Methodological Note

In the previous chapters, I have discussed results obtained by means of PET and EPR brain examination techniques. However, relatively recently attention has been paid to the methodology of these techniques, and various issues pertaining to the epistemological problems generated by the usage of the techniques are being addressed (Bechtel 2002; Bechtel and Stufflebeam 2001; Bogen 2002; Hardcastle and Stewart 2002). Thus, a short discussion of some of the relevant problems is in order to make clear the way I employ the relevant evidence. I will address specifically two issues that are closely related to the ways I employ evidence generated by positron-emission tomography and event-related potential techniques. The first concerns the nature of PET scanning results; the second concerns the use of ERP recordings.

PET data are usually provided by subtracting cerebral blood flow between two conditions. As Bechtel and Mundale (1999, p. 189) argue, one chooses tasks (say, A and B) that are thought to include the same operations and to differ in only a few operations (operations that are required by task A but not by task B). Then one subtracts the activation level registered for performing one task from the activation level registered in performing the other task. The difference in the image is designed to indicate areas employed in performing the additional psychological functions required by task A. Thus, the aim is to find one area in the brain that corresponds to the additional information-processing operation required for the task.

The success of the whole process hinges significantly on the task analysis that is used to identify the set of operations that would perform the task, and thus, task analysis helps to identify the types of operations that are required in one condition but not in another. The subtractive method correlates the additional brain areas with these additional operations, which thus become good candidates for performing these additional operations (Bechtel 2002, p. 56). One assumes that cerebral blood flow in an area of the brain reflects overall neuronal activity in that area. For instance, suppose that condition A involves reading one type of material and that condition B involves reading another type of material. When one subtracts blood flow during condition A from blood flow during condition B, one is able to say that in condition A there was more activity in area X of the brain *relative* to condition B.

Suppose that area Y was equally active in both conditions A and B. If so, the common activity will be subtracted out and therefore we shall see nothing in area Y. Thus, one cannot infer from PET data that area Y was or was not involved during conditions A and B, but one can infer that there was *more* activity in area X in condition A relative to condition B. Though one can say that area X was more active in condition A relative to condition B, one cannot say that X was not involved in condition B. It may have been involved, but to a lesser extent. Thus, from PET scanning one can only infer that area X is more active during condition A than during condition B. One cannot infer that it is not active in condition B, and one does not know what other areas (e.g. area Y) are equally activated by conditions A and B. Whether this is an important statement depends on the hypothesis being tested. What one cannot do is compare activity between conditions A and B and hope to find all the areas activated during condition A. One will see the areas that show differential activation between conditions A and B, but one will not see the areas that show common levels of activation. Thus, PET cannot be used to determine all the areas of the brain that are activated when a task is being performed.

Could PET be used to determine whether an area in the brain is active during one task but not during another? Could one, say, determine whether brain area X, which is associated with semantic processing, is active when the visual form of a string of letters is being attended to? PET by itself does not suffice to settle this, since even if PET highlights area X when subtracting purely visual tasks from semantic tasks, this only means that area X is more active when the subject performs semantic processing, not that area X is not activated when the detection of purely visual form task takes place.

To determine which area of the brain performs which activity, one has to consider additional evidence coming from behavioral data, and from lesion studies. In other words, one has to align different techniques to obtain complementary information about the phenomenon (Bechtel 2002, p. S49). Price et al. (1999) argue that functional imaging studies and neuropsychological studies jointly delineate both sufficient (PET studies) and necessary (neuropsychological studies) conditions for neural systems and their role in processing. To determine, for instance, whether semantic areas in the brain are necessary for detecting visual form, one must examine neurophysiological evidence pertaining to semantic memory impairments. Damage in the left hemisphere (De Renzi, Scotti, and Spinnler 1969) is accompanied by semantic impairments such that knowledge of the objects' category, of object classification, and of properties and functions is degraded or inaccessible. Studies by Warrington (1975) show that the same patients have normal viewer-centered, and object-centered representations, since they succeed in matching tasks, drawing objects, recognizing objects seen from unusual views, and maintaining object constancy. Thus, the semantic impairments leave intact both the viewer-centered and object-centered representation. This suggests that semantic areas in the brain are not involved in detection of visual form.

In PET scans, thresholds must be set high enough to ensure that above-baseline neuronal activities are detected when the subject performs a task. Thus, sub-threshold activity that does not show statistically significant increase in blood flow and which is significant for the task will not be detected. Whether this is a serious problem depends on the question asked. Suppose the question is whether a semantic area in the brain participates in visual form detection (problem *A*), and not the determination of all brain areas that participate in visual form detection and semantic processing (problem *B*). Then the subtractive method (and the other techniques with which it is combined) suggests an answer to question *A*, although it certainly does not answer question *B*. (For a similar argument, see Bogen 2002, p. S70.)

The second problem concerns the use of ERP scanning. ERPs have a poor spatial resolution and cannot be used to locate the brain areas from which recordings are being taken. Thus, these areas must have been specified beforehand by means of other localization methods—usually PET scanning, behavioral data, and recordings of single-unit activity. But it is not quite true that ERPs cannot be used to locate brain areas: the differences in ERP morphology between distinct recording sites on the scalp can be related to underlying sources, and dipole modeling makes it possible to pinpoint sources of scalp potentials.

In the studies to which I have referred thus far in the book, ERP recordings are usually combined with PET scanning. If PET studies provide us with an idea of where activity is located in the brain when various tasks are performed, then this information guides us in applying the electrodes that record electrical activity in the brain to the appropriate sites on the scalp (Posner and Raichle 1996). This combination provides a convenient way to trace the rapid time-dynamic changes occurring when subjects process information in various tasks. This way, one can determine the time course of brain activation previously identified via PET. Mangun et al. (2000), for example, integrated ERP with PET in their studies on attentional selection. ERP provide information regarding the time course of early attentional selection. However, ERP provide little information regarding the neuroanatomical loci at which attention exerts influence on stimulus analysis. PET imaging helps determine the brain regions that are active during sensory, perceptual, and cognitive processing. More specifically, the PET activations are used to determine the possible locations and numbers of active areas in the attentional task. Mangun et al. (ibid.) use brain electric source analysis (BESA) to examine whether electrical activity in the regions of the brain that were found active during the PET in spatial attention tasks could have yielded the ERP effects. Accordingly, the dipoles of ERP are placed at those locations at which PET indicated attention-related activations. Thus, Mangun et al. claim, a cognitive operation (early attentional filtering) was localized both in time and in space. As Ziegler et al. remark (1997, p. 759), "measures of blood flow and measures of event-related activity show convergence in the brain regions they identify as differentially active. . . . Such convergence allows conclusions to be drawn from the ERP data about the timing of the activation of these regions." In other studies, Luck and Hillyard (2000) combine ERP with single-unit activity recordings to study the locus of selection within perception. To determine the neuroanatomical sources of the ERP attention effects, single-unit activity in specific areas of visual cortex in monkeys is recorded. Having clarified this methodological issue, I will proceed now to examine what these scanning techniques reveal about the role of attention in visual processing.

Taking Stock

Now that I have clarified the terminological and methodological issues, let me restate my main theses thus far. I have argued that a pre-attentional segmentation mechanism is designed to provide a short-lived, vulnerable representation of proto-objects as discrete spatio-temporal entities. Thus, it functions as an individuating (which includes indexing) mechanism that focuses on proto-objects and on particular locations within objects. Experimental evidence shows that object individuation is based primarily on spatio-temporal information (information about location, relative position, and motion), may override featural information, and on certain occasions may pick up objects without any regard even for their spatial location (Scholl 2001). If spatio-temporal information by itself does not suffice to individuate the objects in a scene, information about shape, size, and color can be also used to that effect, although this information may not be encoded. The same evidence shows that object individuation on the basis of spatio-temporal information precedes object identification— not surprising, since the latter presupposes the encoding of featural information and its comparison with information stored in memory, which the former does not require. In other words, spatio-temporal object individuation precedes object feature identification. When featural information is used for object individuation, then there is evidence that object feature individuation also precedes object feature identification (Scholl and Leslie 1999).

The claim that the individuating and indexing process is pre-attentive amounts to the claim that the indexing process is purely perceptual and thus nonsemantic, in the sense that it is not affected by top-down flow of information from higher semantic cognitive centers. Thus, it comes as no surprise that the kind of information used by the visual system to parse a scene is information that can be retrieved in a purely perceptual bottom-up

way from a visual scene. This is a theoretical reason why object individuation should precede object identification, which is what experimental
evidence suggests; the former can be a process that involves no concepts
whatsoever, whereas the latter unavoidably involves the conceptual apparatus of the organism. In other words, the system that assigns indexes uses
representations whose content is nonconceptual and of which it has no
access awareness or report awareness. Thus, these properties need not be
conceptually encoded, in which case they would be potentially within the
realm of access awareness. Note that even though the properties used by
the precognitive or preconceptual indexing system may be properties represented in the feedforward sweep, they may also be properties whose
representations require recurrent processing. In the latter case, the system
can be phenomenally aware of them.

These remarks allow us to address Kahneman's claim that object-files are
required for conscious seeing and that they may contain the name of the
object. Though conscious seeing certainly requires object-files or some
other form of object representation, the object-files (or, better, the process
by which they are opened) do not require consciousness. This is entailed
jointly by the fact that object individuation is accompanied by the opening
of an object-file and by the demand that a preliminary parsing of a scene
that individuates objects take place in a pre-attentive and thus early stage
of visual processing. (Even if one rejects that, it is clear that parsing a scene
occurs very fast and certainly before the recognition and categorization
of objects.) This implies that object-files are constructed during the pre-
attentive stage, or at least very early in the visual process. Consciousness,
however, is delayed in time; recall that according to Treisman and
Kanwisher (1998) object recognition usually occurs within 100–200 ms
after stimulus onset, but it takes another 100 ms before this information
is brought into awareness so that the perceiver is conscious of the presence
of an object. Thus, object-files are constructed before consciousness enters
the picture.

I have presented evidence supporting the thesis that objects are individuated in a scene during a pre-attentive, purely perceptual and thus bottom-
up stage of visual processing. This means that no cognitive top-down
information modulates this process, which entails that when an object-file
is opened in the course of the process of object individuation no semantical information (that is, information that requires the conceptual arsenal
of the perceiver) can be included in it. However, names (including names
of kinds) are usually assigned only after an object has been identified and
categorized; I have to recognize an object as (say) a horse to be able to attach

to its object-file that particular piece of information. Thus, the object-files cannot contain names for the individuated objects.

At this point a distinction must be made between the object-files constructed during the individuation process and the full-blown object-files that provide the representations of objects as they are experienced by the perceivers. (This distinction will come handy when I discuss a causal theory of reference based on the object-individuating mechanism in chapter 6.) The former representations contain only information that is retrieved bottom-up from a scene, whereas the latter may include all kinds of semantical information about an object (its function, its relationships to other objects, and so forth). The former representations allow only the individuation of an object, whereas the latter representations allow the identification of objects and their categorization. In chapter 3, I called the former representations "weak representations" and the latter semantic representations "strong representations."

Charting the Road

Let us grant that the arguments developed in chapters 1–3 are sound and that the main conclusion of those arguments regarding a stage of visual processing (to wit, perception) that is bottom-up or cognitively impenetrable is nearly correct. What would be the impact of this thesis on philosophically minded readers, and how do psychology and neural science inform philosophy? In other words, what does philosophy get from all this discussion about whether there is a cognitively impenetrable part of visual processing? Answering this question will be the subject matter of part II of the book.

In chapters 4 and 5, I discuss how and why the existence of a cognitively impenetrable perception vindicates the claims of those who argue that there is a nonconceptual content of perception, where 'perception' is used in the usual sense to mean what I have referred to as 'visual processing'. In addition, the discussion regarding the nature of perceptual processing (with 'perception' used in my sense, designating the cognitively impenetrable part of visual processing) will illuminate and extend the already rich discussion pertaining to the nature or content of the nonconceptual content. To avoid terminological confusion, I will be using 'perception' in my "technical" sense (defined above), and I will be using 'late vision' to refer to the conceptually modulated part of visual processing, and 'visual processing' or 'vision' to refer to the whole visual process that leads to seeing the world.

In chapter 6, I develop a theory of direct reference according to which reference to objects in a scene is secured through a direct, interest-free, theory-free, and concept-free causal link that the perceptual system establishes when a visual scene falls within the receptive field of the eyes. The key to this direct nonconceptual reference is the nonconceptual content of perception.

In chapter 7, I address the theory-ladenness of perception, focusing on the debate between Churchland and Fodor. I argue that there is a theory-neutral part of visual processing. (The reader will have already guessed that cognitively impenetrable perception is also theory-neutral.) I discuss the merits and shortcomings of Churchland and Fodor's respective theses, and I argue that a modification of the definition of 'modules' to avoid the problematic aspects of Fodor's notion can account for the empirical evidence regarding visual processing.

In chapter 8, I address the controversy between realism and anti-realism (the latter in the guise of constructivism) and argue that there is a limited form of realism that can be successfully defended against constructivism. This limited form of realism restricts the "items" in the world toward which one can justifiably adopt a realistic attitude to the contents of perceptual nonconceptual content.

II Philosophy

4 The Nonconceptual Content of Experience

In this chapter I discuss the notion of the nonconceptual content of experience. In section 4.1, I present in a nutshell the main theses of the theory of vision for which I argued in part I of the book and define some important terms. In section 4.2, I introduce the notion of nonconceptual content of perception, defining it as the content that is retrievable from a scene by means of the cognitively encapsulated processes of perception. I delineate the relation of this notion of nonconceptual content to the notion of phenomenal content employed in the philosophical literature, and I offer some criticisms of the method traditionally used to determine the phenomenal content of perception, which I call "the phenomenological method" or "the method of introspection." According to that method, to determine the phenomenal content of experience, one introspects the way an experience is presented, or seems, to one, and tries to determine those aspects of the experience that one could have even if one did not possess the relevant concepts. A more detailed criticism of that method will be developed in the next chapter. I say from the outset that I am not going to argue for the existence of nonconceptual content in the way of, say, Bermudez (1995), Heck (2000), and Peacocke (1998, 2001), though I agree with most of their discussion. The reason is that the theory of vision that has been presented here, if true, renders the existence of nonconceptual content (NCC) indisputable.

4.1 A Short Overview and Some Definitions

At this point it would be helpful to recapitulate the main results of part I of the book about the theory of vision developed there. To that effect I use Lamme's (2003, 2004) studies on the relation between attention, perception, and awareness, which I examined in detail in chapters 1 and 2. Lamme argues that there are two kinds of visual processing in the brain:

the feedforward sweep (FFS) and recurrent processing (RP). In the FFS, the signal is transmitted only from the lower levels of the brain to the higher ones. No signal can be transmitted top-down to influence the visual processing at that stage, as there is no feedback from higher to lower brain areas at that stage. Feedforward connections can extract high-level information, which is sufficient to lead to some initial categorization of the visual scene. In RP, signals flow to both directions. The FFS is succeeded by local RP, that is, recurrent processing that involves lateral flow of information and top-down flow of information that is restricted within early vision and does not involve memory or other cognitive functions. (I will call this kind of top-down processing "local top-down processing.") Further up in the hierarchy of visual processes we have global RP, which involves memory circuits and in which visual processing is modulated by cognitive centers higher in the brain.

Awareness is defined as the occurrence of recurrent processing. Without RP there is no awareness. The processes in the FFS are necessarily unconscious. When there is RP, awareness arises. When RP is limited to early areas, we have phenomenal experience of the content of our perceptual states, and thus this form of awareness is called "phenomenal awareness." When RP includes output areas, then attentional selection has an influence; because of attentional selection, there is "access awareness." Since the content of this awareness can be typically reported, this form of awareness is also called "report awareness." Thus, the type of information of which one is phenomenally aware is situated between feedforward (unconscious) and globally recurrent (access-conscious) processing. According to Lamme (2003, p. 3), the information of which one is phenomenally aware is a short-lived, unstable, vulnerable, and not easily reportable form of visual experience. "Access awareness" (that is, the awareness that accompanies our normal experience) is more stable and easily reportable.

I will now recast the preceding discussion in a way that will allow me to introduce a tripartite distinction between sensation, perception, and observation, which will illuminate the discussion that follows. To that end I will repeat here the definitions of 'sensation', 'perception', and 'observation' that I put forth in the concluding pages of chapter 1. The distinction is based on the account of visual processes discussed in part I of the book, most notably on the distinction between early vision and high vision, on the one hand, and the distinction between feedforward processing and local and global recurrent processing. Recall that these two distinctions are not coextensive but overlap.[1]

All processes that apply to the information contained in the retinal image fall within the scope of *sensation*. Thus, we have processes that compute information on light intensity. Sensation includes parts of early vision, such as those processes that compute changes in light intensity by locating and coding individual changes in intensity. Sensation includes Marr's *raw primal sketch* that provides information about zero crossings, bars, blobs, boundaries, edge segments, etc. The idea is that much of the information about surfaces is encoded in changes in the intensity of reflected light on the retina. Thus, the task of the very early visual system is to decode this information by locating, representing, and interpreting both changes in intensity and the ways in which the intensities are reorganized at various spatial scales by more abstract properties, such as the alignment of termination. Sharp changes in intensity, for instance, are interpreted as surface boundaries. Since, however, the world is not a world of uniformly illuminated smooth flat surfaces, the visual system must also represent and interpret gradual changes in intensity. The properties of stimuli recorded at this level (high temporal and spatial frequencies, anti-correlated disparity, etc.) never reach awareness. There are non-attentional selection mechanisms involved here that filter out information (Lamme 2003, 2004). In neuroscientific terms, sensation consists in those processes that belong to Lamme's feedforward sweep. The "image" resulting from sensation, initially cognitively useless, is gradually transformed along the visual pathways in increasingly structured representations, via *perception*.

The processes that transform sensation to a representation that can be processed by cognition constitute *perception*. The output of these processes is a cognitively impenetrable content that is retrieved from a visual scene in a bottom-up way. A subset of this output, consisting of that which can be brought to a kind of awareness called *phenomenal awareness*, is the "phenomenal content." In Lamme's theory, phenomenal awareness requires local RP. Another subset is the content of subdoxastic states. These are the late states of the FFS that bind features in the image and which, occurring outside the influence of local RP, have contents that are not available to any form of awareness. As an example of perception, consider Marr's various grouping procedures applied to the edge fragments formed in the *raw primal sketch*. They yield the *full primal sketch*, in which larger structures with boundaries and regions are recovered. Through the *primal sketch*, contours and textures in an image are captured in a purely bottom-up way, although processing at that level involves lateral and local top-down flow of information. This lateral and top-down flow of information, however, being within early vision, does not threaten the bottom-up character of the relevant processes.

Perception comprises intermediate-level vision, which includes processes (e.g., the extraction of shape and of spatial relations) that cannot be purely bottom-up but which do not require information from higher cognitive states, since they rely on lateral and local top-down flow of information (Hildreth and Ulmann 1995). Note that since the extraction of shape and of spatial relations require local RP, they are within the scope of phenomenal awareness. As we saw in chapter 1, the same holds for the extraction of size, of motion, and of the surface properties of objects. Being nonconceptual, perceptual processes are not affected by our knowledge about specific objects and events. In Marr's model, the $2\frac{1}{2}$D sketch is the final product of perception. As we have seen, spatial relations, position, orientation, motion, size, viewer-centered shape, surface properties, and color are all bottom-retrievable by low-level vision processes. It may be that, in Lamme's framework, perception consists in those stages of the FFS that bind features in the image, such as edge fragments, and thus result in states that have a rudimentary structure, and in the stage of vision that involves local recurrent processing. Both sensation and perception constitute Pylyshyn's (2001, 2003) early vision.

All subsequent visual processes fall within *cognition*, and include both the post-sensory/semantic interface (at which the object-recognition units intervene) and the purely conceptual processes that lead to the identification and recognition of the array (high-level vision). At this level, we have observation (or, to use Pylyshyn's term, late vision). The objects as we experience them are the products of "late vision." In Marr's theory, the culmination of visual processes is the 3D model of an object. The recovery of the objects cannot be purely data-driven, since what is regarded as an object depends on the subsequent usage of the information and thus is cognitively penetrable. Several theories of vision hold that object identification is based on part decomposition, which is the first stage in forming a structural description of an object and seems to depend on knowledge of specific objects. Other theorists propose that objects are identified by template-matching processes (Edelman 1999). Object recognition requires matching between the internal representation of an object stored in memory and the representation of an object generated from the image. Similarly, template matching relies on knowledge of specific objects, and is, consequently, cognitively driven, since the templates result from previous encounters with objects that have been stored in memory.[2]

By introducing a distinction between a bottom-up, nonconceptual perception and a conceptual late vision, I join a long tradition of similar distinctions. Jackendoff (1987) distinguishes "visual awareness" from "visual understanding" and, interestingly enough, considers Marr's 2½D sketch an exemplification of the former, and Marr's 3D sketch an exemplification of the latter. Similarly, Dretske (1993) distinguishes "thing-awareness" from "fact-awareness" and also (1995) distinguishes a "phenomenal sense of see" from a "doxastic sense of see." The first parts of the aforementioned pairs clearly correspond to a non-epistemic sense of perception. They involve nonconceptual content. The second parts of the pairs correspond to an epistemic sense of perception. In the latter case, the content delivered is the content of judgments and beliefs; it is clearly a conceptual content.

Before I proceed, I would like to explain the qualification "knowledge about specific objects," although the reader is referred to the discussion in chapter 3 of the operational constraints employed by the visual system in its function. Even if perception turns out to be of bottom-up character, it is still not isolated from knowledge. Knowledge intrudes on perception, since early vision is informed and constrained by some operational constraints that reduce indeterminacies in information (mainly the underdetermination of the 2½D structure from the 2D retinal stimulation). The operational constraints are general assumptions about the world constraining visual processing (Marr 1982; Spelke 1990; Pylyshyn 1999; Ulmann 1979). These constraints are not the results of acquisition of knowledge about specific objects but are reliable regularities about the optico-spatial properties of our world. This "knowledge" is implicit, in that it is available only for the processing of the retinal image and cannot be overridden, whereas explicit knowledge is available for a wide range of cognitive applications and one can decide not to use it.

4.2 Nonconceptual Content, Phenomenal Content of Perception, and Phenomenological Experience

4.2.1 Nonconceptual Content: Why Do We Need It?
Philosophers (Bermudez 1995; Crane 1992; Cussins 1990; Dretske 1995; Evans 1982; Heck 2000; Kelly 2000; Lowe 1992; Peacock 1992, 2001; Smith 2002; Shoemaker 2002, Tye 1995, 2000, 2002a, 2006; Vision 1998) recognize the necessity of and argue for a kind of experiential content that is not conceptual and yet it is evaluable as correct or as incorrect. Having correctness conditions (NCC) presents (Heck 2000) or represents (Peacocke 2001)[3] the world as being in a certain way, though the representation does

not have the structure of discursive judgments. Being nonconceptual, NCC is not the content of beliefs.

Several reasons have led to the endorsement of a nonconceptual content.

First, there is the demand to account for how concepts or symbols are grounded in the world and not just in more concepts or symbols (Evans 1982; Lowe 1992; Peacocke 1992; Shoemaker 2002; Tye 2002)—"the symbol-grounding problem." According to the descriptive theories of reference (with which I deal in length in the next chapter), a symbol is associated with a concept in the mind that constitutes its meaning. This concept determines reference, since it allows one to pick out the objects in the environment that are "described" by the concept. Certain of the descriptions associated with the symbol fix its reference. Descriptive theories of reference are incomplete (Devitt 1996, p. 159). By explaining references by descriptive means, they appeal to the descriptions of other symbols; thus, they explain reference by appealing to concepts and to the reference of other symbols. To escape the infinite regress, there would have to be some symbols whose reference does not depend on that of others, symbols that are founded directly in the world. Since perception provides us with an immediate contact with the world, it is at the level of perception that this direct contact should be sought.[4] This would also do justice to the grounding problem, and at the same time it would justify the claim that in perception there is an immediate sensory presence of physical objects, which is usually called the transparency of perceptual experience (Martin 2002; Tye 1995, 2000, 2002). This immediacy can be captured only by making the relation between our perceptual awareness and the world direct and not mediated by concepts, and by postulating the nonconceptual content as the direct causal imprint of the world in us. As I will argue in chapter 6, perception and more specifically perceptual demonstratives put us in a direct *de re* relationship with objects in the world by directly receiving information from these objects—or, as Smith (2002, p. 84) puts it, by embodying information about them.

Second, nonconceptual content allows one to continue to refer to objects while their features or one's beliefs about them undergo radical changes— the problem of reference stability (Devitt 1996; Pylyshyn 2001, 2003). Suppose that the concept of an object is defined by a set of descriptions. Assume that some of the features of the object change. How can one assign the new properties to the same object if one does not have a nondescriptive way of referring to the object? Relying exclusively on descriptions makes this impossible, since a change in description implies a change in reference. If one could pick out objects by nonconceptual means, the problem would be solved. Since one's immediate access to one's environment is through one's experience, finding such a nonconceptual way of reference requires that at least part of the content of experience be non-conceptual. Pylyshyn (2001, p. 138) claims that to assign properties to an object requires a "demonstrative" reference, a kind of reference that somehow picks out the object but encodes none of its properties. In addition, nonconceptual content makes it possible to say that one sees an object while one forms the wrong perceptual beliefs about it, as in the case of an illusion. This is so because were perception mediated by concepts then what one would see would be determined by what one believes to be the case about the object. Thus, it would not make any sense to say that I see a red triangle but I believe it to be green. However, if some non-conceptual content determines the content of one's perceptual states, then what one perceives is independent of any perceptual beliefs one might form about the object of perception.

A third reason for the introduction of nonconceptual content is the necessity to account for the fine-grained character and richness of the "phenomenal content" of experience (Crane 1992; Evans 1982; Heck 2001; Peacocke 1992, 2001; Tye 2002; Shoemaker 2002). Usually, the phenomenal content of our experiences is much richer than any attempt to report it could be; it cannot be described conceptually. The phenomenal content of an experience is what is responsible for the "phenomenal character" of experience—that is, for what it is like to have an experience. "The view I accept," writes Tye (2002, p. 448), "is that what it is like to have a visual experience (the 'phenomenal character' of experience) is a matter of a certain sort of representational content that the experience has." One notes the slide from the nonconceptual content of experience to the phenomenal content of experience. Sometimes in the literature, phenomenal content is nonconceptual representational content (Tye 1995, 2000, 2002); but there is nonconceptual representational content that is not phenomenal, in the sense that it a subject cannot be aware of it, namely the content of subpersonal information-processing states (Bermudez 1995).

Hereafter, in this chapter, I will write "NCC" whenever what I discuss applies to either phenomenal or nonconceptual content in general. Since not all NCC is phenomenal, it goes without saying that phenomenal NCC has properties that NCC in general lacks (most importantly, one is neces-sarily aware of phenomenal content but not necessarily of nonconceptual content). Thus, when I refer to "phenomenal content," what I say concerns nonconceptual content too, except on those occasions in which I discuss the property that phenomenal content has to be content of which one is aware. When I discuss nonconceptual content other than phenomenal content, I will refer to it as "subpersonal content" or "nonconceptual content of subdoxastic or subpersonal states."[5] Note also that, as will emerge from the discussion that follows, there is nonconceptual content that is not representational at all—to wit, the content of the states of sensation. When I refer to nonconceptual content, I usually mean nonconceptual content that is representational, though some of the properties of that content are also properties of nonrepresentational nonconceptual content.

To get a first glimpse of what phenomenal content is, suppose that X views an object Y. Then, the phenomenal content of the perceptual states of X consists in representations of the properties of Y that Y has in virtue of appearing to X, or being disposed to appear to X, in certain ways. These certain ways are the phenomenal properties of perception. There is a convergence of views as to the kinds of properties that figure in the list of the phenomenal (and thus nonconceptual) properties of experience. I restrict myself to discussing the phenomenal properties of visual experience. Spatial relations among objects, size and orientation of objects, location of objects, and colors and their properties (shades) figure in this list. Peacocke (1992) and Bermudez (1995) include the representations of viewpoint-independent objects (Marr's 3D objects) in the list of nonconceptual properties.

The discussion in part I of this book adds one more reason to accept the existence of representational perceptual content that is nonconceptual. We have seen that there is a pre-attentional (where attention is understood as object-based attention) stage of visual processing or early vision, in which information is retrieved from the environment in a purely bottom-up (that is, cognitively encapsulated) way. For reasons I explained in the interlude, information that is retrieved in such a manner from the environment is conceptually encapsulated and thus constitutes the nonconceptual content of the relevant perceptual states. If the account of vision I presented in the chapters 1–3 convinces one that perception is cognitively impenetrable, then one has to cede that nonconceptual content exists, as the content of the states of early vision.

4.2.2   Nonconceptual Content: What Kind of Content?

The kind of content nonconceptual states have depends, of course, on the definition of content. I will say (see also Crane 1992) that a state has a representational content if it represents the world as being a certain way (round, for instance). In this case the state has a correctness condition; that is, the world can make the state come out true or false. Peacocke (1992) calls the correctness condition "the minimal account of content posses- sion." This correctness condition, and the possibility of falsehood (that is, the possibility of misrepresentation), render nonconceptual contents intentional in the sense that they are about something in the world. According to Bermudez (1995, pp. 344–347), that a state should be seman- tically evaluable is a necessary but not a sufficient condition for the state to have representational content. Bermudez (ibid., pp. 348–349) adds some further interrelated conditions that the content of a mental state must meet in order to be representational. I agree with Bermudez that the minimal criterion for representational content possession is not enough to determine representational contentful states and that further criteria are needed. I am going to accept Bermudez's criteria as a step toward a more adequate account of content possession, but I do not attempt either to justify them or to show that they are sufficient and/or necessary conditions for a mental state to have representational content. Here I present them with a short explanation of what they mean. As will be evident when I have finished my analysis of the constituents of phenomenal content, phenomenal content, and nonconceptual content in general[6] satisfy all these conditions.

First, a representational content should be able to figure in explanations of intentional behavior—to wit, in the explanation of the connection between sensory input and behavioral output that cannot be explained by invoking some lawful regularity (in other words, an invariant connection), as when the behavior is the result of some dedicated transducers. Second, representational content should allow cognitive integration, in the sense that it should be able to interact with other representational states. Third, representational content must have structure. This entails that its constitu- ent elements could be constituent parts of other contents, and that the content could be decomposed into its elements, which could then be recombined with the constituent elements of other states having represen- tational content.

In view of this definition of representational content, and in view of the theory of vision developed in part I of the book, the NCC includes both content that is not representational and content that is representational. More specifically, sensation and perception consist of processing states with nonconceptual content, since they are both parts of the cognitively encapsulated and, thus, conceptually impenetrable early vision. I will argue later that sensation consists of states that do not have representational content, whereas perceptual (in the sense defined above) states have representational content.

According to the philosophers who argue for NCC, to be in a perceptual state with a certain content does not require that one possesses particular cognitive capacities; hence the characterization of this content as nonconceptual. Crane (1992, p. 149) writes that X is in a state with nonconceptual content iff X does not have to possess the concepts that characterize the content in order to be in that state. Similarly, Tye (2000, 62: 2006) holds that a mental content is nonconceptual if its subject need not possess any of the concepts that enter into the specification of the correctness conditions for that content.[7] Cussins (1990) also calls the content of such representations "nonconceptual," by which he means those properties that are canonically characterized by means of concepts, which are such that the organism need not have those concepts in order to have that property. More specifically, for any state S with content, S has nonconceptual content P, iff the fact that X is in S does not imply that X possesses the concepts that canonically characterize P, meaning that X does not need to possess the concepts that would normally enter in a report of the content of S that adequately specifies that content. These definitions constitute the "usual" way of understanding nonconceptual content. Notice that these definitions do not require that the subject be aware of the nonconceptual content, and in that sense they are definitions of nonconceptual content in general. If one adds to these definitions the condition that this content be subject to the perceiver's awareness, then they become the usual definitions of phenomenal content.

Stalnaker and Martin also hold that the content of perception is independent of the conceptual repertory of the perceiver. Stalnaker (2003) maintains that the content of a state is nonconceptual if it is fixed externally to anything that the bearer of the state believes or knows (the externality criterion for NCC). In other words, NCC must be determined directly through causal links to the world, independent of what cognitive states the person, whose perceptual states have the content, is in.[8] Martin (1992, p. 759) claims that how things appear must not be constrained by what concepts the perceiver has and that NCC is restricted only by one's sensitivity to the world (ibid., p. 763). Thus, NCC should be the content of experiential states that is sensitive only to world-states with which it is related through direct causal links, and also should be unaffected by the conceptual states of the perceiver.

Burge (1977) offers an account of the direct link between perception and the world that acquaints the perceiver with worldly objects and their properties. According to Burge, being acquainted in perception with an object means that one is in direct (without any conceptual intermediaries) contact with the object itself and retrieves information regarding that very object from the object itself and not through a description. On that account, perception puts us in a *de re* relationship with the object (as opposed to a *descriptivist* relationship). When one forms a *de re* belief, one stands in "an appropriate nonconceptual, contextual relations to objects the belief is about" (ibid., p. 346). Thus, the content of a mental state is non-conceptual if its reference is determined independently of any descriptive content that the mental state might have under a canonical description. Since a description involves sortals, a non-descriptivist *de re* relationship with objects that allows the fixing of reference of perceptual demonstratives does not involve any sortal concepts.

Nonconceptual content represents the world as being a certain way. At the same time, the same content does not require that one who has it possess the concepts that would linguistically describe it, or that one exercise these concepts if one possesses them. Nonconceptual content, thus, is not representational in the subject-predicate sense. Nevertheless, it represents the way the world is. Heck (2000, p. 509) calls this feature of nonconceptual content its "presentational aspect."

As Tye remarks (2006, p. 23), "given the usual understanding of the thesis of nonconceptual content, as far as the nature of the content itself goes, there need be no distinction between conceptual and nonconceptual content," since the difference between nonconceptual and conceptual content is a matter not of the properties of each kind of content but of whether the person who possesses the relevant contentful states also possesses the corresponding concepts. In other words, your nonconceptual content may be my conceptual content. This leaves open the possibility that there are visual nonconceptual states that have conceptual contents. They are nonconceptual for me, simply because I do not possess the required concepts to describe them. It seems, thus, that the traditional definitions of nonconceptual content do not do a thorough job of distinguishing the two kinds of contents. Moreover, they may lead someone to draw the wrong conclusion that nonconceptual content and conceptual content are in the whole the same, as Crane (1992, p. 155) does, although he is also probably motivated by an attempt to explain the evidential relation between perceptual states and perceptual judgments and beliefs. That conclusion is the wrong one to draw. As we shall see, nonconceptual content and conceptual content are different kinds of contents, not contents whose sole difference lies in the fact that conceptual content is accompanied by the possession of the relevant concepts on the part of the perceiver. Put differently: Conceptual content is not simply non-conceptual content + concepts (that is, nonconceptual content that gets conceptualized).

To overcome the difficulties of the traditional definitions of nonconceptual content, Tye (2006, pp. 508–509) claims that "visual experiences have contents that are robustly nonconceptual, and, insofar as they have such contents, they are nonconceptual states." The robustly nonconceptual content is a possible state of affairs that contains entities of this world. The possible states of affairs consist of two basic types. First, structured complexes of specific particular items, properties, and relations. Second, structured existential states of affairs involving properties and relations and plausibly the subject of the experience. NCC belongs to the second category. To explicate what he means, Tye provides the following example (ibid., p. 508):

Suppose . . . I see the facing surface S of an object O and it looks red to me. My visual experience intuitively represents S as having the property of being red. At this level my experience is accurate if and only if S is red. But my experience has also something important in common with certain other visual experiences not directed at S. Suppose, for example, that O is replaced with another object O' that looks just like O or that I am hallucinating a red surface so that phenomenally it is for me just as it is in seeing S. Intuitively, in all three cases, it seems to me that *there is* a red surface before me. At this phenomenal level, my experience is accurate if and only if there is a red surface before me. This content is existential, not involving S, though it does also include the subject of the experience.

This passage suggests that Tye draws a distinction between visual experiences whose content represents a type "a red surface" and a visual experience whose content represents a certain token "the red surface S." At the phenomenal level, what matters is whether there is a red surface (a type) before me, not whether that surface is of S (a token). What both experiences have in common is a red surface. Thus, they are both instances of the same type of experience: "There is a red surface before me." This is entailed by (a) the fact that at the phenomenal level the correctness condition is the same both for the case in which I see O that has S, and in the case in which I see O' that does not have S (recall S is the surface of O); my experience is accurate iff there is a red surface before me, not if there is object O with surface S before me, and (b) the minimal account of content possession, which states that a state has representational content if it describes the world as being some way. Thus, at the phenomenal level only types can be represented, not tokens; phenomenal content is about types, not tokens. From this follows that the nonconceptual phenomenal content is about types of entities, not about entity tokens. It is not about structured complexes of specific particular items, etc. It is about structured existential states of affairs involving properties and relations, etc. Notice that "specific particular items" are not among the possible contents of nonconceptual phenomenal states in Tye's account. Thus, the structured existential states of affairs that characterize nonconceptual contents are types of structured states of affairs that assert the existence of an object or rather of a surface facing the viewer bearing the structured properties (a surface that is red) and relations, although the object is not specified, and that is why those states are not about object tokens.

Notice that the correctness condition is not satisfied in the case of the hallucination, for in that case there is not a red surface before me, and the correctness condition specifically includes the clause "there is (a surface before me.)" Tye presumably adds the existential qualification to exclude hallucinations from having the same nonconceptual content with the other two cases, despite the fact that the hallucination "feels" exactly like the other two cases; that is, when I hallucinate a red surface it seems to me that there is a red surface before me, in exactly the same way as in the other two cases.[9] Thus, Tye brings in externalism to allow him to distinguish between hallucination and "normal" visual experiences. Externalism holds that any mental state cannot be specified independently of the relationship of the bearer of that state with the environment. This means that one's mental states cannot be determined solely by introspection of their contents. Thus, even when the content of the state I am in when I am hallucinating a red surface before me is phenomenally exactly the same as the content of my visual experience when I do really see a red surface before me, the two states are not identical, since in the latter but in not the former the red surface exists. The two states may have the same "inner content," but they have different "wide content."[10]

I fully agree with Tye's construal of nonconceptual content as coarse grained in that sense. Recall that in the first chapter I argued that nonconceptual content represents types of objects, not object tokens. That view was based on the findings of cognitive sciences concerning the mechanisms that retrieve information from a visual scene in a bottom-up manner before the onset of attention. In that chapter, I presented Kanwisher's claim that the representations of objects that can be formed without attention (which thus constitute nonconceptual contents of perceptual states that are accompanied at best by phenomenal awareness) correspond to representations of types of objects rather than to representations of tokens of objects. Representation of object tokens involves not only the individuation of objects in a visual scene and the activation of the relevant perceptual properties, but also the further construction of an organized representation in which these visual properties are attributed to their source in external objects and events. In other words, NCC does not represents objects *as* having properties and *as* standing in certain relations. Also, we saw in Lamme's and Rensink's accounts that in the absence of attention it is possible to construct only fleeting unstable representations of objects that contain sparse information and lack specific details about objects. Now, since (a) the phenomenal content is nonconceptual content, (b) nonconceptual content is retrieved bottom-up before the onset of object-based attention, and (c) without attention the visual system constructs representations of types and not of tokens, it follows that phenomenal content represents types rather than tokens and in this sense it is abstract. Thus, it is plausible that these representations correspond to types rather than tokens of objects, types being at a more general level of abstraction and thus containing less information than tokens.[11]

At this juncture, one might raise the following question: If nonconceptual content is about types of objects and events and not about tokens of objects, then how could nonconceptual content represent object *qua* objects? This seems to cast doubt on one of the main theses of the present book, namely that nonconceptual content is primarily about representations of objects *qua* objects, that is, that nonconceptual content represents objects as individual entities that persist in space and time. How could nonconceptual content that is about types represent "objecthood"? My discussion on Tye's remarks provides an answer to that question. The fact that nonconceptual content is about types of objects does not mean that it does not represent the existence of specific objects. It is about structured existential states of affairs in which *the existence of an object bearing properties is asserted*. However, *the object is not specified*. Recall now the distinction I drew in chapter 3 between *object individuation* and *object identification*. Nonconceptual content allows the former but not the latter. Thus, *nonconceptual content cannot specify objects*, although *nonconceptual content individuates them* (that is, represents them as individuals). This is consistent with the claim that nonconceptual content is about types and not tokens.

Tye's account of nonconceptual content does not refer to the conceptual framework of the perceiver; it refers only to the content of her states.[12] A visual experience is robustly nonconceptual if it has the content described above, which (I repeat) is a representation of types of states of affairs and not a representation of a token entity. Though Tye does not address what determines this kind of content, I think he would not reject the view that the determinant of this content is the causal link of perceivers with a specified perceptual system to the world, which is the view defended in this book.

The account of perception in this book is a causal theory of perception. For A to perceive X as being F, A must be related to X in such a way that it is necessary both that X is F and that if X were not F then A would have had an experience with a different nonconceptual content. What ensures the right kind of causal relation between how things are and the way they are represented through the nonconceptual content of the perceptual states they induce is the fact that in perception information is retrieved bottom-up, and in that sense directly, from the environment. If the environment is so-and-so, then, in veridical perception, it will be perceived as being so-and-so; if it had been different, the perceptual states it induces would have been different.

This account supports the right kind of counterfactuals. It also captures one of Noa's (2003) insights with regard to the appropriate way to analyzing perception and its content. Noa (ibid.) argues that perceptual content[13] is two-dimensional. It varies along a factual dimension and along a perspectival dimension. The first concerns how things are, the second how things look from the perspective of the perceiver. A perceptual experience is veridical if it is veridical along both dimensions of its content.[14] Thus, an adequate causal account of perception must also account for the perspectival aspect of perception. As we shall see in the next chapter, one constituent of the nonconceptual content is the scenario that determines the relative spatial relation between the perceiver and the visual scene. For the same reason that applies to the case of the causal counterfactual account of the factual dimension of content, had the relative spatial relation between the perceiver and the visual scene been different, the visual scene would have looked different to the perceiver. Nonconceptual content as construed here provides the right sort of counterfactual supporting relation along the perspectival dimension of perceptual content.

References to causal links to the world are found in Martin's (1992) and Stalnaker's (2003) accounts of nonconceptual content. They maintain that the content of a state is nonconceptual if it is fixed externally to anything that the bearer of the state believes or knows (the externality criterion for nonconceptual content). I take this to mean that nonconceptual content is determined through causal links to the world, independent of what cognitive states the person whose perceptual states have the content is in. X is in a representational state with nonconceptual content Y if X has (or is being disposed to have) a content that is causally (or nomologically) connected in a certain way to instantiated *Y*-hood. This definition avoids the aforementioned problem of the traditional definitions of nonconceptual content, since it severs the definitional link between nonconceptual content and concept possession.

Nonconceptual content has been defined in this book as the content of the states that are formed during early vision. Nonconceptual representational content has been defined as the content of the states of perception. Early vision extracts information from the environment in a purely bottom-up way, which thus excludes any top-down cognitive effects; early vision processes are cognitively impenetrable. Hence, the contents of those states are necessarily nonconceptual. Furthermore, they are pre-attentional (the attention being object-based attention), and they represent types of objects and not specified objects (that is, tokens of objects). In this view, conceptual and nonconceptual contents are the products of two different stages of vision; the former result from late vision or observation, whereas the former result from early vision or perception. The former require global RP and thus involves both bottom-up processing and top-down effects from cognitive centers, whereas the latter require the FFS and local RP, which involve bottom-up, lateral, and local top-down processes. (The top-down processes are restricted within the system of early vision and thus do not infuse early visual processing with cognitive influences.)

When the conceptual framework is being applied to visual processing by means of the modulation of visual processing by top-down flow of information from cognitive centers to visual areas through the mediation of attention, the nonconceptual content does not simply get conceptualized. The conscious access to the content of experience through attention means that conceptual content permeates nonconceptual content. Owing to the role of attention, the nonconceptual content acquires a coherence in space and time that it lacked before. Its parts are combined in various ways to give rise to the rich percepts of our ordinary experience, whose details stand in opposition to the dearth of information of nonconceptual states. Thus, conceptual objects are usually identified as being such and such, and our experience with previous instances of these objects or similar ones invests them with a host of properties that go far beyond what can be retrieved directly from a scene, such as membership to a category, its possible uses that go beyond its affordances, and so forth. Furthermore, nonconceptual content concerns types of entities, not tokens of entities. In that sense it lacks the specificity of conceptual contents of experience. As a result of that, we cannot make subtle or fine-grained distinctions between things of which we are phenomenally aware (more about that in the next chapter). Thus, it is clear that conceptual and nonconceptual contents have different properties and are different kinds of contents.

To see to what mistakes the construal of phenomenal content as content of the same type as conceptual content could lead to, consider an issue that Campbell (2005) raises when discussing Evans's (1982, 1985) solution to Molyneux's problem. This is the problem of whether a blind man who has learned by the use of touch to discriminate cubes from spheres and who later gains his eyesight and is presented with a cube and a sphere of the same size will be able to tell, using vision alone, which is the cube and which is the sphere. Evans recasts this as a problem concerning the acquisition of concepts through different sensory modalities: are the concepts of properties learned or constructed on the basis of vision the same as the concepts of the same properties learned or constructed on the basis of touch? Evans's solution is that they are the same. I will not address Evans's argument or Campbell's criticism here. Instead, I will examine some of the views of nonconceptual content and its relation to phenomenal content that Campbell put forth in his discussion.

The notion of nonconceptual content figures in Evans's discussion because of his view that concepts must be accounted on the basis of the nonconceptual content of experience (the grounding thesis that I discussed when addressing the reasons that prompted philosophers to posit the existence of a nonconceptual content of perception). Evans distinguishes between the content of propositions whether in language or thought and the content involved in the various information processes that take place in the brain. The former is conceptual whereas the latter is nonconceptual. Evans (1982, pp. 157–158) also distinguishes between nonconceptual content of perceptual sub-personal informational states and the nonconceptual content of perceptual states at the personal level,[15] that is, the experiential or phenomenal content. The latter is content of which the subject is aware or conscious, the content of her conscious perceptual experiences. The way Campbell (2005, pp. 18–20) reads him, Evans construes experiential content as being the nonconceptual content of brain information-processing states that at some point becomes available to the subject's consciousness. Thus, phenomenal content is of the very same type as information-processing nonconceptual content. According to Evans (1982, p. 158), the nonconceptual information-processing content becomes available to the subject's consciousness when it is used as input to the higher cognitive concept involving centers of the brain.

Campbell's (2005, p. 4) objection concerns Evans's construal of phenomenal content simply as nonconceptual content that is available to consciousness. According to Evans (as Campbell reads him), the phenomenal content of experience is to be accounted for in terms of nonconceptual content. However, Campbell believes that "the appeal to nonconceptual content does not give a convincing account of the phenomenal content of experience." The reason is that when it comes to nonconceptual content, as the content involved in information-processing states, the sameness or difference of nonconceptual content is not necessarily transparent to the subject. However, sameness or difference of phenomenal content, as content that is available to consciousness, is obviously transparent to the subject. Whether Campbell's reading of renders justice to Evans is immaterial here. What is of interest is Campbell's construal of phenomenal content. But some clarifications are in order.

First, Evans and Campbell take the phenomenal nonconceptual content of perception to be the content of experience or experiential content. However, as I have argued, the content of experience, as experience is usually understood, is conceptual, or rather is conceptually contaminated. Visual experience is the final output of the sensory modality of vision, the output of higher vision or observation, and that output is a combination of bottom-up and top-down processes, which means that it involves conceptual contents. Perception or early vision, on the other hand, is conceptually encapsulated, and thus its contents are nonconceptual. Thus, in my account, the phenomenal content is not the same as experiential content; as I have stated several times, they are different kinds of content. For that reason I eschew the term "experiential content" when nonconceptual content is involved.

Second, both Evans and Campbell take phenomenal content to be nonconceptual content that is available to awareness or consciousness, even though for Campbell this does not suffice as a definition of phenomenal content. However, there are two kinds of awareness or consciousness: "phenomenal awareness or phenomenal consciousness" and "access or report awareness or access or report consciousness." The former does not involve the possession of concepts and results from local RP that appears at some point along the ventral visual pathway in Lamme's account. The latter does require the exercise of concepts and results from global RP in the visual pathway. In this framework, it does not make sense to talk about nonconceptual content that is available to awareness without qualification for one cannot have report awareness or access awareness of nonconceptual content. It only makes sense to talk of phenomenal awareness of nonconceptual content.

In view of these clarifications, the issue that Campbell raises has been transformed to the following: Nonconceptual content, as the content involved in information-processing states that is not available to awareness, is not transparent to the subject. However, sameness or difference of phenomenal content, as nonconceptual content that is available to phenomenal consciousness, is obviously transparent to the subject. Hence, phenomenal contents have a property that nonconceptual contents lack: they are transparent. From that it follows that the appeal to nonconceptual content does not give a convincing account of the phenomenal content of experience.

Now, it is not clear to me what Evans has in mind when he states that phenomenal content is nonconceptual content of brain information-processing states that at some point becomes available to the subject's consciousness. If this means that phenomenal content is nonconceptual content plus phenomenal consciousness, and thus that there is non-conceptual content that is not the content of an experience (which for Campbell means that it is not available to awareness) and that *the same nonconceptual content* can be the content of an experience, then Campbell is right that Evans is wrong. For phenomenal consciousness is the result of local RP, and RP is not something that is simply added to the content of the processing states up to that point to transform them to conscious states. The RP radically changes the content of the processing states and allows them to represent much more complex aspects of the environment. Thus, if Evans's thesis is that the content of experience or, as I recast it, phenomenal content is the same as the content of information-processing brain systems except that is available to consciousness, he is wrong; these are two different contents.

However, Evans might simply mean that the phenomenal content is a subset of nonconceptual content, and that there is nonconceptual content that is not phenomenal—that is, something along the line that Bermudez (1995) takes by distinguishing between the nonconceptual content of subpersonal or subdoxastic states, which is not available to the subject's consciousness, and phenomenal content or nonconceptual content of experience, which is available to the subject's consciousness. According to this reading, there is nonconceptual content that is not the content of a phenomenal experience, and there is other nonconceptual content that is the content of a phenomenal experience. In that sense, the phenomenal content is different from the nonconceptual content of subpersonal states, and Campbell (2005, p. 24) is right to claim that "phenomenal content does not have to be identified with either conceptual or information-processing content." But this is not necessarily something with which Evans would have disagreed.

Furthermore, Campbell's claim that sameness and difference in nonconceptual content, as the content of information-processing states other than phenomenal content, are not registered by the subject is confusing. For the nonconceptual content that is not phenomenal content is not available to consciousness at all. In view of that, what sense does it make to ascertain that sameness and difference in that content cannot be registered? Thus, Campbell's point that phenomenal content is transparent whereas nonconceptual content is not, and that therefore the former cannot be accounted solely in terms of the latter, reduces to this question: How could phenomenal content, as a phenomenon that belongs to the realm of consciousness, be explained in terms of a content that does not belong to that realm? In other words, how could consciousness emerge from nonconscious states? Or, equivalently, what is the cause of the phenomenal character of mental states? Why is it that a certain neural state causes me to see red rather than green, or to feel pain and not a tickle? Well, that is one of the million-dollar questions in philosophy, and I am certain that Campbell would not attack Evans on the ground that he does not offer an answer to those questions. But then, nothing remains to be said against Evans's thesis that phenomenal content must be accounted in terms of content that is not conceptual. What else could it be? After all, Evans (1982, pp. 157–158) is certainly right to claim that, both phylogenetically and ontogenetically, we were equipped to handle nonconceptual content and to interact successfully with our environment on the basis of such content well before we were endowed with conscious experience. How could have the phenomenal content (or the conceptual content) have emerged if not supervening on the older nonconceptual subpersonal content? Campbell (2005, p. 24) agrees with that when he writes "we have to acknowledge that the conscious experience of a subject is causally explained, in part at any rate, by the content of the information processing carried out in that subject's brain. Part of the reason why the subject has a conscious experience with this particular phenomenal content is that the brain-processing had a particular informational content." Campbell leaves the issue at that, but this is not a convincing account of phenomenal content either.

More relevant to the point of this book is another claim of Campbell's about phenomenal content that is instructively false. Since phenomenal content is conscious content, Campbell argues, sameness and differences in such content are transparent to the subject. This means for Campbell, who applies to phenomenal content Evans's "Intuitive Criterion of Difference" for conceptual content (Campbell 2005, p. 15), that whenever two phenomenal contents are the same, this will be immediately recognized by the subject, and the subject will not be able coherently to take conflicting attitudes toward them. I remind the reader that the argument Campbell tries to drive home is that, since phenomenal contents meet the "Intuitive Criterion of Difference" whereas subpersonal contents do not, the former cannot be accounted for convincingly in terms of the latter.

Recall that phenomenal content does not require possession and/or exercise of concepts. Curiously enough, Campbell does not commit himself to that claim. He says that for Evans the content of experience or phenomenal content is nonconceptual. He notes that those who are looking for the neural correlate of consciousness are looking for the point at which, and the mechanisms by means of which, subpersonal nonconceptual content becomes available to consciousness. He says that phenomenal content needs to be distinguished from both information-processing content, which is nonconceptual, and conceptual content. But he does not say whether he thinks phenomenal content is nonconceptual. Perhaps the fact that in drawing a distinction between phenomenal content and subpersonal content Campbell refers to the latter as information-processing content only and does not add the characterization "nonconceptual" (which information-processing content is, according to him) suggests that he does not distinguish phenomenal content from information-processing content on account of the nonconceptual nature of the latter, but for some other reason. If this is indeed the case, then Campbell considers phenomenal content to be a species of nonconceptual content, to wit that nonconceptual content that is subjectively available to the subject. This also means that the nonconceptual content of information-processing states is not subjectively available to the subject. But then how does this fit with Campbell's statement (2005, p. 17) that even if information-processing content is "subjectively available" to the subject, there is no reason that sameness and differences in those contents to be transparent to the subject? This comment makes information-processing content available to awareness. One is drawn to conclude that for Campbell, after all, it may be that the difference between phenomenal content and information-processing nonconceptual content is not one of availability to awareness but one of the type of content involved. The content in "phenomenal content" is transparent to the subject, whereas the content in "nonconceptual information-processing content" is such that it is not transparent to the subject even if it is subjectively available. In my account, these are indeed two different kinds of content, in that the phenomenal content is formed along the visual pathway through local RP whereas the information-processing content is formed during the FFS. This difference shows in the kind of information the two types of contents carry. Thus, though the information-processing content is not subjectively available (recall that awareness requires RP that does not occur in the FFS), while phenomenal content is subjectively available, the property of being subjectively available is not the main difference between information-processing content and phenomenal content. This is so because phenomenal content is the corollary of the presence of RP that induces other differences in content *per se* as well. But none of this is available to Campbell, and as a result he cannot account for the difference between the two kinds of contents other than to say that the one is transparent and the other isn't.

However, this claim is wrong, on account of the nature of the type of content that phenomenal content is. Transparency as intended here means that when a subject perceives two tokens of exactly the same type of phenomenal content she perceives them as being the same content. This requires the existence of a "re-identification condition" on nonconceptual content modeled on the "re-identification condition on demonstrative concept possession" (Kelly 2001, p. 403). This is the condition that subject S must satisfy if it is correct to say that she possesses the demonstrative concept for X: "In order to possess a demonstrative concept for X, a subject must be able consistently to re-identify a given object or property as falling under the concept if it does." The condition on nonconceptual content would be the condition that subject S must satisfy if it is correct to say that she perceives phenomenal content X. That is, "in order to perceive phenomenal content X, S must be able consistently to re-identify a given content as being the same content as X, if it is the same phenomenal content." However, such a condition is not necessary for perception and therefore, transparency as used by Campbell cannot be said to characterize the content of our phenomenal states. To see why this condition is not necessary for perception of phenomenal content, consider a case in which a subject can discriminate between two colors yet cannot re-identify any of them at some later time. Kelly (ibid., pp. 410–412) argues that "it is perfectly conceivable . . . and there is nothing about the nature of perception to keep it from being true, that our capacity to discriminate colors exceeds our capacity to re-identify the colors discriminated." Kelly asks us to imagine that a subject can discriminate but not identify an attribute, and says that whether perception can be like that is an empirical question, although that it can be like that is certainly perfectly imaginable.

Well, Kelly is perfectly right. If the account of nonconceptual content argued for in this book is on the right course, and if Tye is correct that phenomenal content is coarse-grained (in a sense that I discuss later and which does not contradict the thesis that phenomenal content is also fine-grained), then the phenomenal content (re)presents to a perceiver entity types and not entity tokens, and a perceiver could not identify two different tokenings of the very same type of content as being the same, simply because at that level she does not perceive tokens but only types. Saying that X and Y are of the same type is not the same as saying that X and Y are the same tokens; the latter requires a fine-grained analysis of content, whereas the former requires a coarse-grained analysis of content. Only the coarse-grained analysis is available to phenomenal content in virtue of its nonconceptual character, and the fact that this kind of nonconceptual content is available to consciousness cannot change that, *contra* Campbell.

If the preceding analysis about Campbell's views is correct, the main reason underlying Campbell's misgivings about the account of phenomenal content in terms of nonconceptual information-processing content vanishes, leaving the usual questions about the emergence of the idiosyncratic characteristics of phenomenal content from the basis of nonconceptual content in which it supervenes. The root of Campbell's mistaken instructive error, which leads him to apply the re-identification condition of conceptual content to phenomenal content, is that he takes for granted that, although phenomenal content is different from conceptual content, it is basically content of the same type; in that, Campbell follows Crane (1992).

My thesis that nonconceptual content is retrieved from a scene in conceptually unmediated ways is in line with Martin's and Stalnaker's "causal" accounts, because information that is retrieved in conceptually unmediated ways is information that is retrieved bottom-up in a cognitively encapsulated way from a visual scene. This information is determined solely through some causal links with the world, links that are established by the visual system. Thus, it is at the nonconceptual level delivered by one's perceptual systems that the circle of representations breaks down and one touches, as it were, the world. That level itself is the causal product of the world's acting on our perceptual systems, and of our encapsulated processing of the data input.[16]

The causal definition of nonconceptual content is independent of any considerations about the conceptual arsenal that the perceiver might have or might exercise while she perceives. Let me explicate this. As a matter of course, if the perceiver does not have the appropriate conceptual arsenal, she will not be able to observe (see in the doxastic sense) some things; she will be able only to perceive them (see in the phenomenal sense). However, even if she had the required concepts, she need not have exercised them in order to perceive the world, though the possession of the concepts might allow her to observe the world. This is a direct consequence of the cognitive impenetrability of perception; the possession or not of concepts has nothing to do with nonconceptual content, since nonconceptual content is defined as the content of the cognitively impenetrable perceptual states. Thus, defining nonconceptual content as the content of cognitively impenetrable states of vision allows us to avoid the pitfall of the "usual definitions" mentioned by Tye (2006). In that sense, the distinction between conceptual and nonconceptual content is not "internal" to the perceiver; that is, it does not depend on whether the perceiver possesses the relevant concepts, but is located in the contents of her respective states and the way they are formed during visual processing. One should expect that anyway, to the extent that nonconceptual content is external, in the sense that the content of a state is nonconceptual if it is fixed externally to anything that the bearer of the state believes or knows.[17]

4.2.3   Phenomenal Content

Let us now dwell on how nonconceptual representational content is related to the phenomenal content of experience, in an attempt to specify the latter notion.

In my view, perceptual states have a phenomenal character in virtue of having some kind of representational content.[18] Thus, phenomenal content is a species of representational content that makes things look certain ways. The content of perceptual experience includes representations of properties of things, events, or places, these things, events, or places have in virtue of appearing to us, or being disposed to appear to us, in certain ways. The ways properties or relations are given in experience are as important in characterizing the content of experience as the properties or relations that things are represented by the experience as possessing (Peacocke 2001, pp. 240–241; Shoemaker 2002, p. 471; Tye 2002). The ways things, events, or places seem to us are the phenomenal properties of experience; that is, the qualitative character of perceptual content, the way content is experienced by the perceiver.

Tye (2002a, p. 447) distinguishes between the conceptual content of a visual scene (the fact that it represents, say, a tiger) and the phenomenal content of the same scene (which includes colors, shapes, and spatial relations obtaining among blobs of parts). Tye argues that the scene has the conceptual content it has partly in virtue of its phenomenal content. The phenomenal content of an experience is what is responsible for the "phenomenal character" of experience—that is, for the "what it is like to have an experience." "The view I accept," Tye writes (ibid., p. 448), "is that what it is like to have a visual experience is a matter of a certain sort of representational content that the experience has." It follows that the conceptual content is grounded in the phenomenal content.

Shoemaker (2002, p. 461) echoes Tye. He defines the objective properties of things as they appear in perception, as those properties that the subject perceives in Dretske's (1995) "doxastic" sense of 'perceive'—that is, those properties that the perceiver judges that things have when she takes her experience at face value. These objective properties are grounded in the ways things appear phenomenally, to wit, in the ways they look in Dretske's "phenomenal" sense of looking to the perceiver. Similarly, according to Lowe (1992, p. 89) "such intentional content as a visual experience has must ultimately be grounded in its phenomenal or qualitative content."

The phenomenal content plays a decisive role in the solution of the grounding problem. The reason for this is that a solution to the problem requires that the reference of the representational states with phenomenal content be determined not descriptively but causally. If phenomenal content should be determined by means of causal links with the world, then this content should be retrieved bottom-up from the visual scene through our visual system, without any conceptual involvement on the part of the perceiver; it should be nonconceptual. This is a natural link between "phenomenal" and "nonconceptual" content, in that the latter describes a characteristic of the former.

Peacocke (2001, p. 241) argues that the phenomenal content of experience represents things, events, or places and times in a certain way, as having certain properties or standing in certain relations, "also given in a certain way." Tye (2006) rejects this view. He claims that Peacocke models the awareness of qualities on the awareness of particulars. This is a mistake, because although individuals can look various ways depending on the perspective of the perceiver, the qualities of which we are aware when we see these particulars do not look any way; they just show, as it were, their quality. Does it really make sense, Tye asks, to talk about the way a shape is presented in experience or the way a color is presented? Redness, is not experienced as being given in a certain way, other than as belonging to the thing (ibid.).

Tye's view echoes Smith's (2002) claim that only the perceptual experience that makes us aware of objects can enjoy different perspectives (that make things look different ways to us), whereas sensations (that is, Tye's properties) do not allow different perspectives. This is because perceptual experience presents objects as literally external to our bodies and this gives us the ability to examine perceptually various aspects of these objects from different perspectives. One cannot have a perspective of properties or qualities; properties cannot be experienced as being given in a certain way. It makes sense to say that I see a table that looks round from this view angle but looks elliptical from that view angle; I simply experience a change in the object of perception. One cannot do the same with the property "round." If one perceives in the phenomenal sense "round" and then some time later from another perspective one perceives "elliptical," this is not the way the property "round" looks from another perspective; it is a new property, because in this case we have a change of experience, which signifies the presence of a new property, and not the experience of a change in the object of perception (Smith 2002, p. 170).

The way object X can figure in the phenomenal content of an experience is the mode of presentation of X in that experience. On account of the fact that properties cannot be experienced as being given in a certain way, our awareness of the relevant qualities is direct. It involves no mode of presentation (Tye 2006). Thus, it does not make sense to say, as Peacocke does, that experience represents properties as given in a certain way.[19]

The phenomenal content of the philosophers is accessible to introspection; thus, phenomenal content is accessible to consciousness. But which consciousness? We have seen that there are two forms of awareness. Phenomenal awareness and access or report awareness are defined in terms of the kinds of processes that support them: in the first case, local recurrent processing that excludes memory and other cognitive areas of the brain; in the second case, global recurring processing involving memory brain areas. The part of the nonconceptual content that can be brought to consciousness, the phenomenal content, is accompanied by "phenomenal awareness," which is distinguished from "report awareness" or "access awareness."[20] The difference between the two is not primarily one of accessibility to conscious introspection; such accessibility is found in both cases. The difference is due to the role of attention. Phenomenal awareness does not require object-centered attention, whereas access awareness does. Access awareness is within the conceptual realm (since it denotes contents that are reportable or contents to which we have cognitive access, and thus contents that could be conceptually articulated in principle), whereas phenomenal awareness is not within the conceptual realm; the content of which one is phenomenally aware is retrieved bottom-up and thus is nonconceptual. Thus, conscious awareness plays no role in the distinction between phenomenal nonconceptual content and conceptual content. One can be made aware of both conceptual and phenomenal content. However, the two kinds of content are subject to different kinds of awareness. As a result, the two kinds of awareness have phenomenological differences. Things of which we are phenomenally aware have a shaky existence (in the sense that they have limited spatial and temporal coherence) that differs from the stable percept of which one has access awareness or report awareness. We have a fleeting "experience" of things of which we are phenomenally aware, since nonconceptual content, being about types and not about tokens, lacks the coherence and specificity of conceptual content.

Notice the difference between phenomenal awareness and access or report awareness that are defined in terms of the kinds of processes that support them; Local recurrent processing that excludes cognitive areas of the brain, and global recurrent processing that involves memory and cognitive brain areas, respectively. Phenomenal awareness characterizes phenomenal content and is distinguished from report awareness or access awareness. As I said before, the difference between the two is not one of accessibility to consciousness or not; they both are accessible by consciousness. The difference is due to the role of attention. Phenomenal awareness does not require attention, whereas report awareness does.

To repeat a point made before, when the conceptual framework is being applied to visual processing, the NCC does not simply get conceptualized. Owing to the role of attention and of the cognitive information that flows top-down, the nonconceptual content acquires a coherence in space and time that it lacked before. Its parts are combined in various ways to give rise to the rich percepts of our ordinary experience. That is, the objects that we see in the world, whose details, which include semantic information, stand in opposition to the dearth of information of NCC that is restricted to what can be retrieved directly from the visual scene. These objects are usually recognized and identified, and our experience with previous instances of these or similar objects invests them with a host of properties that go beyond what can be retrieved directly from a scene— membership in a category, functionality (that is, possible uses that go beyond affordances), and so forth. All these constitute seeing in the doxastic sense of the word. Thus, the conceptualization of NCC and the ensuing doxastic seeing that corresponds to the visual episode with the

NCC import extraneous contents to the visual episode (see also Vision 1997, chapter 4).

However, conceptual content is at the same time impoverished compared to the NCC whose entrance in the global workspace and memory caused that conceptual content. Recall from chapter 1 that when NCC enters the workspace and is stored in working memory it undergoes transformation. When perceptual information enters the mnemonic circuits of the brain, the sensory and perceptual information extracted pre-attentively from the scene is augmented with a more abstract higher-level visual representation, which consists of abstract visual categories that are formed in more anterior areas (medial and inferior temporal cortex) and which is stored in short-term visual memory (Hollingworth et al. 2001; Hollingworth and Henderson 2002). Although the higher-level representations contain information about the visual form of the scene and preserve a great deal of visual information, they are more abstract than the sensory representations in that they do not have the iconic form of the latter; for example, they do not retain the metric of the scene, as the iconic perceptual representations do. They also do not encode the perceptual content in all its detail. For example, they do not encode the exact shade of a color (but only the class of the color with a rough description of its brightness) or the exact texture of an object (this is the neural underpinning of the richness argument for NCC).

To recapitulate the point about the kinds of awareness accompanying phenomenal content and conceptual content, the two kinds of content, conceptual and nonconceptual, are subject to different kinds of awareness; they are experienced differently. Things of which one is phenomenally aware have a limited spatial and temporal coherence that differs from the stable percept of which one has access awareness or report awareness.

For the benefit of the clarity of the discussion that follows, let me clarify the interrelations among phenomenal content, conceptual content, phenomenal awareness, report awareness, phenomenal seeing, doxastic seeing, perception, and observation. The perception/observation or early vision/late vision distinction runs along the distinction between *seeing something* and *seeing something as being such and such*.[21] Perception corresponds to *seeing*, whereas observation corresponds to *seeing as*, that is, to identifying or recognizing visual patterns that are *seeing*. Dretske (1993, 1995) distinguishes between seeing in the phenomenal sense (seeing$_{ph}$) and seeing in the doxastic sense (seeing$_{dox}$). The latter involves concepts; the former does not. Thus, seeing$_{ph}$ coincides with perception, and seeing$_{dox}$ with observation. Seeing$_{ph}$ is pre-attentive and characterized by phenomenal awareness;

seeing$_{dox}$ is attentional and is characterized by report awareness or access awareness.

The content of perceptual states of which one is phenomenally aware is structured. In perception, objects are segmented in a scene, and many of their physical properties are extracted bottom-up and are represented by perceptual states. Hence, objects are *perceived* as being in a certain way, although this involves no concepts. Perceptual states represent worldly states of affairs, and the content of these states nonconceptually represents the way the worldly states of affairs are perceived.[22] Put differently, the content of a perceptual state is how it represents the worldly state of affairs (Bermudez 2007, p. 56)—that is, how it represents the world as being. Thus, perceiving something as being such and such should not be confused with the "as being such and such" that characterizes seeing$_{dox}$ in which objects are being *recognized*. To avoid the usual confusion between perceptual states as representational vehicles and their contents, I will say that perceptual states *qua* vehicles represent the world as being such and such, whereas the contents of those states present the world as being such and such.

Notice, however, that the above remarks about the phenomenology of phenomenal content stem from considerations pertaining to the perceptual processes that give rise to the phenomenal content. They are not the result of any introspection of the states with phenomenal content one has. Even if one could isolate, as it were, a certain qualitative characteristic of one's experience, one would have a "fleeting" experience that would lack the sharpness of ordinary experience, on account of the fact that phenomenal contents, being properties of proto-objects, lack spatial and temporal coherence. Recall that information retrieved bottom-up from a scene is processed within 120 ms after stimulus onset and produces representations of proto-objects in a visual scene. Although, as we saw in chapter 1, proto-objects can be complex structures, they are coherent only over a small region and over a limited amount of time, because they have limited spatial and temporal coherence (where 'coherence' means that the structures refer to parts of the same system in space and time—in other words, that their representations in different locations and over different times refer to the same object). Proto-objects are very volatile, in that they are either overwritten by subsequent stimuli or else fade away within a few hundred milliseconds; the volatile representations last about half a second. Each time the eyes move and new light enters the eye, the older proto-objects fade away and new ones are generated. The objects of our experience, on the other hand, are stable structures due to the role of attention.

That is why it is very difficult to retain a particular shade of a color, as the phenomenal content of an experience and not as a concept that articulates that shade, in one's memory for a long time, whereas a person can retain an object's 3D shape for his or her entire life.

Thus, all attempts to pinpoint exactly what it is to have a certain phenomenal content, and therefore any attempt either to determine the contents of which we are phenomenally aware or to discuss the phenomenological differences between experiencing phenomenal content and experiencing the world in our ordinary conceptual experience, are hindered by the fact that, owing to the volatile and short-lived nature of the phenomenal contents, we do not have direct cognitive access to (and, consequently, we cannot directly report) the pure phenomenal content, only our ordinary experiential conceptual content. We cannot tell how we would experience the world or, to be precise, how we would perceive the world, if we did not exercise concepts in seeing.

When we see a 3D shape, we are consciously aware of a specific shape. We can store it in memory and talk about it. However, try to understand what it means to say that one is aware of some phenomenal property of perception, say a segment edge or the viewer-centered $2\frac{1}{2}$D shape of an object or the orientation of an object in space or the particular shade of a color. Or try to introspect what is like to "feel" the affordances of objects. It takes mental effort to abstract from the objects as we experience them to introspect the segment edge or the orientation of the object or a viewer-centered $2\frac{1}{2}$D shape. Notice that this abstraction, if it is to capture some qualitative (i.e., nonconceptual phenomenal) aspect of experience, should not result in the formation of a concept for the qualitative character of the particular experience as in chapter 9 of Dretske 1981. Dretske discusses the notion of abstraction by which one could acquire a concept of the specific qualitative character of experience. Abstracting away, for instance, all the differences from tasting experiences that involve "sourness" except that characteristic feel that they all share, one can form a concept of something that all tasting experiences share: "sourness."

However, the process of abstraction that is needed if one aims to unearth from experience its phenomenal content should not result in a concept for a qualitative characteristic of an experience; rather, it should, as it were, revive that characteristic in visual memory. It is not an abstraction that takes place after the experience, as in Dretske's case, because that mental act requires attentional focusing and working memory, and thus requires concepts. It should be an "on-line abstraction"—that is, a process of isolating a qualitative characteristic of an image from other qualitative characteristics while the image lasts without involving attention and top-down semantic information.

To recapitulate: Very often, if not always, report awareness or access awareness, by providing stable and coherent descriptions of scenes, masks (for lack of a better verb) phenomenal awareness. The objects of our access awareness are the objects of our conceptual experience, not the phenomenal content of perception, though of course we are phenomenally aware of it; we are aware of a specific tiger, not of a type of a shape with a type of a color, though of course the tiger has a certain shape and color. Furthermore, the phenomenal content of perception is not accessible to report awareness or access awareness; the particular shade of a color, for instance, cannot enter report awareness, because it cannot be conceptualized, as far as its qualitative character is concerned, although one could conceptualize à la McDowell the specific experiential episode by uttering "That shade." The reason it cannot be conceptualized is not that one lacks a concept-term for that specific shade but that it cannot be stored in memory. (Remember Block's (2007) statement that phenomenology overflows cognitive access.) The fact that the specific shade of a color cannot be stored in memory means, in turn, that one cannot form a symbol that could act as a stand-in for other occurrences of the same shade. This entails that one cannot have a phenomenal concept for that particular shade. When one attempts to cognitively access phenomenal content, the content is necessarily embedded in one's conceptual framework and ceases to be nonconceptual and thus phenomenal. In other words, phenomenal content, being nonconceptual, cannot be accessed introspectively, because if it gets introspected it gets conceptualized, since introspection involves necessarily concepts. Thus, whereas phenomenal content refers to the content that an experience has in virtue of the perceiver simply having this particular experience and, consequently, the sense of awareness involved in being aware of a particular phenomenal quality is simply a matter of having the experience, "when a subject is introspectively aware of a phenomenal quality, the awareness is conceptual; it involves the application of a concept to the phenomenal quality" (Ellis 2007, pp. 48–49). Introspective awareness is different from phenomenal awareness.

We now see the root of the confusion that led philosophers to take phenomenal content to be of the same kind as conceptual content except that it is conceptualized. When philosophers distinguish a nonconceptual "phenomenal sense of see" from a conceptual "doxastic sense of see," they assume that both are within the realm of consciousness. In the literature, the phenomenal content is thought to be that subset of nonconceptual content of which one is aware (as opposed to the nonconceptual content of the subpersonal states). Owing to the lack of a distinction between phenomenal awareness and access awareness, both phenomenal (nonconceptual) content and conceptual content were thought to be accompanied by the same kind of awareness. Thus, these senses of seeing seem to concern basically the same kind of content, whose only difference lies in the fact that the one but not the other is conceptualized. This led philosophers to lose sight of the fact that conceptual content cannot be phenomenal content (in that it relies on fine-grained distinctions that one could not make on the basis of phenomenal content, such as the distinction between an eikosiaendron and an eikosipendaendron). They also lose sight of the fact that the awareness of a shade or of the $2\frac{1}{2}$D surface of an object is not the same as the awareness of the 3D shape of an object.

I retain the conceptual/nonconceptual distinction, but I do not subscribe to the latent thesis that both kinds of content are consciously accessible in the same way. Seeing in the doxastic sense is necessarily access conscious, since it requires the employment of concepts. Seeing in the phenomenal sense on the other hand, is not access conscious, although its contents are accessible by phenomenal awareness. This renders the two contents different in kind.

Therefore, 'phenomenal' is used here in a way different from the way it is employed in the philosophical literature, first on account of the difference between phenomenal awareness and access awareness (a distinction that is lacking in the majority of the philosophical discussions of the issue) and second on account of the different mechanisms that subserve the two kinds of awareness.

The distinction among "sensation," "perception," and "observation" sheds light on another issue as well. As has been widely argued (Churchland 1988; Dretske 1995; Gregory 1974; Hanson 1958; Kuhn 1968; Marr 1982), the content of experience that identifies objects as being such and such and categorizes them as members of a kind has a strong conceptual component, in the sense that the identification of objects is based on learned knowledge about specific objects that is stored in memory. The experiential content is already an interpretation of the input from the distal objects, an interpretation that is based on one's conceptual system; to identify a perceived object as being such and such presupposes that one possesses the relevant concepts. The semantic acts of the identification of an object and of viewing it as the member of a category (I saw a tiger) belong to observation as defined above. Clearly, the act of perceiving that I call here observation amounts to Dretske's (1993, 1995) "perceiving" in its doxastic sense. A subject who views a scene has access awareness (or report awareness) of the contents of her observational or late visual states. Henceforth, I call the kind of consciously accessible content of observational or late visual states, be it imagistic, auditory or whatever, the "experiential" content of our experience.

I have argued that the phenomenal content of experience is different from the conceptual content of our experiential states. Fodor and Pylyshyn (1981) and Goldstone and Barsalou (1998) suggest that the world delivered to us through our perceptual processes—the phenomenal world—differs from the world as we experience it through conscious access to the content of our experiences (experiential world). This is to say that the phenomenal content of perception differs from the content of the same experiences when consciously accessed.

In contrast to perceptual experience, Pylyshyn (1999, p. 361) claims, the classes provided by the visual system are, at a first approximation, viewer-centered shape classes expressible in the vocabulary of geometry, and thus differ from the classes of objects into which we cut the world. Pylyshyn argues that the product of perception is the $2\frac{1}{2}$D sketch, which delivers not the usual objects of experience but representations of shapes (structured representations of $2\frac{1}{2}$D surfaces of objects) and some of their transducable properties that allow us to index and track proto-objects. Recall the discussion in chapter 1 of the output of early vision or perception. That output consists in the proto-objects that are parsed in a visual scene, which are represented as types rather than as tokens in the sense discussed above. Thus, the output of the visual processor does not consist in the experience of objects, but in a more abstract form of categories of such objects, classified according to their generic shapes. Thus, a distinction should be drawn between phenomenal and experiential content. This is a distinction between a content that is perceptually retrieved in a bottom-up manner from a scene and a content that is formed by means of both top-down and bottom-up processes and thus has a strong conceptual component.

If what I have said is right, it follows that the world delivered to us through perception—the "phenomenal world"—differs from the world as we experience it through conscious access to the content of our experiences. Hence, I disagree with Crane's claim (1992, p. 155) that the nonconceptual content of perceptual states and the conceptual content of the beliefs for which our experience provides reasons can in the whole be the same; it cannot be since the former is about types of objects, that is, classes of structured representations of $2\frac{1}{2}$D surfaces of objects, whereas the latter is about object tokens. On the other hand, I agree with Heck (2001, pp. 514–515) that the conceptual content of our experiences and the ensuing perceptual beliefs that articulate them *reflect* but do not *record* the nonconceptual content of our perceptual states. The contents of perceptual beliefs, moreover, conceptualize the nonconceptual contents of perceptual states. Herein lies the grounding function of nonconceptual content: experiential content (that is, the content of perceptual beliefs) is systematically related to, and is dependent on, the content of the perceptual states.[23]

Let me explain the sense of 'reflect' and what I mean by saying that experiential content, which is conceptual content, is systematically related to the content of perceptual states. What is the evidential relation between nonconceptual content and conceptual content of experience? Our beliefs about the world, as we perceive it, are justified on the basis of the content of our sensory experience, that is, the representational content of mental perceptual states. Perception justifies these beliefs by means of the fit between the descriptions provided by these beliefs and the nonconceptual content they purport to describe. According to BonJour's (2003, pp. 16–19) internalist account of justification of empirical beliefs, to justify an empirical belief about (say) X one must appeal to (1) the specific character of the experience of X, (2) the propositional content of the occurrent belief as if one had X before one's eyes, and (3) the match between the character of the experience and that propositional content, that is, the awareness on the believer's part that the belief describes or records the character of one's experience. This is a mental act of direct apprehension of or immediate acquaintance with the content of one's perception, which does not require an aditional mental act of comparison.[24] To these conditions, Sosa (2003, p. 137) adds the requirement that there be some causal counterfactual connection between the phenomenal character of the experience and the propositional content of the judgment about the phenomenal content of the experience. Conditions 3 and 4, taken together, convey the meaning of 'reflect' that I used above to say that the conceptual content of our perceptual beliefs reflect the nonconceptual content of our perceptual states; they also clarify the sort of systematic relation between the content of perceptual beliefs and the content of nonconceptual perceptual states that must exist in order for the latter to ground the former.

Phenomenal content consists in the qualitative aspects of our perceptual states. In this sense, it coincides with the sensations or qualia that characterize our experience, and it is accompanied by awareness. In the literature, "sensation," "phenomenal content," and "awareness" are intermingled. When the term "nonconceptual content" was introduced, it was used to capture an aspect of the phenomenal content (namely, that to be in a state with phenomenal content does not require either the possession or the exercise of concepts), and thus it became inextricably related to awareness. Bermudez (1995) saw that the studies of vision reveal a whole class of processes that are unavailable to awareness and yet have representational content (that is, content that concerns the way the world is). Furthermore, some of the contents of these processes have no natural analogues in language and thus are nonconceptual (ibid., p. 353). As a result, Bermudez argued that there is also another kind of nonconceptual content, which is not accompanied by awareness: the content of a class of certain computational subpersonal or subdoxastic states. Though, as we shall see in the next chapter, there are problems with Bermudez's way of handling the nonconceptual character of these subpersonal states, the move is very welcome, since it opens up a way to severe the link between phenomenal content (and hence awareness) and nonconceptual content. The necessity of such separation is dictated by the fact that, as the theories of vision discussed in part I of the book suggest, perception and awareness are separate phenomena. Hence, it would be better, in discussing the content of perceptual states, to severe the link with awareness. From that it follows that we should define nonconceptual content independently of awareness, lest we miss an important class of contents of perceptual states that are not available to conscious introspection. Then we could get back to discussing the relation between the contents of our perceptual states and awareness. This is what I have attempted to do in this book. In the first part of the book, I distinguished between perception and awareness and argued that perception can occur without awareness on the part of the perceiver. I also introduced in this chapter the notion of nonconceptual content as content retrieved bottom-up from a visual scene, and I said that a subset of the nonconceptual content (that which corresponds to states of perception in which local recurrent processing occurs) is the phenomenal content of experience, since it is at that stage that the content of the processing states becomes available to a form of awareness, namely phenomenal awareness. Nonconceptual content is defined independently of consciousness, a thesis that follows naturally from the fact that perception is defined independently of consciousness.

My account concentrates primarily on the kind of information retrieved from a scene and not on whether one is consciously aware of this information. In that respect I agree with Kanwisher (2001, p. 90) that perception and awareness are different phenomena, since perception refers to the extraction of information from a stimulus without any assumption that such information be experienced consciously. In this framework, and in view of the demand to study the contents of visual processes independently of awareness, I have defined 'sensation' in a way that differs from the standard meaning assigned to it in the literature, in which 'sensation' is used to denote the qualitative aspects of experiential awareness (or the qualia, to wit, the properties of our perceptual states of which we are aware.) 'Sensation', as I use it, is defined in neural-processing terms; it is a set of neural visual processes that have certain characteristics (for example, they are purely feedforward) and that process a certain kind of information impinging on our transducers (for example, differences in the intensity of light).

5 What Is the Phenomenal Content of Experience?

In this chapter I employ the theory of vision presented in part I of the book to answer, paraphrasing (Bermudez 1995, p. 336), "the substantive question of how phenomenal content is actually specified." In section 5.1, I specify the phenomenal content by examining the output of the bottom-up, lateral, and top-down processes that constitute local recurring processing and make up perception. In section 5.2, I discuss the representational nature of phenomenal content. Also in section 5.2, I answer the criticism against nonconceptual content that introducing nonconceptual content revives the "Myth of the Given," where "the Given" is construed as the unstructured raw sensation or impression, which is the purely sensory result of the world's causal impact on our senses. In section 5.3, I relate the present construal of phenomenal content to other accounts of phenomenal (or nonconceptual in general) content addressing some problems besetting these accounts.

5.1 Determining the Phenomenal Content

Several ways to put an item in the list of phenomenal properties are found in the literature. One is by considering whether it is conceivable for a perceptual state to have a certain content without the perceiver applying the related concept, even though she possess the concept that articulates the content. Another is by considering whether an individual can be in a perceptual state with some content even though the perceiver does not possess the concept articulating that content. These two ways are "phenomenological" in that they rely on the introspection of experience to pinpoint its phenomenal part. One can see a certain shape without possessing the concept that conceptualizes that shape. Another method of putting an item in the list of phenomenal properties is by considering cases in which some intentional behavior could be described as being caused by certain concepts (as when adults see an object disappearing behind a screen and, because they know that objects do not just simply vanish into thin air—information that derives from their possession of the concept "object"—they decide to search for it); however, we have reasons to believe that the organism that engages in such a behavior does not possess the requisite concepts and may not possess any concepts at all. This is Peacocke's (1992) *Autonomy Thesis*, which states that a creature can be in states with non-conceptual content even though the creature possesses no concepts what-soever. This is the case with infants and animals, which exhibit intentional behavior that in adult humans could be explained by reference to concepts, which the infants and the animals clearly do not possess. Children look for hidden objects without possessing the concept "object." The content of the states that the animals and the infants have is nonconceptual, and the part of which animals and infants are is the phenomenal content of their experience.

Yet another way of determining phenomenal content in particular and nonconceptual content in general is by considering cases in which the content cannot be described conceptually because language does not have the requisite resources. Consider the large number of different shades of colors that one can perceive. Few among them can be described con-ceptually; natural languages simply do not have the required conceptual arsenal. In that sense, the shade of a color one perceives is part of one's phenomenal content. Furthermore, the content of many computational sub-personal states cannot be described conceptually. Natural languages, for instance, do not conceptualize the contents of some of the early stages of visual processes (Marr's "zero crossings," to use an example given in Bermudez 1995). Thus, their content, whatever it might be, is nonconceptual.

Some of the aforementioned methods associate perception with aware-ness and seek the nonconceptual content of perception through the intro-spection of the content of perceptual states. These methods are beset by many problems. I will discuss some among them here; I will cite others when I deal with Bermudez's (1995) account of nonconceptual content.

First, the awareness on which introspection relies is usually construed as report awareness or access awareness, since, as we saw in the preceding chapter, introspection involves concepts. The experiential content to which one has access awareness is conceptual content. To unearth the nonconceptual content, one has to think, and argue for, whether it would be possible to be in states with such contents if one did not possess or exercise the concepts that conceptualize those contents. But we have seen that conceptual content is not simply nonconceptual content plus concepts; they are different kinds of contents.

Second, even if one expands the notion of awareness to include phenomenal awareness, the problem is that due to the limited spatio-temporal coherence of the proto-objects and their properties (recall that phenomenal content consists in the proto-objects and their properties that are formed during perception), phenomenal representations are formed very quickly and do not last long and thus it is very difficult to isolate them in experience. One could not attempt to retrieve them from memory either, first because proto-objects are quickly overwritten as new information enters the retina and second because retrieval from memory brings in attention and the conceptual apparatus that comes with it, thus "contaminating" the scene.

Moreover, pertaining to the determination of nonconceptual content in general, there is nonconceptual content of which one cannot be aware, even where awareness is construed as phenomenal awareness. Thus, the phenomenological method restricts the nonconceptual content to items of which one can be aware, where awareness includes both phenomenal and report awareness. Even when Bermudez (1995) notes this problem and, to alleviate it, introduces a distinction between the nonconceptual content of perception and the nonconceptual content of subpersonal computational states, his discussion hinges either on the possession and exercise of concepts or on the availability of the requisite concepts in language. This proves problematic for reasons that I will discuss later when I address in detail Bermudez's view of nonconceptual content.

Another serious shortcoming of the phenomenological method is the inclusion in the list of phenomenal properties of properties of things that are extracted from the scene by visual processes that are cognitively modulated and thus can only be conceptual contents. As an instance of this problem, consider the inclusion in the list of the 3D shape of objects. One wrongly imagines that one could perceive the 3D shape of an object even if one did not possess the concepts that correspond to that shape, and because of that one is led to believe that the 3D shape of an object may be the nonconceptual content of one's perceptual states. However, we have seen that the 3D shape of an object is extracted from the scene in observation or late vision that is a cognitively modulated process (which means that its extraction requires concepts and memory of other objects) and thus the 3D shape cannot be nonconceptual content.

Instead of the aforementioned methods, I propose to determine the nonconceptual content in general and the phenomenal content in particular of an experience by combining a study of the perceptual mechanisms that deliver that content with a study of what introspection of perceptual states reveals. (I will explain shortly why introspection is required to complete the search.) The reason is that if there are no mechanisms that retrieve information from a visual scene in bottom-up conceptually unmediated ways—that is, if the processing at all stages of perception is modulated by top-down conceptual influences—then there is no nonconceptual content and no philosophical argument could resurrect it. Furthermore, if there are perceptual mechanisms that retrieve information from a scene bottom-up then this information is the nonconceptual content of the states produced by these mechanisms. Thus, the existence of cognitively impenetrable mechanisms is both a necessary and a sufficient condition for nonconceptual content.

This approach to the issue of nonconceptual content makes possible a new method for determining the nonconceptual content in general and the phenomenal content in particular: identifying those components of perceptual mechanisms that retrieve information in a cognitively impenetrable way and analyzing their output. This output is the nonconceptual content of experience. This method avoids problems associated with the traditional phenomenological methods discussed above. In addition, it is faithful to externalism, which holds that any mental state cannot be specified independently of the relationship of the bearer of that state with the environment. This means that one's mental states cannot be determined solely by introspection of their contents, as in the phenomenological method. To the extent that the inquiry about nonconceptual content is based on the examination of the causal chain of processes that retrieve information from the environment and lead to the formation of the content of perceptual mental states, such content is determined by considering the relationship of the bearer of the mental state with the environment, which is exactly what externalism demands.

Bearing in mind that it is important that only features retrievable in bottom-up ways enter the list of the components of the phenomenal content, let us start our quest for the determination of the phenomenal content of experience. The guiding criterion is that the search be focused on the contents of perceptual (that is, nonconceptual) states of which we can have phenomenal awareness (recall that these are the states of perception in which local recurrent processing occurs). Thus, I shall look first for the outputs of the bottom-up processes of perception. Insofar as perception consists of bottom-up processes, this ensures that the content thus found will be nonconceptual. Since I am searching for the *phenomenal* content of experience, I shall restrict my search to those elements of nonconceptual content of which one could have phenomenal awareness. To that effect, I shall use two methods. First I shall theoretically examine the contents of perceptual states that require local RP, which is the neural trademark of phenomenal awareness; second, I shall rely on good old introspection. The reason introspection is deemed necessary is that our current knowledge of brain processes does not allow us to draw safe conclusions about the precise kinds of interactions and the sites of those interactions in the brain. Accordingly, our knowledge of the precise functioning of local RP and of the exact sites it involves is far from complete. Even if it were complete, it would not be enough, because all it would give us is neural activities and the sites at where they take place. To translate talk about neural activities in the brain into talk about the representational contents they realize requires access to the contents that subjects experience when in those states. That requires experimentation that, in the last analysis, relies on the phenomenological experiences of the subjects. This means that relying on a purely neuroscientific method alone to determine the phenomenal content of experience is futile. Despite the dangers inherent in introspection, the combination of the two methods diminishes the danger of "misclassifying" in the list of the phenomenal conceptual contents. It will avoid, for instance, including in the list the 3D (Marr 1982) shape of objects, which introspection alone has led philosophers (Bermudez 1995; Peacocke 1992) to consider it as part of the phenomenal content.

The first thing one does upon viewing a scene is parse objects; that is, one separates figure from ground. In chapter 3, I discussed theories of indexing mechanisms that index and track the objects parsed in a scene. As we saw there, perception opens object-files for these objects mainly on the basis of spatio-temporal information. The object-files initially *individuate* the objects and allow us to perceive objects *qua* objects that persist in space and time, but they do not *identify* the objects. Although the object-files are constructed on the basis of spatio-temporal information, this information is not initially represented in the files. In this sense, the content of perceptual states consists first in information about "objecthood"—that is, information that makes us perceive objects *qua* objects (and not, say, undetached object parts or fleeting color patches). Haugeland (1998) claims that this constitutes the objective character of perception—that is, the fact that perception is about objects *qua* objects. Gradually, spatio-temporal information is represented in the object-files. Later, further information about the observable properties of the indexed object that is retrieved bottom-up from the scene is represented in the object-file of that specific object. This allows for object individuation on the basis of featural information other than spatio-temporal information.

Viewer-centered shapes are standard items in any list of phenomenal content. The study of vision in part I of this book justifies this analysis, in that studies show that some form of Marr's $2\frac{1}{2}$D models of the objects present in the scene—that is, representations of viewer-centered shapes (structured representations of surfaces of objects as viewed by the observer)—are retrievable in a bottom-up way from the scene. Visual processes that process information about surface shading, orientation, color, binocular stereopsis, size, shape, spatial relations, and analysis of movement are referred to as "early vision." The stages of early vision purportedly capture information that is extractable directly from the initial optical array without recourse to higher-level knowledge. Moreover, the studies of vision that I reviewed in part I of the book suggest that the extraction of most of the aforementioned information from a scene requires local RP (that is, lateral and local top-down flow of information); this makes this information available to phenomenal awareness, which, as we have seen, is subserved by local RP. Thus, most of the results of the method of examining whether it is conceivable to be aware of something without exercising the relevant concepts or any concepts at all are supported by experimental studies of perceptual processes; one could be aware of the viewer-centered shape, the color, the orientation, the size, and so forth even if one did not possess the corresponding concepts. It comes as no surprise, then, that these features are among the items in the list of the phenomenal content of perception.

All information processed in visual perception is retrieved from the morphology of the scene in a bottom-up manner. Since the mechanisms that extract this information are those of vision, it is natural to assume that the resulting frame is a viewer-centered frame of reference. This frame of reference defines the center and the orientation of the spatial and positional information and provides the framework within which featural information is located. Parallel to this consideration, the literature on image schemes (Johnson 1996; Lakoff 1997) emphasizes the role of the human body and of its orientation in the formation of several image schemes—up-down, inside-outside, the scheme of containment, and so on. One can assume, thus, that the viewer-centered frame is constructed on a frame provided by the human body—that is, it is a body-centered coordinate system.

Before I proceed, I should emphasize that the claim that the frame of reference in which information retrieved in vision (which includes processing along both the ventral and the dorsal system) is cast is a body-centered frame does not contradict the claim that the ventral system represents objects in a relational or scene-centered frame, whereas the dorsal system represents them in a egocentric or viewer-centered frame. Here is why. Our awareness of space has a different origin than our aware- ness of the other sense features in that visual directions constitute an omnipresent grid that overlays every scene, indexing the features repre- sented in it. In that sense, "direction" is part of the form of a visual repre- sentation, whereas "distance," being a feature, is part of the empirical content of vision (Matthen 2005, p. 274). Perceptual states always (re)present the world within a coordinate system; visual scenes are always perceived as being in a space that is structured by means of a Cartesian coordinate system whose center is the body of the perceiver and whose axes correspond to the top-down and left-right directions as defined by the body of the perceiver. In that sense, the Cartesian grid indeed constitutes the form of the representation and not its content. It is this grid that enables the representation of the content of a perceptual state, and there- fore it could not be part of that content.

Within this spatial framework, objects can be represented in two ways: in a scene-based, allocentric, relational form (used by the ventral system), and in a perceiver-centered egocentric, absolute form (used by the dorsal system). In the latter case, all featural information is computed within an absolute, body-centered frame of reference, in which features are com- puted with respect to the body of the perceiver (first her retina, then the center of the distance between the eyes, or the center of gravity of her body, depending on the aim of the perceiver). Size, for instance, is com- puted in an absolute metric, that is, with respect to the perceiver, and not relationally with respect to the sizes of other objects in the scene. In the former case, information is cast in a relational object-centered or scene- based frame of reference in which the object features are computed with respect to the other objects and features in the scene. In this spatial frame- work, objects are still perspectivally seen; that is, they are being represented in a Cartesian framework whose center is the body of the perceiver, but they are organized within this grid with respect to their relations to the other objects in the scene. To avoid confusion, henceforth I will refer to the overarching frame of reference in which information in vision is cast as the *spatial framework* of vision and will retain the terms 'object- centered frame' and 'viewer-centered frame' for the frames of reference in which information is cast in the ventral and the dorsal system respectively.

Evans (1982), and Gibson (1979) before him, proposed the "egocentric space" as an egocentric viewer-centered frame of representing space and spatial properties. This space is defined by the three axes that center on the viewer's body, to wit the axes right-left, up-down, and in front-behind. I think it is safe to assume that the frame of reference intended here is the spatial framework of vision. Campbell (1999), argues that there is a direct, non-observational knowledge of our own bodies, which he calls a "body image." This image gives the system a practical grasp of the ways it can act. It is characterized by an egocentric framework, which is suitable both for place identification and for guidance of simple actions (e.g., those involved in "indexical causality"). The framework is defined by a center (the body) and the axes left-right, front-behind, and up-down, and is tied to the system's actions. Campbell's reference to action signifies that the body image is cast in the viewer-centered absolute frame of reference used by the dorsal system.

Peacocke (1992) elaborates on the spatial framework of vision and on its role in experience. He searches for a level of nonconceptual content on which to anchor concepts in a noncircular way. This kind of nonconceptual content is provided by the spatial types "under which fall precisely those ways of filling the space around the subject that are consistent with the correctness of the content" (ibid., p. 62). To specify the spatial types, one must fix an origin and the axes of the resulting frame. These elements cannot be defined with reference to the real world, since a spatial type may be instantiated at different places. Thus, the point of origin and the axes should be defined with respect to a thing that is always present irrespective of the location at which the spatial type is instantiated: the body of the subject. The point of origin may be the middle point between the eyes (Campbell takes the point of origin to be the center of gravity of the body, but the middle point between the eyes seems a more plausible candidate, considering that we are analyzing visual perception), and the axes of reference are right-left, up-down, and back-front, as defined with reference to the subject's body.

Now, many different things can fill a spatial type. If these things are the surface and its orientation, texture, hue, brightness of light, degree of solidity of objects, direction, the intensity and character of light sources (illumination conditions), and the rate of change of location in relation to the origin and axes as defined above, then this type is a scenario. If one assigns time to a scenario and to its point of origin and if one assigns to the axes of the scenario real directions and places in the world, then one has a "positioned scenario." This positioned scenario is the representational nonconceptual content of the spatial type. Thus, the content of a scenario is spatial representational content.[1]

A scenario must be distinguished from any conceptual representation that articulates this same content, although to describe a scenario one must employ concepts. (The concepts employed in such a description are not themselves components of the representational content of the percept.) In other words, one can have a certain type of perceptual experience without possessing the salient concepts that would describe it. Peacocke's scenarios, being types, can be instantiated by many different scenes.

Putting things into the spatial framework of vision, however, does not suffice to ensure adequate representations of the contents of a scene for the purpose of actions. One also must include the relative relations of the objects in the scene in the Cartesian grid that characterizes the spatial framework of vision. Peacocke's (1992) proto-propositions provide such information. They constitute a layer of the nonconceptual content of perception. Their content contains an individual (or multiple individuals) and a property or a relation. The proto-propositional content of a perception represents the property or relation as holding of the individuals it also contains. The relations may hold of either places or regions in space, or the objects located in those regions. Featural information is not represented in proto-propositions, only spatio-temporal information. This content is nonconceptual. At the same time, Peacocke argues, the content has the subject-predicate form, the individual being the subject and the predicate being the relation. This explains the "proposition" in the "proto-proposition." One can, for instance, perceive a symmetrical relation without possessing the concept 'symmetrical'. Peacocke's (1992, p. 77) list of the contents of proto-propositions includes such relations and properties as "symmetrical," "same shape as," "equidistant from," "parallel to," "square," and "curved." I agree with Peacocke that all these spatial relations and properties are aspects of the phenomenal content of perception, first because one need not possess the relevant concepts to be able to perceive them and second (and more importantly) because these properties and relations are retrieved bottom-up from a scene.

The bottom-up processes of vision do more than just individuate objects and yield their observable properties. They also seem to output functional properties of objects or affordances[2] (Pylyshyn 1999) and causal relations such as "X 'transfers' something to Y." Thus, to complete the list of phenomenal content, it is necessary to discuss the functional properties and causal relations of objects. I will concentrate first on the causal relations, then on the notion of functional properties of objects in general.

More specifically, I will concentrate on Petitot's positional content of a visual scene.

Petitot (1995) talks of the positional (local) content structure of the scene. The positional content is nonconceptual, and it conveys information about nonvisual properties, such as causal relations (e.g., X "transfers" something to Y). Suppose that one witnesses a scene in which X gives Z to Y. The semantics of the scene consists of (i) the semantic lexical content of X, Z, Y and 'give' as a specific action and (ii) the purely positional local content. The latter is the image scheme of the "transfer" type. X, Y, and Z occupy specific locations in the space occupied by the scene (just as they are the arguments in the three-place predicate "to give"). In the image scheme, X, Y, Z are thus reduced to featureless objects that occupy specific relative locations, and in that sense they can be viewed as pure abstract places, in the way Descartes reduced matter to space by denuding it of all its properties except that it occupies space. More specifically, X, Y, and Z, which in a linguistic description of the scene are the semantic roles, "are reduced to pure abstract places, locations that must be filled by 'true' participants." These places are related by means of an action of a "transfer" type (ibid., pp. 251–252).

Petitot's places do not refer to the actual locations occupied by the objects in a scene. The whole description can take place without any reference to the actual locations occupied by the objects. What Petitot seems to allude to using the spatial metaphor is the notion of an object devoid of all features (including actual location) except that it persists in time retaining its numerical identity. In that sense, Petitot construes the first representation of an object that is formed in perception the same way that the theories of object-files do. It is this individuation of an object that Petitot seeks to describe by saying that the objects' only property is that they occupy their own space. This is what the notion of objects as "pure abstract places" means.

Petitot draws from Langacker's (1987) cognitive grammar, in which things, relations, and processes are schematic structures, or parts of domains. The domains have a geometric structure. They are built on a set of fundamental "entities" (space, time, color, shapes, etc.), which provide the elementary representational space upon which the rest of our concepts will be built. In this framework, the concepts that are used in the linguistic descriptions of a scene are locational configurations, or spatial structures.

When one perceives a visual scene, one's visual system "scans" the scene, picking up qualitative discontinuities (abrupt discontinuities in luminance, for instance). From the local discontinuities in the retinal image, contours are detected, boundaries are set, and so forth, until the various image schemes that categorize perceptual events are progressively built. What is important is that the global positional information contained in a scheme be retrieved from the morphology of the scene by the mechanisms of early vision in a bottom-up manner. Petitot gives a detailed exposition of the routines and algorithms of early vision that might perform this task.[3]

Let us now turn to the affordances of objects. Consider the interaction of a frog with a fly (Bickhard 1996). The neural activity in the frog is not an internal representation of the fly. The "representational" content of the neural activity induced by the fly consists in the possibility of tongue flicking and eating on the basis of indications about potentialities that are afforded by specific objects in the environment. This content is about the potentialities or possibilities of further interactions that are afforded by the environment for the organism's interactions with it. They implicitly predicate those interactive properties of the environment that could support the indicated interactions of the organism with it. Thus, they have a causal significance for the frog, which does not rest in the internal representation of external things and in the possession of the notion of "causality" but rather depends on the practical grasp by the frog of the implications of the afforded potentialities for the frog's actions. Since this kind of content implicitly predicates the properties of the environment that afford actions to the organism, it is representational and it does require the possession of any concepts.

The potentialities afforded by the environment for the organism's interactions with it have causal significance only with respect to that specific system and not with respect to other systems, no matter how similar they are. This is so because the potentialities correspond to the disposition of the body of the organism and its specific position in space. Campbell (1999) calls this kind of causality "indexical causality," because the content of the term associated with it (e.g., "it is within reach") depends crucially upon the context in which it is used.

As the frog need not have an internal representation of the fly, so it need not know that the fly "is within reach" in order to initiate action. "The notion of something being 'within reach' that we should want to use in characterizing its knowledge is dedicated to its own capacities for movement. . . . Its representation of something as 'within reach' may be quite directly tied to its own initiation of movement. The reason for saying that the representation is precisely a representation of something as 'within reach' is entirely its direct relation to the creature's actions." (Campbell 1999, p. 85) Cussins (1990) calls this kind of nonconceptual content "construction-theoretic content." It allows an organism to navigate through its environment and to interact dynamically with it.

Let me recapitulate my findings about the phenomenal content retrieved directly from a scene. It consists in the content of perceptual states that extract the following from the environment:

- the "individuated object," which persists separately in space and time, has a spatio-temporal history, and is individuated and tagged by the viewer by means of pre-attentional segmentation processes
- some form of Marr's $2\frac{1}{2}$D models of the objects in the scene—that is, representations of viewer-centered shapes (structured representations of surfaces of objects), motion, size, orientation, color, and surface properties of objects
- the relational properties of the components of scene (whether they be places or objects)—e.g., symmetrical relations and topological relations (up-down, left-right, etc.)
- the positional (local) content structure of the scene (Petitot 1995), which conveys information about causal relation and the functional properties of objects or affordances (Gibson 1979).

5.2   Is Phenomenal Content Representational?

I have been assuming that the nonconceptual content of perception in general and the phenomenal content of perception in particular are representational. Here I will argue for this assumption. I will discuss perceptual nonconceptual content in general, since if nonconceptual content is shown to be representational then phenomenal content is representational too. The minimal account of possession of representational content asserts that a state has a representational content if it represents the world as being a certain way. In this case the state has a correctness condition; that is, the world can make the state come out true or false. In the latter case the state would misrepresent the state of affairs in the world. I think it is not difficult to see that phenomenal content as defined in chapter 4 and in this chapter meets this condition. A perceptual state whose content "depicts," say, an object with a certain viewer-centered shape-type, in a certain topological relation with respect to the perceiver, moving toward a certain direction, can be true or false depending on a specific state of affairs in the world, that is, on whether there is out there an object with that type of shape moving toward that direction. The state is semantically evaluable and thus meets the minimal criterion.

Let us see now whether the phenomenal content as determined in this section meets Bermudez's (1995) additional criteria of representational states. Recall that these conditions are (1) that such a content should be able to figure in explanations of intentional behavior (to wit, in the explanation of the connection between sensory input and behavioral output that cannot be explained by invoking some lawful regularity), (2) that representational content should allow the cognitive integration (that is, it could interact with other representational states), and (3) that representational content must have structure. The third condition means that the content's constituent elements could be constituent parts of other contents, and that the content could be decomposed into its elements, which could then be recombined with the constituent elements of other states with representational content.

An infant need not exercise or even possess the concept of "objecthood" or of the specific direction toward which the object, say a ball, is moving (that is, she need not know that the object is moving to the left). As a matter of fact, the infant does not possess these concepts. Yet her reaction in such a situation, say her reaching to catch the ball, is certainly determined by, among other things, the contents of her perceptual states, namely that the object is moving toward that direction and is within reach. This behavior, moreover, is not the result of some dedicated transducers; perceiving the ball and its motion may be the result of the transducers dedicated to perception, but reaching for the ball is not. The action requires visual and motor coordination and a decision to reach for the ball, which in turn presupposes that the infant perceives the object as being within reach (though of course she might be wrong). The infant's behavior is intentional in that it cannot be accounted in terms of reflexes, and thus it cannot be explained by invoking some lawful regularity connecting sensory input and behavioral output. Hence, the contents of the infant's perceptual states figure in explanations of her intentional behavior, meeting Bermudez's first condition. Notice that explanations of intentional behavior need not invoke contentful states of which the subject is aware in general or which the subject can report in particular. All that is required is that the contents of the states are used to explain a connection between sensory input and behavioral output, a connection that cannot be explained by means of a lawful regularity.

It is also easy to see that perceptual states interact with other perceptual states, allowing thus cognitive integration, which is Bermudez's second condition for a state to possess representational content. The various stages of perceptual processing itself constitute a series of gradual information integration, in the course of which various pieces of information retrieved from a scene and processed by distinct processors (motion, shape, and color, to name a few) are integrated to form a more complex representation of parts of a visual scene. Or suppose you are in the jungle and you see an entity with a certain shape and a certain size galloping toward you and, at the same time, you see another entity with a certain shape and a certain size that affords climbing. Your reaction will be to run toward the second entity and climb on it. This reaction results from cognitive integration of the contents of the two perceptual states. You need not possess the concept 'objecthood', 'tiger', 'big', 'right' (as in "it runs to its right toward me"), or 'tree' to react the way you did. It suffices that you perceive danger and the affordance of climbing. To escape danger, you employ the information that climbing is possible, you take into account that what comes toward you can outrun you, and you take that option. Again, you perceive the information that the thing can outrun you; you do not deduce it from the pattern of the thing's motion. The instrumentality of a particular course of action reveals itself in the perceptual content; there is no need to make a decision. All the information needed to initiate action is directly present in the perceptual content, but if you are to act effectively the different pieces of information must be integrated.

Bermudez's third condition is the most crucial, since it imposes the condition that a representational content be a structured content. In fact, the claim that perceptual states with nonconceptual content can have structured content will allow me, in section 5.4, to rebut the criticism that the nonconceptual content reintroduces the "Given." I argue here that phenomenal perceptual content is structured. According to Bermudez, a content is representational if it can be analyzed into constituent elements, and if these elements can be recombined to form new contents. Does phenomenal content meet this condition? The answer is certainly yes. Shapes, colors, sizes, orientations, spatial relations, and other properties of objects that are the constituent elements of nonconceptual content can be recombined in various ways. Colors, orientations, and spatial relations of an object can change, yet we perceive the same object with the same shape, which means that the unchanged shape can be combined with the new color, orientation, or direction of motion to yield the nonconceptual content of a new perceptual state. Furthermore, even when we perceive just a specific shade of a color, the corresponding perceptual state has a rudimentary structure insofar as that shade is perceived as being in a certain relative spatial relation with respect to the viewer-centered frame of reference constructed on a frame provided by the human body; in other words, it takes place within a scenario in Peacocke's (1992) sense.

So phenomenal content is representational. But what about the nonconceptual content of sensation? Recall that the processes in sensation compute information on light intensity, such as those that compute changes in light intensity by locating and coding individual changes in intensity. Sensation includes Marr's raw primal sketch, which provides information about zero-crossings, bars, blobs, boundaries, edge segments, and so on. More specifically, the raw primal sketch is a first description of the zero-crossings that are detected by channels of different sizes. At this level of processing, high temporal and spatial frequencies, anti-correlated disparity, and other properties of stimuli are recorded. Let us examine as an example of such processes "zero-crossings," which Bermudez thinks are states with representational content.

To locate and represent intensity changes in the retina, the visual system must look at the local spatial neighborhood of any given spatial point to determine whether there is an intensity change at that point, and it must perform this process for every point in the retina, which it does in a parallel way. At this stage, both local and parallel computations are involved. Detecting changes in intensity is important because sharp changes in intensity are interpreted as surface boundaries. To detect local changes of intensity, the visual system applies a first-order difference operator to each pixel in the image (Marr 1982). Suppose one views a dark vertical bar and one wants to find the points in the image of the bar on the retina where the intensity values change in the horizontal direction. The first-order operator computes the difference in intensity values between each adjacent pair of pixel values by subtracting the left member of the pair from the right. One then create a new two-dimensional array in which one replaces the intensity of the pixel at a certain point with the values of the first-order operator at that point. This way, one represents the results of the application of the operator to each pixel in the image array. The resulting array, which represents differences in intensity values instead of intensity values, is called a first-order difference or gradient or convolution array. The convolution array contains zero values when the intensity does not change) and nonzero values when the intensity does change). The nonzero values are an approximation of the slope or the first-order derivative of the intensity function in the chosen direction.

Because its operations are local, the first-order operator represents well the surface boundaries (edges) of the bar, but it does not do a good job in cases where the gradient is spread over a region of space and many surfaces may be present in the visual scene. The reason is that in such cases there may be many nonzero values indicating changes in intensity, which in turn indicates the presence of many surface boundaries; the image resembles a manifold molded by peaks and valleys, representing the maxima and minima in the nonzero values. To delineate the surface boundaries of the objects in the scene, the visual system must apply to the image further operations that detect and represent the peaks and troughs. This is done by means of processes that compute the gradient of the gradient (that is, the second derivative of the intensity function at the chosen direction). This is the task of a second-order operator that computes the difference between adjacent first-order differences of light intensity at the points in the array. Here, as was done with the first-order operator, one replaces the two-dimensional first-order convolution array with a second-order convolution or gradient array. The second derivative of maxima and minima show up as zero-crossings in the second-order convolution array. Thus, zero-crossings are the points at which maxima and minima of intensity differences are located, and, thus, zero-crossings are crucial for delineating surface boundaries in a visual scene.

The question I asked was "Are states whose contents are zero-crossings representational, and hence is a zero-crossing a representational content?" Zero-crossings can certainly be true or false of the environment, depending on whether they reflect surface boundaries as they are in the environment. Thus, zero-crossings satisfy the minimal condition of content possession. How do zero-crossings fare with respect to the other three conditions imposed by Bermudez on representational content? Could they, for example, figure in explanations of intentional behavior that cannot be explained by simply invoking a lawful regularity? I think not. The processes involved in the computation of the zero-crossing are within the realm of a dedicated transducer, which is based on some lawful regularities hard-wired in the mechanisms of the early visual system that performs the computations of differences in light intensity that are required for finding the zero-crossings. Furthermore, I cannot see how zero-crossings could be evoked to explain cognitive behavior, including action in the environment. Shapes, motion, and other properties are used in such explanations, not zero-crossings, even though of course zero-crossings are a step in extracting shapes and motions from the image. In other words, zero-crossings are not poised at the right level of processing to allow them to be fed into cognitive processing (Tye 2002). The registration of differences in illuminances on the retina is a level too low, in that it is not registered in a form that can be fed to and used by the cognitive centers.

The same argument shows that zero-crossings fail to justify Bermudez's second criterion, in that they cannot allow cognitive integration—that is, they cannot interact with other representational states. And it is easy to see that zero-crossings do not meet Bermudez's last condition: that a representational content must be structured, in the sense that it has constituent elements into which it could be analyzed and which could combine with constituent parts of other contents. Zero-crossings are mathematical values, the second-order derivatives of the intensity function. They cannot be analyzed into constituent parts, and they cannot be combined with the contents of other states. Thus, "zero-crossings" are not states with representational content, although they are states with nonconceptual subdoxastic content.

The representational character of phenomenal content and the fact that it is the content of states that are produced in perception before the onset of attention account for some of its properties. More specifically, Tye (2002, pp. 454–455) writes that phenomenal content is poised, abstract, nonconceptual, and representational content. We have seen why it is nonconceptual and representational. Let us see whether phenomenal content as determined in this chapter is also poised and abstract. By "abstract" Tye (2002, 2006) means that it is content into which no information about particular objects enters; it is coarse-grained in a sense that I will discuss shortly. The representation of general features and properties is what is crucial to the phenomenal character of experience.

Recall the account of perception synopsized in section 5.1. I have said that perceptual processes are not informed by any knowledge about specific objects. Instead, they observe some operational constraints that constrain visual processing. These assumptions, however, are not the results of explicit knowledge acquisition about specific objects; they are generally reliable regularities about the visual and spatial properties of the world that are hard-wired in our perceptual systems. Furthermore, the output of the encapsulated visual processor does not consist in the regular objects that we encounter in the world; it consists in a more abstract form of categories of such objects, classified according to their generic shapes. And we saw in section 4.2.2 why and in what sense nonconceptual content is about types of objects and not about object tokens. Thus, the phenomenal content, being the outcome of perceptual process, is abstract.

Tye's remark, and the view developed here that nonconceptual and hence phenomenal content is abstract and concerns types and not tokens, sheds light on the fine-grained (as opposed to coarse-grained) nature of the phenomenal content of experience. Philosophers have argued for nonconceptual content in attempting (among other things) to account for the fine-grained character and richness of the "phenomenal content" of experience—i.e., that the content of an experience that is responsible for the "phenomenal character" of the experience, its phenomenal content, is usually much richer than any attempt to report it could be; it cannot be described conceptually without any loss of content.

Tye (2006) argues that nonconceptual content is coarse-grained or robust in the sense that it consists in structured existential states of affairs involving properties and relations and the existence of an object or a surface facing the viewer that carries these properties and relations but not specific particular items, a claim that (as we have seen) amounts to the claim that the nonconceptual content is about types (in the sense explained in the previous chapter), not tokens. This being so, nonconceptual content does not allow one to represent similarities or differences (that go beyond the description of the type of the object) between specific entities in the same state of affairs or between entities in different possible states of affairs.

The reason why one cannot notice fine-grained details of nonconceptual content, Tye (2006) argues, is that if one had been able to discriminate, on the basis of such fine-grained details, between two tokens of, say, a shade, one would have been able to draw fine-grained distinctions between the two instances of a shade. However, if one could find such fine-grained distinctions, one would have phenomenal concepts structured on the basis of these distinctions, which would phenomenally describe the shades that would thus cease to be nonconceptual contents of perceptual states. That is a problem for all nonconceptualists who take phenomenal contents to be able to individuate in a fine-grained manner—that is, to allow one to make fine-grained distinctions between nonconceptual contents. The problem, again, is that if the content of experience is thus fine-grained, how could it fail to be conceptual? Peacocke's (1994, 1998, 2001) view that nonconceptual contents are in that sense fine-grained is rejected.

Thus, it seems that on the one hand nonconceptual content is fine-grained in that it is usually much richer than any attempt to either report it or conceptually articulate it in one's mind could be, and thus, it cannot be articulated conceptually, and, on the other hand, it is coarse-grained in that it does not allow fine-grained distinctions between its contents. However, according to Tye (2006), to think that these two theses are contradictory would be "to confuse different notions of grain." Coarse-grained nonconceptual content in Tye's sense is perfectly compatible with nonconceptual content being fine-grained in the sense implicated in the richness-of-experience argument. The former determines "how its individuation conditions are fixed by sets of possible worlds or by arrangements of properties and relations in possible states of affairs," whereas the latter concerns the kinds of properties (or relations) that can be represented. Those kinds can be beyond the reach of conceptual designation, thus making nonconceptual contents richer than their conceptual descriptions. Let me try to explain this.

We have seen that phenomenal content, by being nonconceptual, is about types and not tokens. In other words, it is about structured representations of $2\frac{1}{2}$D surfaces of objects carrying some properties and standing in certain relations with other similarly structured surfaces of objects (such as a red square surface on the left of a round blue surface viewed from the viewer's perspective) and not about specific object-tokens that are represented *as* having these properties and relations, where "as" is construed as a semantic relation). Nonconceptual representations are not organized representations in which visual properties are attributed to their source in external objects and events. This fact limits the sorts of distinctions that one can draw between the occurrences of different instantiations of the same type of a property or relation. One cannot, for instance, draw fine-grained distinctions between the occurrence of two shades of the same type in a way that would have allowed one to store in memory the results of the comparison and use them to characterize each shade in a way that would allow one to recognize on another perceptual encounter with another similar shade whether the current shade is the same as a shade one had encountered in the past. In that sense, phenomenal content is coarse-grained. This, however, does not impose any limitations on the number of different kinds of properties or relations that can be perceived. As it turns out, one can be phenomenally aware of far more types of shades than one could conceptually articulate. Phenomenal experience is richer than its conceptual articulations, and thus, in that sense, it is fine-grained.

The phenomenal content is "poised," Tye argues, because it is at the right level of processing to allow it to be fed into cognitive processing. The registration of differences in illuminances on the retina is a level too low, in that it is not in a format that can be accessed by the cognitive centers. The phenomenal content as defined here certainly complies with this requirement, since it is the outcome of perceptual processes. Given the way I have defined "sensation," "perception," and "cognition," phenomenal content stands midway between and connects sensation and cognitive processes.

The list of phenomenal contents at which we arrived by combining an analysis of the output of the bottom-up mechanisms of early vision with the phenomenological method of introspection explains the phenomena that suffice for perceptual consciousness in Smith's (2002, chapters 4 and 5) account, offering an empirical confirmation of the conclusions that Smith reaches using a purely phenomenological method (ibid., p. 133).

Smith distinguishes between sensation and perception. Sensations or sensory qualities or qualia are inherent features of experiences themselves. However, they are not properties of some object, a sense-datum, of which one is aware. Sensations lack intentionality; they do not refer to something beyond them. Although sensations are presented as such in consciousness as intrinsic properties of the experience itself, they do not function as the immediate objects of awareness in this experience. When one perceives, one is not aware of these properties as properties of one's experience; one is aware of objects outside one's body that carry these properties. One is aware of sensations only in cases of nonperceptual sensations. These occur when, for example, one experiences darkness, in which case one is aware of or "feels" an inner darkness that is not intentional at all (it does not refer to anything in the world), or when, with eyes closed, one presses one's eyeballs and has a chromatic visual experience, which Smith (2002, pp. 130–131) calls the "inner light show," and which is not intentional either; one only experiences a certain chromatic sensation, an instance of achromatic quale. It is only in cases like these that one is aware of sensations. These, however, are not cases of perceptual experience.

There is, thus, a distinction between having a sensation of something and being perceptually conscious of something. Sensations can occur either perceptually or nonperceptually, depending on whether they are properties of perceptual states or not, respectively. In the former case, they are perceptual sensations (Smith 2002, p. 92). In the latter case, sensations give us no awareness of physical objects, only of some properties. The faculty that makes us aware of objects is perception.

According to Smith, perception concerns the world; only perception is intentional. Perceptual experience presents objects as literally external to our bodies and this gives us the ability to examine perceptually various aspects of these objects from different perspectives; one cannot have a perspective of sensations. Thus, perception, in addition to its sensory character, has a nonsensory aspect that adds intentionality to perception. At the same time, this extra aspect cannot be the possession or exercise of concepts, lest we lapse back to the two-component theories of perception of Sellars, McDowell, and others.

There are, Smith argues, three nonconceptual characteristics or phenomena of perception that suffice to render it, as opposed to mere sensation, intentional—that is, they make it to be about external objects. The first is phenomenal three-dimensionality that accompanies perception, that is, "the spatial over-againstness with which perceptual objects are given to awareness: an over-againstness which involves a part of our body functioning as sense-organ" (Smith 2002, p. 134). The second extra aspect of perception is the integration of self-movement with the sensory fields. "It is only thanks to self-movement that we have a distinction between how sensorily things are with us and how, although they are themselves directly registered in sensation and veridically perceived, things are with the objects of perception." (ibid., p. 145) This self-movement allows perception to represent things from different perspectives. Smith introduces this second characteristic mainly to account for perceptions involving smells and other items that we perceive and which, despite being physical phenomena, are not spatially located. Smell fails to present odors as at any distance from us; we only have sensations of odors; what makes them objects of perceptual awareness is the fact that we can move in relation to them. The third phenomenon that suffices for perceptual awareness is the *Anstoss*—to wit, the phenomenon of check or impediment to our active movement, "an experienced obstacle to our animal striving, as when we push or pull against things" (ibid., p. 153). The term *Anstoss* is appropriated from Fichte, although for Fichte *Anstoss* is a check of an intellectual act, whereas for Smith it is a check of bodily movement.

Nonconceptual content, I have argued, is the content of perceptual states that result from visual processes that pre-attentively parse a scene into distinct objects that persist in space and time. These objects are also situated within a scenario; that is, they are in certain spatial relations to the frame of reference determined by our body. Moreover, they move in certain ways within this spatial framework. Thus, the nonconceptual content includes the perception of individuated and indexed objects as entities that exist and that move in space and time separately from us. That covers the first two of Smith's phenomena that give rise to the intentional perception. What Smith's analysis reveals is the phenomenological counterpart of the neural mechanisms of perception.

Notice that the two characteristics that perception bestows on its objects—the "over-againstness" of objects from the perceiver that characterize perceptual experience as opposed to mere sensory experience and render the former intentional, and the fact that we perceive, through a parsing mechanism, individuated objects that persist in space and time—are akin to Devitt's (1991) "independence" and "existence" conditions of objecthood, and to Kaufman's (2002) "separateness" and "continuity and distinct existence" conditions for objects experienced as separated from the perceiver.

Anstoss is somewhat more difficult to account for within the current framework. I think it is related to the solidity of objects, which does not allow one object to be at the same location as another—in other words, to the fact that solid objects are impenetrable. Recall that in chapter 3 I discussed the basic principles that guide visual processing by being hard-wired in the mechanisms of visual system. Among these principles were the solidity and the impenetrability of solid objects (Spelke 1988, 1990), which are among the assumptions that the visual system makes in order to solve the many problems of indeterminacy besetting the computations over the incoming information, and which underlie the formation of the nonconceptual content. In that sense, the account offered here explains to some extent the *Anstoss*.

5.3   Notions of Phenomenal Content

Though the findings about the nature of nonconceptual content agree with many of the results obtained through the usage of the other methods I discussed in the introduction to this chapter, there are also some striking discrepancies. Peacocke (1992) and Bermudez (1995) include in their list of nonconceptual contents the object-centered three-dimensional representations of objects that allow objects to be identified and recognized. I disagree with this inclusion. As I said above, most theories of vision consider the 3D representation of an object to be a product of bottom-up nonconceptual and top-down conceptual flow of information. My list of phenomenal content also includes the functional properties that objects have in relation to some organism and some causal relations between objects in a scene. Moreover, as we saw in section 5.2, nonconceptual content and thus phenomenal content is about $2\frac{1}{2}$D surfaces of objects and their properties and relations, not about object tokens. However, the conceptual content of experience is about object tokens.

The notion of nonconceptual content defended here sheds light on a problem noted by Bermudez (1995). Bermudez distinguishes the nonconceptual content of perception from the nonconceptual content of subpersonal (or subdoxastic) computational states. The difference between the two lies in the fact that one can be aware of the former but not of the latter. As examples of such subpersonal states, Bermudez mentions various computational subpersonal stages of visual processes as presented in Marr's theory of vision.

It seems that for Bermudez the content of perception is nonconceptual because it can be detected by means of what I have called the phenomenological method; though one may possess the requisite concepts, one need not apply them in order for one's experience to have the phenomenal content it does; in addition, one can be in a state with such a content even if one does not possess the corresponding concepts. This may work well to a certain extent (remember the case of 3D objects) with phenomenal content, but it does not work well with subdoxastic states and their information-processing content. Subdoxastic states are outside the realm of awareness, and the methodological method does not apply to them. Thus, Bermudez needs another criterion by which to classify subdoxastic states as states with nonconceptual content. This criterion is that the content of the subdoxastic states is nonconceptual because language does not have or cannot have the requisite concepts.

More specifically, Bermudez (1995, p. 353) claims that subpersonal states that are candidates for having content have nonconceptual content because, owing to the recondite nature of the requisite concepts (the concept "zero-crossing," for instance), language does not have the relevant terms. An obvious problem with this account is that we do have a term that conceptualizes zero-crossings, namely "zero-crossings." It may be that the average person does not possess this concept, but a vision theorist does. To discuss the problem, one must first understand what Bermudez means by 'recondite'. For Bermudez, 'recondite' means several interrelated things: requiring special knowledge in order to be understood, dealing with a material that is too difficult to be understood by those without special knowledge, and hidden from view or knowledge.

For Bermudez, the recondite nature of content X makes it nonconceptual content. More specifically, Bermudez answers the question why "zero-crossings" are states with nonconceptual content by stating that contents with recondite nature are nonconceptual contents. Since 'recondite' means "not available to awareness" and/or "very difficult to understand without special knowledge," and since subpersonal states are not available to awareness by definition and positing lack of awareness as a criterion for nonconceptual content would make subpersonal content trivially nonconceptual, one can conclude that Bermudez takes subpersonal states, such as zero-crossings, to have nonconceptual content because one does not have the special knowledge to understand what the term 'zero-crossings' means and therefore one does not possess the requisite concept.

But this linguistic criterion for nonconceptual content is contingent. Language may acquire a concept that directly conceptualizes this content. Suppose that some future civilization, for various reasons, happens to have a language that includes a concept that directly articulates the content of zero-crossings, in the way "red" articulates perceptual states whose content represents a red thing. Suppose, for example, that in that future civilization theories of vision are taught in high school and nearly everyone acquires the special knowledge of zero-crossings and thus learns the requisite concept. Zero-crossings will cease to have a recondite nature. Remember that it cannot be argued that even in that civilization one cannot be aware of zero-crossings and that is why zero-crossings are nonconceptual, because that would make them nonconceptual in a trivial, if not circular, manner. Would that mean that for that civilization the content of zero-crossings is conceptual? And what would that mean for the individuals in that civilization who are unaware of these concepts? And what about a civilization that has not developed theories of vision in which zero-crossings figure as theoretical terms? Bermudez has to accept that for that civilization zero-crossings are states with conceptual content, so that the nonconceptual character of a perceptual state is a contingent fact. I am certain that none of the nonconceptualists, including Bermudez, would be happy with that conclusion.

Suppose, however, that no natural language could ever have such concepts, because the content of the states whose content they are supposed to conceptualize is so fine-grained that it exceeds the limits of the expressive capabilities that the structure of any language can attain. Then an independent noncircular account (meaning an account that does not involve the notion of conceptual or nonconceptual content) must be given of how fine-grained a content must be in order to exceed the expressive capabilities of a language. Such an account is lacking thus far. Only by taking recourse to the cognitively encapsulated mechanisms of perception could one escape these problems.

Furthermore, how could something of which we are not aware (either phenomenally or in access), and which we posited in developing a theory of visual processes, ever enter discussions without being conceptualized, or at least without being described linguistically (recall that is exactly how I presented zero-crossings)? The answer is that it cannot. Thus, in some sense, zero-crossings are already conceptualized. We are not phenomenally aware of them, and thus we can only discuss them and hypothesize about their existence. Does this make zero-crossings states with conceptual content? The answer, of course, is negative. Zero-crossings are nonconceptual contents not because of any linguistic restrictions or because of their recondite nature but because they are formed in a stage of visual processing that is cognitively impenetrable. Let me explicate this further.

If Bermudez's "linguistic" criterion fails to account for the nonconceptual character of subpersonal states, then in what sense are zero-crossings nonconceptual contents of experience? If one were to argue that even if we did possess the requisite concepts we would not exercise them to perceive zero-crossings, the retort would be "How do you know that?" More specifically, using one version of the phenomenological method, to say that *X* is nonconceptual content of experience means that *one can be aware of X without exercising that concept* (or perhaps any concepts whatsoever). However, we are never aware of zero-crossings, either conceptually or nonconceptually. Therefore, that method cannot justify the nonconceptual character of zero-crossings.

We have seen that the traditional methods of determining the nonconceptual character of the content of some state fail. To answer the question as to why zero-crossings are nonconceptual, one has to take recourse to the following argument: Though one may possess the relevant concepts, and independent of whether one possesses them, one need not exercise those concepts to perceive zero-crossings. Thus, zero-crossings are nonconceptual content because one need not exercise concepts to perceive them. The question then is "Why does one not need the exercise of concepts in order to perceive zero-crossings?" The reply is as follows: Zero-crossings are the contents of perceptual states that are formed during the FFS in visual processing, a stage of processing that is cognitively impenetrable and thus conceptually uncontaminated. This is why concepts are not exercised in the formation of zero-crossings. Notice that awareness nowhere enters the discussion of the nonconceptual content of zero-crossings. This move is not available to Bermudez. Recall that he has appealed to the recondite nature of the zero-crossings to account for their nonconceptual character, a move that points the contingent fact that language lacks the concept that is needed to account for their nonconceptual nature. None of these factors plays any role whatsoever in the considerations that lead to the designation of zero-crossings as nonconceptual content in the account I offered in the preceding paragraph.

Thus, it seems that, although Bermudez avoids several problem for an adequate account of the content of subdoxastic states by positing the existence of nonconceptual content of which one is never aware, the criterion he uses relies on the contingent fact that the subjects' language does not or cannot contain concept terms that conceptualize some content or other, and it may even bring back the notion of awareness, depending on the meaning one assigns to the word 'recondite'. But this criterion has its own problems. Bermudez must accept that if zero-crossings are nonconceptual just because one does not have the appropriate concepts, as he has claimed, then for our imaginary civilization zero-crossings and other computational states might indeed become conceptual states. This does not mean, of course, that in order to perceive-zero crossings one must possess the corresponding concept, otherwise zero-crossings would be conceptual contents to begin with; it means that this content can be conceptualized. The way Bermudez deals with this issue suggests that for him nonconceptual content is conceptual content minus concepts. However, we have seen that this is not the case; nonconceptual content and conceptual content are different kinds of content. Even if one possesses the concepts that conceptualize zero-crossings, the kind of processing that results in states with zero crossings being cognitively encapsulated, these states have nonconceptual content.

Thus, the content of the states that correspond to zero crossings is nonconceptual not because language does not or cannot contain the requisite concept terms, but because that content is retrieved bottom-up from a visual scene. To justify the nonconceptual character of the contents of phenomenal and subpersonal stages, one need not take recourse to the resources of the language of a community; it suffices to invoke the fact that these contents are retrieved from visual scenes in conceptually unmediated ways. Nonconceptual content is independent of whether we are aware of it, and independent of whether we possess or exercise the corresponding concepts. The content of perceptual states, whether this content be conscious or not, is nonconceptual because it is retrieved by the visual system from the environment in a bottom-up way, that is, without any cognitive modulation. Thus, my account offers a unified explanation of why certain personal and subpersonal states have nonconceptual contents.

Moreover, this account specifies that the only kind of awareness that could accompany nonconceptual content is phenomenal awareness. Phenomenal awareness is different from the awareness that accompanies our experience of the world, whose content I have called "experiential content." This immediately suggests that one should not hasten to draw conclusions about the nature of nonconceptual content based on introspection alone, because introspection is about conceptual experiential content. As I said above, it may be that one lacks a concept that describes one's experience, but that does not mean that no concepts are involved in the formation of the content of that experience. Or one may think that one can see things in the phenomenal sense, since one judges that one could have the content of the relevant states without exercising concepts, but in reality there is a cognitive modulation of the processes that led to the mental state with that content, of which one is unaware, as in the case of the 3D shape. This also restricts the awareness of nonconceptual content, which stem from the nature of phenomenal awareness; we can be phenomenally aware of types of objects (this is different, of course, from seeing objects as belonging to categories).

5.4 Phenomenal Content, Sense-Data Theories, and the Myth of the Given

Churchland (1988), arguing for the cognitive penetrability of perception, claims that, even if there is some rigidity and theoretical neutrality at some early perceptual process, this *sensation* is useless in that it cannot be used for any "discursive judgment," since sensations are not truth-valuable and do not have conceptual content. Only "observation judgments" can, because they have content, which is a function of a conceptual framework. In other words, even if there is such a thing as the nonconceptual content of our experience, this sensation is epistemologically useless. Brewer (1999), McDowell (1994), Sellars (1956, 1963), and Sedivy (2004a,b) have gone even further, rejecting the existence of this epistemologically uninteresting "sensation" as a distinct stage of perception and arguing that perception is inherently, and thus from its onset, conceptual. Although they concede that the external world is the cause of the experiential episodes, in that it causes in the perceiver certain experiential states, they reject the view that the external world is the cause of the contents of these experiential states, since these contents are inherently conceptualized.[4] They reject the "Myth of the Given"—that is, the view that there is a raw sensation, which involves no judgment at all and thus is nonconceptualized, that awaits interpretation, an interpretation that results in the formation of our ordinary experiences.[5]

Sedivy (2004a, p. 1) describes the myth as follows: "Classical empiricism, you might recall, holds that perception consists of minimal experiences (or impressions) which are the purely sensory result of the world's causal impact on our senses, and more complex experiences which involve our understanding or conceptual capacities as well." Davidson (1984, pp. 189–190) also had renounced the idea that one can distinguish a conceptual scheme from the thing of which it is the schema (i.e., that one can distinguish between a generic unstructured thing that exists and waits to be conceptualized in order to be perceived) as "the third dogma of empiricism." So the myth that is rejected is the view that these minimal experiences (minimal in the sense that they are unstructured or generic) are the raw materials or raw sensations that affect our faculty of receptivity and yield the "Given" (McDowell 1994),[6] which is then infused with the conceptual element to yield our experiences. In other words, what is criticized is the claim that there exists a nonconceptual content of experience. In the terminology used in this book, what is rejected is the thesis that there exists some stage of vision (the one I have called 'perception') that is cognitively impenetrable or encapsulated. The motive behind denouncing the Myth of the Given is, roughly, the following: Since experience stands in justificatory relations with the beliefs and judgments that we may form on its basis, and since these relations can hold only between conceptually articulated contents, experiences must have conceptual content. In other words, experience must be within the "space of reasons."[7]

Churchland argues that the deliverances of perception, if they are to have cognitive importance, must have conceptual content and must be within the space of reasons (to be discursive judgments). If there is such a thing as a nonconceptual content, it is epistemically useless, for it cannot be used to justify and explain beliefs based on experience. This is the standard criticism of the traditional sense-data theories, according to which the immediate object of our experience is something purely sensational that is caused by the world—"the given." Being such, it lacks conceptual content. It has no representational content, either; sense data are not about the world. The notion of phenomenal nonconceptual content is not vulnerable to this critique, though. First, it is semantically evaluable and representational in that it is about entities of the world in virtue of its representational character. Furthermore, it satisfies Bermudez's conditions for being representational. In particular, and at the heart of the charge against it that it resurrects the "Myth of the Given," phenomenal content has structure. The charge against the Myth is based on the assumption that the immediate objects of perception are unstructured raw impressions that await interpretation, these impressions being the purely sensory result of the world's causal impact on our senses. According to the causal account offered in this book, nonconceptual content is indeed the pure result of the world's causal impact on our senses. However, far from being raw or uninterpreted, it comes loaded with structure. Nonconceptual content "shows" (in the sense that it makes us perceive) a physical object that exists as a separate entity in space and time, that has a certain viewer-centered shape, size, location, spatial relations to other objects, orientation, and that moves in a certain way. This structure determines its interpretation by the perceiver, that is, the way the nonconceptual content seems to the perceiver, with her perceptual apparatus. "What is given is not 'raw sensation,' something that awaits an 'interpretation.' What is given is a physical object, or at least a physical 'phenomenon,' in space." (Smith 2002, p. 264)

The structure of nonconceptual content renders possible the evidential relation between perceptual states with nonconceptual content and perceptual judgments made on the basis of these states. We do not make judgments about our internal perceptual states first and then proceed to use them as reasons for our beliefs. To paraphrase Evans (1982, p. 227): although our judgments are based on our nonconceptual informational states, they are not about these states. When we make judgments, we gaze at the world inducing in ourselves a perceptual state or informational state; but we do not gaze at this internal state. We form these beliefs because the world induces in us informational states that have enough structure to sustain evidentially these beliefs (for a similar argument see Heck 2000, pp. 503–504, 517).

Vision (1998) makes a similar claim. He argues that perception induces in us nonconceptual states that have the structure required to allow them to stand in evidential relations with perceptual judgments based on these perceptions. "But if the kinds of divisions into persisting solids, together with some range of their traditional sensory qualities,[8] are available to receptivity from the outset ... this would overcome the problem of fit between what we perceive and what we judge because the former would already come in a form suitable for judgment and inference." (Vision 1992, p. 406) This way, many of the properties of things (the properties that figure in the list of nonconceptual content; that is, motion, orientation, color, viewer-centered shape, surface properties, spatio-temporal properties, relative spatial relations, etc., but most importantly our pre-attentional nonconceptual parsing of a scene in individual persisting objects) as they are perceptually experienced, which McDowell (1994) views as applications of our conceptual faculty to perception from its very onset, are present in perception before one even acquires the relevant concepts. It goes without saying that connecting perception with exercises of reason (contemplation of possibilities, nonperceptual assumptions, and so forth) requires that the perceiver have internal capacities. The dual component theories of perception have it that perceivers contribute these notions to make sense of their experience. But if we perceive a structured or featured reality, then perception is by itself commensurate to interact as premise with the higher exercises of reason; "to be sufficiently commensurate to interact as a premise our perceptual output must already be apprehended with classificatory notions as well as principles of identifying and individuating individuals" (Vision 1998, pp. 417–418).

Vision's divisions into persisting solids and some of their perceptible properties find natural analogues in the individuation and indexing of objects in a scene and in the bottom-up retrieval of some of their properties through the mechanisms of perception presented here. The divisions into solids and their properties endow perceptual states with structured content. In that sense, Vision (1998, p. 409) is right that perception (which corresponds to the Kantian term of intuition) provides us with a featured external reality, or, if one wishes to emphasize the bottom-up way of retrieving information form the environment in perception, that perception (intuition) *receives* this structured external reality.

Vision construes the kinds of divisions into persisting solids and some of their sensible qualities[9] as innate or as appearing very early in life, which means that they precede the acquisition of the concepts that would conceptualize them. He even notes that as more experimental techniques become available for probing into infants from the very first days of their lives, one might eventually show that these divisions and the structure they impose on perceptual images may indeed be innate. If these divisions precede the acquisition of sortal concepts, it goes without saying that perceiving them cannot be the result of the application by spontaneity of these concepts, as McDowell (1994) would have it. These aspects need not be contributed by our spontaneity, insofar as they are present in the perceived image as a result of the way perception functions. To substantiate his claims, Vision (1998, p. 406) cites much of the experimental work that I discussed in chapter 3. However, as we saw there, and in view of strong reservations about innatism (see, e.g., Elman et al. 1996), there is no need to espouse a strong form of innatism to account for our perceptual (meaning noncognitive or nonconceptual) ability to parse a scene into persisting solid objects and extract from it some of their perceptible properties; some constraints hard-wired into our perceptual system will do. This also allows us to avoid unnecessary complications about whether, and if yes which, animals are endowed with concepts.[10]

According to the traditional sense-data theories, the sensory qualities of perceptual experience (the sense data) are really and not intentionally involved in perceptual experience, and they feature in experience as the immediate objects of awareness. This means that experience involves awareness of sense data or of subjective qualities (the qualia), which are mind-dependent not physical entities that cannot be identified with objects in the world around us. The remarks about perceptual nonconceptual content having structure and thus being different from the raw sense data do not remove the lurking threat of sense-data theories being reintroduced in perception disguised in some form of the representational theory of perception. In such a theory, the deliverances of perception are not pure nonrepresentational entities, to wit, the raw sense data or impressions. Instead, the immediate objects of our experiences have intentional properties; the sense data have structure and represent the world. This is a variation of the traditional theory, since its main tenet is that there is an epistemic intermediary, a perceptual intermediary, between the world and our beliefs of it, the perceptual intermediary being not the sense data but the representations that the world induces in us.

Phenomenal content as construed here is immune to that criticism too. The present account of phenomenal content assumes that perceptual states have a representational nonconceptual content, not that sense data have such a content. The phenomenal level is not a representation to a person; it is wrong to claim that one has access only to one's representations of the world and not to the world itself. When we perceive, we are in some causal contact with objects in the world. Now, though this contact is certainly mediated by some psychological and neuronal states of the perceiver, we do not perceive by perceiving these states and examining their content. By having them, we perceive the world; we do not perceive these states. "On this view to experience the world as a certain way is . . . to take it, or represent it, to be that way." (Martin 2002, p. 377)

Thus, we are not aware of either perceptual states or sensory qualities; we are aware of physical objects and their properties and of physical phenomena. The sensory qualities (the qualia) are inherent features of experiences themselves (that is, they are properties of the representings), being the physical properties of the neural states that subserve experience (Block 1995), or they are reduced to (or supervene on) the representational nonconceptual content of perception that meets certain further conditions (Tye 2000, 2007, forthcoming) (that is, they are properties of the represented); they are not properties of sense data, of which we are aware. When one experiences X, one experiences X as a property of an object, not as a property of one's own experience; it is an experience that represents an object as being X. Hence, as Tye (2002a, p. 160) remarks, when one delights in the intense blue of the Pacific Ocean, one is delighting not in the phenomenal aspects of one's experience but in some specific aspect of the content of one's experience, namely the blue of the ocean. It is that content that is immediately accessible to one's experience, and nothing else.[11] This view of experience and its content is known as *intentionalism*.

It is worthwhile at this point to address an objection that Martin (2002, pp. 382–383) raises on behalf of a sense-data theorist against Tye's claim that by being delighted in the ocean and its blueness one is delighted in an aspect of the content of one's experience. Though in the end Martin dismisses the objection as misplaced, the discussion is helpful because it will allow us to delineate some fine points about the nature of the content of perception, and because it will underline Millikan's (1999) point that one should be very careful not to confuse content with vehicle or form.

A sense-data theorist could (Martin 2003, p. 382) object first that Tye uses the word 'content' in a way that combines with 'representational' or 'intentional' or 'propositional' and picks up on what is talked of in terms of propositions. This is the modern sense. So Tye's content of perception is representational or intentional or propositional. Second, given this construal of content, one must distinguish sharply between the content itself and what the content is about; that is, one must distinguish between the sense of content and the reference of the content. Martin (ibid., p. 382, note 8) notes that this distinction is based on Frege's conception of contents as abstract entities. In this view, contents are propositions that have a reference (the state of affairs they describe) and a sense (the propositions, as meanings, themselves, or, as Martin says, "the contents themselves").

Tye's alleged construal of contents is contrasted with an old tradition that distinguishes between the form and the content. In modern terms, this is a distinction between the representational vehicle, be that a sentence or a mental state, and the representational content of that vehicle, be that a proposition or the content of a mental state. According to this reading, being aware of the Pacific Ocean and its blue color through seeing the ocean makes the ocean and its color contents in the older sense. That is, it makes them representational contents of the corresponding perceptual states that are the representational vehicles or the form of the content. However, it is not clear whether the ocean and its color, as the objects of awareness through seeing and reflecting (that is, introspecting) of one's experience, count as contents (or aspects of content) in the modern sense of content; it is doubtful that the ocean and its color are propositional contents. In other words, it is not clear whether they are aspects of the sense or content itself. From Martin's remark that, given the distinction between sense and reference of contents/propositions, "delighting in the blue of the ocean will not be delighting in an aspect of the content of the experience," one may conclude that the ocean and its color, as objects of awareness through seeing and introspecting, constitute the referents of the terms contained in the proposition expressing the experience. This is why, in delighting in them, one does not necessarily delight in an aspect of the content (sense) of the experience.

That Martin means that the ocean and its color in Tye's statement of delight should be construed as referents and not as senses of the content is corroborated by Martin's remark to the effect that, if one endorses a Russellian conception of propositional content and takes objects and properties literally as constituents of contents, then one is able to assert that by delighting in the ocean and its properties one is delighted in an aspect of content. The Russellian conception of propositional content is that the terms of a proposition contribute to the proposition their referents and not their senses. This being so, one might indeed assert that "by delighting in the ocean and its properties one is delighted in an aspect of content," since the ocean and its color as the referents of terms are literally parts of the content or proposition.

Now, it does not follow from being aware of the ocean and its color as the referents of the terms in the relevant proposition that the content (sense) of the experience is immediately accessible to one's consciousness. For that, one must assume that in being aware of a constituent of a content (the referent of a term, assuming the Russellian conception of propositional content) one is aware of the content (the sense of the propositional content or the content itself). In other words, and putting the issue in terms of experiences, one must assume that when one is aware of the referents of an experience one is also aware of its sense or its content itself.

However, Martin (2002, p. 383) continues, the last assumption is doubtful, because it is not at all clear that in being aware of the ocean and its color (as referents) one is aware of the experience's representational properties. The representational properties of experience are properties of the experience itself, not of the ocean and its properties; that is, "they must rather be the properties the experience has of representing things to be a certain way" (ibid., p. 383, note 9). Martin's wording is interesting. Whereas in the last paragraph on page 382 he discusses the content of the experience, construing it as the sense of the content or the content itself, and questions whether this content is immediately available to awareness, in the next paragraph on page 383 he switches from the content itself to the representational properties of the experience (that is, the properties of the experience itself not of the objects it represents) and questions whether these are immediately available to awareness.

Thus, for the sense-data theorist the content of the experience is reified and is construed as being involved really and not intentionally in experience. The experience becomes an entity that has properties—to wit, the representational properties, which become distinct properties that characterize the experiences as mental events. In this view, Tye is delighting in a blue experience of the ocean. It goes without saying that, if this is true, we can be aware of a thing—the content—through some of its properties in virtue of which it has its representational capacity, namely its nonrepresentational properties.

Martin's subsequent discussion corroborates this reading. Martin argues on behalf of the sense-data theorist that, as we become aware of the representational properties of public representations (such as postcards or public signs) through being aware of their nonrepresentational properties in virtue of which the representation represents the environment, so in the case of one's representational states of mind "awareness of how one's experience represents the environment as being is mediated through awareness of some of the properties in virtue of which it represents them" (2002, p. 383). And the most plausible candidate to play this mediating role is the old sense data.

Indeed, it follows from the above discussion that the only obvious examples of being aware of representational properties would take us back to the view Tye is opposed to, namely the old sense-data theories, according to which in experience one is immediately aware of sense data that are traditionally taken to be *the* representational properties. The moral of Martin's discussion is that, for the sense-data theorist, if one insists that by being aware of the ocean and its properties one is aware of aspects of the content of one's experience, one reverts to the sense-data view that "awareness of how one's experience represents the environment as being is mediated through awareness of some of the properties in virtue of which it represents them" (Martin 2002, p. 383). Thus, sense-data theories are vindicated.

Martin argues that only by assuming that in being aware of a constituent (referent) of a content one is aware of the content (sense) could one conclude that from being aware of the ocean and its blueness (the referents) one is immediately aware of experience's content (sense). He then comments: "Indeed, one might complain not only that it is not clear whether in being aware of the ocean and its color one is aware of the experience's representational properties, but also that the only obvious candidate examples of being aware of representational properties would seem to land us back with the kind of view that Tye wishes to oppose." (2002, p. 383) Before the cited passage Martin talks about whether the content of the experience (as the sense of the experience, or content in the old tradition in which content is opposed to form) is immediately available to awareness. But in the cited passage he slips from "content (as representational content) being immediately available to consciousness" to "the representational properties of the experience being immediately available to consciousness." But the representational properties, for which Martin substitutes the content of the experience, are properties of the experience as a real entity, not as representational content. This means that "experience" is now construed as a representational vehicle, whereas the substituted content was construed as representational content. I think this is a clearcut case of confusion between representational vehicle and representational content.

To recapitulate the argument against Tye's intentionalism: The sense-data theorist distinguishes between the reference and the sense of content, and from that it follows that delighting in the blue of the ocean will not be delighting in an aspect of the content of the experience—apparently because the blue of the ocean is within the realm of reference of the content, whereas the aspects of the content of experience are within the realm of the sense of the content, and these two should be distinguished. So the sense-data theorist seems to have in mind the following schema: Tye's contents are (or can be translated into) propositions. Propositions have reference and sense. Reference concerns what propositions are about, whereas sense concerns the mode of presentation of "the what they are about"—the contents of the propositions themselves. Thus, the fact that an experience is about the ocean and its properties does not imply that one is aware of these things as constituents of the content of experience, because the former is awareness of the reference of the content and the latter is awareness of the sense of the content. To put it differently: Being aware of the ocean and its color does not mean that the content (sense) of the experience is immediately accessible to one's consciousness (refuting thereby Tye's intentionalism). Instead, one can be immediately aware only of the representational properties of experience (the sense data).

Now let us see why this criticism is unfounded. The view that the representational contents of experience are things with properties, of which one is aware through perceiving other nonrepresentational properties in virtue of which the reified contents can represent the environment, is the view that is being rejected in this book (and of course by Tye). The states of mind *qua* representational vehicles are entities in the world, in fact in the brain. But when one perceives, one is aware neither of these entities nor of their nonrepresentational properties. One is aware of the representational content of a representational vehicle, that is, of the objects and the properties the representational content is about (reference), as they are represented in experience as being (the mode of presentation or sense). Thus, one is not aware of "how one's experience represents the environment"; one is aware of the environment as it is represented in the experience as to be. To be aware of how one's experience represents is to be aware of how the representational vehicle represents what it represents. That, indeed, requires that one should perceive the nonrepresentational properties of the vehicle, but this is not what we do when we perceive. Tye, in perceiving the ocean, does not have a blue experience of the ocean; he has an experience of the blue ocean. The qualitative content of Tye's experience, the blueness, does not constitute a distinct representational or phenomenal property that characterizes a mental event, namely seeing the ocean; rather, "seeing the blue ocean" refers to a mental property or a type of mental event, namely seeing the ocean.[12]

Unlike public signs (which are available as objects to perceiving subjects, in that they, as objects, stand against the subject to be perceived), one's mental states are not public signs. One cannot perceive, or introspect them; one perceives through the intentionality of their representational content what the content is about in the way the content presents it as to be. One could introspect this content, but certainly one cannot introspect the experience as a representational vehicle. That is why "Tye needn't, and shouldn't, claim that one is aware of the representational properties of one's experience as such when one introspects one's experience" (Martin 2002, p. 383).

To put it in slightly different terms: The representational vehicles are not images on some perceptual screen; they are neural states of the brain. The phenomenal contents of our experience are the contents of the patterns of neural activation that arise during perception; that is, they are the neural states and their records that underlie perception. With this statement I am not endorsing any form of reductionism. I am just stating the physical form of the representational vehicle that carries the relevant information. This format is not accessible to conscious introspection, since it is not the way in which information is encoded but only its experiential content that introspection reveals. Although in our brains there are stored perceptual representations that have a nonconceptual content caused by the outside world, it does not follow that these representations are the immediate objects of perception. Perception consists in having representational states with phenomenal content, not in seeing some intermediate mental images of objects (the sense data) on a perceptual screen. In other words, nonconceptual content, which has replaced the traditional sense data, is involved intentionally and not really in experience. It is easy to see that this construal of the phenomenal content of our experience evades the problems that plague the traditional view of "sense data." It also allows the possibility that some aspect of the phenomenal content assumes the form of picture-like image schemes.

6 Object-Files, Nonconceptual Content, and Demonstrative Reference

It is common to perceive an object and then refer to it, on the basis of one's perception, by using a demonstrative such as 'that' or 'this'—for example, to refer to "That mountain over there." The word 'that' or 'this', when used to point to an object currently perceived, is called a *perceptual demonstrative*. How is the referent of a perceptual demonstrative determined, and how can the corresponding thought be about "That mountain"?

Campbell (1997, 2002) has developed an account of demonstrative reference in which spatial attention (that is, attention that focuses on the locations of objects) plays a paramount role in fixing the reference of perceptual demonstratives. For Campbell, spatial information and information about motion are important in allowing one to refer to an object through a perceptual demonstrative. Moreover, Campbell seems to suggest that this information fixes the reference of a demonstrative without adding anything to the demonstrative's content—that is, without providing a description of the referent. Campbell takes the mode of presentation of a demonstrative to include information that could individuate the demonstratum on the basis of its observable features, and specifically on the basis of its spatial location (which, according to a theory posited by Treisman and adopted by Campbell, binds the other features of the object-referent) without providing a description of the demonstratum. For reasons that will become clear later, these two characteristics of Campbell's account, namely the roles of spatial and motion information in fixing the reference of a perceptual demonstrative without providing a description of the referent, are highly desirable. That is why I will start this chapter by presenting that account in some detail. As I will explain later, however, Campbell's account faces some problems that undermine its adequacy as a theory of demonstrative reference. For that reason, I will model my account of demonstrative reference on work on the same subject by Garcia-Carpintero (2000).

According to Campbell (1997, 2002), reference of the most basic kind occurs when one perceives a thing and refers to it, on the basis of one's perception, by using a perceptual demonstrative. Campbell (1997, p. 55) thinks that the problem of referring to objects by means of perceptual demonstratives is the problem of relating concepts to imagistic content: "[T]he idea that there is a distinction between propositional and imagistic content is familiar and compelling. The problem is to explain the relation between the two types of content."

"Imagistic content" is the content involved in imagistic or pictorial representations, which largely preserve the spatial structure of the scene they represent. It is the content of our experience as we consciously access it and use it to see things as being such and such: "looking out of the window, then we may discuss the castle before us, identifying it as 'that castle,' the one we can see." (ibid.) Let us call this kind of consciously accessibly content, be it imagistic, auditory, or whatever, the *experiential* content of our experience. Since this content can be the content of judgments and beliefs, it is clearly a conceptual content.

For Campbell, the reference of a perceptual demonstrative is determined by selective spatial conscious attention, which is the selection of "imagistic" information from a perceived scene that will be used for further processing. It is not determined by the linguistic meaning of a word used in conjunction with the demonstrative, as in "That castle." Campbell's reasoning is simple: To be able to demonstrate, one must select a certain point in one's visual field—the point at which the object of demonstration is located—and pay attention to it. One must also be conscious of that object; otherwise one could not "point" to it. From these requirements, it naturally follows that spatial selective conscious attention is necessarily involved in acts of perceptual demonstratives.

Before I proceed, let me remind the reader of the notion of deictic pointers[1] put forth by Ballard et al. (1997), since this will be of use both in putting Campbell's discussion in a framework and in following the discussion in the present chapter. Eye fixation exemplifies the role of deictic mechanisms, or pointers, as binding devices—i.e., as devices that bind objects in the world to internal representations through deictic reference. Suppose that the eye fixes at some location in a scene at which an object is located and, as a result, the relevant neurons in the fovea compute information from that location. The act of fixation assigns to this object a pointer that allows object individuation and tracking; this is due to the fact that the fixation of the gaze creates a reference to a point in space and time and the properties of the referent can enter computations as a unit.

Fixation and grasping are mechanical external pointing devices, and localization by attention is a neural internal deictic device.

Campbell's (1997, p. 69) main theme is that the "ability to perceive spatial relations between perceived items is needed for reference to spatiotemporal objects," and that selective attention is the notion needed to describe the relation between imagistic and propositional content, since selective attention fixes the reference of terms figuring in propositional content.

Campbell starts with a promising move. Unlike Davidson (1984) or Stalnaker (1984), for whom representational relations should be analyzed at the level of relations between propositional content of whole sentences and states of affairs in the world, Campbell takes the view that the appropriate level for the analysis of representation is that of the relations between represented objects and properties and the "signs" that purport to represent them (i.e., the atomic constituents of the sentences that express linguistically the representation of states of affairs).

However, Campbell's account faces two problems. I will foreshadow them here and discuss them in detail later.

First, the use of conscious attention and the use of concept-involving consciously accessible experiential "imagistic content" for an account of the reference of demonstrative thoughts are problematic, since both propositional content and experiential content are conceptual representations, and the issue of reference is a matter of relating conceptual representations to the world, not of relating conceptual representations to one another (the grounding problem). To break the circle of representations, one needs a way to fix the reference of perceptual demonstratives without using descriptions, since the latter involve concept terms.

The second problem is about Campbell's reliance on FIT. Campbell's theory assumes that objects are reconstructed in vision by binding together features found at the same location; object individuation presupposes encoding of features. However, as we saw in chapter 3, conscious attention and feature detection may not be indispensable for object individuation; that is, picking out objects in a visual scene or parsing the scene occurs to a significant extent in a pre-attentive parallel stage of visual processing. This may occur at an earlier stage without feature encoding, by means of the mechanisms of object-centered segmentation that index objects and attach mental particulars to things (Pylyshyn 2003, 2007).

To eschew Campbell's first problem, one should analyze the role of some causal interactions in relating the semantic content of demonstrative concepts (such as "That round shape") to the world in a way that, at a last analysis, does not rely on the possession of concepts. This presupposes that before one attempts to ground demonstrative concepts in the world, one should first solve the problem of the reference of perceptual demonstratives in a nonconceptual way. That is, one should provide an account of the way deictic acts refer to objects in the environment in a nonconceptual way. For if one seeks to address the grounding problem, one must first find a level at which we touch the world without any conceptual involvement on our part. Perceptions are not of objects in virtue of relating imagistic to propositional content, both of which depict or encode (meaning conceptually represent) the objects. The intentional relation between perception and events in the world (that is, the of-relation between perceptual mental states and events) should be sought at the level of the direct causal relation between perception and the world.[2] To paraphrase Harnad (1990): The problem is to show how is symbol meaning to be grounded in something other than just more meaningless symbols.

The above remarks are important in view of the attempt to explain reference by relating the symbols that represent in one language to entities in another language, in the manner of model-theoretic semantics. To escape the problems related to the interpretation of the non-Euclidean geometries, David Hilbert sought to relegate matters of meaning outside mathematics to metamathematics. In his formalistic program, mathematics is the study of meaningless symbols, and mathematical proofs are sequences of strings of uninterpreted symbols that receive interpretation in metamathematics. The study of the interpretation of symbols lies outside formal mathematics, in model-theoretic semantics. Model-theoretic semantics assigns meanings to abstract symbols of a formal system by mapping these symbols into elements of a model structure. A model is a structure that consists of a set of entities, sets of n-tuples of entities, and ordered pairs. The symbols in the formal language are mapped into entities in the model structure, the predicates into subsets of the set of entities in the model, and the relations into ordered pairs of entities in the model. Thus, the symbols get interpreted. The models are meaningless, since they have only set-theoretical structure.

Putnam (1980) showed that any model-theoretic semantics is inconsistent, insofar as truth (satisfaction of a sentence in a model) underdetermines reference. A sentence may remain true in a model even though the references of its terms change. Putnam's argument relies on the Lowenheim-Skolem theorem, which tells us that there is no unique interpretation for a formal set of sentences that can be singled out—i.e., our sentences are satisfied by non-intended models. Since the symbols acquire their meaning by referring to entities in a model, the underdetermination of reference undermines the whole enterprise of assigning unique meanings to symbols.

The problem one faces, therefore, is how to account for the meaningfulness of the representations in a language, if the model-theoretic semantics approach fails. Putnam (1980, p. 442) and Dennett (1987, pp. 144–147, 154) suggest an answer to this problem by identifying the source of the problem, which is none other than the fact that we conceive a language as something whose use is completely specified and yet still lacks something, namely its interpretation. Once one starts with this assumption, then one "can only have crazy solutions." (Putnam 1980, p. 442) The only way out is to assume that some kind of interpretation of the symbols exists from the beginning, an interpretation that grounds the representational system. This interpretation can only be the product of some causal chains that ground the symbol directly in the world.

There is another, more general, problem associated with the approach of model-theoretical semantics, which problem is shared by all theories that seek to explain the formation of concepts in terms of a correlation between representations and represented entities. This is the problem faced by encodingist theories (Bickhard 1993, 1998, 2000). Encodingist models assume that all representations (or concepts, or symbols) are connected with the represented entities via some kind of correspondence. These models may be valid and useful when both ends of the encoding relation and the correspondence are already known. If not, encodingist models suffer from "the symbol grounding problem" or "the infinite regress problem." To explain how a given conceptual representation (symbol) X acquires its meaning, one must invoke a Y representation which is already known; then, to explain the Y representation, one must invoke Z; and this goes on *ad infinitum*. The only way to escape the infinite regress is for the process of explanation of the meaning of a symbol to be terminated in something that is not a conceptual representation At the same time, this nonconceptual representation should be structured in such a way that it could be to some extent conceptually articulated.

I claim that the level of the nonconceptual representation that grounds symbols is to be found in our singling out objects and some of their features in a visual scene. Thus, the philosophical problem I address in this chapter is the fixing of reference of perceptual demonstratives whose intended referents are objects in the environment. My aim is to show how one can single out and refer to objects and some of their perceivable features in a nonconceptual way. (In linguistic terms, the issue here is to show

how one can fix the reference of a perceptual demonstrative in a noncon-ceptual nondescriptive way.)

Such an account would explain how one could be in a demonstrative mental or perceptual state with respect to objects about which one does not possess any concepts that would conceptualize either them or their properties. This happens when one views an object with properties whose concepts one lacks, or properties whose conceptualization is not possible (the specific hue of a color, the pitch of a sound, a strange shape, and so forth), and is asked to point to what one is looking at, and one points to the object and says "That." This would also solve the problem of how nonlinguistic animals refer to objects in their environment through a per-ceptual demonstrative. Recall that perceptual demonstratives do not neces-sarily involve pointing to an object; when one fixes one's gaze at a certain point, this is a perceptual demonstrative. It would also explain the way infants, who do not possess concepts, employ perceptual demonstratives to refer to objects in their environment.

To that end, I need to show that reference to objects and some of their properties emerges in conceptually unmediated purely causal ways from our viewing a scene, and that this referring induces in us perceptual states with nonconceptual content. Visual conceptual content is subsequently built upon this nonconceptual content by means of the mechanisms of observation or high vision. In that sense perceptual concepts are grounded in the world.

When I examine demonstratives, I do not mean to examine the linguis-tic expressions of the form "That X" (or, as Kaplan (1989) put it, "dthat + [demonstration]"); I mean to examine the mental perceptual state that could be linguistically articulated by such demonstrative expressions. Such a mental conscious "demonstrative" state occurs when some object is picked up in a visual scene and indexed; one is in an internal mental state whose content is somehow causally related to the object and its features. If asked "What are you looking at?" one could have replied "That X" point-ing to the object or feature. What is important is that a demonstrative mental state can occur pre-attentionally, when one perceives a visual scene and segregates objects (or, to be correct, proto-objects) from one another and from the background, by individuating and assigning object-files of the kind discussed in chapter 3 to those objects. Notice that to be able to do that, one need not know what X is; one need not be able to identify it or describe it using any concepts whatsoever; one need not even possess the concept "objecthood." This is the reason I examine one's perceptual mental state when one employs a perceptual demonstrative, and not the linguistic expression that could articulate it. The latter, being an utterance, has a conceptual structure; it contains the concepts articulating the terms involved in the description accompanying the "dthat" and it also presupposes the concept of objecthood—that is, the knowledge that it is an object that one is attending to. But, as I explained in chapters 4 and 5, one can be in contentful mental states about objects without possessing any concepts whatsoever.

Here is another way to make this point, which I borrow from Smith (2002, p. 92): Suppose one perceives a red object, one possesses the concept "red," and one utters the perceptual judgment "That is red." When one perceives the red object, the natural analogue in the perceptual mental act of the word 'that', which occurs in the linguistic expression of the demonstrative, is the occurrence of the perception itself that constitutes a demonstrative reference to the world. Thus, the perception of red has the cognitive force of "That is red." As I shall say in section 6.2, this means that perception eventually allows one to make a *de re* judgment about the world. It is exactly this "natural analogue" that I purport to examine here and which I have called "the mental act of perceptual demonstration." Henceforth, I will call perceptions viewed from that perspective "mental perceptual demonstratives." In a similar vein, Perry (2001, p. 130) distinguishes between demonstratives as used in perception and linguistic indexicals. According to Perry, the analogue in perception of the linguistic indexicality is the operation of "buffers" that collect information about things that one perceives. (I will elaborate on Perry's notion of "buffer" and on its relation to the notion of "object-files" that I use here.)

I argue that some causal chains that relate the world with mental acts of perceptual demonstration single out the demonstrata and attach mental particulars to things. Recast in a linguistic context, my claim amounts to asserting that these causal chains fix the reference of the perceptual demonstratives. The causal relation is provided by the nonconceptual content of perceptual states that is retrieved in bottom-up ways from a visual scene by means of the object-centered segmentation perceptual mechanism that I discussed in detail in chapters 1 and 3. The objects that are singled out (or individuated) as the demonstrata of perceptual demonstratives are not, initially, the objects as we experience them; they are invested only with properties that are retrieved bottom-up, which Pylyshyn (2003) calls "transducable" properties. The causal chains typically start with a perceptual encounter with an object—a kind of "grounding" (Devitt 1996, p. 164)—that grounds the demonstrative in the world. Thus, I emphasize that there is a level of object individuation that does not encode features and does not presuppose concepts, and that, consequently, the process of object individuation precedes object identification.

The chapter consists of two sections. Section 6.1 is divided into two subsections. In the first, I rely on the theory I expounded in chapters 1–3 and refresh the discussion on the object-files and the ways they are opened and maintained. According to that theory, there are perceptual mechanisms that retrieve information from a visual scene in purely bottom-up ways, that is, in conceptually unmediated ways. Perceptual mechanisms open, mainly on the basis of spatio-temporal information that is retrieved bottom-up from a scene, a dossier or object-file for objects, which initially individuates and indexes a featureless object and allows its tracking; in other words, perceptual mechanisms assign to the object its objecthood and its persistence in space and time. This file is then filled with information that is retrieved from a scene in conceptually unmediated ways. In the second subsection, I explore the problem of demonstrative reference and present a view of reference to show that the senses of demonstratives, which consist in the information retrieved from a visual scene in conceptually unmediated ways, individuate the demonstrata in purely causal ways. To that end I employ Garcia-Carpintero's (2000) and Devitt's (1996) theory of demonstratives. I claim that reference is fixed by opening a dossier or object-file for the referent of the demonstrative. As expected, the object-file is allocated to objects and maintained entirely on the basis of the nonconceptual content of perception. Once the opening of an object-file has picked up the referent, information can be predicated to the object by being added to the object-file. Since this information is being assigned to the object-file of that object, the information is about that object. As the discussion will reveal, spatial representation plays an important role at this level, and in that sense Campbell is right that the representation of space constitutes the solid ground on which conceptual content is subsequently erected. However, this is not because of the role of spatial attention, but because spatial information plays an important role in pre-attentional object individuation and in the formation of the "weak kind of representation," namely the nonconceptual representation of "objecthood" that is acquired through the object-based segmentation processes of perception and which allows access to objects for further investigation without initially encoding any featural information and without even presupposing the concept of "object." In section 6.2, I contrast my account with some other theories of reference of perceptual demonstratives, especially Campbell's (2002) and Haugeland's (1998). Then I relate it to Putnam's (1975, 1981, 1983,

1991) and Kripke's (1980) "causal theory of reference." Finally, I suggest ways in which the account offered here may overcome some problems that have traditionally plagued the notion of causal reference. My main thesis is that the conceptually unmediated causal connection between the nonconceptual content of the object-files and the world provides a conception of causal chains that might help overcome some of the problems associated with causal accounts of reference of perceptual demonstratives.

My overall strategy in this chapter is as follows: The argument supporting my main thesis rests on empirical evidence supporting both the retrieval of bottom-up information in early vision and suggesting that the initial object-files that are used for object individuation do not encode features. Object-files are used to individuate and not identify the object. Thus, an object-file does not represent object conceptually or descriptively. This evidence was discussed in part I of the book. (b) the epistemological requirement that the reference to object tokens take place at a nonconceptual, nondescriptive level.

By means of (b) I establish the epistemological necessity of the initial object-file having exclusively nonconceptual content and by means of (a) I substantiate the existence of such a file and the existence of perceptual mechanisms that implement it.

6.1   A Theory of Reference of Perceptual Demonstratives

6.1.1   Nonconceptual Object Individuation

Despite its shortcomings, Campbell's (2002) theory of demonstrative reference includes an important insight, namely the role that spatial and motion information about the object that is intended as the demonstratum of a perceptual demonstrative plays in providing a nondescriptive mode of presentation of the demonstratum, which fixes the reference of the demonstrative. Thus, I start by discussing Campbell's theory in some detail. I aim to foreshadow its shortcomings and to propose a way the theory could be amended so that one could come up with a theory that retains Campbell's insight while avoiding its problems.

Campbell (1997, 2002) proposes a theory of reference of perceptual demonstratives that purports to be nondescriptive. Campbell thinks that the problem of the sense of a perceptual demonstrative is a problem about selective attention, given that he considers the mode of presentation to provide imagistic information related to the demonstratum. It is the role of selective spatial attention to isolate that information in a scene that pertains to the demonstratum. Campbell uses Treisman's (1993) theory of selective attention, or Feature Integration Theory (FIT), according to which, in vision, information from different feature maps is bound together by extracting the location encoded implicitly in any feature information. Spatial attention makes the implicit location explicit. Information localized at the same location is bound together and thought to pertain to a certain object that occupies that space. Campbell takes the mode of presentation of a demonstrative to include information that could individuate the demonstratum on the basis of its observable features, specifically on the basis of its spatial location. As his example of a tree viewed from different windows by two subjects that refer to the same tree using two different perceptual demonstratives reveals, on certain occasions difference of locations in which the subjects are situated alone suffices to establish difference in the mode of presentation of the same object by two different demonstratives (Campbell 1997, p. 61).

Campbell (2002) argues that demonstrative reference takes place through conscious selective spatial attention that picks out objects' features, forms feature maps, and integrates those features that are found at the same location into forming objects in the way FIT claims. This is essential to Campbell's account because it renders conscious spatial attention indispensable to object construction and thus indispensable for the individuation of objects. Campbell holds that feature integration is necessary for object individuation, and thus that encoding of features precedes object individuation. Furthermore, he thinks that consciousness is required if one is to be able to perceptually demonstrate an object, since one needs to be conscious of the presence of the object one demonstrates. Campbell is wrong on all three accounts.

First, FIT assumes that objects are reconstructed in vision by binding together features found at the same location; object individuation presupposes the encoding of features. However, my exploration in chapters 1 (section 1.1) and 3 (sections 3.1 and 3.3) suggest that attention and feature encoding are not indispensable for object individuation; that is, picking up objects in a visual scene or parsing the scene occurs to a significant extent in a pre-attentive parallel stage of visual processing. Thus, object individuation occurs at an earlier stage, without feature encoding, by means of the mechanisms of object-centered segmentation that index objects and attach mental particulars to things (Pylyshyn 2003, p. xiv). Thus, attention is not necessary to object individuation. This amounts to the claim that object-files can be opened and maintained before any attentional effects modulate perceptual processing.

Second, Campbell's assumption that object individuation presupposes that object features have been encoded (which for Campbell means that the subject identifies and recognizes object features and thus exercises sortal concepts) implies that the application of sortals precedes object individuation. This view, apart from reintroducing the grounding problem that Campbell attempts to solve, is simply wrong. The evidence adduced in part I of the present book, and especially in chapter 3, shows that object individuation through the opening of object-files precedes feature and object identification. Even when features are used to individuate objects (in cases in which the spatio-temporal information does not suffice to parse effectively a scene), these features are not encoded; the subject does not recognize or identify them as such, and thus she does not apply any sortals; she uses featural information to individuate the objects in a scene.

Third, Campbell construes "consciousness" to mean that when one is conscious of an object one applies sortals to it and can identify at least some of its properties, although not necessarily the object itself. In other words, Campbell uses "consciousness" as synonymous to what is called "access or report consciousness" (Block 2005; Lamme 2003). Recall that access consciousness presupposes attention, which is exactly what Campbell requires of perceptual demonstratives. One might hypothesize that it is his construal of consciousness as access consciousness that has led him to claim that sortals are necessarily involved in perceptual demonstration despite his claim that no descriptions are involved in perceptual demonstration. But we have seen that involving sortals in fixing the reference of perceptual demonstratives (apart from the problem that the use of sortals in reference fixing commits one to descriptivism, insofar as the sortals could be used to describe the object and one could demand that the referent of the demonstrative is the object that satisfies that description or, alternatively, the object that has such and such properties) undermines the attempt to ground them directly in the world and also renders problematic the idea that infants or animals that do not exercise concepts may demonstratively refer to objects in their environment.

Campbell's demand that one should be conscious of the object of demonstration in order to be able to demonstratively refer to that object is problematic for two reasons. First, one may refer to or single out objects in the environment for the purpose of action, which is one of the functions of perceptual demonstration, without being aware that one does so, since, as the reader recalls from the discussion in chapter 3, the coordination of vision with action takes place primarily in the dorsal system, whose processes are mainly outside the realm of awareness. In addition, the studies on blindsight (or implicit perception in general) that I reviewed in chapter 1 suggest that one can register information, which may prime behavior in the appropriate context, from objects in a scene of which one is not aware. Second, even if one insists that consciousness is required in perceptual demonstratives, insofar as a demonstration is a mental act that presupposes that the perceiver be aware that she is perceiving the demonstratum, one needs a notion of consciousness that does not require concepts. Though this kind of consciousness cannot be the access awareness that Campbell envisages, phenomenal awareness could well play this role. First, phenomenal awareness is a kind of awareness; second, it does not involve concepts, only nonconceptual phenomenal content.

In view of all these shortcomings[, Campbell's attempt to found the reference of demonstratives on spatial attention through FIT seems to be in trouble. The findings I discussed in chapters 1 and 3 suggest the following: First, spatial attention is not necessary for object individuation. Second, the main burden of parsing a scene and selecting discrete objects seems to be falling on the object-centered pre-attentional segmentation processes, which provides the basis for the perception of objecthood. Third, feature integration is not necessary for the perception of objects as discrete entities—that is, for object individuation. Objects in a scene are singled out before any feature encodings take place. Fourth, even if one assumes that consciousness of the demonstrated object is presupposed by all acts of perceptual demonstration, this consciousness is not the "report or access consciousness" that Campbell has in mind, but "phenomenal awareness." To help Campbell escape from these problems while retaining his useful insights, it suffices to show that object identification is not necessary for fixing the reference of perceptual demonstratives, and that object individuation is enough to single out the demonstrata of perceptual demonstratives. So, I will discuss here the notion of object-files as important factors in establishing the existence of a nonconceptual object individuation. (In the next subsection, I will explore a theory of reference that shows how object individuation determines the reference of perceptual demonstratives.)

Let me briefly refresh the notion of "object-files," drawing from the discussion in chapter 3. Object-centered segmentation processing individuates objects in a visual scene and creates object-files for the discrete objects it parses in a scene. The object-files index objects as discrete persisting entities. Recall that the object-centered segmentation processes are mainly pre-attentional. Although (as we saw in chapter 1) object segmentation takes place at many levels and may involve semantic information relying on top-down flow of information, the visual system performs in a first pass an initial or provisional object segmentation of a scene, before attentional bottlenecks occur. The objects segmented by these pre-attentional processes should, thus, be construed as proto-objects rather than as objects. From now on, for reasons of simplicity, I will use the word 'objects' to refer to *proto-objects*, but the reader should bear in mind that in all pre-attentional processes, such as the object-centered segmentation processes the individuate objects in a scene, the objects involved are the proto-objects that I discussed in chapter 1. Though features (e.g., color and shape) that can be retrieved by early vision in a bottom-up way may be used for parsing a scene and allocating object-files, the object-files are allocated and maintained primarily on the basis of spatio-temporal information, to wit, temporal synchrony or continuity and proximity, which in turn is based on information pertaining to location, relative position and perhaps motion. Individuated objects can be parsed and tracked without being identified, and even when an object is mis-identified and then correctly recognized it is all the time deemed to be one and the same object (Scholl 2001).

Studies reviewed in chapter 3 confirm that featural information is also used to individuate objects when the scene is complex enough, and that feature individuation (i.e., the perception of features as distinct properties of objects without the exercise or possession of concepts) precedes feature identification (i.e., the application of sortals that conceptualize these features). To the extent that spatio-temporal information is retrieved from a scene faster than any other featural information, object individuation precedes representations that support awareness of all other features. Recall from chapter 3 than 10-month-old infants use spatio-temporal information to individuate objects but do not use featural information, such as shape or color, to individuate objects, whereas 12-month-old infants do. This may mean either that featural information is not available at that early age and becomes available later (which if true would mean that 10-month-old infants are feature blind, and this is wrong) or, more probably, that although such featural information may be available for other purposes, it is not used to individuate objects except when spatio-temporal information fails to do so. In either case, it is clear (a) that spatio-temporal information retrieved directly from a visual scene precedes and overrides other featural information also retrieved directly from the scene and (b) that both kinds of information are used first to individuate objects and then to identify objects as being such and such. This goes against the view that feature perception requires the application of sortals, or, equivalently, the view that any perception inherently involves the exercise of concepts. Campbell (2002, pp. 68–74) calls this view "the Delineation Thesis"; Smith (2002, p. 94) calls it "Conceptualism."

The information on which individuation is based does not play the role of the binding parameter that binds the features observed at one location, as spatial information does in Campbell's account, but it ensures that a single object is being individuated. In other words, it provides the object that will eventually carry the features observed at one location rather than binding first the features that are found in one location to form the object (as in FIT, on which Campbell relies). Once an object has been individuated, it becomes the carrier of properties. The properties that are first attached to objects are those retrieved bottom-up from the visual scene.

Object individuation and the retrieval of some of the object features (the transducable features) take place in a nonconceptual manner, which means that this information is retrieved bottom-up by the mechanisms of vision from visual scenes. The mechanisms of vision that process this information induce perceptual states whose nonconceptual content is information about the existence of an individuated persisting object and its shape, size, surface properties, orientation, motion, affordances, and color.

The processes involved in indexing or individuating an object and in retrieving its spatio-temporal features are not cognitively accessible in any form. One does not "know" or "believe" that an object moves in continuous paths, that it persists in time, or that it is rigid, though one uses this information to index and follow the object. Their function relies on certain operational constraints whose role was discussed in chapter 3. Object individuation may eventually result in the belief that an object is here or there, or that two objects must be behind a screen, but this individuation does not appeal to principles regarding objects stored in some knowledge-basis that are used as premises in inferences. These principles, rather, constitute the *modus operandi* of the cognizer, without been represented in an accessible form of "knowledge."

The perception of "objecthood" relies on spatio-temporal information and, should this be not enough, on further featural information (shape, color, orientation, size, and so forth), which allow tracking of the spatio-temporal history of the object and thus render its individuation possible, but this information is not encoded, that is, stored in memory and conceptually represented.[3] Weak representation of objects as discrete entities that persist in time (that is, representations based on spatio-temporal information) precedes representation of the same objects based on featural information retrieved bottom-up from a scene. Both forms of representation allow object individuation, and both precede representations based on semantic information that allow object identification. Thus, weak representations allow access to the object for further investigation, but they do not encode any of its properties. The object is indexed as an individual rather than as something that exists at a certain location and/or has a certain shape and color, although this information is perceived and has been used to allocate the object-file to that object. These properties are not used in the designation of the object *qua object*. That is why the object's features may change while the object is still perceived as being the same object whose features change. This needs some explication.

In perception, upon viewing a scene, certain information is retrieved bottom-up from the scene before attention has been allocated and concepts start modulating visual processing. This information, as the reader might recall from chapter 1, individuates the object as a persisting separate entity and leads to the formation of the proto-objects, which have an unstable short-lived existence, in the sense that they are rapidly erased by new incoming information. Suppose that one perceives an object with such and such features, which undergoes some featural changes. In both cases, before and after the featural change, none of the features are encoded, although they are perceived (the subject may even be phenomenally aware of them). Instead, spatio-temporal information is used primarily to individuate the objects in the scene; if the object satisfies certain principles of spatial and temporal continuity before and after the change, it is perceived to be the same object, featural changes notwithstanding. In other words, although proto-objects have an unstable existence, the proto-object *qua object* that carries certain features is perceived as persisting in space and time and undergoing change for so long as no new information enters the retina to erase the existing pre-attentional object-files and provided that certain spatio-temporal conditions are met. Thus, in perception, it is not the binding of features that constructs the object, as in FIT; rather, the proto-object, as a persisting individual that can carry features, is constructed first.

I have used the verb 'construct' in referring to the object-centered segmentation processes that open object-files for, and allocate object-files to, the objects parsed in a scene. I have done so in order to emphasize that these processes construct the weak representation of an object. In other words, the object-file of an object is a weak representation of that object. In this kind of representation, there is no conceptual information involved (information about fragility, temperature, weight, usage, functions, etc.), and that is why it constitutes a weaker sense of representation.

The object-file thus construed does not require the existence of concepts associated with that object, insofar as the relevant information is retrieved from a scene bottom-up. That is, the spatio-temporal and featural information involved in indexing an object is not conceptualized, since it is retrievable from a scene in a bottom-up manner.

Peacocke (2001, p. 241) argues that the nonconceptual content of experience represents things, events, or places and times in a certain way, as having certain properties or standing in certain relations, "also given in a certain way." Peacocke (ibid., p. 257) distinguishes between ways that help to determine which object is perceived and ways that do not. The determination of what object is perceived amounts to the individuation of an object and its indexing, which may be the product of the object-centered segmentation processes discussed in part I of the book. The other ways refer to the ways features (say, shapes and colors) are perceived. In this subsection, I have argued both for the existence of bottom-up object-tracking mechanisms that construct weak representations of objects in a scene (and thus allow us to determine which objects are perceived) and for the retrieval from a scene of bottom-up information that determines the way shapes and some other observable properties are perceived.

6.1.2 A Causal Account of Fixing Demonstrative Reference through Object Individuation

I have said that I am interested in the way mental states of perceptual demonstration are related to the world. In Ballard's (1999) terminology, I am interested in how "deictic reference" works. "Mental" demonstratives involve two factors. First, there is an object that is intended as the demonstratum of the demonstrative. Second, there are the features of that object, as the viewer perceives them. Consequently, there are several problems concerning the way such a state is related to the world. How is the object that is being attended to singled out in a visual scene? How does the shape that one perceives when one sees an object, even though one may not possess the relevant concept, is an objective property of an object in the world, as opposed to a mental construction that does not present a feature of the object? Finally, what is the role of the objects' features, if any, in singling out the object attended to? I have already sketched the framework in which these questions will be dealt with, so let me now elaborate.

To address these problems, I model the examination of this issue upon discussions concerning the way the expression "That $[\ldots X \ldots]$," as it occurs in a judgment based on the perception of an object X, refers to the object. The reason is twofold: First, the problem of singling out the object in a mental perceptual demonstrative is, in some respects, parallel to that of fixing the referent in the linguistic articulation of the perceptual demonstrative. Second, the issues involved in the linguistic domain, namely issues pertaining to the content of the demonstrative and its mode of presentation, are relevant to the problems of sense and reference of demonstratives as they pertain to mental demonstratives.

When one perceives a round object, points toward it, and utters "That shape is round," then the perceptual demonstrative 'that' exemplifies the most linguistically direct way of referring to something in the world. My account draws on Evans's (1982) work on "demonstrative reference" of experiential concepts. According to Evans, these concepts refer through the use of perceptual demonstratives. The experiential concept F refers through use of the experiential demonstrative "That object is F" while pointing to an object that is F. An experiential concept is a concept *of* a particular object X or of one of its features if one's attitudes toward contents containing that concept are sensitive in an appropriate way to perceptual information about X. Evans claims that this perceptual information cannot be conceptual; if it were, it could not explain how an experiential concept is related to the world.

As Heck argues (2000), if that information were conceptually articulated (that is, if it had the conceptual articulation "That object is F"), one would attempt to explain a concept by reference to other concepts, and that would initiate a vicious circle. Although some concepts are being understood by means of other concepts, say by falling under a certain description involving other concepts, this process must bottom out at some point, lest the relation of our conceptual apparatus with the world be severed. Demonstrative reference is supposed to intervene exactly at this level to break the circle of representations and allow us to "touch" the world. Thus, the information involved in establishing this reference must not involve any concepts; hence, if the vicious circle is to be broken, it must not be a description.

I claim that the information involved must be that contained in purely causal chains that relate us with the world. I agree that, although there is nothing conceptual in these causal interactions, they can ground semantic content by fixing the reference of the concept terms. Thus, when one individuates an object with a certain shape in a scene, or sees a certain shape and says "That" by pointing to the shape, the reference of the demonstrative concept that articulates the shape involved is fixed in a nondescriptive way by means of the causal chains implemented in the mechanisms of vision. The last remark makes it possible that the same way of fixing reference is involved when one sees (in the phenomenal sense) a round object without possessing or exercising the concepts "round," "objecthood," and "shape," and when if asked "What do you see?" one points to the round object in the environment.

In fact, as will become clear from the discussion that follows, the act itself of pointing to the object (either with a hand, with one's head, or with one's eyes) is the motor analogue of the individuation of the object in perception, in that its execution relies on exactly the same information that individuates the object in the first place, and on certain occasions, when objects move, it is the process that fixes the referent. Recall that opening and allocating object-files allows one to individuate and track objects in a scene. Tracking involves following the motion of the tracked object with the eyes, which is an act of "pointing." In that sense, the act of pointing is the fixer of the referent of the demonstrative, in that it is that act that ensures that the same objects is being tracked.

Back to demonstratives now. The reference of demonstratives as used in written texts depends on the context in which they occur and on the grammatical relations between its terms. The reference of perceptual demonstratives in utterances is determined by an external context, i.e., by the relations between the token demonstrative and the state of affairs of the world, including the producer or the token. It also depends on a "lexical" convention that determines the way the type of the demonstrative can be used in language. Thus, a token of the type 'I' conventionally refers to the speaker, a token of 'that' refers to an object "pointed to" by the speaker, and so forth.[4] This convention purports to capture that part of the meaning of a term that does not vary from occasion to occasion.

There are two very influential accounts of demonstratives. The first is the standard Fregean analysis of demonstratives, which treats them like any other expression, assuming that their tokens have a reference by virtue of their sense, i.e. "the way in which the reference is given," their "mode of presentation." As Sellars (1963) would put it, a perceptual experience one has when one uses a perceptual demonstrative to refer to some object is of a certain object if the subject has a perceptual belief that correctly represents and thus describes at least some of the object's properties. The description fixes the reference of the demonstrative in the sense that the object that fits that description, as it is specified in the perceptual belief, is the referent of the demonstrative. The standard problem of this account is that if one takes demonstratives to function like definite descriptions (as Katz (1994) does), then demonstratives cannot be rigid designators—but Kripke (1980) has given us very good reasons to think they are.[5] Another problem of the descriptive theories of reference is that such descriptions involve concepts. However, as I noted a few paragraphs back, this is undesirable when one attempts to show how the reference of perceptual demonstratives is grounded in the world. Though I will examine the shortcomings of the descriptive theories of reference in detail in section 6.2, I think it is clear now that I do not agree with Frege that the reference of demonstratives is determined by a descriptive sense. Rather, I argue that the reference of demonstratives is determined by causal chains that ground them in the world, as argued by Devitt (1996), Kripke (1980), and Putnam (1975, 1991). I go further, though, to elaborate on the nature of information contained in the causal chains, and to explain how these causal chains are established through our perceptual mechanisms.

Even though I think that demonstratives are not definite descriptions, I agree with Garcia-Carpintero (2000) and Devitt (1996) that the difference between definite descriptions and demonstratives does not discredit the role of the senses or modes of presentation of the demonstratum of demonstratives in determining their content. The content of a perceptual demonstrative is both its reference and its sense, although the sense is not the Fregean mode of presentation in thought but the mode of presentation in perception. Meanings notoriously are not in the head, and, paraphrasing Wittgenstein in his *Philosophical Investigations* (1958), one could say that the mind is not the appropriate place for God to look when he tries to find out which object is referred to when one uses a demonstrative. I will not argue for this view in any detail, however, because it is not crucial to the main argument developed in this chapter, namely that reference construed as object individuation can be fixed by means of bottom-up perceptual processes that involve nonconceptual content. What is important to this argument is the existence of such bottom-up processes that assign the referent to the demonstrative, and this claim is independent of whether the referent is part of the meaning of demonstratives. The argument essentially involves the "mode of presentation" of the demonstratum of a perceptual demonstrative in individuating objects in conceptually unmediated nondescriptive ways.

Thus, my thesis goes against a second important construal of demonstratives. This is the direct-reference theory, according to which the only content of a demonstrative is its denotation—in other words, the only linguistic function of a demonstrative is that it refers to its demonstratum (Kaplan 1989; Salmon 1981). Paraphrasing Kaplan's (1989) account of the theory, one could say that a demonstrative does not describe its referent as possessing any identifying properties, it only refers to it. Although I agree that perceptual mental demonstratives do not describe their referent as possessing identifying properties, direct-reference theorists and I part company when the issue is the ways of determining the content of the demonstratives and, hence, the ways of determining the referents. What I have said thus far entails that the mode of presentation of the demonstrative in perception—the perceptual nonconceptual analogue of what Recanati (1997) calls the psychological mode of presentation—is essentially what determines the referent of the demonstrative, albeit in a nondescriptive manner. This is nicely put by Campbell.

Campbell insists that spatial and motion information about an object constitute its mode of presentation in a perceptual demonstrative and that this mode or sense fixes the reference of the demonstrative by drawing attention to the object. He also insists that one should not associate the sense of the demonstrative with a description of the object's features and location. The role of location consists in providing the binding parameter for singling out objects and not for providing some sort of descriptive identification of the object. Location organizes the information-processing procedures that process information about that object. It is in this sense that "the description completes the character of the associated occurrences of 'dthat' but makes no contribution to content. It determines and directs attention to what is being said. . . . The semantic role of the description is pre-propositional; it induces no complex, descriptive elements to content." (Campbell 2002, p. 107)

I have already noted my misgivings about Campbell's attempt to determine the reference of demonstratives. I prefer to model my account of demonstrative reference on Garcia-Carpintero's (2000) descriptive account, modifying it to suit the fact that I do not wish to examine the way the linguistic expressions of demonstratives refer; instead, I am interested in the way mental acts of perceptual demonstration might refer to objects in nondescriptive and purely causal ways, without possession or exercise of any concepts whatsoever (retaining this way Campbell's useful insights). Garcia-Carpintero (ibid.) and Devitt (1996) offer a thorough account of the senses of demonstratives. They claim that indexicals establish their reference by means of their denotation and of their senses. The latter, according to Carpintero, are ingredients of "presuppositions of acquaintance" with the demonstratum, by which Garcia-Carpintero means "propositions that are taken for granted" when a statement is uttered.

Suppose one sees something as being a house and utters the statement "That is F" while pointing at a certain object (the house) and assigning it the property F (being mine). 'That' is a singular word associated with the description "the F object." According to Garcia-Carpintero (2000), when one uses the singular word 'that' one takes oneself to be acquainted with an object by having a dossier for "the F object," which picks it out. The truth condition of the term is the object itself. The presupposition in our case is the proposition "There is a unique object most salient when the token t of 'that' is produced and t refers to that object." Now, the proposition "most salient when t occurs" is equivalent to the expression "object in such and such a location with such and such visual features." "In such and such a place with such and such visual features" is the mode of presentation of the demonstrative 'that' which individuates the object to which the demonstrative refers. (Notice that the mode of presentation includes spatial information.)

The dossier of the object, by means of which the acquaintance with the object takes place, can be updated by new incoming information. A distinction between an object being singled out as the demonstratum of a demonstrative and its dossier should be noted. The latter ontologically presupposes the former; one needs an object to create its dossier. (I do not discuss fictional, illusional, and abstract objects.) One also needs to ensure that the object with such and such features at time t_1 is the same object with such and such features at time t_2.

In Garcia-Carpintero's account, the dossier may contain any kind of information that the user associates with the referent and that helps the user to individuate and/or identify it. Since my project is to show how perceptual demonstratives can single out their demonstrata in nonconceptual ways, I have to modify the term 'dossier' to fit my requirements. It is very important for the success of reference fixing that the whole process be carried out in a purely bottom-up conceptually encapsulated manner. In chapters 1–3, I discussed the mechanisms of perception that retrieve such information from a scene in a bottom-up way and that, on the basis of that information, allocate and maintain an object-file on objects in the scene. Thus, I am going to use 'dossier' so that the contents of the dossier are restricted to information that can be retrieved in a bottom-up and conceptually encapsulated way from a scene and that allows object individuation. The information in the dossier, in the sense of 'dossier' intended here, does not suffice to identify the object as being such and such. However, it suffices to individuate the referent. Since the information contained in the dossier is nonconceptual, the dossier attached to the object does not carry any descriptive information that would identify the referent. The best candidate for the substitution is, of course, the term 'object-file'. Hereafter I will be using 'object-file' to play the same role in fixing the reference of a perceptual demonstrative as does Garcia-Carpintero's 'dossier of an object," except that in my case reference fixing takes place entirely before the application of any sortals whatsoever, whereas Garcia-Carpintero's account involves the conceptual articulation of the properties of the objects involved. To recapitulate the distinction: Whereas Garcia-Carpintero's dossier of an object may carry any sort of information, including semantic and thus conceptual information that is being used to describe and thereby determine the referent, the object-file that I use carries only information that is being retrieved from a scene in a bottom-up way. This information individuates or indexes the object that is the referent of the demonstrative. My claim is that this individuation suffices to fix the referent of the perceptual demonstrative. As a result, although I agree with the direct theories of reference that demonstratives do not provide identifying descriptions of their referent, I argue that demonstratives allow the individuation of the referent as a singular persisting object by means of object-centered segmentation processes that provide the causal chains that ground the demonstrative, and that the information which these processes process constitutes the sense or mode of presentation of the demonstrative. More specifically, these processes use spatio-temporal information, and perhaps other transducable information, that constitutes the nonconceptual content of the mental states induced by these processes. The nonconceptual content of these states is the mode of presentation of a perceptual demonstrative. As such, it is causal and not descriptive. It is not descriptive in that it does not involve concepts that would describe the content. It is causal in that the information involved, being retrieved directly from the environment, precludes the conceptual framework of the perceiver from intervening between the world and her, thus allowing direct and purely causal contact with the world. In this sense, modes of presentation play a decisive role in fixing the referents of demonstratives. So, this is how senses individuate the demonstratum, and thus, acquaint one (in the Russellian sense) with it.

Being acquainted in perception with an object means that one is in direct (meaning without any conceptual intermediaries) contact with the object itself and that one retrieves information about that very object from the object itself and not through a description that would individuate or identify the object, and thus, by depicting it, refers to it. On that account, perception puts us in a *de re* relationship with the object (as opposed to a descriptivist relationship), and the ensuing perceptual judgments are *de re* judgments; when one forms a *de re* belief, one stands in "appropriate nonconceptual, contextual relations to objects the belief is about" (Burge 1977,

p. 346).[6] Recanati (1997) calls the *de re* relation or relation of acquaintance between the perceiver and the objects in the visual scene that she perceives "a fundamental epistemic relation," borrowing the term from Perry (1992).

Therefore, in perception, the reference of perceptual demonstratives is fixed through the nonconceptual information retrieved directly from the environment that allows one to individuate the objects in a visual scene by assigning to them object-files. Thus, Smith (2002, p. 87) is right to claim that "without doubt, contextual, nonconceptual relations are involved in the perception of any normal object, but such relations help put us in a situation in which we can receive information from the world in a way that is sufficient for acquaintance with objects in it." It is my main thesis in this chapter that this nonconceptual information constitutes the nondescriptive mode of presentation of the demonstratum in perception. Thus, the nonconceptual information (or, to be more precise, the nonconceptual content of the perceptual states) functions as a *de re* mode of presentation of the object in perception. This allows one to be in a position to make *de re* judgments or form *de re* beliefs about the world.

Let me elaborate: Perception individuates objects in a visual scene by assigning them object-files based on spatio-temporal and, occasionally, other featural information. The content of an object-file, which is not encoded and thus it is not descriptive, is the nondescriptive *de re* mode of presentation of the object or demonstratum in perception. Recall that when one perceives an object, the natural analogue in the perceptual act of 'that', which occurs in the linguistic expression of the demonstrative that the perceiver could use to point to that object, is the occurrence of the perception itself. The perception itself constitutes a demonstrative reference to the world and, thus, the perception of the object has the cognitive force of "that object."

The objects of perceptual demonstratives are determined relationally in a sense very similar to that defined by Bach (1987, p. 12), which means that for an object to be an object of a perceptual state it must stand in a certain kind of relation to that same perceptual state. I have said that the nonconceptual content of an object-file is the nondescriptive *de re* mode of presentation of the object or demonstratum in perception. Since object-files index objects and secure reference to them through their content, one could claim that perceptual *de re* modes of presentation function as mental demonstratives. Furthermore, in accordance with Evans (1982), the causal relationship between a visual scene and the content of the object-files the perceptual system assigns to the objects it parses in the scene is such that it allows the perceiver to individuate (Evans uses the word 'discriminate', but in the case of perception 'individuate' is more apt) the objects in perception. Now, the content of an object-file is idiosyncratic to the relationship of the viewer with the visual scene, which means that different viewers may use different information to parse a scene or that the same viewer may use different information to individuate the same objects, depending on the viewer's perspective on the scene. This entails that the *de re* relationship of the perceiver with a visual scene (a relationship that allows her to retrieve information about the scene from the scene itself and not from a description of it) is highly contextual. This, in turn, means that a *de re* perceptual mode of presentation determines reference given or within a certain context. This may be taken as aligning me with Bach (1987) and Recanati (1997) and against Evans (1982) and McDowell (1984, 1986), the latter claiming that senses or modes of presentation determine reference independent of a context, but this aligning is not necessarily true. I would be aligned with Bach and Recanati if I construed modes of presentation as belonging to the narrow content of a perceptual state.[7] However, I do not take this stand. The main reason is that, owing to the relational nature of the content of an object-file (the *de re* mode of presentation of the object in perception), the *de re* sense cannot be construed as the narrow content of the mental perceptual demonstrative, which, augmented with contextual factors, would determine reference. Instead, the contextual *de re* mode of presentation of the demonstrative determines reference. However, one should be careful at this juncture not to interpret "the contextual *de re* mode of presentation of the demonstrative" in the preceding statement to mean that the context is added to the mode of presentation, because that would deny the relational character of the perceptual mode of presentation. The relation between perception or the perceiver and the object of perception is constitutive of the *de re* perception that acquaints the perceiver with the object, since in perception information is directly retrieved from the visual scene and, hence, the objects in the scene and their properties contribute directly to the contents of the perceptual states that, *qua* representational vehicles, represent them.[8] The nature of information used to individuate the objects in a scene and determine that the relevant perceptual demonstratives refer to them may depend on the context in which the perceptual encounter takes place, and therefore, the determination of reference involves context, but the context (that is, the causal link between the visual scene and the viewer) that participates in the reference fixing process is not something external to the mode of presentation but part of it.

The object-file individuates the referent; by opening a dossier fixing the object to which the demonstrative refers, one indexes the object and can track it. In this sense, my theory of reference resembles in some respects that of Pylyshyn's (2001), in which when one speaks of reference, one means that one is able to access the thing being referred to in certain ways. This kind of reference fixing is what Pylyshyn (ibid.) calls "deictic reference." Object individuation and not object identification is indispensable for fixing the referent of a perceptual demonstrative.[9]

The indexing system of perception initially provides access to an object but does not encode or represent its features, although the indexing system uses information (mainly spatio-temporal information) to individuate the object and open an object-file for it. This has two important consequences. First, although spatio-temporal and other featural information is retrieved from the scene and is being used by the perceptual system to individuate objects and assign to them object-files, this information is not retrievable by the perceiver and one is not aware of that information at that stage of visual processing (it is situated at the subpersonal level), and there may be aspects of that information of which one will never be aware. The object-individuating processes are faster than the processes that construct representations of the information used in the individuation of objects. This means that the relevant information is used without the subject being phenomenally aware of it, and, *ipso facto*, that this happens before the information is stored in memory so that it becomes available to access awareness. We saw in chapter 1 that the feedforward sweep that retrieves information from a scene in a purely bottom-up manner precedes the local recurrent processing that is required for phenomenal (and, *ipso facto*, access) awareness. Second, the object-file initially does not encode any information at all. Spatio-temporal information, for example, is used to individuate objects, and this information relies, in turn, on information on the relative positions of objects, locations of objects, and changes in these parameters over time. Object individuation, thus, presupposes that all this information be retrieved from a scene. However, none of this information is encoded in the initial object-file that is being opened for the proto-objects in the visual scene.

Now, I have claimed on several occasions that the information employed to individuate and index objects in a scene is not encoded. Let me explain what I mean by that claim. The object-file indexing an object will eventually represent a host of information about that object, information that will become available to one's awareness and will be stored in memory, but initially the information it includes, including the information used to open the file in the first place, is not stored in visual short-term memory or in long-term memory. Furthermore, the perceiver has no access to that information, and the information is not retrievable. Proto-objects last for a very short period of time for their traces to be consolidated or stored in either VSTM or LTM, although, as we have seen, sensory information used by the perceptual system is stored in sensory visual memory. However, neither is one aware of nor does one have access to the information stored in sensory memory and used in perceptual processing. Thus, when I assert that the information used to open object-files is not encoded, I mean that this information is not stored in a retrievable form, is not conceptualized, and is not content of which one is aware. This precludes this information becoming the content of a description that could be used to fix the reference to the object; hence, it can be used against attempts to defend descriptivism in reference fixing.

Notice that the individuation of objects in a nonconceptual way by the object-centered segmentation processes of perception constitutes a mechanism that allows one to refer to an object even though one misdescribes it by, say, assigning to it the wrong properties, as in the case of an illusion. Nonconceptual object individuation justifies, thus, the intuition that one should be able to say that one sees an object but one formulates the wrong beliefs about it or, in my terminology, that one perceives (that is, sees in the phenomenal sense of the word) a thing but sees (in the epistemic sense of the word) it wrong.

The referent of the demonstrative is not the usual object of one's experience (the house in Garcia-Carpintero's example). The representational content of the perceptual state induced, when one perceives an object and one's perceptual system singles it out from the scene in which the object is embedded and indexes it, is the kind of weak representation that I discussed in the preceding subsection. Recall that the weak representation, being created before attention, is short-lived and unstable. The object that features in it is a proto-object. However, once the object-file indexes the object and allows reference to it, by ensuring that the object with such and such features at time t_1 is the same object with such and such features at time t_2 (always within the time span of a fixation, or, to use Recanati's term, as long as the fundamental epistemic relation stands), further properties may be added. Should the object be important for the behavioral needs of the organism, attention may be allocated to the proto-object. When it does, the proto-object acquires the stability of the objects of everyday experience, and a rich representation of it is formed transforming it to an object.

To elucidate the point I am trying to press home, let me modify Garcia-Carpintero's example to suit my discussion. Suppose one sees a scene and perceives an object in it. This means that the segmentation processes of one's perceptual system have singled out that object and have allocated an object-file to it. Let us assume that one does not possess any concepts whatsoever that could apply to that object, including the concept "object-hood." (Recall that one does not recognize something as an object; one just perceives an object.) Suppose that one is asked what one is looking at, and one replies by pointing to the object and saying "That." I agree with Garcia-Carpintero that when one uses the singular word 'that' one takes oneself to be acquainted with an object by having an object-file for the object, which picks it out. The truth condition of the term is the object itself. However, first, this "be acquainted with" does not mean that one is aware of the existence of the object-file or of the fact that it is through the object-file that the object has been singled out. Furthermore, this acquaintance does not presuppose the possession of any concepts whatsoever. Second, in contrast with Garcia-Carpintero's example, the sense of the demonstrative or presuppositions of acquaintance with the demonstratum are not a (or a set of) proposition(s) that are taken for granted by the subject, because that would presuppose that the subject exercises the concepts associated with the terms of the proposition. The presupposition in our case is the nonconceptual content of the perceptual states, which are induced by the subject's perception of the object. Since the nonconceptual content of such states consists in spatio-temporal information and other transducable information, were one to put this content in a propositional form, this would read as the description "object in such and such a location with such and such visual features." The "in such and such a place with such and such visual features" is the mode of presentation of the demonstrative 'that' that individuates the object to which the demonstrative refers. However, as Campbell (2002, pp. 106–108) states, this "description" completes the character of the associated occurrences of "dthat" but makes no contribution to content. The "description" determines and directs attention to what is being said, and thus directs us to look at the point at which one is pointing to when uttering "That," but induces no complex, descriptive elements to content. In other words, the object has been indexed as an individual rather than as something that exists at a certain location and/or has a certain shape and color (which would mean that these properties would have been encoded, sortals would have been applied and the mode of presentation would have been a genuine description), although this information has been used to allocate the object-file to that object.

This is what I meant when I said above that demonstratives allow the individuation of the referent as a singular persisting object by means of object-centered segmentation processes that provide the causal chains that ground the demonstrative. The information on which these processes are based (the nonconceptual content about spatio-temporal information and other featural information that can be retrieved bottom-up from a visual scene) constitutes the sense of the demonstrative without being encoded as such and, thus, without providing a description that fixes the referent of the demonstrative. Since the information used to open an object-file for an object cannot be stored in a way allowing retrieval and awareness, it cannot provide a description that could be used in the same context or other contexts to fix the reference of a mental demonstrative the demonstratum of which is that object.

Or, if one wishes to assert that the information used is descriptive independent of whether one has access to it or not, one should be careful to distinguish between a description used to open the object-file for an object and a description used to fix semantically the referent of the relevant mental perceptual demonstrative, allowing, thus, one with the same information to individuate the same object just be acquiring this information and without perceiving the scene. In perception, the former is certainly the case, not the latter.[10] To be able to individuate the same objects upon viewing the scene, another viewer is not required to have or understand anything about the information used by the first viewer to individuate the same objects in that visual scene; other information may be used depending on the idiosyncratic relationship between the viewer and the referent of the perceptual demonstrative, since the list of properties that allow object individuation in a visual scene is heterogeneous and may differ from case to case. Soames (2005, p. 60) makes the same point with an eloquent example: "When looking at out firstborn and naming him Greg Soames, his mother and I did not intend the name to have the force of any dthat rigidified description incorporating the content we used in singling him out. Although our stipulation relied on descriptive information to initially endow the name with meaning, that information was not incorporated into either the content of the name, or the conditions required to understand it."

Thus, even if one wishes to claim that a description (provided, of course, that such a term can be aptly applied to a structured set of nonconceptual content) is being used to open the object-file for an object in a scene and endow it with the initial meaning that grounds the mental representation of the object in the world, this description does not semantically fix the reference of the perceptual demonstrative or become part of the conditions required for other viewers to individuate the same objects in that scene. Borrowing the term "foundational facts" from Soames (2005, chapter 8) and adapting it to the contents of the present chapter, one can put the previous point as follows: One should distinguish foundational facts (that is, the facts that originally brought it about that the viewer parsed the scene the way she did and that have sustained the reference to the objects parsed as entities persisting in space and time, always within the time framework of a single fixation) from the facts that other viewers may use to parse the same scene; the foundational facts do not constitute necessary and sufficient conditions for parsing the same objects in a visual scene and thus do not provide a description that semantically fixes the referent of perceptual demonstratives that correspond to the perceptual acts of singling out objects in a visual scene. It is easy to see that the information that is used to open the object-files belongs to the foundational facts. When attention focuses on some of the proto-objects in the scene, and when their object-files are enriched with further visual and semantic information and acquire a kind of coherence in space and time that they lacked before, the updated object-files can be stored in some form of retrievable memory. This allows comparison with other objects, or with future occurrence of the same object, across fixations. Some of the content of the updated object-files may eventually become the meaning of the object and provide, cast in linguistic form, a description that allows reference to the object. However, as Soames (ibid., pp. 183, 185, 297, 299, 321) repeatedly emphasizes for all forms of demonstrative reference, a viewer need not have access to or use the foundational facts that were used in opening the initial object-file. In fact, the viewer whose perceptual system constructed the initial object-file did not have access to the information used to construct the file, since she was unable to control, and did not have access to, the contents of the states during the feedforward sweep in which the relevant information was retrieved directly from the visual scene.

The object-files in the role of constructs that allow reference to or individuation of objects in a scene bear some similarity to Perry's (2001) perceptual buffers and file folders. Perry calls the individual representations of individuals *notions* and the individual representations of universals (properties or relations) *concepts*. For Perry (ibid., p. 52), notions and concepts are not abstract objects defined by the properties that they attribute to the object or the universal at issue, in which case one should have to suppose that notions and concepts are of the individuals or universals that have those properties, but particular structures in the brain. Thus, when one thinks of (that is, has an idea of) Dretske (Perry's favorite epistemologist), this idea is the neuronal structure in one's brain that represents all the information about Perry that one has in mind at that particular instance. This move allows Perry to be able to claim that one could have inaccurate concepts and incomplete notions of universals and objects. But if one's notion of Dretske is not of the person known by that name, then what is it about? Surely, that notion has intentionality insofar as it allows one to represent that person. Perry's reply is that notions and concepts are *of* their origin, that is, *of* what Perry (ibid., pp. 51–52) calls, among other things, the dominant source of information that allowed or prompted one to open a *file folder* for that person. Thus, in Soames's "first newborn son" example, the notion of Greg Soames is *of* the foundational facts that led to the adoption of that particular name. These foundational facts were included in a file folder that Greg's parents opened when they first saw their newborn son. The notion "Greg Soames" is that file folder, and in that sense that notion is not individuated by and, thus, is determined not by content (that content certainly changes as Greg grows up, yet the concept keeps referring to the same person) but by circumstance (ibid., p. 51), namely the relevant foundational facts.

Before Perry met Dretske, he had a notion of Dretske whose origin was the information that Dretske is the author of *Knowledge and the Flow of Information*. That notion, writes Perry (ibid., p. 120), "is sort of like internal file folder, and the ideas like information that has been put in such a folder. This inner file was set up when I first heard about and read articles by Dretske." Since, however, Perry had never met Dretske, his notion of Dretske was not attached to any perception of Dretske. Such attachment occurs when Perry meets Dretske in person for the first time. Perry (ibid., p. 121) defines buffers as the notions associated with the perception that are used to store temporarily ideas one gains from the perception of an individual until the individual whom one perceives is identified and those ideas are stored in some form in memory or the individual is forgotten. Thus, a buffer is a file attached to a perception. Strip Perry's buffers from any conceptual content (and thus reject the term 'notion'), invest them only with nonconceptual content retrieved directly from a visual scene in perception, and one ends up with the object-files discussed in this chapter. In fact, Perry (ibid., p. 135) admits that to be attuned to factors in a situation, one does not need *all of the concepts* that are required to discuss those factors, and adds that belief and attunement are different kinds of doxastic attitudes toward situations. Though it might be tempting to associate Perry's comments with the notion of nonconceptual content, his statement that one need not all of the concepts involved in theoretical formulations of the factors involved in a situation implies that Perry thinks that some concepts are required for attunement to factors in a situation and, thus, that he would not subscribe to the main thesis of the nonconceptualists: that perceptual content is in its entirety nonconceptual content. Perry's calling the attunement to factors in a situation a doxastic attitude toward situations reinforces this conclusion.

As in Perry, so here the object-file contains the fundamental facts that allowed the individuation of the object to which the file is attached, and thus the object-file is determined by and is about the origin that led to its opening. Similar to Perry's buffer, the object-file stores temporarily information from the object directly retrieved from the visual scene, and either some form of this information will be stored in memory, if the object is being attended to, or else, it will be forgotten. Furthermore, Perry's buffers (that is, perceptual file folders) contain information "gleaned from the perception and put directly into that file" (Perry 2001, p. 124)—Perry's way of saying that perceptual content brings *de re* contact with the world.

My account is also similar in many respects to Peacocke's scenarios. Peacocke (1992, pp. 61–62) searches for a level of nonconceptual content on which to anchor concepts in a noncircular way. This kind of nonconceptual content is provided by the spatial types, "the type being that under which fall precisely those ways of filling the space around the subject that are consistent with the correctness of the content" (ibid.)). To specify the spatial types, one must fix an origin and the axes of the resulting frame. These elements cannot be defined with reference to the real world, since a spatial type may be instantiated at different places. Thus, the point of origin and the axes should be defined with respect to a thing that is always present, which is the body of the subject.

If the things that can fill a spatial type are the surface and its orientation, texture, hue, brightness of light, degree of solidity of objects, as well as the direction, intensity and character of light sources (illumination conditions), and the rate of change of location, in relation to the origin and axes as defined above, then this type is a scenario. If one assigns time to a scenario and one assigns to its point of origin and axes real directions and places in the world, then one has a "positioned scenario." This positioned scenario is the representational nonconceptual content of the spatial type, and it provides in part the phenomenal representational content. Thus, the content of a scenario is spatial representational content.

We see that many of the nonconceptual properties that can fill a scenario are those that fall within my description of nonconceptual content. One sees that Peacocke's "the type being that under which fall precisely those ways of filling the space around the subject that are consistent with the correctness of the content" comes very close to be the mode of presentation of a demonstrative used by the subject. The problem is that Peacock (1992) denies that the contents of experience picked out by demonstratives should be individuated in terms of the differences of their mode of presentation by demonstratives. I address this issue in section 6.2.2.

To improve on the understanding of the theory of reference fixing offered in this chapter, consider Loar's (1976) example, which is also used by Garcia-Carpintero to drive home the argument that descriptive senses fix the referents of the terms with which they are associated. Notice, however, that the example by its nature demands from the beginning that the discussion take place in a conceptual framework Suppose that Smith and Jones see a man on the train every morning. One evening they watch a man being interviewed on a television show, they do not know that this man is the same man they meet on the train every morning, and it so happens that while watching the show they are talking about the man on the train. Suppose now that Smith switches his attention to the man on the TV show and says "He is a stockbroker," referring to the man on TV. Jones, unaware of Smith's attention switch, takes Smith to refer to the man on the train about whom they have been talking. Though Jones has identified the referent, since the man in the train is the same as the man on the television, one feels that Jones failed to understand Smith's utterance. This shows that for grasping meaning the mode of presentation of singular terms is important, even in extensional contexts.

The upshot of Loar's example is that although Jones's belief to the effect that the man on the train is a stockbroker has the same truth conditions as Smith's belief that the man on TV is a stockbroker, since the referent in both beliefs is the same person, Smith is justified in holding his belief, for suppose that he had formed this view on hearing some piece of information in the television show, whereas Jones's belief is not justified, since by thinking of the man in the train Jones does not deem this same piece of information to apply to the man in the train. Thus, Garcia-Carpintero concludes, examples like this vindicate the Fregean core claim to the effect that the relation between singular terms and their significations is mediated by semantically significant ways. By "semantically significant" Carpintero means that senses are essential in determining the reference and meaning of the demonstrative.

Why had Jones missed some information that would have justified his belief? Because Jones does not know that the man on TV and the man on the train are one and the same person, and this is why information pertaining to the former does not apply to the latter as far as Jones is concerned. In the terminology of this chapter, Jones has two different object-files (dossiers): one for the person on TV and one for the person he meets on the train. The role of the sense, or mode of presentation, of a singular term is to clarify exactly this point, namely whether the object under consideration has been individuated in the appropriate way. In other words, had Jones had the same object-files for the two persons, then his belief would have been a justified one. Spatio-temporal information purports to do exactly that; if Jones had followed the spatio-temporal path of the person on the train, he would have known that it is the same person as the one that appears on TV and he would have used all relevant information to update that person's object-file, in which case his belief would have been as justified as Smith's.

This discussion provides a solution to a parallaxis of Richard's (1983) "paradox" as well. Suppose A both sees a woman B across the street in a phone booth and is also talking to her through the phone, albeit A does not know that the person whom she sees and the person to whom she talks are one and the same. Suppose also that A perceives an immediate danger to B and waves to warn her of the threat but does not say anything over the phone. C is in the phone booth with B and says to her, while pointing to the man waiving at her,

(1)   That man believes that you are in danger.

At the same time C also says, pointing to the phone,

(2)   That man believes that you are not in danger.

These two beliefs seem to be contradictory, since the referent of the demonstrative 'that' is the same in both utterances, in which case C would be irrational. Yet we feel that we could have very well uttered the same statements and we do not think that would be irrational. Devitt (1996, p. 219) tackles the paradox analyzing the role of 'you' in the two utterances. Although I agree with his discussion, I think that the account of Loar's example provides another solution to the problem. The modes of presentation of the two demonstrative tokens of 'that' in (1) and (2) are different, in that, by ascribing different spatial locations to their referents, the two demonstrative tokens distinguish them. In other words, C has created two different files for the referents of 'that'. For this reason, it is not the case that the referent of the two instances of 'that' is the same thing and the paradox is removed. What the person refers to is the objects individuated in her object-files, and these are two different persons.[11]

My claim is that, as in Loar's example, spatio-temporal information (and, whenever this information is not enough, further featural information) allows singling out objects in a scene as persisting entities in space and time that retain their identity despite changes in location and attributes. The difference with Loar's example is that there need be no description associated with the object in order for it to be singled out and referred to.

How does this "mode of presentation" differ from Frege's sense? What could be the mode of presentation when, for example, one says "That (one)" while pointing at a house (e.g., in response to "Which house is yours?")? For one thing, I am not looking for the lexical difference between the types like "this" and "I" but for the difference between separate tokens of the same type, e.g. of "this," on separate occasions. Frege tried to account for both of these via different senses, which is problematic in the latter case, given the evidence that demonstratives refer rigidly. Instead, I shall construe the mode of presentation as a causal chain that connects a specific token of a demonstrative to its referent. For the reasons explained in previous paragraphs, this is clearly not a descriptive mode of presentation of the demonstratum, as Frege would have it.

The picture I have drawn differs from the standard modern accounts of the Fregean (1962) notion of reference of concepts in a public language as a correspondence between a symbol and something in the world, the correspondence being determined by the inherent descriptive sense of the sign.[12] In the view developed here, concepts, which according to Frege are the references of "concept terms" and which via their senses pick up the entities in the world that constitute their extension, have an inherent meaning that depends of the nonconceptual content retrieved from the world in which they are grounded.

One should expect this. We have seen that the mechanisms of early vision play a crucial role in extracting spatial and perceptual structure from visual arrays. The constitution of our sense organs and the general principles underlying their processing, thus, play a decisive role in the nature of information extracted from the environmental input and the way this information gets organized into contentful structures. Insofar as these structures intervene between one's representations and the world, they mediate the reference of one's concepts. In accordance with Putnam (1981, 1991) one could say that reference is determined within a certain descriptive scheme, which in our case is set by the constitution of the body and its sensory organs.

The discussion of the distinction between object identification and object individuation allows me to address a problem raised by Kelly (2001) in his discussion of McDowell's (1994) and Brewer's (1999) notion of demonstrative concepts. McDowell and Brewer have claimed that the correct way to articulate the conceptual content of experience is by means of demonstrative instead of general concepts. A demonstrative concept (such as "that shape"), unlike a general one (such as "shape"), applies only to one entity, the demonstratum of the demonstrative act, and that entity constitutes its semantic value, being the referent of the demonstrative. This way these authors believe that can discredit Evans's rejection of the thesis that experience has a conceptual content, a rejection in whose defense Evans (ibid., p. 229) had used the Richness Argument (that is, the claim that the content of our experiences is usually much richer than any attempts to report it using states whose content is conceptually articulated).

McDowell and Brewer believe that this way they can escape the richness argument and retain the core of their thesis that the contents of our experiences must be conceptual. The motive behind their thesis is, roughly, the following: since experience stands in justificatory relations with the beliefs and judgments that one may form on its basis, and since these relations can hold only between conceptually articulated contents, experiences must have a conceptual content. In other words, experience must be within the "space of reasons."

Furthermore, the introduction of the notion of "demonstrative concept" allows them to claim that one can conceptualize the content of an experience without acquiring a concept that is independent of that experience. Indeed, for McDowell (1994, pp. 56–57) the demonstrative concept exploits the presence of the sample that constitutes the referent of the demonstrative, and for Brewer (1999, p. 171) the grasp of demonstrative concepts depends essentially on the subject's relation with the actual entities that constitute their semantic values.

Heck (2000), Kelly (2001), Smith (2002), Tye (2006), and Vision (1998) have replied, quite successfully, that such a move fails for many reasons. One of the reasons pertains to the issues discussed in this book. This is that the possession of a demonstrative concept requires that one must be able to re-identify that an object falls under that concept whenever object occurs in one's experience. In fact, Sedivy (2004a) makes this a requirement for perception. Now, the first problem with such a view is that since recognition requires awareness on the part of the perceiver, perceptual experience is made to require perceptual awareness. In part I of the book we saw that this claim is simply false. Perception is independent of any form of awareness. It is false not as a victim of philosophical argumentation but as a result of what our best scientific theories tell us about perception.[13]

Kelly (2001, p. 403) discusses the re-identification condition. He claims that both theses of McDowell's that I presented in the paragraph before the last one require the existence of the "re-identification condition on demonstrative concept possession." This is the condition that subject S must satisfy if it is correct to say that she possess the demonstrative concept for X: "In order to possess a demonstrative concept for X, a subject must be able consistently to re-identify a given object or property as falling under the concept if it does." McDowell (1994, p. 57) speaks of such a recognitional capacity, which reminds us of Frege's "recognition judgments." Kelly argues that such a condition is not necessary for perception, and that, therefore, demonstrative concepts cannot be said to articulate the content of our perceptual states. To substantiate his claim Kelly (ibid., pp. 410–412) adduces as evidence a case in which a subject can discriminate between two colors, yet she cannot re-identify any of them at some time later, and argues that "it is perfectly conceivable . . . and there is nothing about the nature of perception to keep it from being true, that our capacity to discriminate colors exceeds our capacity to re-identify the colors discriminated." Kelly asks us to imagine that a subject can discriminate but not identify an attribute, and says that whether perception can be like that is an empirical question, though that it can be like that is certainly perfectly imaginable.

Well, if my account thus far is correct, Kelly is right. The 10-month-old infants in Xu and Carey's (1996) study use color and shape information to individuate and discriminate objects. But they cannot use color to recognize an object as the same one they had seen before. As our discussion on identification and individuation shows, one's individuative capacity does exceed, in the sense that it precedes and often overrides, the capacity to identify objects and/or properties as being such and such. Thus, one can discriminate objects without being able to re-identify them, and one can discriminate properties without being able to re-recognize them as such in future encounters. The subject can distinguish the two colors by having opened two different object-files for the two patches, without possessing any concepts at all, and being unable, thus, to reidentify these colors. She could "experience a shade without picking it out thus" (Vision 1998, p. 426).

I started by asking three questions: How is the object referred to in a mental demonstration singled out in a visual scene? What is the role of the object's properties in singling out the object? How is it possible that the perceived properties of objects that are the referents of demonstratives are perceptions of real properties of distal objects? The answers provided by the discussion thus far are the following.

There is a very early pre-attentional mechanism in vision that parses a scene into objects by singling them out as separate persisting things in space and time; this mechanism individuates objects. It relies on spatio-temporal information and occasionally on other information about transducable properties, but none of this information is conceptually represented at this stage. The objects thus singled out can be tracked and accessed by the perceiver; the perceiver can make further inquiries about the properties of these objects and this information is stored in the file of the object, which thus becomes enriched with further information. Since this information is stored into the object-file assigned to the specific object, it is information that refers to that object. Thus, the mechanism of early vision by individuating objects allows reference to those objects.

The fact that the information required for object individuation, and hence reference to that object, is retrieved bottom-up from the visual scene by means of the mechanism of perception renders the process a purely causal one, breaking the representational circle, which as I have argued is the main requirement for a successful theory of reference and solution to the grounding problem. Perception makes possible our immediate contact with entities in the world, and this contact precedes the application of sortal concepts that would describe the properties of the object. At the same time, the contact, by singling out objects, renders possible the exercise of our classificatory schemes, since it provides the object to which they will be applied. The discussion of attention in chapter 1 will aid us to understand this point. When one attends to an object, the effects of attention are delayed in time. During that delay, there is a host of information that is retrieved pre-attentively and in a bottom-up way from the scene about the object. This information allows parsing the scene and retrieving individuated objects from it. Thus, even when attentional effects eventually occur, bringing in with them the exercise of concepts, the exercise of concepts has been preceded by the object individuation. In fact, as was discussed in chapter 1, attention captures the proto-objects that have been formed during the pre-attentional processing. In that sense, the formation of the proto-objects, which is none other than the individuation of objects or object parts in a scene, makes possible the act of attention because it provides the material out of which attentional selection occurs. To paraphrase Smith (2002, p. 123): perception is intrinsically directed to objects in the world, prior to the offices of conceptualization. There is something about the character of perception that sustains the ability to refer to entities in the world nonconceptually. If perception yields a unified, coherent (even in a short run, in view of the character of pre-attentional objects as proto-objects), separate object that persists in space and time and undergoes changes, then one does not need conceptualism to explain the unity of the object given the diversity of perception. Object-files assigned by the object-centered segmentation processes of perception can do that.

The object-file that is opened for an object rendering the object the referent of a mental demonstrative individuates the object from other objects in a visual scene. It also contains nonconceptual information about transducable properties of the object, information that acquaints us with the object and which thus, following Garcia-Carpintero, functions as the mode of presentation of the mental demonstrative referring to the same object. In that sense it assumes the role of Fregean senses, although, unlike the Fregean sense, it contains no descriptive conceptual elements. Campbell (2002, pp. 106–108) captures successfully the nondescriptive character of the senses of demonstratives by stating about the information required for singling out an object, and which if linguistically described would provide information about the location and the mode of motion of the object, that it completes the character of the associated occurrences of 'dthat' but makes no contribution to its content. The semantic role of the description is pre-propositional; it induces no complex, descriptive elements to content.

6.2   Object Individuation and Reference

In this section I relate my theory to other theories of demonstrative reference, I discuss it in relation to Putnam and Kripke's causal theory of reference, and I attempt to address some of the problem besetting traditional accounts of causal reference.

6.2.1   Objects Files and Other Theories of Reference

Haugeland (1998) has offered a somewhat similar account according to which we share with non-concept-possessing creatures various innate "object-constancy" and "object-tracking" mechanisms that automatically "lock onto" medium-size lumps. These mechanisms can provide the discriminatory capacities necessary for the individuation and recognition of environmental objects in a bottom-up, nonconceptual way. Haugeland claims that the objective character of perception, that is the fact that perception is about objects *qua* objects, is due to the role of some normative standards that constitute thinghood. Unlike those animals, we have the capability to apply normative standards when we perceive and that it is these standards that allow us to distinguish between possible and impossible object configurations, and thus, render perception objective, meaning perception of objects. The "constitutive standards for thinghood" that Haugeland (1998, pp. 261–262) has in mind are cohesiveness and compatibility. However, the term 'normative' goes hand in hand with the application of concepts that determine what is correct or false, right or wrong, and this seems to commit Haugeland to the thesis that perception must be conceptual.

It is easy to see that these standards are in fact results of the operational constraints on perception that I discussed in part I of the book and which constitute the *modus operandi* of our perceptual systems and which are hard-wired in the circuitry of our perceptual system. Thus, Haugeland (1998, pp. 248–249) is right to claim that neither the perceiver has a discursive cognizance of the standards in some explicit formulation, nor are these standards articulated as rules. But then, Haugeland's appeal to normativity seems displaced, since usually normativity involves application of rules and most importantly involves the application of concepts of right or wrong, or true or false. However, in the case of the operational constraints at work in perception, neither of these prerequisites applies. It is therefore hard to see why Haugeland hastens to exclude animals from using these constraints. It is highly likely that the perceptual systems of animals, to the extent that their experience (for the same reasons as our experience) is experience of objects and not of proximal ambient arrays or undetached object parts, implement some form of operational constraints.

The present account of reference also shares many common themes with Campbell's (1997, 2002) theory of reference. It would be useful, thus, to compare my account with Campbell's account. Campbell (1997, 2002) thinks that the problem of the sense of a perceptual demonstrative is a problem about selective attention: "The understanding of a demonstrative depends on the act of visual attention" (Campbell 2002, p. 7). It is the role of selective spatial attention to isolate that information in a scene that pertains to the demonstratum. Campbell uses Treisman's (1993) theory of selective attention. Campbell (2002, p. 31) distinguishes between two kinds of attentional mechanisms. On the one hand, there is spatial attention that singles out a single location on the map of locations so that all features at that location could be bound together to constitute the object of our experience. This attention can operate without being consciously felt by the subject. This low-level phenomenon is contrasted with the kind of conscious attention that is required for knowledge of the reference of a demonstrative, in the sense that it is through this kind of attention that one could attend the object consciously, keep track of it over time and act intentionally on it. It is the latter attentional mechanism that allows us to verify propositions containing the referent of the demonstrative. It is not clear whether both kinds of attention are needed to fix demonstrative reference. Campbell hesitates to decide whether object individuation and/or object identification are required to fix demonstrative reference. Sometimes it seems that object individuation that does not assume sortals is sufficient, whereas other times reference fixing requires *knowledge* of the demonstratum, that is, object identification. Be that as it may, my account differs from that of Campbell's in that it is based on the thesis that objects can be singled out in a visual scene and can be tracked before the onset of any conscious attention and before any feature encoding.

For FIT, when one attends to an object then one automatically encodes all, or some, of its observable of its features in visual working memory and has them available for further processing. As Campbell (2002, p. 94) notes, the use of a demonstrative is grounded on the fact that you use it on "the basis of your having bundled together all the information from that location as from a single object." Thus, the representation of an object requires feature detection.

However, the evidence adduced here shows that the conscious attention of Campbell's is preceded by the representation of an initially featureless object that persists in time and will be the carrier of features bound together at a later stage. Most importantly, this weak representation allows the perceiver to perceive and track the same object undergoing feature changes, whenever such changes occur, instead of perceiving a new object with different features. The weak representation is provided by preattentional object-centered segmentation processes.

The difference between my account and Campbell's can be viewed from another perspective. For Campbell, conscious attention binds together features found at the same location and constructs the object that carries these features. Thus, for Campbell, conscious attention solves Quine's (1995) reification problem; that is, how one passes from the feature-placing level of experience to the particular involving level of experience. However, as Strawson (1959) has pointed out, perception of a bundle of features does not necessarily mean perception of a thing that carries these features. One may respond to the presence of certain features that one has encountered before without being able to single out an object as an object that carries these features. To use Bermudez's (2003) example, an animal may perceive a tree as affording shelter without perceiving it as a tree; without attributing to it "objecthood" in Haugeland's (1998) sense. Thus, the attentional mechanism invoked by Campbell does not suffice to solve the reification problem (for a similar criticism of Treisman's theory, see Bermudez 2003, p. 75). In my account, it is the object-centered segmentation processes that solve the reification problem, since it is this mechanism that singles out objects as persisting entities in space and time that can undergo featural changes.[14]

Campbell (2002, pp. 90–94) takes the mode of presentation, or sense, of a demonstrative to include information that could individuate (and/or identify?) the demonstratum on the basis of its observable features. Spatial location, along with Gestalt information and information on motion depending on the kind of the object, play the role of the binding parameter that binds the features observed at one location to a single object and constitute the sense of the demonstrative. Thus, spatial attention, which for Campbell means both the low-level unconscious attention to locations and the conscious attention that allows knowledge of the referent of a demonstrative fix the reference of demonstratives. Now, at some parts of his book Campbell insists that one should not associate the sense of the demonstrative with a description of the object's features and location. The role of location consists in providing the binding parameter for singling out objects and not for providing some sort of descriptive identification of the object. Location organizes the information-processing procedures that process information about that object. Location, through spatial attention, renders the object available for further processing and ensures that the information that is being processed is about that object. It is in this sense that the description completes the character of the associated occurrences of "dthat" but makes no contribution to content; it simply directs attention to what is being said.

According to Campbell, the sense of a demonstrative contains all information required to single out an object in a scene, bundling together all the information related to the object. However, this information is not given in a descriptive form. Taking this together with Campbell's (2002, pp. 62, 69, 71, 73) repeated claims that demonstrative reference is a more primitive phenomenon than the application of a sortal concept to the object that is being referred, one draws the conclusion that the content of the sense, that is, whatever information constitutes the binding parameter that allows singling out an object, is nonconceptual.

However, at some junctures Campbell seems to be ambivalent about that. He notes, for instance, that "for there to be a demonstrative referring to the object, there must be involvement of high-level semantic identification of the object involved" (2002, p. 53). Campbell, in general, seems to be confused as to what is involved in singling out an object as the referent of a demonstrative. Sometimes he writes that it suffices to individuate the object (in the sense defended in this chapter) and sometimes he thinks that singling out the object presupposes semantic identification of the object as being such and such. My thesis on that matter is clear. Object individuation requires no descriptions; it takes place at a nonconceptual level.

Thus, a second difference between the two accounts concerns the role of sortal concepts in reference fixing in Campbell's theory. Campbell (2002, pp. 68–74) argues, and rightly, that the ability to refer to objects is more primitive than the application of sortals to these objects. He argues against what he calls "the Delineation Thesis," which holds that for one to be able to single out an object in experience one must apply in a top-down manner the relevant sortal concepts. The sortal concepts allow one to cut the world in the appropriate pieces and avoid problems of ambiguity of reference. His example, however, is ambiguous. He discusses the case of an unknown archaeological artifact that is found by archaeologists who, unable to recognize and identify it, they cannot apply a sortal concept to it. Yet, Campbell claims, they can refer to it. Thus, reference is more primitive than the application of sortals. The objection here is that though the archaeologists cannot identify the object by assigning it a sortal, they can still apply several sortals identifying its shape, color, texture and so forth. One might even claim that it is the ability to apply these sortals that enables reference to the object in the first place.

Recall that for Campbell attention bundles together all information about an object at the focused location allowing reference to the object. Does this binding involve the concepts articulating the content of the salient experience of the object? It is not clear whether Campbell would allow for the possibility of reference to objects by creatures that possess or exercise no concepts whatsoever. Campbell (2002, p. 69) claims that though one cannot intentionally attend to Fs without having the concept for F, one can attend to an F without having that concept. But F is an object and one does not know what Campbell would say were F a feature of the object. In his account of the classical view of attending to objects Campbell (ibid., p. 29) discusses the features of objects. He distinguishes between using an object's possession of a property to single it out visually and verifying propositions about that property. The latter involves conceptual skills, whereas the former does not. In that sense "singling out" is a more primitive phenomenon that can be carried out nonconceptually. Now, although what can be singled out nonconceptually is the object, Campbell may be construed to hold that one could attend to features without possessing the relevant concepts since he says that the singling out does not involve conceptual skills. However, as we have seen, Campbell (ibid., p. 53) also claims that the possibility of demonstratively referring to an object depends on the involvement of high-level semantic identification of the object. This requires that the viewer possess the concepts of the features that allow identification of the object. I suspect that this oscillation on Campbell's part is due to the fact that he considers, justifiably, demonstratives to require awareness but he construes awareness as access awareness or report awareness, which invariably involves concepts.

Be that as it may, the account offered here makes clear that objects and their transducable properties can be singled out in a scene in nonconceptual bottom-up ways that individuate objects and their features. For, if one wishes to eschew the delineation thesis altogether, one must provide an account of how, at least some of, the object features could be perceived without the application of the relevant sortal concepts. The segmentation processes, by individuating and indexing objects in nonconceptual ways, render the individuation process more primitive than the application of any sortals that would describe the object in any way.

Although Campbell is right that intentionally attending to an object requires concepts, this does not mean that there is a nonconceptual attending which is not intentional, and this cannot be taken to mean that reference requires concepts either. Conscious attention brings with it concepts; there is not a nonconceptual attending to objects. Moreover, the nonconceptual singling out of objects fixes the reference of the demonstrative; it is intentional, since it refers to an object. Here again, Campbell is victimized by FIT, which requires that spatial attention bind the features at some location to a single object, constructing thus the object. Campbell knows that attention brings in concepts but at the same time he wants to maintain that the reference of a perceptual demonstrative can be fixed independent of the application of sortal concepts. But, he cannot have it both ways. Only a nonconceptual pre-attentional object individuation could show us a way out.

It seems, thus, that Campbell thinks that reference fixing of perceptual demonstratives could be carried out in a nondescriptive way and at the same time he holds that to be able to attend to the object and demonstrate it requires the application of at least some sortals applying to its features. I think that the problem Campbell faces is this. One the one hand, he has argued that perceptual demonstratives rely on spatial and motion information that does not constitute a descriptive mode of presentation. One the other hand, demonstration requires that one should be aware of the demonstratum, and furthermore, demonstratives usually are accompanied with knowledge of the demonstratum. But awareness, and knowledge, for Campbell involves the high-level attention, which in turn opens the way for concepts permeating acts of perceptual demonstration and making thus the modes of presentation of the demonstratum conceptual structures.

Another factor that might contribute to Campbell's predicament is his missing the fact that even when one attends to an object, the effects of attention are delayed in time. During that delay, there is a host of information that is retrieved pre-attentively in a bottom-up way from the scene that allows a pre-attentional parsing of the scene into individuated objects *even when one attends to it*. Thus, even when attentional effects eventually occur, bringing in with them the exercise of concepts, the exercise of concepts has been preceded by the object individuation. The pre-attentional contents of perception are subject to phenomenal awareness. Campbell could have extricated himself had he construed "consciousness or awareness" as "phenomenal consciousness or awareness." The latter does not require attention, and hence, any concepts. This way, Campbell could have maintained both that some form of awareness is necessary for demonstration and that this awareness does not introduce conceptual structure in acts of perceptual demonstration. This is the line I take in the present chapter.

If, as I have argued here, object individuation can fix reference and if object individuation can be carried out without conceptual involvement, then reference can be fixed in a nonconceptual manner; there is no description involved in the mode of presentation of the demonstrative. This goes against a strong view of reference fixing, the descriptive theories of reference. According to it, a sign is associated with a concept, which constitutes its meaning, thus rendering the sign meaningful. This concept determines what the sign refers to, since it allows one to pick out the objects in the environment that are "described" by the concept.[15] Certain of the descriptions associated with the sign fix the reference of a term.

The fixing of reference by means of descriptions is the standard Fregean analysis of demonstratives which treats them like any other expression, assuming that their tokens have a reference by virtue of their sense, i.e. "the way in which the reference is given in thought," their "mode of presentation in thought." Although Frege never explicitly says that sense specifies sufficient (let alone necessary) conditions for membership in the extension or reference, it still seems fair to paraphrase this as the meaning of his talk about "determining reference." Wiggins (1993) argues that Frege's construal of the "sense" of singular terms amounts to a twofold claim; that there exists an object x that the term presents, and a way in which the term presents that object x. Wiggins (1993, p. 200) calls this "way of presentation" a "conception" and identifies it with a body of information in which the body x itself plays a distinct role. This information may generate different descriptions of x that may serve in suitable contexts to identify x. A conception of x is a way of thinking about x that fixes which object x is, that is, that fixes the referent of the singular term.[16] Similarly, Dummett (1973) argues that Frege's senses of singular terms are criteria identifying objects as the referents of these terms, that is as determinants of reference.

Thus, roughly speaking, Frege takes the reference of signs to be fixed via meaning (sense). Signs have a meaning, which determines their referents by determining a set of sufficient conditions for membership in the extension. Even if, as Wiggins argues, the Fregean sense is object-involving, and thus the meaning of a term is the combination of its sense and of its referent, the point remains that the sense involved contains descriptions of the referent. Thus, reference fixing invariably requires that concepts be involved. It is exactly this claim that I am denying by arguing that the referent of a perceptual demonstrative can, and must, be fixed outside the conceptual realm. I emphasize that reference fixing does not mean identifying the referent as being such and such, but something weaker, namely individuating the object to which the demonstrative refers. Filling the object-file yields object identification.

Kripke (1980) and Putnam (1975, 1983, 1991) have already shown that the standard conception of reference fixing through the sole intermediary of conceptual content is bound to fail. At least for certain kinds of terms, their reference cannot be determined by their meaning, by their sense, but by what the world is really like. As Devitt (1996, p. 159) argues, descriptive theories of reference are incomplete. By explaining references by descriptive means, they appeal to the application of descriptions of other words; thus, they explain reference by appealing to the reference of other words to the world. This cannot go on forever. To escape the lurking infinite regress, there must be some words whose reference does not depend on that of other words, that is, words that are founded directly in the world.[17] Natural-kind words, names and indexicals seem to be the places at which descriptive theories fail and where the referent must be fixed by other means. Our discussion thus far shows that these other means consist in causal grounding chains that are provided by the segmentation mechanisms of perception.

Pylyshyn (2003, chapter 5) raises another problem with descriptive theories of reference: they fail to explain how an object that is described into two different ways could nevertheless be deemed by the cognitive system to be the same object. If all that the cognitive system has access to is the pure description of the referent of an object, then it is stuck with two distinct representations and there is no way to establish that the referents of the two representations are identical. This means that the cognitive system can only represent facts about objects, that is, that an object has certain properties, but it cannot represent a particular object *qua* individual. This is, of course, the reification problem that I discussed before in another disguise. This being the case, how could action on this object be explained? Actions are performed on objects not on object descriptions. "A purely descriptive representation," Pylyshyn concludes (ibid., p. 253), "does not connect with the world in the right way: there remains a gap between representing the fact that there is something having certain properties and representing the fact that this very thing has those properties. . . . You must at some stage have a representation that connects, in this epistemically direct way, with the token objects on which actions must be based."

I have adopted, and expanded, Garcia-Carpintero and Devitt's account of the role of senses in fixing the demonstrata of perceptual demonstratives. Thus, as I have said above, my thesis goes against the direct-reference theory, which claims that the only content of a demonstrative is its denotation, or in other words, that the only linguistic function of a demonstrative is that it refers to its demonstratum[18]; a demonstrative does not describe its referent as possessing any identifying properties, it only refers to it. To put it in Frege's terms, demonstratives have no sense, only reference. In my account, although perceptual demonstratives do not provide identifying descriptions of their referent, they individuate the referent as a singular persisting object on the basis of nonconceptual spatio-temporal information. This information constitutes the mode of presentation of the demonstrative in perception and in that sense the referent is always perceived under a mode of presentation. Thus, against direct-reference theories, there is a mode of presentation of a demonstrative, though it is causal, idiosyncratic to the particular context of the perceptual encounter, it cannot be adequately rendered in linguistic terms since it has nonconceptual content, and is not descriptive.

One of Kaplan's arguments against Fregean descriptivism is based in the observation that directly referential terms like demonstratives that occur in attitude ascription sentences, when in different contexts they still play the same role in each instance; that is, they are used to report attitudes toward a particular object, namely the referent of the demonstrative. Hence, the semantic content of the demonstrative cannot be whatever description may be associated with the demonstrative in each context, these descriptions may differ from context to context, but what remains constant across contexts, which is the referent of the demonstrative. Let us compare this with the case of mental perceptual demonstratives that individuate objects in visual scenes through the employment of object-files. Suppose different persons view the same scene from different perspectives. Their perceptual systems parse the scene and individuate objects in it. Each uses spatio-temporal or other featural information to individuate these objects and the kind of information used is idiosyncratic to each perceiver depending on her perspective. Some viewers may perceive the scene from a perspective in which spatio-temporal information suffices to individuate objects whereas others do not have such a clear taking of spatio-temporal information. An object, for instance, may have not clearly visible boundaries from another from that particular perspective, or it may partly hide another object, and other featural information is required to individuate objects from other objects and the background. Since all the viewers have the same perceptual make up and barring cases of hallucinations and illusions, they all individuate the same objects in the scene, since they all use nonconceptual information that is directly retrieved from a scene. Thus, the perceptual demonstratives used by all viewers have the same referents, namely the objects in the visual scene, even though those objects may be perceived under different modes of presentation, depending on the information used to individuate the objects in the scene.

Hence, there is a sense in which the account that I have provided is similar to Kaplan's. We both think that the referent of a demonstrative is independent of its mode of presentation (for epistemological realists this means that the objects in a scene are independent of the ways one uses to individuate them). However, we differ in that for Kaplan this means that the semantic content of the demonstrative is solely its reference and that the sense is irrelevant to that content, whereas I hold that there is a kind of sense or mode of presentation of the demonstratum that is part of the content because in perception it is the nonconceptual mode of presentation that individuates objects in the scene and, thus, provides the referents of the demonstratives. It must be said, though, that the content that I am talking about is somewhat different from the content that Kaplan talks about. Kaplan talks about content that constitutes part of the meaning of the demonstrative (hence the term "semantic content"), whereas I talk about a peculiar kind of content, which although it cannot be part of the semantic meaning of a demonstrative since mental perceptual demonstratives do not have semantic contents (recall that the contents I am examine are semantically evaluable in the sense that they are true or false of the things they represent but they are not semantic in the way Kaplan intends, that is, they do not have linguistic meaning, they are not descriptions, and thus they are not contents in that sense), still it causally grounds the demonstrative in the world and relates mental representations with the world. It is because of the role of the mode of presentation of perceptual demonstratives in grounding mental perceptual representations in the world that I take the mode of presentation of a demonstrative to be part of its content.

It is interesting to examine how the causal notion of reference discussed in this chapter relates with Putnam's (1975, 1983, 1991) and Kripke's (1980) new theory of reference, or direct-reference theory ("direct" in that it avoids the mediation of conceptual content as the sole factor in establishing reference).[19] According to Putnam (1983, p. 71) "the extension of certain kinds of terms is not fixed by a set of 'criteria' laid out in advance, but is, in part, fixed by the world." In other words, descriptions ascribing properties to some terms do not suffice to fix the referents of the signs. The world has a saying on the fixing, what Putnam (1991) will later call the "contribution of environment," in reference fixing.

To be more specific, Putnam argues that there is an indexical component that participates in reference fixing. When one takes a liquid sample to be water, one does so because one thinks that this liquid sample has a property, namely "the property of behaving like any other sample of pure water from our environment" (1991, p. 33). This property, Putnam argues, is not a purely qualitative property (meaning that membership to it is not determined by a set of pre-specified criteria); its description involves a particular example of water, one given by pointing or focusing (hence the term 'indexical'; note also that pointing and focusing correspond to Ballard's mechanical and neural pointing devices) on something that it is considered to be water. The stuff out there, to which the act of pointing is an essential part of fixing reference of the natural-kind term 'water', is the contribution of the environment. This brings immediately into mind the notion of causal chains by means of which demonstratives refer; causal chains that are established through the object based on the object-centered segmentation processes discussed in this chapter. It is in that sense that reference is determined by things that are given existentially and not by a set of criteria.

A word refers to something if it stands in the right relation (causal continuity in the case of proper names; sameness of "nature" in the case of kinds terms) to these existentially given things. In the case of proper names, the existentially given thing is the person or thing originally 'baptized' with the name; in the case of natural-kind words, the existentially given things are the actual paradigms. Kripke (1980, pp. 80, 135) refers to this kind of assigning names and using demonstratives as "initial baptisms." Suppose, Kripke writes (1980, p. 95), that one points to a star and says "That is to be Alpha Centauri." By this, one commits himself to the following: "By 'Alpha Centauri' I shall mean that star over there with such and such coordinates."[20] The gist of the idea lies in Kripke's remark that "the original concept of cat is: *that kind of thing*" (ibid., p. 122).

Kripke dismisses the descriptive theories of reference that assign reference by means of a conjunction of properties of the relevant term. Kripke attacks both the view that the referents of singular terms or direct referring expressions and the referents of natural-kind terms are determined to be those objects that satisfy the descriptions, and the view that the meanings of these terms are given by the descriptions associated with them. I confine my discussion to the case of reference. Kripke tries to explain reference fixing by "touching" and "pointing," all of them being deictic pointers. These pointers assign primarily spatio-temporal information, and tag objects through object-based attention, thus providing "deictic reference." I have claimed that information retrieved in a bottom-up manner from a scene is the mode of presentation of a singular term, a mode of presentation that is causal and not descriptive. In this sense, despite Kripke's (1980, p. 135) claim that singular terms do not have connotations, that is, modes of presentation, I think that Kripke's position and the thesis developed in this chapter are compatible.

Kripke's examples (e.g. that involving Alpha Centauri) clarify the role of spatial information and of object individuation in fixing the reference of singular terms. The causal chain that grounds the term starts with spatio-temporal information. In the case of singular terms, the reference can be fixed in various ways. An initial baptism ostentation or a description that belongs to what we have called "the foundational facts" typically fixes it. Otherwise, the reference is usually determined by a chain, passing the name from link to link. The vast majority of names have, for Kripke, their reference semantically fixed by a historical chain of reference transmission and not by a family of associated semantic descriptions. The same observation holds for such a general term as 'gold'. In general, natural-kind terms may acquire reference in one of two ways. Either by direct presentations of samples of the term and the stipulation that the term is to apply to all and only instances of the unique natural kind, or, by using a description involving some contingent properties of the sample. When the term passes from user to user the original description stating the foundational facts does not play any role so long as both users agree that they refer to the same stuff.

This way of fixing the referents of singular and natural-kind terms captures adequately Kripke's intuition: "Don't ask: how can I identify this table in another possible world, except by its properties? I have the table in my hands, I can point to it, and when I ask whether *it* might have been in another room, I am talking, by definition, about *it*. I don't have to identify it after seeing it through a telescope. If I am talking about it, I am talking about *it*. . . ." (1980, pp. 52–53) Though Kripke and Putnam speak of proper names and natural-kind terms, their analysis easily transfers to all singular terms, and thus, to perceptual demonstratives. (See Garcia-Carpintero 2000 for a justification of this claim.) Singular terms, that is, names and indexicals, are associated with something extralinguistic, their referents. Some existentially given thing, Putnam claims, is essential for fixing these referents.

This existentially given thing is precisely the object individuated in the "object-file" introduced above. The object-file establishes the causal continuity with the object originally "pointed to" by the perceptual demonstrative, satisfying Putnam's criterion for reference fixing (recall our discussion of Loar's example). The object-file, in other words, is based on the indexical component that participates in reference fixing. The fact that the content of the object-file is retrieved in a bottom-up manner from the scene warrants the central claim that its content is the contribution of the environment and not the contribution of conceptual content.

Thus, the theory expounded in this chapter, shares many common features with the direct theory of reference. However, it has a less ambitious scope that its cousin, since it is restricted to the reference of perceptual demonstratives and needs extension to cover natural-kind terms *qua* natural-kind terms. Furthermore, it fixes reference by invoking a restricted range of information, namely only what can be retrieved in conceptually unmediated ways from a scene, a restriction that clearly does not apply to the original causal theory of reference.

It is these restrictions that allow the theory to avoid many of the problems associated with the two aforementioned theories. First of all, by proposing to fix reference through conceptually unmediated chains between the world and the perceiver, breaks the circle of representations associated with the descriptive theories of reference and offers an adequate springboard for building a solution to the grounding problem. I think, thus, that the present account of reference fixing captures particularly useful insights of the causal theories of reference. It shows that descriptive identification is not necessary for a term to denote something (see also Evans 1993, p. 210) and that for an item X to be the referent of some term entertained by Y, it suffices that X be placed in a context which relates Y to X.

6.2.2 Object-Files and the Role of Senses in Reference Fixing

I examine here some problems pertaining to the role of senses in fixing reference. Let me deal, first, with Peacock's (1992) problem that led him to deny that the contents of experience picked out by demonstratives should be individuated in terms of the differences of their mode of presentation by demonstratives. Peacocke uses the example of two distinct lengths, the length of a column and the length of a window that are perceived as the same. This means that their mode of presentation is the same. Yet the perceiver may reasonably wonder whether they are the same. Thus, should this perceiver be informed that they are indeed the same, this would be informative. According to the Fregean criterion of the identity of senses, if the two senses were identical, then the information that the two lengths are equal should not be informative ("The morning star is the morning star"). This is the case, however, in the above example, which means that senses do not individuate the contents of the perceptions of the two lengths.

Peacocke's conclusion is warranted only if one restricts the individuative information about the two lengths to their perceived length. If one includes in that information the perceived location of the two lengths, then it is clear that the mode of presentation of the two lengths is not the same, simply because they are perceived in different locations, the one at a column the other at a window. In discussing Kripke's well-known example, Devitt (1996, p. 236) draws a similar conclusion discussing the apparently contradictory character of statements such as "Flora believes that this ship (pointing to the bow) is not that ship (pointing to the stern)" in a context in which Flora sees the two ends of the same ship, whose mid-section is occluded by a large obstacle and Flora does not know that it is one and the same ship whose stern and bow she observes. Devitt claims that the statement is meaningful because the meanings of the two demonstratives are different, in that they ascribe different spatial perspectives that individuate the referents of the demonstratives as two different things, removing the apparent contradiction. Thus, Peacocke's problem is solved without rejecting the thesis that the contents of experience picked out by demonstratives can be individuated in terms of the differences of their "mode of presentation," provided the latter is properly understood as the object-file.

Another problem surrounding the role of "senses" in fixing the reference of singular terms is the controversy between Evans (1990) and Dummett (1973) over the relation between sense and reference when it is applied to the fixing of the referents of perceptual demonstratives. According to Dummett, the sense is a way of determining reference, whereas for Evans it is a way of thinking of reference. Evans (1990, p. 73) argues that if Dummett's thesis is correct, then the sense of a singular term is a way of recognizing, or identifying, the referent of the term. This leads, according to Evans, to the unacceptable consequence that the sense is existence-independent, that is, that a singular term without a referent can still have a sense. To block that conclusion, Evans construes the sense as a way of *thinking* of reference, that is, as a mode of presentation of the referent in thought, not as a way of determining reference. However, if we apply Evans's idea to the case of perceptual demonstratives and to the way their referents are fixed we see that Evans falls back to the descriptive theories of reference. For, if the sense of a perceptual demonstrative is a way of *thinking* the reference, then reference involves the usage of concepts (it becomes like Wiggins's (1993) conception of the referent). Thus, the sense provides ways of describing the referent, and this leads back to the vicious circle of descriptivism. This, in addition, contradicts Evans's (1993) claim to the effect that descriptive identification is not necessary for a term's denotation.

We can avoid the undesirable consequence of Dummett's analysis without falling back to "descriptivism," by admitting that the sense determines reference not by identifying the referent but by individuating the referent, or as Evans himself states, by providing the appropriate (and spatio-temporal, I add) context that disambiguates reference. This construal of senses blocks on the one hand "descriptivism," and on the other irrevocably connects senses with the existence of the demonstratum, because there can be no object individuation on the basis of spatio-temporal information without the existence of an object that provides this information.

Brandom (1996, p. 417) argues that recognition judgments, whose form is assumed by identity claims, express recognition of an object when given or referred to in two different ways. These two different ways are, of course, two different modes of presentation of a singular term, which this way has two different senses. "To associate an object with an expression as its referent requires settling of what would count as another way of picking out the same object." (Brandom 1996, p. 424) Only then, one would be entitled to apply two different concepts to the same object. Thus, if a is a round object entering a screen and b is a square object exiting the screen then a recognition judgment should be $a = b$, where a and b are two different ways of presentation associated with the singular term denoting the object. Now, the main point of indexing theories is that this identification need not assume the form of a judgment but it can take place at a purely non-conceptual level, in which the identity (as the same object) and individuation are guaranteed by the indices that tag and track objects through their time histories.

The nonconceptual way of reference fixing defended in this chapter captures another of Evans's insights into the relation between sense and reference. Evans (1990, p. 80) writes that it would be wrong to construe a Fregean sense as an intermediary between a thinker and a referent as "something which must, from a certain point of view, get in the way, or anyway render indirect what might be direct." Evans concludes that a way of thinking of an object does not get in the way of thinking an object and does not render thinking of an object indirect. This passage is puzzling. Evans starts by denying the indirect character of the sense and reference relation and ends up defending the direct relation between "a way of thinking of an object" and "thinking of the object." But although the latter claim is trivial (a mode of something is a way this something seems to be and does not render this something indirect), it does not say anything in defense of the former claim, namely that the relation between sense and reference is direct. For thinking, and any mode of thinking, can get and does get in the way between a thinker and the reference of a term she has uttered. It gets in the way because it invests the denoted object with the panoply of the conceptual framework in which thinking resides. And here we are back to descriptivism.

To understand and assess Evans's puzzling argument, one must consider the context of Evans's discussion. Evans targets direct-reference theories that claim that some singular terms refer directly without the mediation of a Fregean sense. To defend his notion of Frege's theory Evans must block the movement from the role of sense in reference fixing to the conception of an existence-independent Fregean sense. The problem here is that if one allows senses to play a role in fixing the referent of demonstratives and other singular terms, then one runs the risk to assign referents to nonexistent things, insofar as nonexisting things may have a sense or a mode of presentation. Direct theories of reference block this by denying that sense is a part of the meaning of some singular terms, only reference determines the meaning of singular terms. Evans insists (correctly in my view) on the indispensability of senses in reference, and consequently, must defend the existence-dependent character of sense, that is, he must show that admitting senses to be a part of the meaning of singular terms does not lead to the assignment of referents to nonexistent things. To do so, he must argue that sense does not get in the way between the thinker and the referent masking the object and allowing, thus, the possibility of thinking of nonexistent objects. But as I said, thinking does get in the way and the only way out is to defend a way of reference fixing that does not involve thinking. This is exactly what I tried to do in this chapter, by tying reference, through the thinkers' causal direct relations with the world.

Evans comes close to the account of reference offered when he discusses understanding sentences containing the word "here." Such an understanding requires a *knowledge* of which place is in question, which partly consists in a disposition to judge the sentence as true or false—"[a] disposition which he can have vis-à-vis just one place in the universe in virtue of his occupying it, and which in no way depends upon the capacity to recognize that place as the unique satisfier of some description. If these accounts are on anything like the right lines, it is very easy to understand how these 'ways of thinking' are irreducible to any other way of knowing which object is in question, certainly no descriptive way, can guarantee the existence of the relevant dispositions." (Evans 1993, p. 81)

Though Evans talks of "knowledge," this is a peculiar kind of knowledge, for it consists in a disposition, which the person uttering the sentence acquires by being at that place, and not by endorsing a set of discursive sentences. Furthermore this disposition is irreducible to any set of descriptions, and thus the ensuing knowledge is irreducible to any other form of knowing. It may be, thus, that Evan's "thinking" in his identification of senses with "ways of thinking" may not necessarily be "thinking" in its discursive semantic sense, but a term used to signify the kind of the nonconceptual states of an organism in its interactions with the environment, akin to Bickhard's (1993, 2000) practical grasp on the part of an organism of the implications of the afforded potentialities by the environment for the organism's actions or to Campbell's (1999) indexical causality. But then "ways of thinking" come close to "ways of individuating" objects and "assessing" their causal significance for the organism.[21]

6.2.3 Object-Files and Problems of Causal Theories of Reference

I will discuss now some problems of the causal theories of demonstrative reference. I will apply the theory of reference developed in this chapter and argue that it contributes positively in addressing these issues. In particular, the notion of "object-file" through which reference gets fixed and the way object-files are opened and maintained, if incorporated into a causal account of reference, could help overcome some of the difficulties traditionally associated with the account of Putnam and Kripke.

First, the theory of reference fixing of perceptual demonstratives that I have offered clarifies the role of context in disambiguating reference. Brandom (1996, p. 416) bases the intelligibility of judgments directed toward objects on the availability of a context of practices of identifying objects as entities persisting in time. He argues that the use of singular terms is associated with an implicit identity criterion that provides the authority to pick out particulars as persisting, subsistent objects that can be recognized as the same again, that is, to identify objects as being the same objects, even when their properties change.[22]

Indexing theories provide that context of identifying objects as one and the same, and individuating them. The difference between Brandom's account and mine consists in the fact that according to Brandom "recognizing an object as the same again is making a certain kind of judgment," whereas in my account object individuation does not require judgments (which necessarily involve concepts) but takes place instead at a nonconceptual level, in which information is retrieved in a bottom-up manner. According to Brandom, a singular term can pick out an object only if the issue has been settled when it is correct to recognize the object as the same again by making an identity judgment. According to my account, at the appropriate level, one does not have to *judge that an object is the same* despite featural changes; one *perceives the same object* changing.

Similarly, Evans argues that although causal theories correctly state that a causal relation between the utterance of a singular term and the item concerned is essential for fixing the referent of the term, they mislocate the causal relation because they ignore the role of the context of the utterance in determining what is referred. "What gets said is going to be determined by what name is used, what items bear the name, and general principles of context disambiguation." (Evans 1993, pp. 217–218)

For causal theories of initial baptisms, the important causal relation is between the item's being dubbed with a name and the speaker's contemporary use of it. For Evans, however, the essential causal relation is between the item's states and doings and the speaker's body of information. If one substitutes the "object-file" that contains information about "objecthood" and other information about size, shape, color, orientation, and surface properties for "the speaker's body of information," the account of a bottom-up reference fixing emerges, since the important causal relation is that between the item's spatio-temporal states and doings and the object-file that the speaker opens based on these doings and states for the item.

Furthermore, the way object-files individuate objects sheds light on the problem of indeterminacy of reference raised by Quine (1960) with his famous "gavagai" example. The upshot of that argument is that an observational singular term (e.g. "gavagai") that gets uttered by the members of a tribe, whose language the linguist is trying to translate, in the presence of a rabbit, need not be translated as the sortal "rabbit" but can be rendered, in an alternative translation, as, say, the sortal "undetached rabbit part." Since linguistic practice constrains only the interpretation of sentences there is, as Brandom (1996, p. 409) argues, "considerable slack in how responsibility for the use of those sentences is indirectly apportioned between the subsentential linguistic units the theorist chooses to discern."

The "gavagai" argument led Quine to talk of "ontological relativity," a thesis which states that to ask what really exists independent from or distinct from any framework is unanswerable (and thus, for the neo-positivists still among us, this question is meaningless). The reason is that is possible to adopt two or more different frameworks that equally succeed in describing the verbal and nonverbal behavior of the native whose language the linguist is trying to translate. In a first framework the world is divided up into discrete objects. For this reason the framework contains all the necessary linguistic arsenal of logical, and single term referring expressions that allows one to refer and talk about rabbits. However, there exists a second framework, with different referring single term expressions and perhaps different logical concepts, in which the world is divided not into discrete objects but into rabbit-parts or other rabbity moments (a finer-grained framework, if you will). If these two frameworks are equally successful in describing the behavior of the native, then they both have equal claims to be the correct descriptions. Since no one can decide which one is the correct description, it does not make sense to ask which one is the right description. Hence, the issue of what entities do exist in the world, rabbits or rabbit-parts (or other rabbity moments), is relative to some framework, from which it follows the thesis of "ontological relativity."

Brandom claims that the difficulty with the general strategy of re-individuation (that is, the adoption of translations that individuate the world at a finer level, instead of individuating "rabbits," for instance, they individuate "rabbit parts") consists in the fact that re-individuation does not ensure that the language contains the apparatus to individuate the terms it sorts. In other words, if terms invoking parts of wholes are to function in the language as genuine singular terms, there must some ways of predicating them that do not construe them through the wholes in which they appear, but as independent entities. Notice that for Brandom's argument to bear its full brunt, one need assume that the native's language does not contain singular terms referring to parts independent of terms that construe them through the wholes of which they are parts. It is only under that condition that the re-individuation strategy has difficulties. I am not certain that this move is successful in blocking Quine's argument. Quine talks of an alternative framework with different single term referring expressions and different logical concepts and it is not clear whether one can preclude such a framework from containing the apparatus to individuate rabbit parts as opposed to whole rabbits. Only if one argues that humans, as a species, cannot have a linguistic framework with such referring terms, one could block Quine's inference to ontological relativity.

Brandom cannot supply this additional demand, but I think I can. Here is why. I share Brandom's assessment and I think that the theory of reference through object individuation offered here supports Brandom. The way demonstrative thought works through deixis precludes the possibility of referring to parts of wholes at the nonconceptual level. The reason is that early vision picks up objects according to several general operational constraints hard-wired in the visual system. Recall that among these constraints are those that determine that adjacent elements are combined, that two edge-segments could be joined even though their contrasts differ because of illumination effects, that the shapes of natural objects tend to vary smoothly and usually do not have abrupt discontinuities, and that a pair of image elements are matched together if they are physically similar, since they originate from the same point of the surface of an object). Finally the rigidity and no action at a distance principles specify that bodies move rigidly.

The operational constraints, which are at work in vision, are the constitutive standards of vision, that is, those "rules" that determine what the perception is of, and also that we perceive objects as integral bearers of properties (Haugeland 1998, pp. 253, 260–261). Thus, undetached rabbit parts that occur whenever rabbithood is instantiated and move together are perceived as a rabbit and not as parts that move together. The sortal associated with the singular term "gavagai" or with the perceptual demonstratives elicited in the presence of rabbits, is "rabbit" and not "undetached rabbit parts." It is because of the function of the operational constraints that there is no possibility of an apparatus individuating rabbit parts independently of the whole of which they are parts, as opposed to rabbits; object-files are opened for rabbits not for undetached rabbit parts, because object-centered segmentation processes parse the scene into rabbits and not into undetached rabbit parts. In other words, these principles necessarily join together the "undetached parts of a rabbit," and induce thus the perception of a whole rabbit and not of rabbit body parts.

This being the case, there can also be no predications addressing "undetached rabbit parts" independently of the whole, justifying thus Brandom's claim to that effect; for predications are allowed only for objects for which an object-file has been opened. This means that one's perceptual system, or to be accurate, the way one's perceptual system function, precludes the existence of the alternative "rabbit part" framework. Human perception simply does not work that way. Quine's inference to ontological relativity from the possibility of existence of different frameworks fails because the premise is wrong at the species level. This of course leaves opens the question of ontological relativity with regard to species with other perceptual systems, but I will not pursue the issue here.

The preceding discussion shows the way to addressing a classical problem with causal theories of reference. As Putnam (1981) pointed out, this is the problem of how to single out the "right" causal chain that determines reference. This occurs in the model-theoretic argument (ibid., 34ff.) and concerns the need to single out what one means by "cause," given that any event has several causes, whereas one needs the one "explanatory" cause. It is supported by Wittgensteinian arguments to the effect that deixis is necessarily ambiguous. When Quine's native pointed at the rabbit, saying "gavagai," was he pointing at a rabbit, an ambient optical array, an animal, a color, a symbol? This is the traditional problem of picking out what is perceived among the causal antecedents of the perceiving. Why does one say that one sees objects and not the retinal projections (proximal stimuli) that causally mediate between the percept and the object in the environment?

The problem is that of choosing the distal strategy that must be used to determine the distal cause of some stimulus. One popular approach to identifying distal stimuli is that of Dretske (1981). It consists in employing two or more intersecting causal chains of covarying event-types that elicit a response of the appropriate type. Brandom calls this method "causal triangulation." Dretske uses this strategy to identify the distal cause that allows a thermostat in a room to control room temperature. If the thermostat has only one way to measure temperature (by the bending of a bimetallic strip), then there is no way to say that the system responds to the change in room temperature rather than to curvature of the bimetallic strip. But suppose that the thermostat has another way to measure temperature (say, by means of a column of mercury, which supports a float with an electrical contact that completes a circuit that can turn the furnace on or off). Though the second route does not provide a means for identifying changes in room temperature as the distal cause, both routes together can do that. The distal cause is the point where the two roots intersect.

Brandom (1996, p. 429) objects that one may take the distal cause to be the disjunction of the two proximal causes (the curvature of the bimetallic strip or the height of the mercury column). Thus, again, one cannot determine the distal cause of the reliable differential responsive disposition of the thermostat. To achieve this, Brandom argues one must supplement "causal triangulation" with "inferential triangulation," that is, one must also consider the inferential role, and thus, conceptual role of the responses. In other words, one must consider how claims that contain the involved terms function in language, that is, how they are connected to other claims by inference, what claims can be derived from them, from which claims they are derivable and so forth.

Though I agree that the solution of the "disjunction problem" requires at some level of analysis conceptual triangulation *at the level of the nonconceptual content* conceptual triangulation is not necessary for fixing reference. Object-based segmentation processes by individuating and indexing objects, provide immediately and directly (i.e., in a bottom-up manner) the organism with information pertaining to the distal objects that cause the flow of information. One does not have to triangulate anything to "know," for instance, that the same object has undergone a color or shape change during its movement in time. Similarly, one does not have to choose which "packages of reality," to borrow the term from Vision (1998, p. 415), to select from the environment when viewing a scene. The object-segmentation processes of perception see to that.[23] When the scene is more complicated and objects overlap then the mechanisms of vision and the principles they implement execute some kind of causal triangulation to disambiguate objects; there is, however, nothing conceptual about this triangulation.

Brandom (1996, chapter 7) extends this analysis to demonstratives. All subsentential expressions, acquire their significance indirectly through the significance "their occurrence has for the inferential involvements of the sentences in which they occur" (ibid., p. 472). Similarly, demonstratives and all unrepeatable tokenings, such as deictic usages of singular terms, are inferentially contentful in virtue of their links to other tokenings in sentences. Since unrepeatable tokenings can participate in substitutional, and thereby inferential, commitments only through their depending anaphors, deixis presupposes anaphora (ibid., p. 462). No tokens can function as demonstratives unless other tokens function as anaphoric dependents. Since Brandom (ibid., chapter 5) has analyzed "reference" in terms of substitutions, inferential relations and anaphoric expressions, he draws the conclusion that deixis cannot determine reference, since pointing is understood only in terms of anaphors, and thus, reference. Now this claim undermines the project of finding a naturalistic bottom-up, cognitively impenetrable way of explaining reference in terms of in terms of deixis.

Let us examine Brandom's arguments closer. Pointing, Brandom argues (ibid., p. 461), is the core phenomenon underlying demonstratives, and it is thought, especially by fans of causal theories of reference, that pointing could provide a purely causal way of picking out objects (put it differently, pointing could explain reference). But this is an idle hope, for bare demonstration is empty. Even when one points to a book, one still needs an account of sortals to determine whether the act of pointing refers to a book, or to its cover, its title, etc. But an account of sortals, Brandom has argued when discussing Quine's indeterminacy of translation and Dretske's causal triangulation, need to be supplemented by a conceptual, or inferential, triangulation if it is to pick out the proper distal objects. Conceptual triangulation involves inferential substitutions, which presuppose token repeatability, and thus, anaphora.

As I argued when discussing the "gavagai" and "causal triangulation" problems, however, the way demonstrative thought works through deixis precludes both the possibility of referring to parts of wholes at the nonconceptual phenomenal level (addressing thus the former problem) and the possibility of referring to disjunctive proximal causes (addressing thus the sufficiency of causal triangulation at the phenomenal level to determine reference to distal causes). At the nonconceptual level of spatio-temporal and other transducable information at which I propose to ground demonstrative reference, the act of "pointing" to a book picks out the book, or to be precise the proto-object which has the transducable features of the book, which is thus, the referent of the demonstrative. Once the object-file has been opened, featural information may be assigned, and hence refer, to that object. And then, the original demonstrative can be substituted by anaphoric expressions, which inherit the reference to that object in virtue of their being dependent anaphors of the original demonstrative, whose reference has been independently established. On my account, anaphora presupposes reference based on deixis.

Brandom employs another argument to support his thesis that pointing can not be used as a means of solving by purely causal means the problem of reference: "[O]ne using a tokening of 'that pig' demonstratively in many cases need not *do* anything in order to have indicated or demonstrated one particular pig in the barnyard, provided that the unique salience of that pig has somehow already been established." (1996, p. 461) Agreed. But then, what act could ultimately have established the required unique salience of that pig, if not an act of deixis? Otherwise how could the existence of the pig, which the use of a demonstrative requires, be established?

My disagreement with Brandom lies in the fact that he does not address the problem of how conceptual content is grounded into the world, but only how, given that this grounding has taken place, terms are used in the language game. Though he admits the existence of an entry-level to the linguistic game (borrowing the term from Sellars 1963) at which non-inferential differential responses are elicited by objects and events in the world, he does not seek to examine the way these responses are elicited (probably he thinks that this is the work of psychology, which as such, cannot offer any semantical significant insights). Brandom (1996, p. 235) acknowledges that entry moves (observational claims, for instance) have also an empirical content (acquired by means of their non-inferential elicitation). However, the task of analysis for him begins at the conceptual level. Brandom points to the root of the problem, that is, the reason that everything has to be solved at the conceptual level, when he writes (ibid., p. 466): "The use of a demonstrative may be elicited non-inferentially as a response to an environing stimulus. What makes it a term referring to an object rather than a mere conditional response, like 'ouch,' is its role as an anaphoric initiator of claims that can be subjects of substitutional commitments. It is in virtue of those anaphoric connections that a demonstrative token can play a conceptual role."

Conceptual role semantics is the only way to assign content to the differential responses of an organism and differentiate them from mere conditional responses. It is only at the conceptual level that epistemically significant content can be found. Thus, reference (being semantically significant) can be settled only at the conceptual level. Hence, demonstratives refer through their conceptual roles. My answer to that is that an epistemically significant nonconceptual content needs to be explored, if one wishes to solve the grounding problem.

Haugeland (1998,) approaches the problem from a different angle. Haugeland's asks how and why "the structure of objectivity" (i.e., the fact that we see objects *qua* objects) is "imposed on the physics and physiology of sensation?" He criticizes (1988, pp. 250–251) Dretske's attempt to solve the problem by means of interconnecting causal chains though he agrees that such intersections in part do specify distal objects instead of proximal stimuli as the objects of perception. Haugeland claims that this strategy works only if supplemented by a "letting the standards govern perception" strategy. As we have seen, it is these standards that Haugeland charges to carry the load of imposing the structure of objectivity upon perception. Though Haugeland is right that much of the work in perception that makes us perceive objects *qua* objects is due to the operation of some "standards," there is nothing "normative" or "conceptual" involved. Perhaps the term 'standards' is not appropriate here, because it refers to the notion of normativity with its conceptual connotations. The standards at work in perception are the restrictions that the operational constraints that I discussed in detail in chapter 3 impose on the processes of perception, and more specifically, the restrictions they impose on the possible solutions to the equations in the algorithms involved in perceptual processing. Thus, it is the operational constraints, as I called them, which supply Haugeland's standards. There is nothing conceptual or normative in its usual sense involved.

Let me recapitulate the main thesis I have advanced in this chapter: In using a demonstrative one, opens a file for the demonstratum. The first thing that this file does is to establish "objecthood" and individuate the object. This ensures the existence of a distinct object whose paths in space and time can be tracked down. In that sense, a version of Carpintero's "dossier," a dossier that contains spatio-temporal information only, becomes an "object-file." The objects involved in the object-files are reduced to entities whose predominant "property" is that they exist, persist in time and through motion, and that occupy some space.

Representations including such information are used to index the objects of a visual scene and follow their movements; they also function as the loci that integrate feature maps, and preserve the identity of the object through changes. Thus, they lie in the midway between the proximal stimuli and the objects of our cognitive lives. Pylyshyn (2001, p. 361) calls such objects "proto-objects" and claims that the classes provided by the visual system are, at a first approximation, viewer-centered shape classes expressible in the vocabulary of geometry. Featural information may be assigned to the object-file of a specific object, and that makes this information to be about that object, to refer to it. The features that have priority for inclusion in the extended object-files are color, size, and viewer-centered shape. These features are extracted directly, that is, bottom-up from a scene.

Thus, the reference of perceptual demonstratives is fixed through object individuation, which opens object-files that are subsequently filled with spatio-temporal information and information about surface properties, sizes, shapes, and orientation. This is the level at which we touch the world directly, in the sense that this information is directly retrieved in bottom-up. It is at this level that the causal chains grounding representations reside. They do this by providing the substratum on which demonstrative concepts refer to objects in the world; the object-files individuate objects and allow featural information to invest these objects, whose identity as spatio-temporal objects is independently established, allowing thus the conceivability of the same object undergoing featural changes. This way conceptual content of demonstratives is grounded in the world without the mediation of concepts. Pylyshyn (2001) calls this representation a "demonstrative" thought, in that one can perceive an object without having any concepts, not even the concept "object."

7 The Theory-Ladenness of Perception: Churchland vs. Fodor

The evidence from PET and ERP scans that we examined in part I of the book shows that there is a part of perceptual processing that precedes semantic interference from cognitive centers higher in the brain. Similarly, Lamme's work on visual processes and on attention and awareness suggests that there is a stage of visual processes at which there is only feedforward sweep and a recurrent processing that is limited within early visual circuits and outside the effect of cognitive signals. I have called that stage of vision, which encompasses the FFS and the LRP of Lamme's theory and in which an initial coherent perceptual interpretation of the scene is provided, *perception*. It is evident that the term 'perception', as employed here, does not designate the same processes as it designates in its usual occurrences. This part of visual processing, to wit perception, is opposed to the whole processing that takes place in vision and results in the formation of our conscious percepts and thus of our experience of the world, which I have called *vision*.

Armed with the theory of perception expounded in part I of the book, let me now address the controversy over the theory-ladenness of perception, focusing on the debate between Paul Churchland and Jerry Fodor.

In an article titled "Observation Reconsidered," Fodor (1984,[1] p. 120) argues that observation is theory-neutral, since "two organisms with the same sensory/perceptual psychology will quite generally observe the same things, and hence arrive at the same observational beliefs, however much their theoretical commitments may differ."

Later in "Observation Reconsidered" (p. 127), Fodor concedes that a background theory is inherent in the process of perceptual analysis. In this sense, observation is theory-laden and inference-like. But this theory-ladenness does not imply that observation is theory-dependent in the way relativistic theories of philosophy of science and holistic theories of meaning intended it to be. The reason is that these theories require that the perceptual analysis have access to background knowledge and not just to the theory that is inherent in the system. But this is not true in view of the various implasticities of perception (e.g. the Müller-Lyer illusion) which show that how things look is not affected by what one believes. This argument is best understood in the light of Fodor's (1983) view of the modularity of the perceptual systems, which, unlike reflexes, are computational but informationally encapsulated from information residing in the central neural system.

The input systems, or perceptual modules, are domain-specific, encapsulated, mandatory, fast, and hard-wired in the organism, and they have a fixed neural architecture. Their task is to transform the proximal stimuli that are registered by the sense organs to a form that is cognitively useful and which can be processed by the cognitive functions. This transformation is a computation that relies on some general assumptions whose role is to reduce the sensory ambiguity and allow the extraction of unambiguous information from the visual array.

The perceptual modules have access only to background theories that are inherent in these modules. The modules, in this view, do not have access to our mental states and theoretical beliefs. Fodor (1984, p. 135) distinguishes between "fixation of appearances" or "observation," which is the result of the functioning of the perceptual modules, and "fixation of belief," which is the result of the processing of the output of the modules from the higher cognitive centers. The former is theory-encapsulated; the latter is not. Fodor's target was the "New Look" theories of perception, according to which there are no significant discontinuities between perceptual and conceptual processes. Beliefs inform perception as much as they are informed by it, and perception is as plastic as belief formation.

Fodor's (1984) argument is that, although perception has access to some background theories and is a kind of inference, it is impregnable to (that is, informationally encapsulated from) higher cognitive states (desires, beliefs, expectations, etc.). Since relativistic theories of knowledge and holistic theories of meaning argue for the dependence of perception on these higher states, Fodor thinks that his arguments undermine these theories, while allowing the inferential and computational role of perception.

Churchland (1988[2]) attacks Fodor's thesis of the theoretical neutrality of observation on two grounds. He argues, first, that perceptual implasticity is not the rule, but rather the exception, in a very plastic brain, in which there is ample evidence that the cognitive states significantly affect perception. Thus, he rejects the modularity of the perceptual systems. Second, he claims that even if there is some rigidity and theoretical neutrality at an early perceptual process, this "pure given," or sensation, is useless in that it cannot be used for any "discursive judgment," since sensations are not truth-valuable or, equivalently, semantically contentful states. Only "observation judgments" are semantically contentful states, because they have content, which is a function of a conceptual framework. Thus, they are theory-laden.

In this chapter, I address Churchland's claim about the plasticity of the perceptual systems and his arguments against their modularity, and I assess their effectiveness as a critique of the theoretical neutrality of observation. The conclusion is that, although Churchland is right that observation involves top-down processes, there is also a substantial amount of information in the perceptual stage of vision or early vision, which is clearly bottom-up and theory-neutral. (As I explained in the interlude, I take the terms "theory-laden" and "cognitively penetrable" to be coextensive.)

The difficulty with both Fodor and Churchland is their conception of the sensation-perception-cognition distinction, and an adequate account of this distinction will help us delineate what exactly is at stake in their arguments. Both Fodor and Churchland, moreover, view perceptual learning and the structural changes it induces as threats to the cognitive impenetrability of the modules—Fodor because he thinks that the input systems have a fixed neural architecture, Churchland because he thinks that perceptual learning demonstrates the cognitive penetrability of perception. Both views fall short of the truth.

Finally, I will address Churchland's claims that recent neuropsychological research provides evidence in favor of the top-down character of perception. I will claim that Churchland misinterprets this evidence, and that these findings can be reconciled with a modularized view of human perceptual systems in which modules are meant as systems that are semi-impregnable to top-down penetration—that is, although these systems receive information from cognitive centers, this information arrives with a time delay such that it allows the systems to process initially information in a purely bottom-up manner and to participate subsequently in cognitive processing.

Before I proceed, some terminological discussion is in order. The terms 'perception' and 'observation' will be employed frequently in this chapter and will be carefully distinguished from one another. These terms are not employed consistently in the literature. Sometimes 'perception' purports to signify our phenomenological experience and thus "is seen as

subserving the recognition and identification of objects and events"
(Goodale 1995, p. 175). In Goodale's sense, perception is a wider process,
which includes recognition and identification of objects. As the reader
might recall, I use 'perception' in a more restricted way, excluding identification and recognition of objects, which belong to observation.

'Sensation', as I use it, refers to all processes that lead to the formation
of the retinal image (the retina's photoreceptors register about 120 million
pointwise measurements of light intensity). This set of measurements,
which initially is cognitively useless, is gradually transformed along the
visual pathways in increasingly structured representations that are more
convenient for subsequent processing. I call the processes that transform
sensation to a representation that can be processed by cognition 'perception'. Perception includes both low-level and intermediate-level vision,
and is bottom-up in that it extracts information retrievable directly from
the scene only. In Marr's (1982) model of vision (discussed below), the
$2\frac{1}{2}$D sketch is the final product of perception. In other models, perception
encompasses all processes following sensation that produce their output
independent (in an on-line manner) of any top-down information,
although information from higher levels may occasionally select the
appropriate output. Perception is cognitively impenetrable, in that perceptual processing is not modulated by top-down semantic information. All
subsequent processes are called 'cognition', including the post-sensory/
semantic interface at which the object-recognition units intervene as well
as purely semantic processes. At this level we have observation, which
results in object recognition and identification. Observation is cognitively
penetrated by top-down information from higher cognitive centers; thus,
it uses information stored in mnemonic circuits. The formation of Marr's
3D model, for example, is a cognitive activity. The recovery of the objects
cannot be purely data-driven, since what is regarded as an object depends
on the subsequent usage of the information and thus is cognitively penetrable. Several theories of vision hold that object identification is based on
part decomposition that is the first stage in forming a structural description
of an object and seems to depend upon knowledge of specific objects.
Other theorists, including Edelman (1999), propose that objects are identified by template-matching processes. Object recognition requires matching
between the internal representation of an object stored in memory and
the representation of an object generated from the image. Similarly, template matching relies on knowledge of specific objects and is, consequently,
cognitively driven, since the templates are results of previous encounters
with objects stored in memory.

7.1 The Argument from Illusions

Churchland's first argument against the thesis of impenetrability of the perceptual systems consists in an examination of various illusions and visual effects (the Necker cube, the well-known rabbit/duck figure, etc.), which reveals that there is "a wide range of elements central to visual perception—contour, contrast, color, orientation, distance, size, shape, figure versus ground—all of which are cognitively penetrable" (Churchland 1989, p. 261).

The interpretation of visual illusions is controversial. There is disagreement about their causes and about the extent to which their resolution depends on top-down flow of information. The whole issue hinges on exactly how much of a top-down process vision is, and on the nature of the top-down influences. In the next section I attempt to show how Churchland's observations concerning illusions can be accommodated in a semi-Fodorian framework, I will use Marr's (1982) theory of vision as an example of the kind of modular theory Fodor is arguing for. I will start with a brief presentation of Marr's theory of visual processing.

7.1.1 Marr's Theory of Vision

According to Marr (1980), there are three levels of representation. The initial level is the primal sketch, which captures contours and textures in an image. The second level is the observer-centered $2\frac{1}{2}$D sketch, which yields occlusion relations, orientation, and depth of visible surfaces. Recognition of objects requires an object-centered representation, Marr's 3D model. Marr considers the $2\frac{1}{2}$D sketch to be the final product of the bottom-up, data-driven early vision—that is, perception. Its aim is to recover and describe the surfaces present in a scene. Visual processes that process surface shading, texture, color, binocular stereopsis, and analysis of movement are referred to as *low-level vision*. The stages of low-level vision purport to capture information that can be extracted directly from the initial optical array without recourse to higher-level knowledge.

Hildreth and Ulmann (1989) argue for the existence of an intermediate level of vision. At this level occur processes (such as the extraction of shape and of spatial relations) that cannot be purely bottom-up, but which do not require information from higher cognitive states. These tasks do not require recognition of objects, but they require the spatial analysis of shape and spatial relations among objects. This analysis is task-dependent in that the processes involved may vary depending on the task being accomplished, even when the same visual array is being viewed.

The recovery of the objects present in a scene cannot be the result of low-level and intermediate-level vision. This recovery cannot be purely data-driven, since what is regarded as an object depends on the subsequent use of the information and thus is task-dependent and cognitively penetrable. In addition, most computational theories of vision (Marr 1980; Biederman 1987) hold that object recognition is based on part decomposition, which is the first stage in forming a structural description of an object. It is doubtful, however, that this decomposition can be determined by general principles reflecting the structure of the world alone, since the process appears to depend on knowledge of specific objects (Johnston 1992). Object recognition, a top-down process that requires knowledge about specific objects, is accomplished by late vision. Object recognition requires matching between the internal representation of an object stored in memory and the representation of an object generated from the image. In Marr's model of object recognition, the 3D model provides the representation extracted from the image, which will be matched against the stored structural descriptions of objects (perceptual classification).[3]

Against Marr's model of object recognition, Lawson, Humphreys, and Watson (1994) argue that object recognition may be more image-based than based on object-centered representations, which means that the latter may be less important than Marr thought them to be. Neurophysiological studies by Perrett et al. (1994) also suggest that both object-centered and viewer-centered representations play substantial roles in object recognition.

Other criticisms address Marr's thesis regarding functional modularity—that is, his idea that a large computation can be split up and implemented as a collection of parts that are nearly independent of one another. As we saw in chapter 1, it is highly likely that the early-vision module consists of a set of interconnected processes (submodules) for shape, color, motion, stereo, and luminance that cooperate within it. These are functionally independent, and they process stimuli in parallel. Thus, early vision consists of a continuum of multiple, parallel, task-specific modules. This (internal to early vision) "horizontal" or "lateral" flow of information, however, does not threaten the cognitive impenetrability of early vision, since it leaves no room for penetration of knowledge from higher extravisual cognitive centers. Neurophysiological evidence (Felleman et al. 1997) also suggests that information flows in a top-down manner from loci higher along early vision to earlier stages of early vision. Being within the early-vision module, however, this top-down flow of information does not support the cognitive penetrability of early vision from extravisual information.

Thus, despite criticisms of Marr's program, his distinction between early representations (which most likely are bottom-up) and higher-level representations (which are informed by specific knowledge) remains valid. His notion of functional modularity also holds, provided that one views Marr's modules as consisting of a set of submodules with lateral and top-down channels of communication that process in parallel different information extracted from the retinal image.

A host of neurological and neuropsychological findings support the above conclusion. Consider the cases of visual agnosias. Visual agnosias can occur for different kinds of stimuli (colors, objects, faces), and may affect either the ability to copy or the ability to recognize objects. Research (Newcombe and Ratcliff 1974; Warrington and Taylor 1978; Warrington 1975, 1982; Humphreys and Riddoch 1984, 1985; Campion and Latto 1985) shows that there is a relative autonomy of the components of the visual processing routines. Damage to the early visual routines causes impairments at high-level vision, but damage to high-level vision usually leaves low-level vision intact.

Impairments of the object-centered representation, for instance, leave intact the lower viewer-centered representation. More specifically, difficulty in identifying objects that are seen from unusual views (Warrington and Taylor 1973), difficulties in matching by physical identity (Warrington and Taylor 1978), and difficulties in recognizing that an object has the same structure even when its view changes—that is, in recognizing object constancy (Humphreys and Riddoch 1984, 1985), suggest an impairment in the formation of the 3D model (the object-centered representation). Insofar as the patients perform normally in categorization tasks, their viewer-centered representation is intact.

Impairments of semantic memory leave intact both the initial viewer-centered representation and object-centered representation. Damage in the left hemisphere (De Renzi, Scotti, and Spinnler 1969) is accompanied by the so-called semantic impairments, in which knowledge of the objects' category, classification, of properties and functions is degraded or inaccessible. Studies (Taylor and Warrington 1971; Warrington 1975) show that the same patients have normal initial, viewer-centered, and object-centered representations, since they succeed in matching tasks, drawing objects, recognizing objects seen from unusual views, and maintaining object constancy. Thus, the semantic impairments affect neither perception nor observation (observation being the formation of object-centered representation).

The neuropsychological evidence provided by studies of the various forms of visual agnosias suggests that there is a relative autonomy of the various components of the routines of visual processing. Damage to the early visual routines causes impairments of high-level vision, but damage to the high-end routines usually leaves low-level vision intact. Thus, although sensory visual deficiencies and/or impairment in the formation of the primal sketch affect performance in tasks that require the $2\frac{1}{2}$D sketch and/or the 3D model, impairments at this latter level are not reflected in deficiencies in tasks that depend on the formation of the primal sketch. Similarly, impairments of the object-centered representation leave intact the lower-level viewer-centered representation. Finally, impairments of semantic memory that affect object categorization and deprive the patient access to her background knowledge of specific objects seem to leave intact not only the perceptual initial and viewer-centered representations but also the more cognitive object-centered representation. Therefore, the various parts of the visual processing system seem to satisfy Marr's principle of modular organization, and they seem to enjoy a cognitive impenetrability *à la* Fodor.

7.1.2   Implicit vs. Explicit Knowledge and Theory-Ladenness

According to Fodor (1983), perception has access to some background theories and is a kind of inference. Still, it is impregnable to higher cognitive states, such as desires, beliefs, and expectation. A distinction is drawn, thus, between the theories informing perception and the specific knowledge about objects that constitutes the representational content of our cognitive states (beliefs, expectations, desires).

The computations involved in all levels of vision are constrained by some principles or operational constraints. In section 3.1, I provided a somewhat detailed account of those operational constraints. Here I repeat the main point of that discussion: These constraints are needed because perception is underdetermined by any particular retinal image; the same retinal image could lead to distinct perceptions. The problem is accentuated with the underdetermination of the $2\frac{1}{2}$D structure (which is three-dimensional) from the 2D retinal stimulation (two-dimensional). Unless the observer makes some assumptions about the physical world that gives rise to the retinal image, perception is not feasible. Thus, even if perception is bottom-up, it is not insulated from knowledge. Knowledge intrudes on perception, since early vision is informed and constrained by some general operational constraints that reduce indeterminacies in information.

Many theories of vision, including those of Ulmann (1979) and Marr (1982), hold that these constraints substantiate some general approximate truths of our world and are not assumptions about specific objects acquired through experience. In this sense, they are general principles about our world. Moreover, they seem to be hard-wired into the system. Thus, even the early stages of vision, insofar as they involve some built-in physical constraints or theories, are theory-laden. These constraints provide the body of background knowledge stored in Fodor's perceptual modules. In this sense, and if one metaphorically interprets the processes involving the general constraints as "thinking," one could agree with Spelke (1988, p. 458) that "perceiving objects may be more akin to thinking about the physical world than to sensing the immediate environment." These principles, however, do not result from explicit knowledge acquisition about specific objects; they are general reliable regularities about the optico-spatial properties of our world that are hard-wired in our perceptual systems.

This knowledge is implicit in that it is available only for the processing of the retinal image, whereas explicit knowledge is available for a wide range of cognitive applications. Implicit knowledge cannot be overridden. The general constraints hard-wired in the visual system can be overridden only by other similar general constraints with which they happen to compete (although no one knows yet how the system "decides" which constraint to apply). Still, one cannot decide to substitute the body of knowledge hardwired in the perceptual system with another body of knowledge, even if one knows that under certain conditions this implicit knowledge may lead to errors (as is the case with the visual illusions). Hence, one would not be justified in calling this set of constraints a "theory." This theory-ladenness, therefore, cannot be used as an argument against the existence of a theory-neutral ground, because, first, perception based on a shared theory is common ground, and, second, the body of operational constraints implemented in the visual cortical areas can hardly be said to constitute a theory.

7.1.3 Ambiguous Figures

Let me now turn to cases in which the internal organization of a figure or a scene is such that it deceives one in constructing the wrong organization, or is so ambiguous that its resolution seems to rely on higher cognitive factors. Similar problems occur in linguistics, where syntactic analysis yields, for instance, more than one possibility for the grammatical role of a word.

Fodor (1983, p. 76) is aware that context may be invoked to solve certain syntactic ambiguities. The problem he considers is whether this top-down process determines the output of the syntactic module. If the top-down flow of information affects the module before its production of output, there is no cognitive impenetrability. But Fodor believes that, although the context solves the disambiguity, it does not determine the output of the modules. What happens is that the module proposes all possible syntactic analyses, and the higher-level processes then determine which interpretation is acceptable. All other analyses are deactivated and do not participate in further processing. Thus, the effects of sentence context are "post-perceptual" in that these processes operate after the input system has provided a (tentative) analysis of the lexical content of the stimulus.

The "filtering interactive" model allows weak interaction between higher and lower levels of processing, since the channel of communication between the levels allows a very limited feedback: the only information that passes is "yes" (that is, acceptable) or "no" (unacceptable). The channel of communication functions as a filter that modulates what receives further processing. As such, it is contrasted with Gregory's (1974), Neisser's (1976), and Churchland's "strong interactionism," which holds that top-down processes affect perceptual processing.

Research in linguistics shows weak interactionism to be quite plausible, especially if it is augmented by the assumption that the bottom-up processes propose their alternatives in parallel (Forster 1979; Crain and Steedman 1985; Altmann and Steedman 1988; Ferstl 1994). The conceptual information that is brought to bear on the syntactic or the phonological processor must be available after these processors have formed some hypotheses regarding the syntactic structure. Then conceptual information intervenes to select the appropriate structure in the specific context. The same model applied to vision may be able to account for most if not all of the cases that strong interactionism cite as evidence in its favor.

I will now address some of Churchland's arguments about illusions. In the Müller-Lyer illusion, the operational constraints applying to the projection of three-dimensional objects onto two dimensions deceive us into seeing the two lines as different in length. Fodor used this case to argue that, since we cannot help seeing the lines as unequal notwithstanding our knowledge to the contrary, the visual input system is informationally encapsulated. Churchland (1989) answers that using this illusion to support impenetrability is a poor choice because, as Fodor admits, children with less experience with edges and corners are less susceptible to the illusion.

This means that this illusion is the result of learning from experience, which shows the cognitive penetrability of perception. There are three rejoinders against Churchland. First, it is by no means certain that this illusion is the result of misplaced depth constancy. Second, even if it is, and perceptual learning is involved (as will be argued in section 7.3), perceptual learning does not necessarily involve cognitive top-down penetrability; it may involve only data-driven processes. Third, there are other, low-level explanation of the illusion, based on filtering weak interactive models.

The duck/rabbit figure and the Necker cube, for instance, are typical ambiguous figures in which a figure is so ambiguous that its resolution seems to rely on higher-order cognitive factors. The context may dictate whether the rabbit/duck configuration is perceived as depicting a duck or a rabbit, or the way the cube is perceived. Thus, perception is allegedly shown to be cognitively penetrable. This need not be the case, however. The weak-interaction model can account for this phenomenon. The bottom-up processes of vision propose in parallel both duck and rabbit, and higher cognitive states select one. Since the production of the output of the visual input systems is not affected by any top-down processes, their impenetrability is not undermined. Fodor (1989) offers another reply. That reply is worth discussing, since it paves the way for another account of ambiguous figures that does not rely on the problematic weak interactionism while, at the same time, it does not relapse to strong interactionism and hence does not imply the theory-ladenness of perception. Fodor argues that one does not get the duck/rabbit configuration to flip by changing one's assumptions, and that "believing that it's a duck doesn't help you see it as one." What does the trick is fixation at the appropriate parts of the configuration. Whether Fodor is right or wrong is a matter of empirical investigation. Research by Taddei-Ferretti et al. (1996) confirms some of Fodor's claims but also suggests that top-down processes may determine how reversible figures are perceived.

It has been found (Kawabata 1986; Magnuson 1970; Peterson and Gibson 1991, 1993) that subliminal stimuli that reach perception but not cognition affect the reversal rate of reversible configurations, confirming the effect of bottom-up information on the perception of such ambiguous patterns. This research also shows that fixation at some crucial "focal areas" of the ambiguous pattern may cause reversion of the schema, thus justifying Fodor's claim that fixation may do the trick (see the discussion in chapter 1). But research on reaction times in responses to such patterns shows that perception of the pattern is influenced by the previous interpretations of the incoming sensory information, suggesting that background information affects the way the ambiguous pattern is perceived. It may be, therefore, that specific-object information affects in a top-down manner the way ambiguous patterns are seen. Still, this does not mean that there is early cognitive penetration of perceptual processing, since the context may bias one of the interpretations that the perceptual system produces without affecting perceptual processing itself (which is the main contention of weak interactivism) or, alternatively, the context may determine the focus of spatial attention without affecting perceptual processing *per se*.

Let me delineate this issue by examining in some detail the case of ambiguous figures (or, as they are preferably called nowadays, bi-stable figures).

The Duck/Rabbit Figure   Consider first the duck/rabbit ambiguous figure (figure 7.1a). During perception, figures are individuated from the ground and from other objects that may appear in the scene (figure-ground segmentation). Properties of the object (size, shape, color, orientation, motion, spatio-temporal continuity, etc.) are also bottom-up retrieved from the visual scene. Thus, the image phenomenally perceived (seeing$_{ph}$) consists in a configuration with the aforementioned properties. However, on certain occasions multiple figure-ground segmentations in an image are possible, in which case the figure is ambiguous. Or perceptual ambiguity may arise because a figure may be decomposed in multiple ways, or may have more than one internal organization. In the case of the duck/rabbit figure, although none of the properties retrieved bottom-up from the image allows by itself the distinction between a rabbit-like and a duck-like figure, it is the way the figure is decomposed and organized that determines whether a duck or a rabbit is perceived.

Studies with ambiguous figures suggest that seeing a duck or a rabbit when presented with the ambiguous configuration depends on where spatial attention focuses on the image. Attention enhances or attenuates the availability of certain perceptual categories. Folk et al. (1992) use the term *attentional control settings* to denote all those factors that guide perceptual acts and consist in the perceptual goals held by the observer during the task. Such goals may include either the experimenter's instructions (search for such and such object, or focus at that location) or the subjects' plan of action. Indeed, in ambiguous figures there are some crucial points attention to which may lead to different decompositions of the image and therefore to experiencing different objects.

a. Ambiguous figures

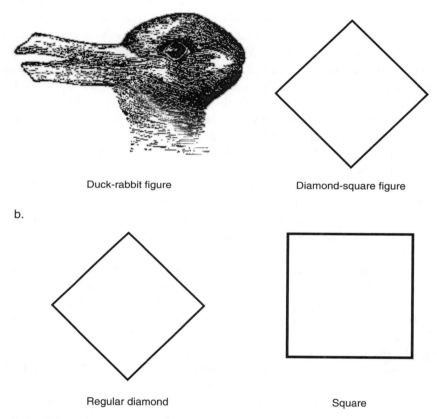

Duck-rabbit figure   Diamond-square figure

b.

Regular diamond   Square

Figure 7.1
Ambiguous figures.

Spatial attention can be bottom-up and image-driven (exogenous attention) or top-down and conceptually driven (endogenous attention). In exogenous attention it is the features of the image that "pop-up" and capture attention by making more salient the crucial points, whereas in endogenous attention attentional focus is determined by the conceptual framework of the perceiver. Suppose a view of the duck/rabbit configuration of figure 7.1a that is not stationary but moves from left to right. Then one's attention would focus on the right side of the figure, where the direction of motion is, and the figure would be decomposed and organized in such a way that a rabbit-like figure (that is, a figure that could be described or identified as a rabbit should the perceiver possessed the salient concept) would be perceived. If the figure were moving from right to left then one would perceive a duck-like figure (that is, a figure that could be described or identified as a duck), since one's attention would have focused on the left side of the figure and would have decomposed the figure in another way. In the latter case, the image perceived would be determined by exogenous attention, since the locus of attentional focus would have been determined by the moving image. If the perceiver possessed the concepts "rabbit" or "duck," she would see$_{dox}$ a rabbit or a duck respectively. Notice that even if the perceiver had not possessed these concepts she would still have perceived a different figure in each case—that is, she would have had different phenomenal contents in each case.

In the case of endogenous attention, on the other hand, the activation of perceptual set may explain the process by which perceptual set operates with bi-stable stimuli (stimuli that support two perceptual interpretations), in tasks in which only one stimulus is present and there is not a target object that must be selected amidst other distractors. Perceptual set facilitates one interpretation over another. Work with bi-stable stimuli by Attneave (1971), Driver and Baylis (1996), and Peterson and Hochberg (1983) sheds light on the mechanisms that underlie the way perceptual set biases object segmentation. Their findings suggest that the cognitive states of the observer that determine her perceptual set do not by themselves affect the organization of the stimulus. Some crucial points of fixation influence the organization of the stimulus. In other words, the way a bi-stable stimulus can be visually interpreted depends on where the observer fixes her attention, because there exist in the figure crucial points fixation on which determines the perceptual interpretation. This means that the mechanism underlying the effect of perceptual set in ambiguous figures involves the voluntary control of spatial attention; the perceptual set induces observers to allocate their attention to a specific region in the stimulus (Peterson and Gibson 1994). This is supported by Leopold and Logothetis's (1996) research, which suggests that the perception of bi-stable figures is determined not during early visual processing (for example, by suppression of monocular cells), but in higher visual areas (such as V4 and MT) in which shape is encoded.

As I discussed in chapter 2, endogenous attention is related to working memory; when one looks for a spoon, one's working memory informs one that spoons are usually in the kitchen, and one searches the kitchen. Working memory stores information and performs executive control governing retrieval, encoding, and commands for the expression of attention.

These two functions underlie the distinction in the attentional control processes between expectancy of an upcoming event and preparation for that event. However, the expectation of an event is not necessarily accompanied by an attentional preparation for it. The top-down attentional control of perception amounts to the attentional expectation for an upcoming event, not necessarily to the preparation for that event. That is, cognitive factors determine the expectation for an event, but this is not sufficient for attentional preparation for that event. Information about the upcoming display of an object may be kept in working memory, whereas attention may be directed elsewhere. Attentional preparation for an event follows expectation if the event is task-relative.

Suppose, now, that a stationary duck/rabbit configuration is viewed by a perceiver X who possesses both concepts but who, for some reason, has activated the concept "rabbit" before the ambiguous figure appears. In other words, cognitive factors have created a context in which X is biased toward rabbits or (equivalently) X is in perceptual readiness for rabbits. This has resulted in an expectation in X's spatial attention. Suppose, second, that X performs a task that is related with rabbits. This leads X to be prepared for rabbits. This preparation combined with expectation means that spatial attention focuses on points in space where previous experience indicates that, with an acceptable probability, the information contained at those points suffices to determine the presence of a rabbit. Such characteristic information may be the relative position of the ears with respect to the face, which depends on the orientation of the image. In the case of a perceptual readiness for ducks, the characteristic information pertains to the relative position of the beak with respect to the face. If at some time X is presented with a rabbit/duck ambiguous shape, then X, focusing her attention on the location at which she expects the characteristic ears, will see a rabbit. If X were expecting a duck, she would have focused elsewhere in the picture and would have seen a duck.

Thus, when the ambiguous figure appears, the perceiver, because of the perceptual set, focuses on some part of the image and retrieves from it bottom-up, and therefore is phenomenally aware of, either a duck-like or a rabbit-like figure. This image is fed to higher cortical areas where Global Recurrent Processing (GRP) occurs and working memory activation affects visual processing. At this stage, cognitively driven object-based attention intervenes and determines, depending on the kind of perceptual readiness, whether one sees$_{dox}$ a duck or a rabbit. Object-recognition contributions play a significant role at this stage (Chambers and Reisberg 1992; Peterson and Gibson 1994). It is known that familiar objects have an advantage over unfamiliar objects in object figure-ground segregation (Peterson 1994; Vecera and O'Reilly 2000) and in object attention (Vecera and Farah 1997). According to Desimone's (1999) account of attention as biased competition, familiar objects that are stored in visual long-term memory, when they become task relevant, activate cells in visual working memory that represent the familiar objects' features, providing top-down feedback that enhances the activation of neurons in the visual cortex that respond to these objects giving them an edge in their competition against neuronal assemblies that respond to the unfamiliar objects. This is, in a nutshell, how object-centered attention operates and how the effects of perceptual set bias image perception.

The above analysis shows in what sense the duck/rabbit configuration is perceptually ambiguous. The image that is formed during the first stages of the FFS is neither a duck nor a rabbit but, rather, the duck/rabbit configuration. There is no separation between a duck-like and a rabbit-like image during the first stages of visual processing, since how the image is eventually seen does not affect early processing. About 70 ms after stimulus onset, spatial attention, whether endogenously or exogenously driven, decomposes that figure in ways that the ensuing phenomenal content of perception is that of a duck-like or a rabbit-like figure. This takes place in areas V4 and MT, in which shape is encoded. That content may eventually be conceptualized as either a duck or a rabbit (respectively) and become available to the report awareness or access awareness of the perceiver; the perceiver passes from representational states in which she sees$_{ph}$ a duck-like or a rabbit-like figure to representational states of seeing$_{dox}$ a duck or a rabbit.

The Diamond/Square Figure   There is some confusion in various accounts of the diamond/square figure. Sometimes the ambiguity that is discussed is about the fact that the *two* figures in figure 7.1b are seen as a diamond and a square, respectively. But strictly speaking there is no ambiguity here. Each of these figures is consistently reported as a diamond or a square, respectively. What is at issue is not that there are two different reports, one for each figure, but that one figure is a tilted version of the other and yet is reported as a different figure. This, however, is not ambiguity regarding the perception of an image but failure of shape-constancy. Other times, the ambiguity refers to the fact that *one and the same* figure, though it is usually reported as a diamond, could on certain occasions be reported as a tilted square.

Palmer (1983, 1992) offers an account of the various theories that have been proposed to explain ambiguous figures and the contextual effects on perceived ambiguous figures. I will concentrate here on a relatively current theory that purports to explain the square/diamond ambiguous figure by invoking differences in the frames of reference that can be imposed on the ambiguous figure (Ferrante et al. 1997). The reason is that this theory provides an adequate account of the perception of the diamond/square figure and it is consistent with the theory of perception presented in section 7.1.

Ferrante et al. (1997) argue that it is the frame of reference that is applied to the ambiguous figure that induces subjects to report seeing a diamond or a square. This frame of reference is a Cartesian system of coordinates whose vertical axis coincides with the axe of vertical symmetry of the square. In the case of a square, the vertical axis of symmetry bisects the edges of the square whereas in the case of the diamond it bisects the angles. Thus, the frame based on the vertical symmetry of the figure cuts the two figures differently inducing different representations. More specifically, if a tilted frame is applied to the figure (see figure 7.2b), the subjects report seeing a square. If a non-tilted frame is applied, then the subjects report seeing a diamond. If this is what happens, representationalists could argue that when seeing the ambiguous figure the nonconceptual content that subjects retrieve from the image is represented in one frame of reference

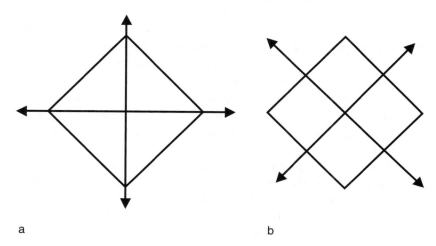

a   b

Figure 7.2
The regular diamond figure cast into two different frames of reference. Left: The frame of reference bisects the angles of the figure, which is readily seen as a diamond. Right: The frame of reference bisects the sides of the figure, which, as a result, may be seen as a square.

and, as a result, the figure that is seen$_{ph}$ has a different NCC from the figure that would have been seen$_{ph}$ had a different frame of reference been applied to the ambiguous figure. In other words, different contents are represented in the two cases, despite there being only one physical input. Hence, differences in phenomenal content are caused by differences in NCC. Furthermore, this account explains the finding that when subjects view the figure they first report seeing$_{dox}$ a diamond. If the NCC is represented in a non-tilted Cartesian frame of reference, then the figure that is automatically retrieved from the image is diamond-like, and that is why subjects at first report seeing a diamond. If, for some reason or other a different frame of reference had been applied to the image a different figure would have been seen$_{dox}$, namely a square.

Why should the Cartesian system of coordinates in which the figure (or, to be precise the content of the scene that is retrieved bottom-up, since we are talking about NCC) is cast be sensitive to the vertical symmetry or symmetry around the vertical axis. Why should the system of coordinates that the perceptual system applies to frame the NCC content retrieved from a scene be sensitive to vertical symmetry? In other words, why has the perceptual system been evolved in such a way as to be sensitive to the detection of vertical symmetries? We have seen one reason, to wit that NCC is represented with respect to the body of the perceiver with the center of the axes being either the center of gravity, or the center between the eyes, or the center of the head, depending on the perceiver and the circumstances prevailing in the environment. In this case, the two axes represent the dimensions up-down and right-left, with the vertical dimension being the more important, since it is this that matters mostly for the orientation of the organism in its environment. Another explanation is provided by the work of Braitenberg. Braitenberg (1984; also see Dennett's discussion on pp. 303–304 of *The Intentional Stance*) offers a very interesting hypothesis why this may be the case. Braitenberg's main point is that in the natural world the perception of vertical symmetry counts because it allows the animal to detect other animals that are facing it. This is important because this may signify another animal that is looking at, and therefore has detected and may be interested in, the fist animal. This means, in turn, that the second animal may be a potential threat, or mate, or antagonist, and this is very important for the first animal to "know." Finally, another reason why the detection of vertical symmetries is so important that an organism must be quite sensitive to its detection is proposed by Leyton (1992), who argues that the determination of axes of symmetry in combination with local perturbations on the surface of objects may lead to the representation of Marr's (1982) generalized cylinders or Biederman's (1987) generalized cones that figure prominently in theories of vision as providing fast and easy solutions to determining with a good approximation the shapes of objects. Leyton also argues that the detection of symmetries or rather the lack thereof signifies for the organism the action of causal forces that are likely to have acted to form the shapes of the objects, the detection of these forces being apparently important to the survival of the organism.

In view of the above, what happens when subjects view only the square/ diamond figure? The image that is perceived (i.e., retrieved bottom-up from the scene) is a figure with a certain shape and a certain orientation (i.e., with non-normal right angles). Recall, furthermore, that NCC is framed in a relational coordinate system that is best captured by Cartesian coordinates, in which the directions top-down and right-left are determined with respect to the position of the body of the perceiver. In the square/diamond figure, the application of the coordinate system bisects the angles of the figure. Thus, what is phenomenally perceived is something like the configuration shown in figure 7.2a. This phenomenal content is readily conceptualized as a diamond. Since almost all subjects report seeing a diamond, there is some controversy as to whether this figure is really an ambiguous figure. Recently it has become more common to call this figure "reversible"—that is, a figure the perception of which may change under certain circumstances (by rotating the figure, for instance). Here, as in the case of the duck/rabbit figure, spatial attention can influence the way the square/ diamond figure is perceived. One could, for instance, shift spatial attention to the axes that bisect the sides of the square/diamond figure, and then one could report seeing a square. Such an attentional shift may be due to either an exogenous or an endogenous reason. A cue, for example, may appear at the middle of one side and may cause attention to disengage from one of the corners and shift to that middle point. This is a case of exogenous attention. Or, in endogenous attention, the subject may be in perceptual readiness for squares and may, as a result, decompose the configuration in her visual field in a way that results in the perception of a square-like figure. In either case, the ensuing phenomenal content is that of a square-like figure. It is not certain what happens in these cases, that is, how attentional effects cause what is usually perceived as a diamond to be perceived as a square. It is probable that the subject performs a mental rotation that changes the orientation of the figure so that it acquires normal right angles. There is abundant evidence (Pylyshyn 1979; Shepard and Cooper 1982) that, under various conditions, subjects perform mental rotations in order to identify and classify figures. If, for example, there is a perceptual set for squares, and a subject comes across a figure that might be a square even though it does not look like one (say, the diamond-like figure), the subject will rotate the figure to find out whether it is a rotated square.

Be that as it may, the phenomenal content of the rotated figure (which could be conceptualized by the concept "square") is different from the phenomenal content of the figure with the non-normal right angles (conceptualized by "diamond") in that the two figures have different orientations and the Cartesian framework cuts them differently. Since these attributes of the image are retrieved bottom-up from the scene, they are parts of NCC, which means that the original figure and the rotated figure have different NCC. This being so, the two figures have different NCC and they also have different phenomenal contents, which is all that representationalism demands.

Alternatively, the subject may be in perceptual readiness for (say) squares, and may search the scene for squares. The phenomenal content that corresponds to a diamond is first retrieved bottom-up from the scene, on account of the nature of perceptual processing and the way the figure is oriented in space. When GRP is implicated in the processing, object-based attention modulates the processing, as a result of the perceptual readiness for the class "square," and the conceptual framework of the perceiver applies to the phenomenal content of perception and the object is identified as a square. The content of the relevant neural states along the visual system is now conceptual and that allows the perceiver to have access to, and be able to report, that content. The subject sees$_{dox}$ a square even though she is seeing$_{ph}$ a diamond; there is only one phenomenal content, but there are different conceptualizations of that content. If this is the case, then there is no gestalt switch in seeing a diamond or a square, since the switch is not a change in phenomenal content but a change in content of which one has report awareness or access awareness; it is a change in conceptual content not phenomenal NCC. If this what happens—that is, if there is no change in phenomenal character but only different cases of doxastic seeing—then infants and animals, lacking concepts and thus unable to see$_{dox}$, should see$_{ph}$ the same figure.

Which of the two alternative accounts that I have offered here is a more adequate account of the perception of the square/diamond ambiguous figure is a matter for empirical research to solve. If it could be shown, for instance, that infants or animals do not undergo the gestalt switch upon viewing the square/diamond figure (which would mean that the figure is not ambiguous for them), that would tip the scale in favor of the second account.

This analysis implies a potential difference between the duck/rabbit and the square/diamond ambiguous figures. If it is possible that in the latter case there can be only one NCC content retrieved from the image (a diamond-like figure), and the ambiguity results from the conceptualization of that NCC as a square, then the square/diamond figure is not perceptually ambiguous, or at least is not ambiguous in the same sense in which the duck/rabbit figure is ambiguous. The duck/rabbit is ambiguous because it can be decomposed perceptually and can be perceived (seeing$_{ph}$) into two different ways. The square/diamond figure, on the other hand, can be seen$_{ph}$ only in one way (as a diamond-like figure) but can be conceptualized either as a diamond or as a square.

Here is another way to make the same point: In the case of the figure with non-normal angles (the diamond), the configuration that is phenomenally perceived readily elicits the application of the concept "diamond." That is why subjects who are shown that figure usually report seeing a diamond. Herein lies a difference between the duck/rabbit and square/diamond ambiguous figures. The former figure is neutral with respect to its possible conceptualizations in the sense that both are equally possible and in the sense that it is the cognitively driven attention that determines the interpretation that prevails; furthermore, subjects with no attentional set will see$_{ph}$ as either a duck-like or a rabbit-like figure. The NCC of the diamond-like figure (its orientation and the way the system of reference cuts the figure), on the other hand, is such that the phenomenal character of the experience is unmistakably that of a diamond-like figure, which readily elicits the concept "diamond," and the figure is reported as a diamond (unless the subject is conceptually driven to see$_{dox}$ a square because she is in perceptual readiness for that class).

The account of the duck/rabbit and square/diamond ambiguous figures is an example of how the resolution of ambiguities could be explained without appealing to context (that is, to top-down, effects that modulate perceptual processing). Thus, Churchland's appeal to ambiguous figures fails to drive his argument in favor of the theory-ladenness of perception home.

However, suppose that I am wrong and that there are some genuine cases in which ambiguities are resolved by means of top-down semantic modulation that does affect perceptual processing itself. Even in that case, it would be rather far-fetched to argue that the rare cases (if any) of perceptual ambiguities that are resolved by means of cognitive interference imply that perception is cognitively penetrable, and that the scientists' beliefs shape what they perceive. The point is that the results of scientific enterprise very rarely result in genuine perceptually ambiguous images, whose resolution requires top-down processes. Scientists may argue over what objects they see (object recognition), but they rarely disagree as to what they perceive (the image extracted from early vision).

Moreover, one does not choose which arrays are ambiguous, nor does one choose the terms of ambiguity. Recall that these illusions arise exactly because they play against the physical assumptions underlying our vision. One does not choose these assumptions; they reflect our world. It follows that, although one may "choose" to see a rabbit or a duck in a duck/rabbit configuration, one cannot "choose" one's illusions. This means that disagreeing scientists cannot argue that they perceive different things, because of the top-down character of perception, because the cases of real perceptual ambiguities that require top-down processing cannot be chosen as it fits their current dispute.

7.1.4   Inverted Frames

Churchland's (1989) favorite example is the case of "inverted fields," in which people who wear lenses that invert the retinal image succeed (after a period of disorientation) in adjusting to the new perceptual regime and behave quite normally. According to Churchland, this is a clear demonstration of the penetrability and plasticity of our vision, since some very deep assumptions guiding the computations performed by the visual system can be reshaped in view of new experiences. Churchland thinks that the adaptation to the inverting lenses is evidence of the plasticity of some deep assumptions implicit in visual processing, such as the specific orientation of the visual field. That these assumptions can be reshaped in a week is evidence that the plasticity and penetrability of perception.

Fodor (1988) concedes to Churchland that if in fact the case of inverting lenses reflects the penetration of perception by experience then the modularity thesis is blown to pieces, since Fodor is committed to the thesis that the perceptual systems have a fixed neural architecture. Fodor, however, denies that such is the case, since one might expect to find this kind of plasticity on good ecological grounds. Fodor claims that there may be specific mechanisms that "function to effect the required visual-motor calibrations" and that are required for the adaptation of the subjects to the new inverted retinal images. Fodor concedes to Churchland the plasticity of perception in this case, but he does not think it damaging for the thesis of the theoretical neutrality of observation, since it is expected on specific

ecological grounds, whereas the thesis of the theory-ladenness of observation requires that the perceptual field be reshaped "by learning physics."

There are several reasons why this may not be the case. First, the weak-
interaction model seems to work here too. In fact, the later stages of
inverted field learning seem more like an oscillation between two competing impenetrable modules than like anything penetrable. Second,
Churchland thinks that the inverting lenses cause true visual effects. This
is disputable, however, as there are accounts of this phenomenon that
explain the reorientation and adaptation, not by imposing changes in the
visual computational mechanisms and the visual representation itself, but
by positing that such adaptations occur in the felt position of the limbs
and the head (Dodwell 1992).

Suppose, finally, that some of the basic assumptions underlying visual
processing do change as a result of experience. Does this mean that perception is cognitively penetrable by top-down processes, and that people who
wear inverting lenses readapt because they know that they see the world
upside down? Or do they readapt because their perceptual mechanisms
readjust? All the phenomenon shows is that perception is data-driven, not
theory-driven, and that, in view of some new experience that upsets its
balance, the system readjusts to achieve equilibrium. Though this undermines the claim of the rigidity of the modules' architecture, it does not
imply that information flowing from higher cognitive levels penetrates the
visual circuits to effect the appropriate changes. As we shall see in section
7.4, both Churchland and Fodor confuse cognitive penetrability with expe-
rience-driven changes in the perceptual systems. Evidence for the experi-
ence-driven changes in the perceptual systems does not entail cognitive
penetrability.

7.1.5   Illusions and the Theory-Ladenness of Perception
If Fodor believes that object recognition is impenetrable, then he is wrong
and Churchland is right to point this out. Fodor (1983, p. 97) argues that
the "visual-input system delivers basic categorizations." He believes that
the 3D sketch is computed algorithmically in a bottom-up fashion, and
that an encapsulated processor can perform object identification. Then, at
a final stage, the 3D sketch is paired with a "form-concept" dictionary,
which selects one of the outputs of the encapsulated processor. Thus, Fodor
seems to think that object identification involves weak interactionism, and
that, in this sense, it is a purely bottom-up process.

Against that, it has been argued that the formation of the object-centered
representation relies on top-down flow of information. Pylyshyn (1999)

argues, in accordance with Marr (1992), that the end product of perception is the $2\frac{1}{2}$D sketch, which delivers not objects but representations of shapes (structured representations of $2\frac{1}{2}$D surfaces of objects). Thus, the output of the encapsulated visual processor does not consist in the regular objects that we encounter in the world, but in a more abstract form of categories of such objects, classified according to their generic shapes.

Fodor's distinction between "fixation of appearances" or "observation" (which is the result of the functioning of the perceptual modules) and "fixation of belief" is misguided. Fodor seems to distinguish between the "sensory" and "cognitive" or "semantic" processes that are involved in the formation of observation statements, and to consider observation as a pre-cognitive activity whose output is processed by cognition giving rise to the observation statements. Philosophers would recognize here the distinction between what we see and how we interpret it. But this distinction is misleading, because object recognition is a cognitive process, and observation involves object recognition. The distinction Fodor wishes to draw between a bottom-up, theory-neutral process and a top-down, theory-laden process should not be cut at the observation/cognition interface, since such an interface does not exist, but at the perception/cognition interface. This criticism of Fodor's views does not imply the rejection of the modularity thesis. What is rejected is the view that observation is informationally encapsulated.

My discussion suggests that Churchland is right in rejecting the encapsulation of observation. He is wrong, however, in arguing for the cognitive penetrability of perception. First, it seems likely that, as the weak-interaction model states, the higher cognitive states affect the products of the visual modules only after the visual modules have produced their product by selecting (acting like filters) which output will be accepted for further processing. Weak interactionism can explain much, if not all, of Churchland's evidence for strong interactions. Second, as we shall see, perceptual learning need not involve top-down penetrability of perception from higher cognitive states. Finally, even if weak interactionism is wrong and there is some top-down flow of information from higher cognitive levels, which through the effects of attention modulates processing at perceptual sites, this modulation is either delayed and does not affect perceptual processing itself if the attention involved is object-centered attention (its role being to enlist these sites to participate in higher cognitive tasks), or, if the attention involved is spatial attention, the attentional effects on perceptual processing do not entail the cognitive penetrability of perception, as I argued in chapter 2 and I will elaborate further in the next chapter. In this sense, the input systems are cognitively impenetrable.

7.2   The Argument from Descending Pathways

Churchland's (1989) second line of attack against the impenetrability of perception consists in evidence that there are top-down links from higher cognitive centers to the peripheral modules. (Here Churchland uses 'module' in the way it is employed in neuroscience, according to which brains are structures, with cells, columns, layers and regions that divide up the labor of information-processing, and each such region is called a module.) Churchland reports findings from cell-staining techniques according to which the ascending pathways from the retinal to the geniculate nucleus (LGN), and from there to the visual cortices and to other centers higher in the processing hierarchy, are matched by descending pathways from the higher level of processing back to the earliest processing systems at the retina (Zeki 1978; Van Essen 1985). Churchland argues that the function of these descending pathways is "centrifugal control," that is, "the modulation of lower neural activity as a function of the demands sent down from levels higher in the cognitive hierarchy."

The existence of descending pathways is hardly disputable, nor is the importance of top-down processes in observation. What is disputable is the function of these top-down pathways in perception. Does their existence imply that even the early levels of vision are penetrable by this top-down flow of information? The answer to this question is No—not because, as Fodor (1988, p. 194) claims, "if there is no cognitive penetration of perception, then at least 'descending pathways' aren't for that" (that argument is apparently a poor one), but because we know something about the function of the neuroanatomical structures in the brain.

To facilitate the discussion, let me repeat here the main results from chapter 2 about the timing of visual processing. When a visual scene is being presented to the eyes, the feedforward sweep reaches V1 at a latency of about 40 ms. Information is fed forward to the extrastriate, parietal, and temporal areas of the brain. The first ERP component, C1, is elicited at about 50 ms after stimulus onset and is not affected by attention, be it spatial or object-centered. By 70–80 ms after stimulus onset, most visual areas are activated. The pre-attentional FFS culminates within 100 or 120 ms after stimulus onset. 70–90 ms after the stimulus onset, spatial attention, by modulating the P1 waveform, enhances visual processing in a voluntary task-driven search at the salient locations. However, P1 is sensitive only to the characteristics of the stimulus. 100 ms after the presentation of the stimuli at those locations, an extensive part of our brain responds to the physical characteristics of the visual array. 150 ms after the stimulus these features fuse to a single form or structural description of the objects in a visual scene by means of LRP. At 150 ms, the onset of N1 indexes the beginning of the registration of differences between targets and distractors and, in general, differences between task-relevant and task-irrelevant items in the visual scene. About 200–300 ms after stimulus presentation, a voluntary task-driven search is registered in the same areas that process the visual features in the FFS and LRP enhancing neuronal activation of the salient objects and/or locations. These attentional effects are indexed by the onset of N2, which also signifies the onset of the biasing of processing by object-centered attention. Thus, the top-down effects of attention to features and objects are delayed in time and involve the same anatomical areas as the FFS and LRP, except that attention amplifies the recordings in these areas. Finally, about 250 ms after the stimulus, some of the same areas participate in the cognitive/semantic processing of the input. Global RP takes place and objects are classified and recognized, a process that is indexed by the onset of P3. In sum, the active attention studies suggest that when top-down processes occur, the activation of some groups of neurons in early perceptual areas is enhanced with a relatively considerable delay and the source of this amplification is higher areas in the brain.

What do these findings suggest? Tasks that require more or less top-down flow of information activate broadly the same areas that are needed to compute the purely bottom-up tasks, in addition to the higher cognitive areas in the brain whence the top-down signals originate. The active attention studies showed that when top-down processes occur, the activation of these areas is enhanced and the source of this amplification is higher areas in the brain. In order for the factors that cause this amplification to be transmitted to the lower areas certain descending pathways are required. The same conclusion can be drawn from the visual imagery studies. Visual imagery demands that activation originate from higher cognitive centers and descend to the visual cortex in which imagined images are formed. The descending pathways accomplish exactly this. Furthermore, since recurrent processing involving both perceptual circuits and cognitive centers is necessary for access awareness or report awareness, which is what makes us conscious of our surroundings, the descending pathways are necessary for consciousness to emerge as well.

Now, the filtering weak interactionist model assumes that in attention-driven tasks perception sends up in parallel all possible interpretations of a scene, that is, all possible proto-objects within the visual field and then attention selects the one that is most relevant to the aims of the perceiver. This means that there is a problem with weak interactionism that stems from the account of ambiguous figures and of the role of spatial attention in determining which interpretation of the ambiguous figure is finally seen. This account suggests that focusing on some crucial points of the image determines the way the image is decomposed and synthesized and, hence, determines the percept. This, however, means that perception does not process all the way up to the cognitive interface both possible interpretations of the bi-stable figure so that cognitive factors select one or the other interpretation. Instead, relatively early on in perception one or the other interpretation is chosen and being processed.

Although the role of spatial attention seems to undermine weak interactionism, it does not compel one to adhere to the theory-ladenness of perception. In the focus attention tasks, attention modulates processing by singling out locations and features that, consequently, are preferably searched. These are the effects of spatial attention that does modulate perceptual processing (the P1 ERP waveform that signals the first effects of spatial attention occurs about 70 ms after stimulus onset and this places the effects of spatial attention well within the time frame of perceptual processing). To see what is at stake here, recall that visuo-spatial attention may act in two ways. It may enhance the base-line activation of the neuronal assemblies tuned to the attended location in specialized extrastriate areas and in parietal regions and perhaps in striate cortex V1. This is the *attentional modulation of spontaneous activity* and indicates the shift of attention to a certain location, that is, the fact that spontaneous firing rates of neurons in all visual pathways are increased when attention is shifted, by means of a cue, toward the location of an upcoming stimulus before the presentation of the stimulus. This is, however, a pre-perceptual effect that does not affect the issue of the cognitive penetrability of perception (Pylyshyn 1999; Raftopoulos 2001a,b).

Now, when one fixes one's gaze at some location before the stimulus onset (say, through the instruction of the experimenter or a spatial cue or in general through some attentional control setting), there are effects of spatial attention, in addition to the enhancement of spontaneous activity of the relevant neurons, that are delayed and this way they pervade early perceptual processing that starts after the eyes have focused on some location. (Recall that the stimulus is presented after attention has focused.) In other words, when one focuses on some location spatial attention modulates the perceptual processing that will follow the appearance of the stimulus. Hence, the argument that the effects of spatial attention are only pre-perceptual and therefore the cognitive driven character of spatial attention does not threaten the cognitive impenetrability of perception fails. Fortunately, for those who defend the theory-neutrality of perception, the effects of spatial attention on perceptual processing are, as I explained in chapters 1 and 2 and as I will elaborate further in the next chapter, stimulus driven and not cognitively driven. This means that once spatial attention has selected some loci for focusing, and once it has enhanced the activity of the relevant neuronal sites and inhibited the activity of the other sites, information is registered at that stage of processing irrespective of task demands and cognitive states. In other words, once spatial attention enhances processing of information coming from some specific loci, and once task-relevant stimuli have been distinguished from task-irrelevant stimuli on the basis of their features and the perceptual setting, what one sees at the relevant location depends on what is there, not on the cognitive stances of the viewer. This is a kind of indirect cognitive penetrability of perception, which, as I shall explain in chapter 8, blocks drawing the conclusion that because of the role of spatial attention perception is cognitively penetrable.

Thus, tasks that require more or less top-down flow of information activate broadly, albeit with a delay, the same areas that are needed to compute the purely bottom-up tasks. How does the brain do this? The answer lies in the reentrant connections or mappings among neurons in the brain (Edelman 1987, 1992). These reentry connections map (as it were) the activity of any system onto the others and reciprocally, by allowing the transmission of information in all directions. Recall now Churchland's argument. We know that there are many neural connections devoted to bringing information back to the sensory systems from higher cognitive centers. This constitutes evidence for the mediation of the output of the perceptual modules by information from higher cognitive states. But, as we saw, the descending pathways most likely have another role to play. The sensory systems are fed back information from higher centers, and signals from higher areas reenter the brain areas that had processed before the signals that were transformed by the higher centers to the reentrant new signals. The same areas that process sensory specific information in a bottom-up way are also involved in higher-level thought (voluntarily attention-driven search, imagery), except that in the latter case they are reentered in a top-down manner, and their activation is amplified. As Lamme and Roelfsema (2000, p. 574) observe, "cortical neurons are not simple detectors of one aspect of the visual scene. Instead, lateral and feedback connections allow them to contribute to different analyses at different moments in time."

The effects of top-down influences on the early sites are variegated. In addition to engaging early visual sites to participate in cognitive tasks, such as visual imagery, they also engage these early sites in representing concepts and in participating in the brain activity that induces report awareness or access awareness. Recall that, as I discussed in chapter 2, according to Treisman (2004) and others attention is needed for some feature binding, for detailed localization, and for conscious perception. The initial unconscious FFS provides the gist of the scene, the gross spatial layout, and some rough bindings of features into some form of objects (perhaps the proto-objects that have been proposed in other studies). Attentional modulation of early visual areas occurs to allow a check of the initial rough bindings through the fine spatial resolution of early visual areas, a check of the initial identifications for selected scene elements against the sensory data (Lamme and Roelfsema 2000), and to form the representations of objects as we consciously experience them.

Another crucial aspect of the role of recurrent feedback connections, which is closely related to the previous point, is that they enhance visual responses in order to integrate them eventually into a coherent representation of items in a visual scene (Lamme and Roelfsema 2000; Rensink 2000a,b). When attention in a target search task enhances processing and induces the identification of the target, it does so by enhancing responses that are selective for the identity and location of the target. This way, attention labels the identity and location of the target item (Lamme and Roelfsema 2000, p. 576). As I have said, Kanwisher (2001) distinguishes perception from awareness and suggests that perceptual awareness involves not only activation of the relevant perceptual properties, but also construction of an organized representation in which these visual properties are attributed to their source in external objects and events. Thus, perceptual awareness presupposes binding of activated features with a representation that specifies a specific token, as opposed to type, object. This binding requires "visual attention," which thus becomes necessary for a coherent representation of object tokens.

7.3   The Argument from Plasticity of the Brain and Perceptual Learning

7.3.1   Plasticity of the Brain, Innatism, and Modularity

Churchland's (1989, p. 267) third argument against impenetrability comes from neuroscientific studies suggesting the plasticity of the visual cortex in particular, and the cortex in general. Its line is that plasticity goes against Fodor's view that the perceptual modules are endogenously specified, are hard-wired, and have a fixed neural architecture. Instead it shows that these systems are developed over time in a highly plastic system and that this development is context driven or environmentally driven (by the characteristics of the input to the cortex). It is true that the cortex can support a variety of representations early in development, and that there are no areas of the cortex pre-specified for a certain function. When inputs are rewired so that they project to a different region of the cortex from what they usually do, then the new region develops some of the properties of the original target (Sur, Pallas, and Roe 1990). When a piece of the cortex is transplanted to a new location it develops projections that characterize the new location rather than its origin (O'Leary 1993). Finally, when the areas for the normal higher functions are bilaterally removed in early infancy, regions at considerable distance from the normal site can take over their function (Webster, Bachevalier, and Ungerleider 1995).

All this evidence supports the "protocortex" hypothesis against its competitor "protomap" hypothesis. The latter states (Rakic 1988) that the differentiation of the cortex into areas with specific functions is determined by intrinsic molecular markers, or by a pre-specification of the proliferative zone. This implies that the areal specification of the cortex is innately determined and hard-wired (specified by interactions at the molecular level and independent of thalamic inputs). The former states (Killackey 1990; O'Leary 1993) that the protocortex is initially undifferentiated and is divided up into specific areas largely as a result of the thalamic input, which means that the specialization of the cortex is not innate but determined through the interactions of an undifferentiated cortex with the environment.

This is hardly the image of hard-wired, innate perceptual systems, since the differentiation of the cortex into specific areas, or maps, is not pre-specified. This is not the end of the story, however. First, all the research showing the plasticity of the cortex involves experiments in vitro. There is some evidence that the thalamus may know about its preferred cortical targets in realistic in vivo situations (Niederer, Maimon, and Finlay 1995). This means that the sites to which thalamic input is projected may be pre-specified, and that the areas in the cortex that will become the perceptual systems are innately determined. Second, even though there is evidence that the representational differentiation of the cortex is not innate, that is, that there are no innate representations in the form of stable connection weights among the neurons, there is strong evidence that there are some powerful innate architectural and chronotropic constraints that restrict the way the cortex develops while interacting with the environment (Thatcher 1992; Shrager and Johnson 1995; Elman et al. 1996; Johnson 1997).

The architectural constraints consist in the types of neurons, their response characteristics, their firing threshold, type of transmitter, nature of pre-synaptic and post-synaptic changes, number of layers, packing density of cells, degree of interconnectivity, whether the connectivity is excitatory or inhibitory, and finally, the way the various modules are connected together to form the whole brain (Elman et al. 1996, pp. 27–30). The chronotropic constraints refer to the timing of events in the developmental process, which often is under genetic control. Shrager and Johnson (1995) propose a model which shows how a progressively grown wave of plasticity that traverses the cortex may govern the way the cortex is parceled into different functional maps.

Evidence for this kind of architectural and chronotropic innatism abounds. Johnson and Morton (1991) show that, whereas face recognition becomes progressively species-specific due to interactions with the environment, infants at birth consistently orient toward species-like faces as opposed to other attractive stimuli. This shows that there is a sub-cortical head start to the process of face recognition. Research in language (Bates et al. 1992, 1997) suggests that, although the child does not begin with innate representations for language, it begins with strong computational constraints that normally lead to the familiar pattern of cortex parcellation, when the child is exposed to its species typical environment (STE). These constraints include computational asymmetries between the right and left hemisphere, and differences in speed and type of processing.

Elman et al. (1996) and Johnson (1997) argue in favor of the existence of some chronotropic and architectural constraints on cognition, while they reject the notion of some pre-specified representations. They consider innate representations, however, as constant connection-synaptic weights. That does not preclude the possibility of representational innateness, in the form of pre-determined initial connection weights, which will reconfigure, up to the limits of initial constraints, with learning.

We know that the development of axons and dendrites, as well as cell death, are postnatal phenomena, and that early in life there is an excess of synaptic connections among neurons. We also know that synaptic changes are related to the information received from the environment, in that those cells that participate in information processing are selected to survive, whereas the inactive ones become eliminated (Changeux and Dehaene 1989; Kolb 1993). However, there is evidence (Ebbesson 1988) that the pattern and timing of neural connection loss is independent of experience and endogenously specified.

Johnson and Karmiloff-Smith (1992) proposed a model of synaptic loss and stabilization that purports to take into account evidence suggesting both the experience-dependent and experience-independent and time-constrained character of postnatal neural development. They distinguish between "timing" and "patterning" of loss and argue that although the specific pattern of synaptic loss is experience-dependent, the timing and extent of this loss is intrinsically determined. According to this view, the basic laminar structure of the cortex is consistent and is relatively insensitive to experience, whereas the differentiation in areas that characterizes the cortex is partly the product of experiential input.

In the same vein, Johnson (1997, pp. 40–41) argues that "while the basic architecture of a network is innate (basic circuitry, learning rules, type, and number of cells etc.), the detailed patterns of (dendritic and synaptic) connectivity are dependent upon experience. In such a case we may say that while the network imposes architectural constraints on the representations that emerge within it, there are no intrinsic representations." Examples of the way some architectural biases can affect and restrict representations and learning can be found in O'Reilly and Johnson's (1994) model of chick-imprinting and in Jacobs, Jordan, and Barto's (1991) model of the "what" and "where" system. The idea is that the macrocircuitry of the brain is pre-specified, whereas the detailed microcircuitry is the product of the interaction of the brain with the environment.

Churchland is right that the cortex can support a variety of representations early in development, and that there are not areas of the cortex pre-specified for a certain function. This plasticity, furthermore, is not just a system response to early injury but is a basic property of neural operations (Antonini et al. 1995; Katz, et al. 1995; Polat and Shagi 1995). But evidence also suggests that the brain is not equipotential for all functions, and that there are deficits, due to brain damage, that persist to some extent. This shows that the brain is not entirely plastic.

If the early brain damage is such that it affects the spatial-analytic processing, a subtle deficit persists, unlike the cases concerning early brain injuries that affect language, in which the initial deficit is almost reversible (Stiles 1995). This suggests that the neural system for processing spatial-analytic information is much more highly pre-specified than the system processing language, and less plastic in its response to early injury. The reason may be that since spatio-analytic processing is phylogenetically much older than language processing, evolution has imposed a more rigid structure on the corresponding neural system. A parallel argument can be made for the visual system, and consequently, one could argue that visual perceptual processing is much more constrained, and much less plastic than the higher, phylogenetically younger, higher cognitive processes.

It seems, thus, that the brain is initially undifferentiated representationally but possesses strong architectural and chronotropic restrictions, which restrict its representational potential and modulate the process of functional parcellation. This, conjoined with the view that there is a progressive loss of synapses due to task specialization, could explain the finding that in early phases of normal language development widely distributed regions of the brain participate in the processing (Mills, Coffey-Corina, and Neville 1993), whereas children who are efficient users of language show a much more focused distribution of brain electrical activity.

Where does the above discussion leave us with respect to the problem of innateness of our perceptual systems? Karmiloff-Smith's (1992, p. 4) "minimalistic" stand toward innateness—shared by Clark (1993a,b)—that a fairly limited amount of innately specified predispositions (which are not strictly modular) would be sufficient to constrain the classes of inputs that the infant mind computes" seems quite plausible. These predispositions include some maturationally constrained attention biases, and some structures that constrain the way the input is processed. The former ensure that some part of the input (which is characteristic of a certain domain) will be processed by a mechanism that is suited to do exactly that and ignore other data, and the latter constrain the way these data are processed.

In order to see what the above means, let us turn to the function of the auditory system with respect to the acquisition of language. Since the infant's exposure to speech is part of her species typical environment (STE-Johnson 1993), we can say that there are cells, with their dendrites and axons, that are sensitive to receiving the correct sensory inputs, and which, in response to the processing demands that this input imposes, reconfigure themselves to handle the task. These are the cells and connections that are selected to survive. This process of selection in response to input typical to the species is called experience-expectant (Greenough et al. 1993). Once this is done, these neural connections are sensitive only to a certain class of input (some particular speech sounds, as opposed to all kinds of sounds), process only this kind of input, and are indifferent to other sensory information.

The conclusion is that, far from being an equipotential medium, the brain starts with some strong innate constraints that restrict the kinds of representations it builds, in response to external environmental input. We also see that the input modules (and the linguistic one) result from development and interaction with the environment rather than being there from the beginning. Thus, current research supports a view of progressive modularization with development that encompasses, in addition to perceptual modules, higher cognitive centers.

Thus, one should amend the claim that there are no domain-specific areas in the brain and should allow the possibility that evolution has imposed on certain areas such strong constraints that, under normal conditions, these areas and these areas alone will perform certain specific functions. Architectural and chronotropic constraints seem to suffice to explain the parcellation of the brain. Jacobs, Jordan, and Barto's (1991) "what and where" connectionist system exemplifies this by showing how the architectural constraints of systems suffice to perform task decomposition and allocate one part of the system to one task, and the other to the other task, creating a complex modularized system consisting of two modules, each of which is domain-specific.

Churchland raised the issue of cortical plasticity to argue that there are no innately specified, domain-specific cortical areas, and thus, that the perceptual systems are neither hard-wired, nor encapsulated, since the idea of cortical plasticity does not "sit at all well with a picture of endogenously specified assumptions unique to each modality" (1989, p. 267). Against this claim, I discussed the kind of innatism and hard-wiring that is supported by current neuroscientific and neuropsychological research, and concluded that the brain develops and functions under certain architectural and chronotropic constraints that restrict the kind of representations it builds when interacting with the environment. The modules are the result of the interaction of a constrained brain with environmental input, and consequently, they appear with development and may become hard-wired, though initially they were not. But this is Fodor's (1983) view of innateness, and thus Churchland's criticism fails.

7.3.2 Perceptual Learning: Evidence for Cognitive Penetrability?

Does perceptual learning entail cognitive penetrability, as Churchland argues repeatedly in his discussion of illusions? Is there a way to reconcile the notion of cognitive impenetrability of perceptual systems with the growing evidence for their diachronic penetrability? According to Fodor (1988), there is no way, and this issue would be resolved with the findings of empirical research. Should empirical research show perceptual learning to be possible, then the encapsulation of Fodor's input modules would prove false. Well, empirical findings exist, and they suggest that perceptual systems are diachronically (meaning in the long run) open to some rewiring of the patterns of their neural connectivity, as a result of learning. Thus, these systems are to some extent plastic. But this does not mean that they are cognitively penetrable. Let us see why.

Research by Karni and Sagi (1995), by Yeo, Yonebayashi, and Allman (1995), by Antonini, Strycker, and Chapman (1995), by Stiles (1995), and by Merzenich and Jenkins (1995) shows that changes can be induced in visual cortical neural patterns in response to learning. More specifically, visual processing at all levels may undergo long-term, experience-dependent changes. The most interesting form of learning is "slow learning," because it is the only type that causes structural changes in the cortex (formation of new patterns of connectivity). Such learning can result in significant performance improvement—for example, one may learn with practice to perform better at visual skills involving target and texture discrimination and target detection, and to learn to identify visual patterns in fragmented residues of whole patterns (priming). Performance in these tasks was thought to be determined by low-level, stimulus-dependent visual processing. The improvement in performance in these tasks, thus, suggests that practice may modify the adult visual system, even at the early levels of processing. As Karni and Sagi (1995, pp. 95–96) remark, "learning (acquisition) and memory (retention) of visual skills would occur at the earliest level within the visual processing stream where the minimally sufficient neuronal computing capability is available for representing stimulus parameters that are relevant input for the performance of a specific task."

Karni and Sagi (ibid.) suggest that slow learning is independent of cortico-limbic processing, which is responsible for top-down processes and is, through the interaction of the limbic system with the visual pathways, responsible for conscious object recognition (Webster, Bachevalier, and Ungerleider 1995). It is also independent of factors involving semantic associations. Yeo, Yonebayashi, and Allman (1995) suggest that priming facilitates the neural mechanisms for processing images and that the cortex can learn to see ambiguous patterns by means of experience-induced changes in functional connectivity of the relevant processing areas. Thus, priming involves a structural modification of basic perceptual modules. Practice with fragmented patterns leads to the formation of the "priming memory" which may be stored in the cortical visual areas. Long-term potentiation (LTP) may be the mechanism implementing these architectural changes by establishing experience-dependent chains of associations.

Architectural modifications induced by slow learning depend on experience, in that they are controlled by the "image" formed in the retina. But, although learning and its ensuing functional modifications occur in those neuronal assemblies that are activated by the retinal image, still some extra-retinal factor should provide the mechanism that will gate functional plasticity. Although many neuronal assemblies are activated by the retinal image, learning occurs only in those assemblies that are behaviorally relevant. This is called "gating of neuronal plasticity." The mechanism that ensures this relevance cannot be the retinal input.

Gating is modulated by the demands of the task. They determine which physical aspects of the retinal input are relevant, activating the appropriate neurons. Functional restructuring can occur only at these neuronal assemblies. The mechanism that accomplishes this is attention. Focusing attention ensures that the relevant aspects of the input will be processed further. There is, indeed, ample evidence for the necessary role of attention in perceptual learning (Ahissar and Hochstein 1995) and for the role of attention in learning to perceive ambiguous figures (Kawabata 1986; Peterson and Gibson 1991, 1993).

Thus, slow learning takes place under specific retinal conditions that are input-dependent and task-dependent. These conditions do not involve cognitive influences and therefore do not imply the cognitive penetrability of perception. Recall that slow learning is independent of recognition and semantic memory. Most of the priming effects are associated with identification and discrimination of relative spatial relations and extraction of shapes. This brings to mind Hildreth and Ulmann's (1989) intermediate level of vision. The processes at this level (the extraction of shape and of spatial relations) are not purely bottom-up, but they do not require the intervention of knowledge of specific objects. They require the spatial analysis of shape and spatial relations among objects, which is task dependent.

So the perceptual systems are to some extent plastic, as Churchland argues. But this plasticity is not a result of the penetration of the perceptual modules by higher cognitive states; rather, it is a result of learning-induced changes modulated by the retinal input and task demands. Fodor's (1988) belief that the perceptual modules have a fixed architecture, made him concede that if evidence were to be found for diachronic changes in the functional architectures of the modules then that would mean the end of the modularity thesis of perception. According to the view of perceptual modules I have presented here, this is not necessarily so, since the data-driven changes in the perceptual modules can be accommodated by the notion that the modules are semi-hard-wired. This view requires only that the functional changes reshape the microcircuitry, not the macrocircuitry, of the modules. Bearing in mind that priming enhances performance in various visual tasks, one cannot see how such learning could violate the general assumptions reflecting our world and thus reshape the basic macrocircuitry.

7.4   Where Do We Stand?

To put things into focus, consider the argument for the cognitive penetrability of perception. We know that there are many neural connections devoted to bringing information back to the sensory systems from higher cognitive centers. This allegedly constitutes evidence for the mediation of the output of the perceptual modules by information from higher cognitive states. But the descending pathways probably have another role. The sensory systems are fed back information from higher centers, and so these same areas that process sensory specific information in a bottom-up way are also involved in higher-level activities (voluntarily attention-driven search, imagery, concept formation), except that in the latter case they are reentered in a top-down manner.

My arguments suggest the picture of a modular organization of our perceptual systems, which is somewhat different from that of Fodor's picture of the perceptual brain. According to this picture, which is based on the distinction between noncognitive perception and cognitive observation, the perceptual semi-Fodorian modules share some properties with the Fodorian ones. Domain-specific, fast, automatic, mandatory, and independent of conscious control, they emerge from the interaction between a constrained brain and the environment. They are different from their cousins, the original Fodorian modules, in that, first, they are informationally semi-encapsulated. The prefix 'semi' is used here to convey my notion of cognitive penetrability that does not affect perceptual processing itself, owing to the considerable delay that results from the time it take top-down information to reenter those early sites, but engages early processing sites to participate in cognitive tasks. Second, the modules have no fixed neural architecture, but are semi-hard-wired, since perceptual learning can modify the patterns of connectivity. Fodor's insistence that the modules have a fixed architecture made him vulnerable to Churchland's attacks. It also committed him to allowing that if perceptual learning occurs then modularity fails. As we saw, perceptual learning is possible and restructures the visual system. But, this does not affect his claim with regard to the module's cognitive on-line impenetrability.

Churchland's argument about reentrant pathways does not entail by itself a top-down flow of cognitive (to wit, extravisual) information. It

seems most likely that the top-down pathways serve to convey information to locations along the route of early vision, or perception, so that
these locations can participate in processing of cognitive tasks and not in
order to carry out their perceptual function. Furthermore, attempting to
demonstrate that the thesis about the cognitive penetrability of our perception, and the theoretical neutrality of observation is false, Churchland
confuses the plasticity of the brain and perceptual learning with cognitive penetrability. But the former does not entail the latter. The only way
out for Churchland is to argue that the experience-induced learning
changes the way we observe the world, and that it does so by means of
some top-down flow of information that affects the way we perceive.
Though it is true that our experiences shape our theories and the way we
see the world, to say that these theories influence the way we perceive the
world is question begging, since one must show that this top-down influences occur. Fodor seems to allude to this when he argues that even
though the perceptual modules may be plastic and amenable to local
functional changes due to environmental pressure, still "these might not
even be perceptual effects of acquiring beliefs; perhaps they're perceptual effects of having the experiences in virtue of which the beliefs are
acquired" (1989, p. 192).

Churchland also claims that even if there is theoretical neutrality at an
early perceptual process, this "pure given," or sensation, is useless in that
it cannot be used for any "discursive judgment," since sensations are not
truth-evaluable, or semantically contentful states. Only "observation judgments" can be truth-evaluable, because they have content, which is a
function of a conceptual framework. In chapters 4 and 5, I attempted to
show why Churchland is wrong. Not only is NCC semantically evaluable,
since it presents the world as being such-and-such, but is also representational content according to Bermudez's (1995) notion of representational
content, which is more stringent than Peacocke's (1992) Correctness
Condition for representational content. This means that NCC has a rich
structure, and thus perceptual states are semantically contentful states.

This theoretical neutrality does not mean that the perceptual modules
function independent of any "theoretical" constraints. Perceptual computations rely on certain operational constraints that are based on some
general assumptions about the world that constitute a powerful "theory"
constraining visual processing. But this theory is not learned. It is a pre-
requisite, if learning is to start off the ground, and this "theory" is shared
by all. Thus, this theory-ladenness cannot be used as an argument against
the existence of a common ground (in the form of some innate principles

predetermined by the structure implicit in the interaction of the perceptual mechanisms with the outside world), because perception based on a theory that is shared by all is such a common ground.

Another finding that emerges from my discussion is the importance of the perceptual "modules" in the execution of higher cognitive functions. Not only does this finding undermine the descending pathways argument for the theory-ladenness of perception; in addition, it shows that our conceptual systems are severely constrained by the architecture of the perceptual modules, since the cognitive processes that give rise to concepts involve in a significant way the perceptual processes. Perception does not serve only as the faculty that provides input to higher cognition and then comes on line, after the cessation of the conceptual processing, in order to test empirically its outcome; it also is an active participant of the conceptual processing itself.

Consequently, my discussion questions the standard distinction between conception and perception. According to this view, conception is thought of as a mental process, whereas perception is deemed to be bodily. The new picture that is emerging, which is drawing attention to the fact that perceptual processes are inextricably involved in higher cognitive processing, rejects this distinction and forces us to extend cognition to encompass the body, insofar as the perceptual bodily mechanisms do considerable conceptual work.

There is a trap lurking here, though. One should not be lured into reading the above statement to mean that (to use the title of Pylyshyn's 1999 paper) cognition and vision are continuous, that is, that cognitive and visual processes are not distinguished in space and time, and that, as a result, visual processing is throughout cognitively penetrable. The latest subscription to the continuity thesis comes from Spivey's recent book *The Continuity of Mind*. Spivey (2007, p. 208) rightly points out that the evidence that has been amassed about the existence both of a rich connectivity of lateral projections within visual cortical areas and of the abundance of recurrent synaptic projections between various cortical areas undermines any linear feedforward systems accounts of vision. Spivey takes the lateral and (especially) the recurrent connectivity to be evidence for cognitive effects influencing low-level visual processes (for example, the feedback projections allow cognitive expectations to modulate the processing of perceptual input), the most prominent among such effects being the modulation of low-level visual processing by visual attention.

To evaluate Spivey's thesis, one must first clarify the meaning of the expression "feedforward linear systems accounts of vision." There is a class of accounts of vision a characteristic representative of which is Fodor's theory of vision in *The Modularity of Mind*, according to which vision is a feedforward linear system consisting of well-distinguished subsystems that are hierarchically structured in such a way that each system informs those that are hierarchically higher in the structure but each system is impenetrable to influences from the higher structures. This is a clear-cut example of a linear feedforward systems account of vision, and, as Spivey points out, it is wrong. The lower-level visual processes are affected by top-down projections from hierarchically higher structures. Attentional effects, as we have seen, do modulate low-level processing (that is, processing that occurs at sites that are hierarchically lower or more peripheral). So, this is evidence that Fodor's modularity theory is wrong, since, after all, low-level processing is not impenetrable.

However, and this is very crucial, this same evidence would support the view that low-level processing is modulated by the information transmitted through the recurrent projections if those influences were found to take place while the lower sites process information in their capacity as low-level processing sites, that is, while those sites process low-level information (information about illuminances, spatial frequencies, surface properties, location, spatial relations, size, orientation, motion, shape, and color) during the first 100–150 ms after stimulus onset. But this is not the case. The evidence Spivey himself refers to, which I discussed in the first two chapters, shows clearly that top-down influences, although they may even reach the primary visual cortex, are delayed in time and thus cannot affect early processing. Consider the evidence from a study by Rolls and Tovee (1995) that Spivey cites to substantiate his claim that low-level processing is affected by top-down influences and that visual processing and cognition form a continuum. Rolls and Tovee recorded from multiple neurons in the inferotemporal cortex of the macaque monkey and found out that that identification of objects takes a few hundred milliseconds. The 50 percent of those neurons reaches its full resonant activity 70 ms after stimulus onset responding to the features of the stimuli. From this Spivey (2007, p. 214) concludes: "When you look at the right time scale for perception and cognition, that is, hundreds of milliseconds, there's nothing instantaneous about it at all. There are no meaningful instants; there is only process." This accords with Spivey's previous statement to the effect that sensory input gradually produces a percept.

The study by Rolls and Tovee (1995) reveals that within 70 milliseconds after stimulus onset activation has reached the IT cortex, whereas recognition of the target takes place several milliseconds later. This suggests that the recognition of an object (a cognitive feat) occurs much later in visual processing. Now, it is not clear whether the identification of the target in the Rolls-Tovee study amounts to mere recognition of the object by the animal or to the animal's awareness that such and such an object is in front of it. Recall that, according to Treisman and Kanwisher (1998), although object recognition can occur within 100–200 ms after stimulus onset, it takes another 100 ms for the required subsequent processes to bring this information into awareness so that the perceiver is aware of the presence of a token object. Be that as it may, the study by Rolls and Tovee shows that it takes time for the target to be identified and that during this time a representation of the target is gradually built. Thus far, there is no discrepancy between Spivey's account and the account presented in part I of the present book; vision is indeed a continuous process, and there is nothing instantaneous about it. But why should this be taken to mean that cognition and perception are continuous in Spivey's sense, that is, in the sense that cognition continuously informs perception? The empirical evidence, bringing to the fore the time delay of the cognitive top-down modulation of perceptual processing, supports the opposite conclusion, namely that there is a stage of early visual processing that is not affected by cognitive effects, even though the sites at which this early processing takes place are later used in cognitive tasks. Spivey's account (which, being dynamic, is entirely based on timing considerations), forgets time when it comes to assessing the connection between cognition and perception, and this is bad because time is not on Spivey's side.

Bearing all these facts in mind, it is much wiser to subscribe to the view (which can be found in the synopsis of Spivey's work at the inner cover of his book) that "perception, cognition, and action are partially overlapping segments of one continuous mental flow, rather than three distinct neural systems." Indeed, the evidence adduced in part I of the present book heavily supports that view, since it makes abundantly clear that cognitive and perceptual processes *partially* overlap in time in that, on the one hand, there is a part of visual processing, namely perception that consists in the FFS and LRP, which is uninformed by cognitive processes, and, on the other hand, that the same sites at which perception takes place receive *with a delay* input from higher cognitive centers through top-down neural pathways and participate in cognitive processes mental imaging, object-based attentional search, access awareness or report awareness, and so forth.

8 Nonconceptual Content, Perception, and Realism

One of realism's most serious opponents is Constructivism. Constructivists claim that material objects are constructed out of representations, and that the objects as mind-independent entities are epistemically inaccessible. Constructivism denies the realist's claims that scientific theories relate mind-independent objects and us. Kitcher (2001) distinguishes two trends in constructivist criticisms of realism, namely epistemological and semantic constructivism. Epistemological Constructivism undermines realism by arguing that our experience of the world is mediated by our concepts, and that there is no direct way to examine which aspects of objects belong to them independently of our conceptualizations. There is no Archimedean metaphysical point from which one could compare our representations of objects and the mind-independent objects we represent. Perception is cognitively penetrable and theory-laden. Semantic Constructivism attacks realism on the ground that there is no direct way to set up the relation between terms and the entities to which they purportedly refer. That relation can only be indirect mediated through the causal relations between these entities and our behavior; it can only be interest-dependent, depending on our theorizing. Since these relations ground terms in the entities to which they refer by fixing their referents, reference becomes theory-dependent (Brandom 1996).

The discussion in chapter 6 and the central thesis of that chapter about the existence of a theory-neutral, conceptually free, direct causal reference to objects in the world are rejoinders on behalf of realism to semantic constructivism's main claim. The claim that there is a cognitively impenetrable theory-neutral stage of vision, namely perception, although a good, and I think the only proper, place to start to form a rejoinder to epistemological constructivism, does not suffice by itself to put the doubts that constructivism has raised to rest or to answer the question regarding what we can know, as realists, about the world. The reason it cannot put all doubts to rest is that a theory-neutral perception may not be enough to bar the incommensurability between competing research programs. After all, scientific debates occur at the level of observational reports not at the level of perceptions and the NCC of perceptual states. Since, as we saw in chapter 7, observation unlike perception is theory-laden, constructivism's threat remains unscathed. Only if a way were to be found to ensure communication of observational reports on the basis of the theoretically neutral perception would the existence of a theory-neutral perception matter for rebutting the claim as to the incommensurability of competing scientific theories. The theory neutrality of perception cannot delineate the nature of our knowledge about the world either, because to say that perception is theory-neutral and interest-free is one thing and to say what exactly does perception reveal about the world is another.

In this chapter, I examine both problems and attempt to answer the questions they raise.

8.1   Defending Realism on the Proper Ground

The thrust of epistemological constructivism's argument is that the theory-ladenness of our perception implies that our experience is mediated by our concepts, and thus

• persons within two different conceptual backgrounds experience the world differently,
• they could agree on what they see only if they espoused the same conceptual framework,

and

• there can be no theory-neutral basis on which, eventually, their debates about theory testing, confirmation and theory choice could be resolved. (Being in different conceptual frameworks means that they cannot see each other's data. From this ensues the famous incommensurability thesis that bars communication across paradigms.)

Epistemological Constructivism can be readily detected in the undermining of the theory neutrality of perception, which has rendered the distinction between *seeing* and *seeing as* obsolete (Churchland 1988; Hanson 1958; Kuhn 1962), clearing the way for the relativistic theories of science and meaning. Since the existence of a theory-neutral basis on which a rational choice among alternative theories could be based is rejected, scientific theories become incommensurable, because there is not a theory-neutral perceptual basis that could resolve matters of meaning. Instead, perceptions are modulated by theoretical commitments, and proponents of different paradigms perceive different worlds. Perception becomes theory-laden, and the choice between two alternative and mutually excluding theories cannot be based on empirical testing and confirmation.

In view of the attacks against the possibility of a theory-neutral perceptual basis, any adequate attempt to defend realism against epistemological constructivism must meet two conditions. First, it must show that there is a theory-neutral basis on which debates about theory testing and confirmation will eventually be resolved. Second, since, at a last analysis, debates about theory confirmation are supposed to be resolved on the basis of empirical evidence, the realistic account must show first how observational concepts are grounded in a theory-neutral basis provided by perception and second how abstract concepts emerge from observational concepts. In this book I examine only the first issue. For a sketch of how observational concepts might be grounded in the neutral basis and how abstract concepts might emerge from observational concepts, see Barsalou 1999 and Goldstone and Barsallou 1998.

In this section, I claim that findings in the cognitive science cast some doubt on the thesis of epistemological constructivist. Perception, properly understood as that part of vision that extracts from a visual scene certain properties of objects in a bottom-up way and allows object individuation and indexing, is not theory-laden in a way that justifies the conclusions of constructivism. To undermine constructivism, I put forth the following theses. I argued in part for the first in part I of the book, and I will argue further here. I will also argue for the second here. Finally, I will briefly discuss the third, since a proper defense of the third thesis goes beyond the scope of this book. Consider these claims:

(a) The part of vision that I will call perception (which differs from 'perception' as is usually used in the literature) is only indirectly cognitively penetrated through the effects of spatial attention and in which, because of the indirect character of the cognitive penetration, information is retrieved from visual scenes in purely bottom-up ways.

(b) Because of (a), the content of perceptual states is free of cognitive modulation. Thus, perception, provides a theory-neutral basis, in the sense that when persons with differing conceptual backgrounds view the same visual scene they perceive the world the same way, while remaining within their respective conceptual frameworks (to differentiate my claim from Kuhn's (1962) thesis that one can see the world from another perspective only if one adopts the corresponding conceptual framework). This renders possible communication across paradigms.

(c) Since persons within different conceptual frameworks can perceive the world the same way (thesis b), debates about theory testing, confirmation, and theory choice could eventually be resolved on empirical grounds.

If these claims are correct, epistemological constructivism's attack against realism collapses. One word of caution is due here, though. My claim is that empirical evidence suggests that a part of visual processes, which I call perception, is cognitively impenetrable. I do not claim that the whole visual process (that is, the process that leads to the formation of a conscious percept) is theory-neutral. On the contrary, I take for granted that the visual processes that lead to the formation of our ordinary experience of objects are theory-laden. As I put it in chapter 7, while perception or early vision is theory-neutral and cognitively impenetrable, observation or late vision is theory-laden and cognitively penetrable.

Forty years or so after Hanson's and Kuhn's work, not many philosophers of science take the incommensurability theory seriously, since they feel that the history of sciences proves that communication across paradigms is possible. Thus, it may seem that there is not much of a point in trying to prove that communication across paradigms is possible. However, one may *feel* that Kuhn and Hanson were wrong because scientific practice does not work the way they suggested is one thing, but to *show* that Kuhn and Hanson were wrong one must undermine the "New Look" theory of vision on which their work was based. To do that, one needs a theory of perception. The alternative theory of perception that I propose has been presented in detail in part I of the book, and I hope that the reader recalls its basic theses (if not, the reader could take recourse to the interlude, in which I present the central theses of the theory in a nutshell).

I take for granted, as a follow-up to the theses presented in the preceding chapters, the cognitive impenetrability of perception, the theoretical neutrality of its content, and the nonconceptual nature of its content. I will digress from that strategy only to reopen, in subsection 8.1.1, the issue of the relation between visual processes and cognition focusing mainly on the role of spatial attention in perception. Spatial attention, as opposed to object-centered attention, seems to permeate all stages of perceptual processing, including those that occur very early, and spatial attention can be top-down driven (endogenous attention)—that is, driven by cognitive factors. Hence, it seems that all perceptual processes are cognitively penetrable. To answer this threat against the cognitive impenetrability of perception, I put forth the thesis that the attentional modulation of perception allows an indirect influence of cognition on perceptual processes that does not threaten the cognitive encapsulation of perception.

In subsection 8.1.2, I elaborate on the significance of the existence of perceptual theory-neutral content for the epistemological issue of the empirical comparison of scientific theories. More specifically I examine the second hypothesis stated above and discuss any bearing this might have on theory testing and confirmation. The main claim is that communication across paradigms is possible, since two people with differing conceptual backgrounds can access each other's data.

8.1.1   The Role of Spatial Attention in Vision: How Does It Affect the Perception of Objects?

Before I discuss whether or to what extent spatial attention's modulation of perception undermines the theory-neutrality of perception, I should note two things.

First, when I refer to bottom-up processes, I am interested in examining the cognitive encapsulation of these processes—that is, whether and to what extent visual processing depends on how a visual pattern is interpreted in view of what the viewer knows, believes, expects, and so forth. Thus, when I argue that there is a part of vision that is bottom-up I do not mean that there are not any top-down and horizontal interactions *within* the relevant perceptual mechanisms. Early vision consists of a continuum of multiple, parallel, and task-specific modules that communicate by means of both top-down and lateral flow of information. However, the "horizontal" or "lateral" flow of information, which is internal to early vision, does not threaten the cognitive impenetrability of early vision, since it leaves no room for penetration of knowledge from higher extravisual cognitive centers. Thus, the "bottom-up" should be taken to preclude only top-down semantic flow of information that affects perceptual processing itself. Furthermore, the abundant top-down connectivity in the brain between cognitive centers and perceptual circuits does not imply (as I showed in part I and in chapter 7) the cognitive penetrability of perception, as Churchland (1988) and Estany (2001) would have it.

Second, I am interested in the general form of the output of perceptual processes. No commitment is made with respect to the details of any current formulation of that representation. What is important for my purpose is the overall conception of what information each representation, or level of processing, enables and how the interpretations, levels of processing, interact with each other. Thus, the reference to Marr's $2\frac{1}{2}$D and 3D sketches is only an example from a specific theory.

We saw in chapters 1 and 2 that there are two kinds of attention that intervene in two different stages of the process to perform two different functions. First, in the form of spatial attention via the P1 component in the early stages of perceptual processing to focus attention on the salient locations. Second, object-centered attention, in the form of feature selection, and after some of the features retrieved in a bottom-up manner from the scene (size, shape, motion, spatial relations) have fused to deliver the candidate physical form of the objects, to enable binding of all features to form the objects of our experience and to solve the competition problem.

The effects of object-centered attention, which is cognitively driven, are postperceptual, as they occur after the termination of feedforward processing (FFS) and local recurrent processing (LRP). As such, they do not affect the issue of the cognitive penetrability of perception, as defined here. However, spatial attention, which may also be cognitively driven, seems to threaten the cognitive encapsulation of perception, since it intervenes during the perceptual, as the term has been defined here, processing. Therefore, I will focus on spatial attention.

The studies we examined in chapter 2 about the role and timing of spatial attention in perceptual processing show that the P1 wave (a component of the ERP waveforms) is larger in amplitude for stimuli presented at the attended location than for stimuli presented at the unattended location. Since the difference is due to the attended location, it is reasonable to assume that the amplitude of the P1 wave is modulated by spatial attention. The neural site of P1 seems to be the V4 area in the extrastriate cortex, which implies that spatial attention influences visual processing in extrastriate areas of the visual cortex. Thus, the P1 component may represent the earliest stage of visual processing that is modulated by voluntary spatial attention. The effect begins 70–90 ms after stimulus onset, which means that it is clearly an early perceptual and not a postperceptual effect. Spatial selective attention increases the activation of the neural sites tuned to the selected loci.

This seems to entail that, through the modulation of attention, early visual processing is cognitively driven. To see why this is not the case, I must say first a few words about the control of attention. So, I repeat that account I gave in the preceding chapter. What I will say applies to attention *simpliciter*, and thus *a fortiori*, to spatial attention, which is our focus here. Attention can be controlled either in bottom-up or top-down ways.

Bottom-up control operate either by triggering shifts of attention (attentional capture) or by guiding attention to particular locations. A sudden motion of an object in a scene, for instance, captures attention and focuses it on the moving object. In these cases, attention is driven by stimuli.

Top-down control of attention is related to the working memory, since sites of that kind of attentional control underlie systems of working memory. The exercise of attention depends on the contents of working memory. Working memory stores information, and performs executive control governing retrieval, encoding, and commands for the expression of attention. These two functions underlie the distinction in the attentional control processes between expectancy of an upcoming event and preparation for that event. As I showed in chapter 7, the expectation of an event is not necessarily accompanied by an attentional preparation for it. The top-down attentional control of perception amounts to the attentional expectation for an upcoming event, a form of Bruner's perceptual readiness.

I claimed in chapter 2 that studies regarding the P1 and N1 waveforms of ERPs that are related to spatial attention suggest that spatial attention does modulate perceptual processing in a way that entails the cognitive penetrability of early vision. Note, for example, that the P1 effect of spatial attention that is registered 70 ms after stimulus onset and thus affects the FFS is sensitive to stimulus factors such as contrast and position. It occurs before the identification of the stimuli and is insensitive to the identity of the stimuli. It is independent of the task-relevance of the stimulus, since it is observed for both targets and nontargets. The effect is also insensitive to cognitive factors, with the exception of spatial attention, in that the voluntary control of spatial attention is driven by stimuli and task demands, not by cognitive demands. For this reason, P1 is considered to be an exogenous component of spatial attention.

The claim that the P1 component of spatial attention is not sensitive to cognitive factors amounts to the following. Cognitive factors do not control directly the P1 effect. They determine the expectation for an event, but this is not sufficient to ensure attentional preparation for that event. Information about the upcoming display of an object may be kept in working memory while selective attention may be directed elsewhere. Selective attentional preparation for an event will follow the expectation of that event, if the event is task-relative. Once attentional expectation and preparation is effectuated, the amplitude of the P1 wave that is modulated by spatial attention is only stimuli-driven (it is influenced by factors such as contrast and position). It is worth emphasizing this point. Cognitive

factors control the expectation of an event. Task-relevant factors "translate" the expectation to attentional preparation for that event. Thus, the
preparation for an event is task-driven. Once the latter is in place, neither
cognitive nor task-relevant factors influence the P1 effect and hence that
stage of perceptual processing. Only stimuli factors do. It seems, thus, that
once spatial attention has selected some loci for focusing, and once it has
enhanced the activity of the relevant neuronal sites, information is registered at that stage of processing irrespective of task demands and cognitive
states. In other words, once spatial attention has selected some loci for
focusing, what one sees at the relevant location depends on what is there,
not on the cognitive stances of the viewer. Although things are a bit more
complicated with N1, which is not a clear exogenous component of spatial
attention, the discussion in chapter 2 suggests that N1 does not threaten
the cognitive penetrability of perception in that N1 intervenes relatively
late in visual processing and that it signifies the role of the task demands
in perceptual processing. Task demands affect perception in an indirect
way, which means that once the task has been selected what one perceives
while viewing a visual scene is not cognitively modulated but stimulus-
driven. This is what indirect cognitive penetrability amounts to, and, as I
explain in subsection 8.1.2, this is what blocks the conclusions of epistemological constructivism.

To assess the debate between epistemological constructivism and realism
let us see where all this leaves us with respect to the issue of the theory-
ladenness of perception. Recall our conclusion in the preceding chapter.
Churchland is right that observation is cognitively penetrable. There exists,
however, a part of the visual process, perception, which is only indirectly
penetrated by cognition and conceptually unmediated. The information
delivered by that process is spatio-temporal (that is, information about
location, spatial relations, orientation, and motion) and information about
size, color, orientation, and viewer-centered shape, and is used for object
individuation and tracking. It is retrieved bottom-up from a scene, despite
the interference of spatial attention.

Hence, it is not true that there is no direct way to examine which aspects
of objects belong to the objects independently of our conceptualizations.
All the aforementioned aspects belong to objects, as perceived by our
sensory apparatus, independently of our theoretical commitments. It is at
the level of the weak representation that the world imprints itself on us
through our perceptual systems.

Let us assume that the aforementioned claim is correct. The advent
of the theory-ladenness of perception denied the existence of a theory-

neutral basis. Scientific theories would become incommensurable, because there is not a theory-neutral perceptual basis that could resolve matters of meaning. Now, if I am correct, there is a theory-neutral perceptual basis. Could one resolve, on the basis of this theory-neutral basis, matters of meaning; that is, could one restore access to data across paradigms?

Churchland (1988) denies that there are theory-neutral data. He argues that even if there is some theoretical neutrality at an early perceptual process, this "pure given" (sensation) is useless in that it cannot be used for any "discursive judgment," since sensations are not semantically con-tentful states. Only "observation judgments" are contentful states, because they have content, which is a function of a conceptual framework. However, they are theory-laden. Our "perception," however, is different from "sensa-tion." The content of perception is structured and semantically truth-valuable. It delivers information about objects in the world. It tells us that an object has a certain viewer-centered shape, size, and color, is spatially related to other objects, is located at a certain place, is a separate object that persists in time, and moves in a certain way. This content may be true or false, depending on whether this information reflects events that actu-ally develop in the world.

In subsection 8.1.2, I will elaborate on the significance of the indirect penetrability of perception via spatial attention for the epistemological thesis of constructivism, namely that two persons in two different concep-tual frameworks perceive the world differently because of their differing theoretical commitments and that one of them cannot perceive the world as the other does unless he or she adopts the conceptual framework of the other.

8.1.2   Implications for the Philosophy of Science

Since I have conceded that vision is cognitively penetrable and have restricted my claim to the thesis that only the sub-part of vision I have defined as perception is theory-laden in an indirect way that allows bottom-up retrieval of information from a visual scene, the question comes down to (a) whether scientists with different theoretical commitments and with different experiences could form the same *perception* of the same retinal image and (b) if they do, whether one can see what the other sees, and thus access the other's data, while remaining within his or her conceptual framework.

Suppose that, because of learning through repeated experience in her field, a scientist has somewhat shaped her perceptual sensitivity according to her specific professional needs and can recognize patterns that others cannot. She has learned which dimensions of visual analysis to attend to, and this process has reshaped her basic sensors by selecting the output of certain feature detectors. Suppose that this learning has induced changes in the circuitry of her early vision, thereby altering her visual perception. (Recall the discussion about perceptual learning in chapter 7.) Furthermore, and related to the previous point, her theoretical commitments allow her to focus on specific locations of the visual array in her field and thus to analyze and recompose the picture in a way that is not available to others who do not share her conceptual framework and whose spatial attention does not focus at the same locations of the visual array. As a result, she can detect patterns that others cannot. Hence, scientists who are trained in certain patterns and have stored them in their memory may be able to perceive patterns that others could not. Suppose further that these changes affect the scientist's assessment of experiential evidence about theory evaluation.

Does this pose a threat to the existence of a theory-neutral perceptual basis? It does not, because (a) as the discussion on perceptual learning in chapter 7 suggests, the neural change in early vision neural circuits is task and/or data-driven and not theory-driven and (b) spatial attention influences her perception in an indirect way. The differences are important for the following reasons.

First, all scientists have had experiences of more or less the same objects, share more or less the same scientific education, and work with roughly the same objects and instruments in their experiments. Thus, their brains share a roughly similar basic microcircuitry, insofar as this circuitry bears on the practice of their profession, since the microcircuitry of the brain is formed as a result of experience (Johnson 1997; Quartz and Sejnowski 1997). Notice here that the role of experiment as a means for opening communication channels between scientists working in different paradigms is well established (Franklin 1986; Gooding 1990; Gooding, Pinch, and Schaffer 1989; Nersessian 1984).

Second, even if some of the scientists have stored in memory some patterns and can detect patterns that others cannot, nothing precludes the latter from undergoing the same training, as a result of which they could themselves detect these patterns, thus reestablishing a common ground. Learning of this kind is data driven and task driven, which means that the same training (that is, training in the same task with the same input) will almost certainly produce the same "priming memory." In other words, the fact that induced changes are the results of task and stimuli-dependent conditions means that persons who undergo the same training could learn to perceive the same patterns despite their differing theoretical commitments.

Third, although the allocation of attention is clearly cognitively driven, cognitive factors do not affect perceptual processing once attention has been focused. This is a result of the indirect form of cognitive penetrability of perception, which means that the contents of our cognitive states do not affect the kind of the neural modifications but only determine, as it were, the conditions of learning by means of attentional mechanisms. As Pylyshyn (1999) remarks, arguing that this is a form of cognitive penetrability is like arguing that, because the decision to wear glasses is cognitively determined and because wearing glasses affects perception, perception is cognitively penetrable.

Let me elaborate on the difference between the direct cognitive penetrability of perception by cognition and the indirect penetrability through stimulus-driven and task-driven attention, which in turn is shaped by cognitive factors. In stimulus-driven and task-driven attention, cognition indirectly mediates the process through the allocation of spatial attention. Spatial attention can be controlled, though, since people can be instructed to focus their attention on a certain location and to scan for a certain feature, despite the fact that they may have entirely different intentional states. Once the location of the focus and the task have been controlled, theoretical differences do not affect the course of information retrieval from a scene. In other words, cognition affects the choice of the sites of focusing, not the perceptual process itself. Were information retrieval theory-driven, such a control would not be possible—one cannot control other people's theoretical commitments the same way one can control attention.

Here is an example of how the existence of a theoretically neutral perceptual basis, in combination with the indirect cognitive penetrability of perception through spatial attention, allows the resolution of differences related to seeing: Suppose first that cognitive factors have given rise to a context in which X is biased toward rabbits. This has resulted in an expectation in X's spatial attention. Suppose, second, that X performs a task that is related with rabbits. This leads X to be prepared for rabbits. Had X been solving differential equations, there would have been no such preparation. If X is walking around a farm, where animals are expected to be seen, the preparation is in place. This preparation, in combination with expectation, means that, when the right opportunity arises, spatial attention is ready to focus on points in space where previous experience indicates that, with an acceptable probability, the information contained at those points suffices to determine the presence of a rabbit. Such a characteristic deter-mining information is the ears that are to be found on the upper part of the picture of the animal—on either the left or the right part, depending on the orientation. If at some time X is presented with a rabbit/duck ambiguous shape, then X, focusing his attention on the location at which she expects the characteristic ears, will see a rabbit. If X were expecting a duck, she would have focused on the lower part of the picture and would have seen a duck.

If a picture of a car had been presented to X, she would have seen neither a duck nor a rabbit but probably, a car. Notice also that the image (or, rather, the content of the relevant perceptual states that is formed during the first stages of the FFS) is neither a duck nor a rabbit but, rather, the duck/rabbit configuration. There is no separation between a duck-like and a rabbit-like image during the first stages of visual processing, since how the image is eventually seen does not have any effects on early processing. At about 70 ms after stimulus onset, spatial attention, whether it be endog-enously or exogenously driven, decomposes that figure in ways that the ensuing phenomenal content of perception is that of a duck-like or a rabbit-like figure. Thus, the person who expects a duck and the person who expects a rabbit perceive a $2\frac{1}{2}$D duck-like shape and a rabbit-like shape, respectively.

However, the different conceptual frameworks in which the "rabbit person" and the "duck person" are situated did not affect the perceptual processes that led to the $2\frac{1}{2}$D surfaces. They determined, through percep-tual set, the point of focus, which in turn determined the phenomenal contents of the persons' experiences *given the characteristics of the stimulus image*. In other words, what changes in view of the persons' differing theo-retical commitments is the "where" on which they will focus their atten-tion. Other than that, their differing theoretical backgrounds did not induce them to perceive what they did; that was determined by the image itself. This is what I mean by claiming that the perceptual processes them-selves are not affected by cognitive factors if these factors indirectly pene-trate perception through spatial attention.

To get a glimpse of the repercussions of the preceding analysis of ambigu-ous figures for the philosophical discussions that were inspired by the "New Look" theories of perception, let us assume now that the person who expects (and as a result sees) a rabbit is instructed to lock her attention onto the lower left part of the picture, rather than onto the upper right part (on which her cognitive stances had led her to focus in the first place). Under these circumstances, she would perceive a duck-like figure and would see$_{dox}$ a duck. The important thing to notice here is that the person can shift attention despite her differing theoretical commitments. This is what I mean when I claim that spatial attention could be controlled. Thus, a situation arises in which two persons with differing theoretical commitments could communicate with each other and understand what the other sees even though they initially saw different things.

These considerations suggest that the answers to the two questions posed in the introduction of this section, namely—"Could scientists with different theoretical commitments and with different experiences form the same *perception* of the same retinal image?" and "Can one person see what the other sees while remaining within his or her conceptual framework?"—are both affirmative. Differences in theoretical commitments do not affect perception (as defined here), and, on account of the indirect way spatial attention influences perception, two persons in two different conceptual backgrounds can be led to see the same things. The existence of a common perceptual basis entails that the two persons share the nonconceptual content of their experience. At the same time, visual focus on this content can be shifted through controlled allocation of attention, which can occur despite theoretical differences. Thus, the two persons can be led to see each other's viewpoint, and hence to share data.

The same considerations hold with respect to the remark that the decision as to which task to undertake is theory-laden. More generally, since Duhem and Kuhn at least, what one chooses to inquire about is cognitively determined either directly or (through instruction) indirectly. In this sense, the determination of a task is cognitively driven, and thus the selection of a task is a cognitive matter. However, the selection of a task can be controlled. Scientists in different research traditions may be instructed to perform a certain task, even though, owing to their theoretical commitments, they might have never considered performing it on their own. As with spatial-attentional focus, once the task has been selected, the visual processes that take place are the same for all parties involved. That is why task-driven processes are theoretically or cognitively driven only in the indirect sense described above. In other words, even though a "duck person" would have never thought to look at the upper right part of the picture, she can be instructed to do so, and if she does so she will perceive a rabbit configuration. This means that one can see other's data, and seeing each other's data can lead to communication across paradigms. This should not come as a surprise. Usually the effects of the determination of a task consist primarily in allocating attention to the proper places or objects. Since object-based attention is post-perceptual and thus does not entail the cognitive penetrability of perception, and since spatial attention affects perceptual processing only indirectly, the fact that tasks can be cognitively determined does not entail the cognitive penetrability of perception.

I think, although I will not pursue that here, that considerations like the above regarding the role of attentional focus and the nature of the task in perceptual processing underlie discussions about the role of experiment in rendering possible the communication of "meaning" across paradigms. Experiments bring to the fore the role of the task in experimental design and the role of attention in observing the results. First, they make concrete the task in the design of the experimental devise. Second, they channel the allocation of attention. Scientists from paradigm A who are invited to participate in an experiment designed by scientists in paradigm B, when faced with this specific experiment and told to expect a certain event to occur, will observe the same things as scientists from paradigm B, and this holds reciprocally. This establishes a common observational basis on which matters of meaning could be resolved, despite the fact that the scientists belong to two different paradigms and thus have different theoretical frameworks.

Let us grant that too. Suppose that there exists an epistemologically interesting neutral perceptual basis. How could it be used in matters of theory testing and choice over two competing theories—say, in debates about the theoretical entities posited by two competing scientific theories? Is it useful in settling these issues on an empirical basis, taking the thrust out of constructivism's attack on scientific realism? Well, it certainly does not resolve these disputes. However, according to realism, scientific debates are supposed ultimately to be resolved by recourse to some *experimenta*. It is because of this that constructivism sought to render all entities, not only the unobservables, inaccessible to us. I have reintroduced a theory-neutral perceptual basis into the picture. For this basis to function as the common ground that would resolve scientific debates, it should be able to provide a way to overcome the difficulties posed by the theory-ladenness of observation. In other words, it should show us a way to agree on observational reports, despite differing theoretical commitments affecting them, on the basis of the common perceptual basis.

I claim that the first constructivist obstacle to that has been overcome. Since the allocation of attention and the determination of the task can be controlled over different conceptual frameworks and, once this has been done, what one perceives is stimuli-driven, communication between paradigms becomes possible, since one person (in paradigm A) can see the other's (in paradigm B) data. But that on its own does not solve the problem. To analyze fully the way disputes about theoretical entities could be resolved on the basis of perceptual reports, and thus to address the issue of theory testing and choice, one must first solve two problems. First, one must show how concrete conceptual structure (concepts about observable entities) emerges from nonconceptual content—that is, show how conceptualization is possible. Second, one must show how abstract conceptual structure (concepts about theoretical terms) is grounded on the concrete conceptual structure. These are admittedly formidable problems, but at least there is a neutral basis on which, one hopes, conceptual structure could be grounded.

This point deserves further consideration, lest my account be distorted. I have said that attention is stimulus-driven and task-driven, and that, although cognitive factors determine where attention will be allocated, what one perceives at those locations depends on the stimuli and the task. What is important here is that this claim is valid only so long as we are in the domain of perception—that is, so long as we are discussing retrieval of, say, shape, size, motion, and spatial relations from a scene. The evidence adduced in chapter 3 suggests that a weak representation of objects present in a scene precedes a rich representation of the same objects. Furthermore, the latter is grounded in the former. On the other hand, semantic properties of objects belong to the domain of observation, which is clearly theory-laden. Thus, when I argue that once spatial attention has focused what one perceives depends only on what is there in the visual scene and not on one's cognitive states, I am not claiming that what one sees in a visual scene is independent of one's theoretical commitments. Seeing an electron is, clearly, theory-laden. The search for indications of theoretical constructs in the laboratory and their detection is cognitively driven too. In fact, even the search pertaining to the objects of our ordinary life and the way we experience them is theory driven. What I do claim is that some properties of objects are retrieved in a bottom-up way from a visual scene and that in this case spatial attention, indirectly modulating perception, does not threaten the bottom-up retrieval of the relevant information. In other words, cognitive factors determine where to look for information. However, what one *perceives* at those locations depends on the stimulus and not on one's cognitive states. The "what is there" that can be retrieved in a conceptually unmediated way is none other than the properties of the weak representation of objects, which become, thus, the theory-neutral ground that allows two persons with differing theoretical commitments to agree on what they see while retaining their respective conceptual frameworks, by coordinating, as it were, the allocation of their spatial attention and by agreeing on the task at hand. In the case of the electron, for instance, when one is presented with the appropriate apparatus and is instructed to look for a trail, one will see the trail independent of one's theoretical commitments. That, by itself, does not settle the issue about the nature of the "thing" that caused the trail, but, as I said above, it establishes a common observational report on which eventually theoretical discussions must settle.

Let me wrap up the discussion. I have distinguished perception from observation and presented evidence that perception is cognitively impenetrable. I have claimed that the result of the conceptually unmediated perception is a weak form of object representation that conveys shape, size, motion, and spatial information. I have argued that although spatial selective attention permeates almost all levels of perceptual processing, and although some forms of spatial attention are cognitively driven, the modulation of perceptual processing by spatial attention yields an indirect form of cognitive penetrability that does not justify the epistemological constructivism's claim that perception is theory-laden. This is because the indirect penetrability does not threaten the bottom-up retrieval of information from a visual scene by perception. Perception yields theory-neutral representations of objects, albeit weak ones, which can function as the neutral ground. The neutral ground, along with the fact that the allocation of spatial attention can be controlled and the task can be agreed upon, make it possible that two persons with differing theoretical commitments could be led to *see* the same things, and thus could access each other's data.

With this, the main thesis of Epistemological Constructivism collapses. It is true that there is no Archimedean metaphysical point from which one could compare our representations of objects and the mind-independent objects we represent. However, evidence from cognitive science seems to suggest that there is a level—that of the weak nonconceptual representation that is delivered by perception—at which the world reaches out and imprints (given our perceptual systems), albeit in an egocentric frame of reference, itself on us. At that level, we do not compare anything with the world; we just have perceptual states whose nonconceptual content consists in certain aspects of the world.

Where does this leave us relative to the main aim of this section, namely defending realism? I have only provided reasons to believe that one can be reasonably realist with respect to the contents of nonconceptual representational states (a variant of common-sense realism). But what about scientific realism? I have argued that there are some obstacles that one must overcome in order to be able to defend scientific realism based the neutral perceptual basis. One of the things that must be accomplished is the grounding of theoretical structure to observational structure and from there to perceptual structure. It is not certain that this program could succeed, especially if one bears in mind the complete failure of a similar attempt undertaken by Logical Positivism. In this case, there are two options. One has to concede that, although some form of epistemological realism is defensible (one could be realist with respect to the nonconceptual content of experience), scientific realism cannot be defended. Or one can seek alternative means of defending scientific realism, perhaps in the way of Kitcher (2001) or Psillos (2000).

8.2 Perceptual Systems and Realism

Traditionally, the problem of realism is interwoven with the problem of the truth of perceptual beliefs. The truth of beliefs is relevant to realism because if one's beliefs are true then the objects and their observable properties, as they figure in these beliefs, must really be as one believes them to be. The problem regarding realism from the perspective of beliefs is whether one's beliefs are true and whether one is justified in thinking that one's beliefs are true. Success semantics and reliabilism provide an answer to the first question, which is the only one that I address here; they are true because they successfully negotiate one's interaction with the environment.

However, this view faces serious objections. First, even if beliefs were true, this would not vindicate realism, because the truth of a set of sentences does not fix the reference of their referring constituent expressions and without that one cannot talk seriously about realism. Furthermore, the truth of beliefs says nothing about the perceptual content that causes them, and, as we saw above, to rebut constructivism, realists must show that perceptual content presents the world correctly. Second, there is some serious doubt whether success semantics could establish the truth of beliefs. The processes in perceptual systems depend on operational constraints that are used to solve the problem of the underdetermination of the percept from the retinal image. These constraints ensure only that perception is coordinated with action; they aim to provide a reliable guide for on-line action in interactions with the environment. When it comes to successful action, satisficing and not truth is what matters. It may be that perception computes solutions of distal optical arrays that satisfy action needs without any regard for reconstructing truthfully the distal cause. If so, beliefs may be successful and yet false.

To defend realism against constructivism, one must first show, against epistemological constructivism, that perceptual systems retrieve information from the environment in bottom-up conceptually unmediated ways, and one must also show, against semantic constructivism, that the reference of perceptual units as they figure in perceptual demonstratives (that is, the reference of the constituents of the contents of perceptual states) can be determined in purely causal, interest-free ways. (Part I and chapter 6 of this book were devoted to establishing these two aims.) Second, one must argue that some of the outputs of perception (re)present things as they really are in the world. I argue here for a form of realism according to which the contents of perceptual neural states correctly represent aspects of the world, and that parts of that nonconceptual content present to subjects real independent properties of objects. The term "real independent properties" denotes those properties that objects have independent of the existence of the minds and perceptual systems of organisms.

Thus, my aim is to show that one can be in an appropriate relation with the world so that one's perception extracts correct information from it in conceptually unmediated ways. In this framework, it is not necessary that the perceiver form true beliefs about the world or know them to be true. In that sense, my approach is situated within the wider externalist program in epistemology.[1]

I critically examine the attempt to defend realism on the ground that our beliefs are mostly true. I conclude that the truth of beliefs does not suffice to found realism, because this is not the right level at which to address the issue. The appropriate level is that of the nonconceptual content of perception and whether NCC correctly cuts the world. I start by exploring the possibility of founding realism on the ground that most of one's perceptual beliefs must be true on account of one's success in actions that are caused by those beliefs. If one could show that beliefs are true, would that entail that one perceives aspects of the world as they really are? To show why this entailment does not hold, I use Putnam's arguments that the truth of a beliefs does not fix the reference of the referential terms in the sentence that formulates the belief. I also claim that even if one had succeeded in fixing that reference, still that would not have resolved the issue of how the referents are presented in perception. Although success semantics fixes the truth values of beliefs, it does not address the problem of how perceptual content carves the world, that is, the problem of how the world is presented in perception. This is the problem that should be addressed, because realism would be vindicated if it could be shown that perceptual content cuts the world in the proper places. Then, I reject the view that success semantics could establish the truth of beliefs on the ground that the operational constraints that are implemented in perception ensure that we are satisficers rather than truth seekers.

Finally, I develop my argument for realism based on the theory of perception presented in part I of the book. I distinguish between properties of the world-mind-environment system and the properties of the objects that exist independent of one's cognition and perception, and argue that perceptual content correctly represents the latter.

8.2.1 The Problem

The relation between a perception and a belief is causal, not evidential. Perceptions cause some beliefs, thereby causally explaining the formation of these beliefs. However, a causal explanation of a belief does not provide evidence for its truth value, since it does not show how or why the belief is justified. So, even though perception causes beliefs, their content bears complex relations to the contents of the perception on which they are based. Consequently, the causal relation does not by itself epistemically warrant the truth of the beliefs.

Furthermore, we take it for granted that, since perception delivers shapes, sizes, and other properties of objects, these objects do have such properties. We assume that objects in the world must have such features in order to cause in us states whose content consists in shapes, sizes, and so forth. However, it will not do to argue that, since a property of an object X causes in us a percept of X as being F, then this property is F. Causality does not presuppose identity or even similarity between effect and cause.

Thus, the causal relationships between the world and one's perceptual states and between those perceptual states and one's relevant beliefs do not warrant either the correctness of the former or the truth of the latter.[2] At the same time, the fact that one successfully relies (other things being equal) on perception to guide one's interaction with the world suggests that there probably is some kind of correlation between the content of one's perceptual states (and the ensuing beliefs) and the world states that cause it, otherwise perception would not have been reliable. This means that the content of perception may be suggestive of the correlated physical situations; there may exist a structural isomorphism between NCC and the world states that cause it. But, this correlation being causal, there is not "an immediate apparent basis for thinking that it is in fact dependable, that beliefs adopted on the basis of it [the correlation] are likely to reflect in an accurate way what is really going on in the physical world. And plainly this is not something that can be simply assumed in an epistemological context where it is the very justification of beliefs about physical objects that is in question." (BonJour 2003, p. 83)

Since beliefs conceptually articulate the content of perception, any relation between the beliefs and the world is both complex and indirect, since it is mediated by NCC. Despite that, to address the issue of realism, one might attempt to establish a direct link between beliefs and the world, sidestepping perceptual content. At this juncture reliabilism enters the picture. One's visual experience "as if X is before one" is a reason for believing that "there is an X before one" only because in one's world such a visual experience is *reliably* related to an X being before one (Sosa 2003). To put it in a different way, in one's world such a visual experience would in normal conditions reveal X's presence before one. This is a modal connection, since it is *necessary* that one's visual experience as of X would in normal conditions reveal the presence of X. Note that this reliability is not about experience effectively guiding our interactions with the world (which it certainly does); it is about forming true beliefs about the external world.

As with most arguments, one has to start from premises that are the least contestable. It is hardly disputed that we, and all other existing organisms, have been very successful in negotiating the environment. It is also uncontestable that the perceptual systems of these organisms have played a major role in that success, and that they have been shaped to a certain extent to ensure that success. Thus, one could hardly disagree with the assessment that perception reliably guides our interactions with the environment. It is plausible that the fact that perception reliably guides our interactions with the environment may mean something both about the veridicality of perception and about the truth status of the beliefs we form on the basis of perception. This offers a possibility for realism that is worth exploring.[3]

How do we get from success in action to the truth of beliefs? The answer is given by success semantics, which goes hand in hand with reliabilism. Success semantics holds that the content of a belief is given by its utility conditions (that is, the conditions that would have to obtain for the various desires associated with that belief to be satisfied).[4] More specifically, the truth state of a belief (that is, what makes the belief true) consists in those states of affairs that guarantee that the actions that are based on the belief satisfy the desires with which the belief is associated in causing action. True beliefs are such as to cause actions that, by being successful, satisfy a creature's desires. Of course, it is possible to get the world correct and form true beliefs and yet misconstrue the instrumental relationship between the action and the goal. That is, it is possible to err either on the side of opting an effective strategy that would satisfy one's goal or on the side of thinking that a specific action would satisfy one's goal rather than erring on the side of the beliefs that cause the relevant actions. That shows that getting the world right in our beliefs is a necessary but not sufficient condition for successful action.

Recall that the epistemological problem related to reliabilism and success semantics is whether perceptual beliefs are true. Had we succeeded in solving this problem, would we have settled the issue of realism? That is, could we say that since beliefs are true then perception truly reflects the externalia? The answer is No. Success semantics fixes the extension, that is, the truth value of a belief and not its intentional content.[5] This means that success semantics cannot determine what the referring expressions in the sentence that articulates the belief refer to in the world. Does the subject in a belief correspond to a real thing in the environment? Do the categories that are predicated to that thing correspond to real properties in the world? In other words, one needs to know the intentional content of a belief, not just its extension (its truth value) and examine whether the fillers of the roles of the subject and the predicates do refer to things and properties in the world.

The reason why the truth of a belief does not warrant that its content designates real things and properties is that the truth of a set of sentences or sentence analogues does not fix the referents of the terms and their meanings. Putnam (1981, pp. 39–41) argues that a subset of our beliefs about the world must be true on account of the fact that we successfully interact with the world. Beliefs are interwoven with actions. The beliefs that guide actions or "directive beliefs" have the form "If I do X, I will get Y." (Here Y is the description of a goal.) Were many of our directive beliefs wrong, most of our actions would be unsuccessful. Dennett (1978) offers a similar argument, claiming that natural selection favors inferential strategies that generally yield true beliefs because true beliefs offer a larger adaptive advantage to an organism than false beliefs. True beliefs allow an organism to interact with its environment with greater success than would be achieved with false beliefs. Hence, selection pressures have seen to it that at least our beliefs are true.

Unfortunately, even if one accepts that most of our beliefs must be approximately true on account of our success in interacting with the world, this is not enough to fix the reference of the referential terms of the beliefs. Putnam (1980) showed that any model-theoretic semantics is inconsistent, insofar as truth (satisfaction of a sentence in a model) underdetermines reference. A sentence may remain true in a model even though the references of its terms change. Putnam's argument relies on the Lowenheim-Skolem theorem, which tells us that there is no unique interpretation for a formal set of sentences that can be singled out, i.e., non-intended models satisfy the sentences. Since the symbols acquire meaning by referring to entities in a model, the underdetermination of reference undermines the whole enterprise of assigning unique meanings to symbols. Without unambiguous reference there can be no talk about realism.

Putnam uses this line of thought to argue that evolutionary success "affects linguistically mediated or conceptually mediated survival via its tendency to produce in us representation systems whose sentences or sentence-analogues have certain truth conditions. . . . But the truth conditions for whole sentences were just shown not to determine the reference of sentences parts . . . it is simply a mistake to think that evolution determines a unique correspondence between referring expressions and external objects." (1981, pp. 40–41) Putnam's point is that the attunement of beliefs with the environment does not arise at the level of the atomic constituents of the sentences that formulate one's beliefs; it arises at the level of the beliefs of the whole organism. To initiate successful action there is no need for selection to have exercised pressure to the former level for sensitivity to the aspects of the environment so that the referring expressions of the sentences that formulate beliefs refer to real objects and their properties in the world. This statement should not be construed as a rejection of that possibility. However, if one appeals for any reason to this kind of selective pressure, one must argue for it and show how it is possible.

The above critique is based on the application of the Lowenheim-Skolem theorem. However, it is debatable whether that argument could be applied the way Putnam intended, and this leaves open the possibility of resurrecting the reliabilist defense of realism. In that vein, suppose that the repercussions of the Lowenheim-Skolem theorem could be avoided—say, by resorting to the pragmatics of language, or by arguing that the theorem holds on first-order logic and that there is no reason to restrict oneself to first-order logic only. Now suppose that one could fix the referents of referring expressions of beliefs by means of some form of model-theoretic semantics. Would that suffice to vindicate realism? The answer is still negative. The reason is that even if one had succeeded in fixing the reference, still that would have not illuminated the debate about realism. Realists claim that the contents of perceptual states represent entities and properties as they exist in the world, which means that perceptual contents get the basic "ontological units" of the world right; they refer to the right kind of entities. Thus, to defend realism, one should examine the issue of how perception cuts the world. It is exactly this issue that needs be resolved if one hopes to address ontological issues and gain an insight of how the world is for creatures with our perceptual apparatus or for creatures with perceptual apparatus similar to ours.

In other words, even if the kind of indeterminacy Putnam is arguing for were removed there would be still another kind of indeterminacy left open, namely that concerning the way the perceiver's perceptual system cuts the world (as opposed to the way the referential terms in her expressions refer to the world). To see why this is so, consider the "gavagai" problem (Quine 1960). The native utters "gavagai" in the presence of a rabbit, as the linguist perceives the animal. The term functions as a direct referential term (it may be a natural kind term). Quine's discussion raises two issues. First, one could ask whether the native's term refers to a rabbit, or undetached rabbit parts, or fast rabbits, or whatever else is also perceived whenever a rabbit (as the linguist would categorize the animal) is perceived (this is also Putnam's problem). But one could also ask whether the native *perceives* a rabbit or undetached rabbit parts or fast rabbits; that is, one could ask what is the perceptual content of the native's perceptual states. Now, Quine's (1960) discussion is not motivated by consideration of truth in terms of utility. Quine argues for the inscrutability of reference (that "gavagai" is referentially indeterminate between rabbits and undetached rabbit parts), which is implied by the underdetermination of the reference of singular terms in a language from the sentences that the linguistic community assents to or rejects. At this point Quine's argument seems tangent to Putnam's, but in reality it cuts much deeper, and that is why it undermines attempts to determine reference even if Putnam's argument fails. The reason is that Quine's challenge can be extended from the domain of language and the referents of referential terms in it to the domain of mental states and their contents, and therefore to the domain of perceptual states and their contents.[6] In the latter context, Quine's problem is whether there exists a unique interpretation of the mental states of a being, as opposed to whether it exists a unique translation of a language, which was the Quine's original problem and which he shares with Putnam.

Quine aims to show that in order to determine reference the ontology should be established first (whether there are rabbits or undetached rabbit parts in the ontological framework); otherwise reference is inscrutable. Quine's point in the "gavagai" discussion in the *World and Object* is that there is not a matter of fact as to whether the native, by uttering "gavagai," refers to a rabbit or to undetached rabbit parts. To determine that one cannot rely on any kind of empirical linguistic data; instead issues like this are settled beforehand by fixing the ontology, that is, by deciding whether the world is populated by objects or by object parts. This point, as I argued above, can be extended (and has been extended by Quine himself) to cover the content of the mental/perceptual states of the native.

It goes without saying that in this new framework it is not the linguistic data that would solve or fail to solve the problem of the indeterminacy of the contents of perceptual states but only data concerning perception, perceptual states, and their contents. Quine argues (see the quotation in note 6) that the indeterminacy in the case of mental states arises from the lack of isomorphism between physical mechanisms realizing mental states and distinctions that can be phrased in mentalistic language. Quine's point seems to be that, even though there is a difference between sentences or belief ascriptions (A) "the native perceives a rabbit" and (B) "the native perceives a collection of rabbit parts," this distinction is formulated in mentalistic language and need not correspond to a distinction at the level of physical mechanisms that realize mental/perceptual states. Since Quine admits that behind any genuine distinct mental state there is a distinctive physical mechanism, it follows that for Quine the distinction between (A) and (B) does not map onto a genuine distinction between corresponding mental/perceptual states. This, in its turn, means that at the level of perceptual contents one cannot distinguish between rabbits and collections of rabbit parts.

So if Quine is correct, the question as to whether perception can tell whether as a matter of fact there is only one thing or two different things that occupy the same place at the same time cannot be raised, let alone answered. The reason seems to be that the two properties "being a rabbit" and "being a collection of rabbit parts" are co-instantiated and there is no way to tell which one of them obtains based on perceptual facts alone. To be able to do that, one should determine the ontology independently and beforehand.

Now, as I will elaborate in the concluding section of this chapter, my own view on object individuation is that our perceptual system is so structured that one individuates objects in a scene and not objects' parts. When connected points in space move together, and in that sense they are undetached, one sees an object moving, not a collection of connected points moving in the same direction with the same speed. So our perceptual system has solved the indeterminacy of reference of the kind Quine raises; the native perceives a rabbit, and thus the referent of "gavagai" is that rabbit. The ontology, that is, that at the basic level there are objects and not collections of object parts, is fixed by the way perception works. If one does not know how the visual system individuates the world and, therefore, how a visual scene is parsed and perceived, one cannot determine what the referents of perceptual contents are. This also why I insist that the appropriate level at which to address the issue of realism and defend it is the level at which our perception cuts the world.

One could object here that it certainly makes sense to say that an object, which occupies a specific place at some time, may be presented differently to two perceivers who view it from different perspectives, and that in this sense one should be able to determine the referent independent of its modes of presentation. After all, this is why one distinguishes between transparent and opaque contexts of expressions, where in the former it is the referent of a referential term that participates in the expression, whereas in the latter it is its mode of presentation. Although this is true, note that the discussion presupposes that it is whole objects and not collections of object part that constitute the basic vocabulary. So it is not the case that the referent of the perceptual content is simply whatever is occupying the relevant portion of space at the time, where it is only its mode of presentation (that is, the way it looks to the perceiver) that is not determined. The reason is that one could not determine what occupies the relevant position in space and time (if one wishes to be faithful to Quine's spirit one should say that it does not even make sense to ask that question) unless one had first settled the ontology, that is, unless one had first determined the mode of presentation of the "gavagai" in perception.

Quine's point is that one must have decided on that vocabulary, that is, one should have fixed the ontology, before engaging in discussions about referents of linguistic expressions. My point is that unless one examines how scenes are parsed and, thus, how objects are individuated and things are presented in perception, one cannot tell what is the referent of perceptual content. At that level, at the ontology fixing level, the referent, as an object in space and time, is determined only through its mode of presentation in perception, that is, by the way the perceptual system carves the world.

Quine's concerns, though initially cast in terms of the reference of singular expressions in the native's language, also touch on the problem of the mode of presentation of the referent in the native's mind (for whether the native perceives rabbits or undetached rabbit parts is determined by the mode of presentation of that object in the native's perception). Quine's arguments for the inscrutability of reference also cover the inscrutability of the mode of presentation of the referent. The problem of the inscrutability is very cogent to the issue of realism, because if the mode of presentation of referents in perceptual content could not be fixed then any discussion of realism would be idle, since the defense of realism that I mount is based on the claim (still to be proved) that NCC carves the world in the right places.

To recapitulate: Perceiving a rabbit and perceiving undetached rabbit parts are two states with different perceptual contents, though "rabbit-hood" and "undetached-rabbit-parts-hood" are co-instantiated properties. Both states could be ascribed to the native, and both are stimulus synonymous in that the native will always utter "gavagai" whenever she sees what in the linguist's framework is a rabbit. When the native uses the term "gavagai" under these circumstances, the term correctly applies to both of these states; this is why this fact does not suffice to determine the way the native perceives the world. This shows that, even if one had solved the problem of the underdetermination of reference in Putnam's arguments, one would not have determined the referent in the native's perception, because one would not have known the mode of presentation of that object in the native's mind. One might have determined, for instance, that the "cat" in the sentence "the cat is on the mat" refers to the animal we call "cat" and not to, say, "cherries" ("cathood" and "cherryhood" are not co-instantiated properties), but one could not have answered the question as to whether the perceiver perceives a cat or undetached cat parts. ("Cathood" and "undetached-cat-parts-hood" are co-instantiated properties.)

Having examined the significance of Quine's argument, let us return to success semantics' claims to fix the content of a belief containing "gavagai" via the utility condition of the action caused by the belief. One is led to conclude that the most success semantics could fix is the truth values of the beliefs that cause actions. The reason is that success semantics fail to accommodate the intentional dimension of a belief, in that it does not fix the content of the belief, only its extensional dimension. It fixes its truth conditions via its utility conditions, by specifying under which environmental conditions an action is successful. However, success semantics fails to specify the way the world is presented as being in perception.

The problem is that "there are many stimulus synonymous ways of specifying the utility condition—many different ways of describing the given state of affairs that are compatible with its being such as to result in the satisfaction of the creatures desires" (Bermudez 2003, p. 71). Consider the evidence that is available to Quine's linguist who studies the native's language. It consists in those cases in which the native, under various circumstances, utters "gavagai" in the presence of what is for the linguist a rabbit. So the linguist may infer that whenever rabbithood is instantiated the native uses the term "gavagai," except that (and this is Quine's point) whenever "rabbithood" is instantiated so is "undetached-rabbit-parts-hood," and the issue of which of the two is what the native "has in mind" when using "gavagai" cannot be resolved on the basis of the linguistic evidence alone. Similarly, all success semantics can show is that the utility condition satisfying the native's desires (e.g., eating a "gavagai" or having it as a pet) is met whenever the native gets hold of a "gavagai." But this leaves unspecified which is exactly the state of affairs in the world that corresponds to the utility condition. What does exactly does the native get hold of? Is it a rabbit, as the linguist would have described it, or undetached rabbit parts, as a person with a different ontology would have described it? There is simply no way to specify the state of affairs based on success semantics alone.

As a result, one cannot tell which one among these "equivalent" or "stimulus synonymous" states of affairs describes the native's state of mind—that is, either her belief when she sees a "gavagai" or the content of her relevant perceptual state. Thus, one cannot tell how the creature perceives the environment or how it carves up the world, only that if a certain state of affairs obtains then some desire of the creature is satisfied. The content both of the belief and of the corresponding perceptual state is underdetermined, and thus cannot be specified, by its utility conditions. In Bermudez's terms (2003, chapter 5), success semantics fixes the reference of a belief (that is, the state of affairs that, if it obtains, then the action it causes is successful) but not the mode of presentation of that state of affairs to the perceiver. Similarly, with regard to "gavagai" construed as a direct referential term, success semantics fixes the correctness of its application but does not fix its referent; it cannot tell us whether the native perceives a rabbit or undetached rabbit parts. One must find a way to specify that state of affairs so that it reflects the way the creature perceives the world— that is, one must find a way to fix the content of its perceptual states by specifying how the creature apprehends the world or, equivalently, how the world is presented as being in the creature's NCC of perception.

The argument I have offered here suggests that success semantics and reliabilism by themselves cannot help promote realism's case, as they do not and could not deal with what is the decisive point for realism, namely whether perceptual content carves the world in the right places. Only an argument that takes into account the way the visual system works and the nature of perceptual content could ever hope to succeed, because it is at the level of perception that the kinds of indeterminacy raised by the "gavagai" example could be addressed and the problem of how perception cuts the world be solved. I will explore such an argument in the next section, but before that there is one issue that I would like to address.

One might think that Putnam's argument concerning the reference of the referring expressions of sentences or of the referring constituents of beliefs could be extended to cover perceptual states as structured wholes and thus to undermine from the beginning any attempt to examine whether perceptual content carves the world in the right places. Recall that the problem of realism concerns the relation between perception and the world; one needs to know whether perceptual content cuts the world in the proper places. This is not exactly the same problem as that of fixing the reference of referring expressions in sentential beliefs, although they are closely related. Consider the belief "S believes that O is F," where S is a person, O an object, and F a property. In the brain of S there is a neural state that represents, *qua* representational vehicle, a world state in which an object has a certain property. That representational state has a representational content that presents (assuming veridical perception) O as being F. Let us also assume, to avoid unnecessary complications, that it is this specific perceptual content that causes S to form the aforementioned belief. Putnam's point is that the truth of the sentence (or a set of sentences) does not fix the reference of the referring expressions "O" and "F" of the belief.

Now, "there is an analogy between familiar ways of reporting seeing and the units into which objects of sight may be articulated. The latter are divisible in roughly the way we tend to parse linguistic components of sentences." (Vision 1997, p. 85) Does Putnam's point say anything about the reference of "O" and whether O is presented as being F in the representational perceptual content? Though it seems tempting to transfer Putnam's arguments to perceptual contents and claim that the truth of the content as a whole underdetermines the reference of the referring constituents of the content, I would resist such a move because it presupposes that perceptual contents have sentential form and are propositional representational contents. However, perceptual contents, being nonconceptual, do not have a propositional structure, and thus it is, at best, doubtful whether Putnam's arguments could be applied to NCC. Does this mean that the indetermination problem raised by Putnam does not arise at the perceptual level? The answer, as I argue in section 8.3, is affirmative.

The argument I have offered here suggests that success semantics and reliabilism by themselves cannot help promote realism's case, as they do not and could not deal with what is the decisive question for realism: whether perceptual content carves the world in the right places. Only an argument that takes into account the way the visual system works and the nature of perceptual content could ever hope to succeed. I will explore such an argument in subsection 8.2.2.

We saw that even if success semantics thesis that our beliefs are largely true were correct that would not suffice to vindicate realism. Now, I will cast doubt on success semantics and on Putnam's and Dennett's thesis that successful action requires the truth of the beliefs on which the action is based, and I will argue that the fact that we successfully interact with the environment does not entail that our beliefs are necessarily true.

In chapter 3 we saw that, although perception has noncognitive content, which is retrieved bottom-up from a visual scene and is cognitively impenetrable, the perceptual system does not function independently of any kind of "knowledge." Visual processing at almost every level is constrained by certain operational constraints that modulate information processing. Such constraints are needed because perception is underdetermined by the retinal image. Unless the processing of information in the perceptual system is constrained by some assumptions about the physical world, perception is not feasible. Most computational accounts (Marr 1982; Ulmann and Richards 1990) hold that these operational constraints or principles substantiate some reliable generalities of the natural physical world, which means that in propositional form they become assumptions about the world. They are not assumptions about specific objects acquired through experience; they are general idealizations about the world. In chapter 3 I discussed in detail the kinds of constraints used, and so I will not examine them here, except to mention that there is evidence that the physiological mechanisms underlying vision reflect these constraints; their physical making is such that they implement these constraints, from cells for edge detection to mechanisms implementing the epipolar constraint (Poggio and Talbot 1981; Ferster 1981). Thus, in a sense that will be explicated below, one might claim that these principles are hard-wired in our perceptual system.[7]

The operational constraints reflect general or higher-order physical regularities that govern the behavior of objects in our world.[8] The operational constraints are implemented by mechanisms in the perceptual system and they modulate its processing. As such, these constraints are not available to introspection, and they function outside the realm of consciousness. One does not "know" or "believe" that an object moves in continuous paths, that it persists in time, or that it is rigid, though one uses this information to parse, index, and follow the object. In other words, these constraints are not perceptually salient, but one must be "sensitive" to them if one is to be described as perceiving our world. The constraints constitute the *modus operandi* of the perceptual system.

Even though perception becomes possible on account of such constraints, the perceptual system's dependency on operational constraints that implement general higher-order regularities about (mostly) solid objects in our world poses a threat to realism, because these constraints are not necessarily true of the world; their task is to ensure success in negotiating the environment. They aim to provide a reliable guide for fast on-line action in the environment.

To secure success, not only one need not act on true regularities; in addition, the regularities that guide actions must be schematic and idealized, in that they should abstract many of the complexities of the environment, so that fast and effective action will be possible. At the level of our negotiations with the environment, we are satisficers, not truth seekers. Indeed, if one examines closely the regularities in the behavior of solids behind the operational constraints, one sees that they are too general to capture exactly what is going on in a visual scene. I admit that they allow us to parse a visual scene, that they allow us to perceive solids, and that they allow us to perceive the motions of those solids and some of their features, and that they provide us with a fast and rough estimate of what might be the case; however, they are not meant to provide us with a true image of the state of affairs that obtains, only with an image that would allow us to interact successfully with the environment.

Stich (1985, pp. 123–125) argues, in the same vein, that success does not necessarily mean that the beliefs on which successful actions are based are true, and offers an example of why this is so. Stich adduces empirical evidence from studies of rats that, having been fed a certain food, were subjected to substantial doses of radiation and became ill. The rats developed an aversion to the food they had eaten before the irradiation. Apparently, the rats acted as though they believed that food poisoning was responsible for illness, and as a result they became averse to any food whose taste was more recent among the foods they had eaten before they became ill or was novel. It is likely that this aversion strategy is the result of natural selection. Stich asks us to consider whether in the rats' natural environment the belief that food poisoning is responsible for deathly illness is true. Given that the causes of rats' illnesses are variegated and only a minority concern food poisoning, that belief is most often false. It seems that natural selection has opted for extremely cautious inferential strategies that tend to produce false beliefs more often than true ones. The reason may be that, although the inferential strategy usually results in false beliefs, it provides true beliefs when true beliefs are most important. It is better to ensure that the rats avoid a poisonous food when they come across it, even though that means that they will avoid foods most of which are harmless.

There are many ways to argue that Stich's argument' is flawed. It presupposes, for instance, that there is plenty of food of different kinds, so that the rats have the luxury to avoid harmless food, and we could express serious doubts whether this is ever the case with all animals. Or that the diseases strike the rats at rare intervals, because if they did not, then the rats would have excluded from their eating repertoire most of their food sources, which again would have been a costly strategy. However, Stich's argument is plausible and provides an example of what it means to say that when it comes to successful action we are satisficers and not truth seekers. Pylyshyn (2003, p. 96) does not raise the point that the operational constraints do not guarantee the correct interpretation of all stimuli and that they lead to the correct interpretation under specific conditions common in our physical world. The problem is that "correct" is relativized to the functionality of the perceiving organism. "Correctness" is determined by success and not by true correspondence. One may be in the position of a neural network that successfully learns a task by minimizing its error within acceptable limits not because it has retrieved the regularity governing the data, but because it hit on a local minimum, which, by allowing it to generalize successfully, hides the fact that the "beliefs" formed by the network are not true but only successful. In subsection 8.2.2, to defend realism against this threat, I will argue that the regularities underlying the operational constraints at work in perception could not result in success while perceptual content is inaccurate.

I have claimed that to defend realism against constructivism one should ultimately show how perceptual nonconceptual content is related to the world. Since perceptual content is the representational NCC of perceptual states *qua* representational vehicles, the relation between that content and the world must be established. That would address the issue of realism in that, to make any claims whatsoever about the externalia, one must argue *from* perceptual states *to* the external world. A first step in attempting to capture the externalia is to claim that NCC is directly retrieved from the environment without any conceptual or theoretical contamination that would distort, as it were, the objectivity of perception by imposing on it our forms. A second step is to examine whether perceptual content carves the world in the right places. Thus, a successful argument for realism must show why perception, at least partly, presents true aspects of the world. In the next subsection I provide such an account and show that perception's reliability means that it captures some of the real properties of things and events in the external world.

My argument is based in part on a causal account of perception. It is also based on a detailed account of the NCC of perception. To assert that perception cuts the world in the right places, one must examine the contents of perceptual states. To do this, one must examine the processes of perception and its output. However, to argue *from* these contents *to* the world one must appeal to the fact that perception is reliable (reliabilism gets us from perceptual states to the world because we know that actions based on these states are successful) and show that perception is reliable because these states present aspects of things as they really are. Here is my argument for a restricted form of realism:

(i) To get in contact with the world through vision, one must break the circle of representations;
(ii) To break that circle in an epistemologically informative way, at least some visual states must have nonconceptual *representational* content.
(iii) There is a part of visual processing, which I call perception, that induces in us states with nonconceptual representational content.
(iv) The nonconceptual content has features that we consciously perceive as of properties of objects (the phenomenal content of experience).
(v) Our interactions with the world on the basis of this content are largely successful.
(vi) In order for some of our interactions with the world to be successful, a subset of the NCC must present correctly some of the real properties of the external objects.

Therefore, some aspects of the NCC of perception veridically (or correctly) present in perception real properties of objects in the external world. I have defended claims i–iv in the preceding chapters. I take claim v for granted; otherwise I would not be discussing the issue here. I will now argue for claim vi.

8.2.2 What Does Perception Tell Us About the World?

We saw that success semantics and realism deal with sentences in a language, whereas the proper analysis (which would allow one to address realism) should take place neither at the level of whole sentences nor at the level of the atomic constituents of sentences, but at the level of perceptual NCC, because only at that level can one examine whether one carves up the world in the right places. However, when one decides to take that step, a new problem appears. For that analysis to be possible, one must be able to distinguish at the level of perceptual NCC between what in linguistic form would be the constituents of the sentence—that is, between the predicate and the subject. In other words, one should be able to distinguish between the object and its properties as they are presented in perception. And all this should take place outside the context of a language, and even before the possession of sortals such as 'subject' and 'predicate'.

How do we go on to distinguish at that nonconceptual level between the object and its properties? This is crucial, for only if such a distinction is possible can the perceptual system track objects as they move and undergo featural changes. If, for example, the perceptual system could not distinguish in the appropriate way between objects and properties, then any change in properties would probably be perceived as the appearance of a new object and not as the same object that has undergone some featural change. The answer is that the perceptual system solves these problems.

To see why, we should first examine the specifics of the causal processes involved in perception and develop a causal theory of perception so that we can provide an account of how our representations result from the operation of perceptual organs on the external world. The theory of perception that I presented in part I of the book purports to do exactly that. In perception, information is extracted from the environment in a purely bottom-up way (that is, in an informationally encapsulated or cognitively impenetrable way).

The information directly (that is, with no conceptual intermediates) extracted from the world through perception consists in the following:

- aspectual representations—that is, representations indicating the structure of actions or events, and the potentialities afforded for action upon objects (affordances of objects)
- representations of objecthood—that is, representations of objects (the representation of an object's existence) as entities that persist in space and time[9]
- representations of spatial relations, and spatial location, of spatiotemporal properties, such as temporal synchrony or continuity and proximity, representations of the surface properties of objects viewed from the perspective of the perceiver, and representations of the objects' size, orientation, color, and motion.

I argued in chapter 6 that perception acquaints us with objects and their properties. Being perceptually acquainted with an object means that one is in direct contact with that object and that one retrieves information about that very object from the object itself, not through a description that would individuate or identify the object (and thus, by depicting it, would secure reference to it). On that account, perception puts us in a *de re* relationship with the object (as opposed to a descriptivist relationship). In perception, the reference of "mental perceptual demonstratives" is fixed through the nonconceptual information retrieved directly from the environment that allows one to individuate objects by assigning object-files to them. Thus, the NCC of the perceptual states functions as a *de re* nondescriptive mode of presentation of the object in perception.[10]

Upon viewing a scene, perception parses objects by assigning object-files through the object-centered segmentation processes. Perception uses the objects' properties to segment a scene, which means that these properties are perceived, but this information is not encoded as such, and thus it is not available to the organism for other tasks (say, the identification of an object as being such and such), or for providing semantic criteria for fixing the reference of the object-files. Since objects are individuated in a visual scene long before the onset of any form of awareness, the information that fixes the reference of mental perceptual demonstratives is unconscious (that is, not available to the subjects' awareness).

Recall from chapters 3 and 6 that when one looks at a scene, through eye focusing, a part of it is further processed. Objects located at that part are picked out and individuated. The brain's ensuing internal representations are about, or refer to, those specific objects of the scene. When one's internal representation refers to an object through such a deictic representation, this is a "deictic reference." Thus, when fixating a location, an object, or multiple objects, the neurons that are linked to the fovea refer to information computed from that location, that object, or those objects.

Eye fixation exemplifies the role of deictic mechanisms, or pointers, as devices that bind objects in the world with internal representations and cognitive programs. Suppose that the eye fixes at some location or objects in a scene and, as a result, the relevant neurons in the fovea compute information from that location or from those objects. Those objects are the referents of the deictic reference. The act of fixation assigns to the objects pointers or object-files that allow object individuation and tracking.

Successful interaction requires some form of action memory so that past reliable actions can be learned and repeated when needed. Indeed there is evidence that a motor element in memory for enacted events, stored in the brain, facilitates vision-action coordination. However, the object-files are not supposed to store these actions memories; they are used by the relevant mnemonic circuits in their capacity as reference fixers to objects. Their role is to parse and track objects in a scene. Their function precedes the storage of action memories, since the latter are actions on objects that must have been picked out in a scene first.

Thus, object-files individuate objects and fix their reference in perception by connecting the objects with internal representations—that is, with the representational contents of the neural structures that, *qua* representational vehicles, are related to the objects in the scene through the deictic reference in the way explained above. By opening a dossier for an object or an object- file, one indexes and tracks it. The object becomes the referent of the file, and any information in the file is information that refers to that object. There is, thus, a distinction between "objects" and "properties" inherent in the way the perceptual system processes information without the need for possession of the relevant sortals; One perceives objects *qua* objects as carriers of properties that may change while the object retains its identity as "that" object.

Now, to determine whether perceptual states represent the environment as it really is (that is, whether they correctly individuate objects and register and process the correct information about these objects) one must examine the content of those perceptual states and determine whether it correctly depicts aspects of the environment. So the claim that I put forth is as follows: In order for the perceptual representations to function successfully and guide action reliably (as they do), they must get something right.[11]

Consider a very simple organism-environment interaction: a frog's interaction with a fly (Bickhard 2000). The representational content of the neural activity induced by the fly in the frog's brain consists in the possibility of tongue flicking and eating on the basis of indications about potentialities that are afforded by specific objects in the environment. The representational content is in the indication in the frog that it is in a tongue flicking and eating situation. This content is about the potentialities, or possibilities of further interactions, that are afforded by the environment to the system, not about the fly; the relevant states of the frog are intimately connected with action. The potentialities implicitly predicate those interactive properties of the environment that could support the indicated actions of the frog. This is a kind of functional predication. Since this kind of content implicitly predicts the properties of the environment that afford actions on the part of the cognizer, it is about these properties.

To catch the fly, the frog does not have to calculate the courses of action that are available to it, the chances of success, and the outcome of each course of action, then estimate utilities, as Fodor (1975) would have it. The possibility of eating that the fly affords to the frog is indirectly perceived by the frog (indirectly in that the perception of affordances is based on certain invariant characteristics of the environment that are perceived directly, that is, nonconceptually). Furthermore, the instrumentality of a particular course of action reveals itself in the perceptual content; there is no need for decision making. All the information needed to initiate action is directly present in the perceptual content. If, for instance, there are multiple flies, the frog will go after the one with respect to which it is located in the most favorable eating position. The information that allows the frog's perceptual system to determine which fly that is contained in the environmental information that the frog's perceptual system processes (relative locations, orientation of motion, etc).

The problem now is to determine whether the information that the frog's visual circuit processes merely allows the frog to interact successfully with its environment or whether it functionally represents aspects of the environment as they really are. To answer that, one must consider the kind of information contained in the perceptual states of the frog when it perceives the fly. It certainly indirectly perceives the possibility for eating, but that is not the only information it gets. Affordances are based on certain invariant characteristics of the environment. First the frog sees an object by locking on that object. It also perceives the fly's shape and size (which are essential in making the frog indirectly perceive the affordance of eating), its relative location, its pattern of motion, and the orientation of its motion.

If action is to be successful, the contents of the states of the frog are at least approximately true of the environment; that is, they get the potentialities right. Surely the fly's existence, its size, its motion, its distance from the frog, and its shape are among the aspects of the environment that are essentially involved. If these were not estimated correctly, the frog would catch the fly by accident and not systematically. One might object at this point that it is conceivable that the frog systematically misperceives sizes, distances, and velocities and yet does it in such a way that the errors somehow cancel each other out and the frog systematically catches the fly. Although this possibility is conceivable if applied to only one activity (say, catching food), it loses its appeal if one bears in mind that these errors should cancel one another out when the fly wants also to find a mate, or to avoid a predator. In other words, the systematic misperceptions of sizes, shapes, motions, and distances should be such that they allow the frog to interact successfully with the environment with regard to a wide range of activities.

I think that this systematic misperception is highly unlikely, especially if one bears in mind that perception computes distances, sizes, motions, orientations, and shapes in parallel in both dorsal and ventral visual pathways (although this information is cast in a different coordinate system in each visual pathway) and makes this information available to a wide range of activities that are all subserved by the dorsal and ventral systems respectively. Specifically, information, say, about motion, shape, and color, which is required for an organism's wide range of interactions with the environment, is processed along both visual pathways in each pathway centrally, and then made available for a variety of aims subserved by each pathway. There is ample evidence (Goodale and Milner 2004; Moutoussis and Zeki 1997; Zeki 1993) that the early-vision module consists of a set of interconnected processes for orientation, shape, color, motion, stereo, and luminance. These processes are functionally independent, they process stimuli in parallel, and they provide input both to each other and to other visual areas that bind incoming information and segregate figures from ground. Studies (Moutoussis and Zeki 1997; Zeki 1981, 1993) also show that color, form, and motion are perceived separately and at different times. Color is perceived first, followed by shape and then motion. It seems, thus, that the brain consists of separate perceptual systems that form a perceptual temporal hierarchy in vision. Thus, color, shape, and size are each processed in one visual circuit and then are used by other visual circuits for various purposes.

A systematic misperception of shape and motion will be transferred all of the frog's activities that require information about shapes and motions. Thus, one could not argue that for some tasks (in which mutual cancellation of errors is not possible) perception delivers the true shapes and motions, whereas in other tasks (in which mutual cancellation of errors is possible) it misperceives them, or that different activities might require different sorts of canceling out and thus different estimations of size. So the argument could work only if selection has seen to it that not only the organism systematically misperceives environmental features, but also that it does so in a way that allows the errors to cancel one another out in all possible activities. I think that is unlikely. That perception gets the basic environmental parameters right, and that this is why actions are successful, is a much simpler and more plausible explanation of success.

Thus, successful action is possible only if "its presupposed enabling conditions hold. If those enabling conditions involve particular properties, then success in that interaction detects, differentiates, those properties" (Bickhard 2000, pp. 40–41). Suppose that perceiver P perceives object X as having the property F (say, a specific shape). Suppose further that the object does not have the property F but instead has the property Z. The problem is that if F is different from Z and X ignores that because she is systematically being deceived by perception, then any behavior of X that essentially involves estimation of F will not succeed in satisfying X's purposes except by accident. A perceptual system that functions thus would be detrimental to the organism.[12]

The argument from the success of our actions (as they are guided by perceptual information) to the veridicality of some of the information they deliver (as developed here) avoids the pitfall to which, according to Fodor, many appeals to evolutionary theory are susceptible. Fodor (1994, p, 20) complains that many arguments of this kind appeal to evolution, as if evolution is a mechanism that can explain how things work, and according to Fodor this is not true. Evolutionary explanations are not of the right form to answer that kind of question. The correct answer would be to posit a mechanism that, selected by some Darwinian process, guides perception in its success. The argument offered here does not run that risk, since the explanatory work is done not by evolutionary selection but by the operational constraints that modulate perception, which, by reflecting some reliable regularities about our environment, ensure successful interaction with that environment.

8.3   Concluding Comments

Putnam may be right that from true beliefs one cannot determine correspondence of symbols to objects. However, with respect to the problem of the presentation of world states in perception one need not argue from true beliefs to referential relations of symbols; one can argue from actions and nonconceptual states to referential relations of nonconceptual states with the world. In the latter case, there is no set of sentences whose truth fails to secure unique reference of the singular terms involved. The perceptual system computes certain parameters or perceived features of objects to initiate action. For the action to be reliable, these parameters must be of the right kind and must have the right values. Spatio-temporal properties of objects, size, shape, orientation, and motion must be in the object, as we perceive it to be. One's perceptual system selects to process and represent, or is tuned to, those among the features of objects in the environment that fit one's interactive purposes with the environment.

Thus, although it is true that evolution could not determine a unique correspondence between referring expressions in beliefs and external objects, my argument is not based on the hypothesis that evolutionary pressures have determined the reference of sub-sentential referential expressions. It is based on the claim that our perceptual systems retrieve in a bottom-up direct way information from the environment, and that the object features, *as they are presented in perceptual states that are essential for reliably successful action*, correspond to features of external objects (their actual shapes, sizes, motion, and so on). The way perception parses a scene—by means of processes that open and assign object-files to objects that are updated by incoming information from these objects—establishes the reference to these objects and their properties. One does not have to establish reference to items of the world through the truth of beliefs.

Successful action is all one needs to argue for the truth of (part of) perceptual content. Successful actions require at a minimum that an organism indirectly perceive, say, the affordances of objects and situations in the environment. The affordances rely on certain invariants of the objects' features that the organism perceives directly. If these invariants were not perceived correctly, the animal would never perceive the affordances, and its actions would not be successful. Getting the affordances right certainly requires the correct perception of those object features.

The fact that perception correctly represents only some of the worldly dimensions neither presupposes nor implies that some conceptual scheme is applied to the incoming information. The operational constraints that make us perceive objects that persist and move in space and time involve no concepts whatsoever; they are implemented in our perceptual system, and they make it function the way it does. McDowell (1994, pp. 7–8) claims that, since the world can be carved up in many different ways and perceivers choose one among them, or better, perceivers passively select the one that fits their conceptual scheme, this suggests that the carving up of the world is directed or generated by the conceptual schemes of the perceiver. However, the fact that in perception only certain features are selected and the fact that this selectivity is an inherent part of perception do not entail that perception depends on conceptual schemes; they suggest, in Vision's words (1998, p. 411), that "we are certain kinds of information processing engines and not others."

Let me propose a solution to Putnam's problem and to the "gavagai" problem. Putnam's problem does not arise at all for the nonconceptual content of perception. In perception the NCC functions as a *de re* nondescriptive mode of presentation of objects that fixes the reference of the neural correlates—which implement in neural terms direct referential expressions like demonstratives as they figure in the brain (of the native when she perceives the rabbit and utters, while pointing to it, "gavagai")— that represent, *qua* vehicles, these objects. The perceptual system itself solves the problem by parsing a visual scene and picking up the objects in it by assigning to them object-files. What is more, once that reference is fixed and the object-files are filed with nonconceptual information that is retrieved directly from the scene, the linguistic terms that formulate the "mental referential expressions" have their reference determined.

This is in line with Putnam's own solution. Putnam (1980, p. 482) identified the source of the problem with model-theoretic semantics with the conception of a language as something whose use is completely specified and yet the language still lacks an interpretation. If one starts with this assumption, one can only get crazy solutions. The way out is to assume that some kind of interpretation of the terms in a language exists from the beginning. The object-files, by fixing the referent through the *de re* mode of presentation of the referent, provide such grounding of the directly referential terms; this why the underdetermination of reference does not arise. Furthermore, the approach taken here suggests that the model of semantics that Putnam attacks—the view that the interpretation of symbolic systems comes from the correspondence between the symbols/terms and entities in a model, and ultimately the world—should be rejected. The terms in a language do not start as pure syntactic entities whose meanings should be specified by correspondence to the entities of the model. Meaning, as is provided by the object-file assigned to objects in perception, is embedded in the referential symbols/terms from the beginning, and grounds them in the world.

More generally, the indeterminacy of reference in problems of the "gavagai" kind does not arise, because the perceptual system cannot perceive undetached parts moving together; undetached points that move coherently together are perceived as a single moving object. Recall from chapter 6 that this is due to the structure of the human perceptual system, which has hard-wired mechanisms implementing certain operational constraints. As we saw in chapter 3, studies suggest that perception is constrained by a number of domain-specific principles about material objects and some of their properties. These constraints involve attention biases toward particular inputs and a certain number of principled predispositions constraining the computation of those inputs. Among these principles are the *rigidity* and no *action at a distance* principles, which specify that bodies move rigidly (unless the other mechanisms show that a seemingly unique body is a set of two distinct bodies) and that they move independently of one another. These constraints entail that if a set of points/parts in space move with the same velocity and to the same direction they are perceived as a rigid body moving and not as a set of points/parts moving together. Recall the *local proximity* and *proximity* constraints (discussed in section 2.2), which state that the perceptual system combines adjacent elements into one object and that, since matter is cohesive, adjacent regions usually belong together and remain so even when the object moves. Together, these constraints show that when different objects/parts cannot move independently of one another (they are undetached) they cannot be perceived as distinct objects that for some reason are always connected but must be perceived as a single object. This fixes the ontology in the "gavagai" case. One cannot see undetached rabbit parts, only rabbits.

The operational constraints that are at work in vision are the constitutive standards of vision—that is, the "rules" that determine what the perception is of, and also that we perceive objects as integral bearers of properties (Haugeland 1998, pp. 253, 260–261). Thus, undetached rabbit parts that occur whenever rabbithood is instantiated and that move together are perceived as a rabbit and not as parts that move together. The sortal associated with the singular term 'gavagai' or with the perceptual demonstratives elicited in the presence of rabbits is "rabbit," not "undetached rabbit parts." It is because of the function of the operational constraints that there is no possibility of an apparatus individuating rabbit parts independently of the whole of which they are parts, as opposed to rabbits; object-files are opened for rabbits not for undetached rabbit parts, because object-centered segmentation processes parse the scene into rabbits and not into undetached rabbit parts. In other words, these principles necessarily join together the "undetached parts of a rabbit," and thus induce the perception of a whole rabbit and not of rabbit body parts. This fixes the ontology in the "gavagai" case. One cannot see undetached rabbit parts; one sees a rabbit.

Notes

Chapter 1

1. Strictly speaking, a distinction should be made between object-centered and feature-centered attention. Since, however, the lack of this distinction is not important for the purposes of the book, I will gloss over that difference and keep talking of object-centered attention to denote both kinds of attention.

2. Superior colliculus (SC) is a region in the brain form which the majority of pathways descending to the oculomotor centers emanate. SC consists of multiple layers and maps visual space, in the sense that cells in the upper and intermediate layers have visual receptive fields whose locations are laid out topographically. At the same time, cells in the deeper layers have the property that their stimulations generate saccadic eye movements with the direction and size dependent on the location of stimulation. In that sense, SC also maps oculomotor space. Whenever an animal fixates at a region in space, the cells in the SC that correspond to the foveal region of the visual map are activated and this activity pauses with the animal's saccadic movements. The term "fixation center" applies to those cells. There are two other main cell types in the deep layers of SC. The first is the buildup cells whose activity starts well before the movement of eyes and which reached its peak just before the saccade is triggered. The second is the burst cells that show a brief burst of discharge just prior to the movement and signal the onset of the saccade.

3. The issue of how exactly is an object represented by means of an indexical like "there" or "that" is discussed in chapter 6, where I develop a theory of demonstrative reference. In the same chapter, I discuss the issue of the meaning of indexicals and whether their meaning consists only in their external relation to the object they denote.

4. Philosophers describe the detailed character of perceptual or sensory representations as opposed to the poorer, sensorily speaking, representations stored in memory by appealing to the fine-grained character and richness of the "phenomenal content" of experience; the phenomenal content of our experiences is usually much richer

than any attempt to report it could be; it cannot be described conceptually by invoking the contents of mnemonic representations of that content.

5. This line of work does not consider states with phenomenal content to be conscious and, therefore, does not make the same distinctions that Lamme and Block do, since according to the theory there is only one form of consciousness—to wit, what Lamme and Block have called "report or access awareness," which involves the global workspace and hence the working memory. For further discussion, see Dehaene and Changeux 2005.

6. The issue of binding, or the binding problem, has at least three *different* components: binding at the neural level, binding at the level of awareness, and binding at the level of cognition and performance (Revonsuo 1999). The first form of the binding problem concerns the way the brain integrates information emanated form an object in a visual scene and processed distributively in a multitude of brain areas into a single object representation. The second form concerns the way the brain constructs a neural entity that gives rise to the conscious perception of an object as unique entity in space and time. The third form concerns the way the various cognitive (modular?) subsystems of the brain that separately process information from the same object integrate their results to form a unified representation of objects for the purposes of perception, recognition, memory, and interaction with the environment. Lamme's and Kanwisher's work, by dissociating perception from attention and awareness, open the road for paying the due importance to this multifaceted nature of the binding problem.

7. I elaborate here on the threefold distinction made first by Shrager (1990).

8. It would be useful to remind the reader the basic layout of Marr's theory. According to Marr, useful information from a three-dimensional scene (such as, surface markings, object boundaries, and shadows) can be recovered by finding the places where the intensity of light impinging on the retina changes relatively abruptly. The array of intensity values is created by the way light is reflected by the object the observer is viewing. Marr distinguishes three levels of representation: the initial, the viewer-centered and the object-centered. The initial level of representation involves Marr's *primal sketch*, which consists of the *raw primal sketch* and the *full primal sketch*. The *raw primal sketch* provides information about the edges and blobs present in a scene, their location and their orientation. This information is gathered by locating and coding individual intensity changes. Grouping procedures applied to the edge fragments formed in the *raw primal sketch* yield the *full primal sketch*, in which larger structures with boundaries and regions are recovered. Through the *primal sketch* contours and textures in an image are captured. The primal sketch can be thought of as a description of the image of a scene, but not as a description of the real scene. This latter involves the relative distances of the objects and their motions. This information is provided by the viewer-centered representation, that is, Marr's $2\frac{1}{2}$D sketch. At this level information about the distance and layout of each

surface is computed using various depth cues, and by means of analysis of motion and of shading. This information describes only the parts of the object that are visible to the viewer, and thus is relative to the viewer. One of the aims of vision is the recognition of objects. This requires the matching of the shape of a structure with a particular object, a matching which requires an object-centered representation. This is Marr's 3D model.

Chapter 2

1. So as not to complicate matters unnecessarily, I opt to ignore implicit processing—that is, the processing of stimuli that are unattended, although I have already said a few things about that in chapter 1. The evidence on implicit processing suggests that there are non-attentional visual pathways (or at least that these pathways require a minimum amount of distributed spatial attention) that allow elaborate processing of unattended stimuli even at the level of semantic processing in the absence of attention or awareness.

2. The "gist" of the scene is usually taken to be the semantic content of the scene—that is, whether the scene portrays, for instance, a room or a market. It is problematic to attribute the extraction of the semantic content of a scene during the FFS is that the time course of the FFS ends long before semantic top-down information could affect perceptual processing and invest it with conceptual content, which is certainly required in order to perceive a scene as a market or a room. That is why, when I refer to gist, I construe it as Petitot's (1995) positional (local) content structure of the scene, which is nonconceptual and is contradistinguished from the semantic content of the scene (see discussion in text). It would be interesting to examine whether that nonconceptual notion of a "gist" could account for the properties that Rensink and others take "gist" to have when they claim that semantic content of a scene is retrieved by the mechanisms of early vision. If that is the case, then "gist" should not be taken to mean "semantic/conceptual" content.

3. I hasten to add that this matter is complicated, since there are cases in which feature singletons or sudden motions may not capture attention, as IB studies reveal. However, a discussion of this issue would take us far afield, and the issue is not important to the central topic of this book. Interested readers are referred to Egeth and Yantis 1997.

Chapter 3

1. For an overview of the evidence for object-centered attention, the reader should refer to the discussion in chapter 1 of this book, but mainly to Egeth and Yantis 1997 and Pylyshyn 2003 for psychological evidence, and to Cziger and Balazs 1998 and Olson and Gettner 1996 for neuropsychological evidence.

2. As we have seen, top-down effects, including familiarity with objects or scenes, may override this initial segregation in favor of some other parsing of the scene into objects, and they may also resolve ambiguities when the bottom-up processes do not suffice to segment a scene into its objects (Treisman and Kanwisher 1998).

3. Sensory memory is a rich, rapidly decaying sensory trace of the entire stimuli display. It refers to items detected by sensory receptors and retained for a very short period of time in the sensory registers that are able to hold accurate images of sensory information momentarily. Sensory memory is outside conscious control, in that it happens automatically and is unbidden.

4. See Aloimonos, Bandyopadhyay, and Weiss 1988; Ballard 1991; Brooks 1991.

5. As a result of the relative metric used, the ventral system, unlike the dorsal system, is vulnerable to various illusions that exploit the fact that the ventral system computes sizes relatively (Goodale and Milner 2004).

6. Recent work on the dorsal and ventral systems suggests that the difference between the two systems lies not so much in the kind of information they process (they both process spatial information, information about size and shape, and so forth) as in the functions they serve.

7. As I will explain in chapters 4 and 5, weak representations are semantic in the sense that they have true values, that is, they are true or false depending on whether they correctly (re)present the proto-objects and their features in the visual scene.

8. Peacocke (2001, p. 241) argues that the nonconceptual content of experience represents things, events, or places and times in a certain way, as having certain properties, or as standing in certain relations, "also given in a certain way." Peacocke (ibid., p. 257) distinguishes between ways that determine which object is perceived and ways that do not. Peacocke's determination of what object is perceived may amount to the individuation of an object and its indexing discussed here.

Chapter 4

1. The tripartite distinction is loose and expands a similar distinction by Shrager (1990, pp. 438–439). Shrager (1990) views perception as the link between sensation and cognition. Perception translates sensation to a format that is amenable to cognitive process; that is, it reinterprets sensation so that its information could interface with the cognitive abilities of the perceiver. Sensation *per se* is, for Shrager (ibid., p. 438), the set of transducers by means of which an agent has access to an environment.

2. I am interested here in the general form of the output of perceptual processes. No commitment is made to the details of any current formulation of that representation. What is important for present purposes is the overall conception of what

information each representation, or level of processing, enables and how the interpretations, levels of processing, interact with each other. Thus, the reference to Marr's $2\frac{1}{2}$D and 3D sketches is only an example from a specific theory.

3. Bermudez (1995) thinks that being semantically evaluable does not suffice to render the content of a state "representational." For a state to represent something, certain additional conditions should be met. I discuss this issue in the third section of this chapter and argue that the states with nonconceptual content as construed in this book satisfy all of Bermudez's criteria.

4. There are good reasons, though I will not discuss them here, to assume that this causal contact cannot be on the level of atomic concepts (as proposed by Fodor 1998), so I propose to investigate the possibility that nonconceptual content is what provides this contact.

5. Confusion may lurk here because 'subdoxastic' is sometimes confused with 'nondoxastic'. The former term is used it to signify those perceptual states the content of which does not fall within the realm of awareness, as in Bermudez's (1995) information-processing computational states. In that sense, 'subdoxastic' is roughly synonymous with Dennett's (1993) 'subpersonal'. 'Nondoxastic' is used to signify content that is not propositional or conceptual (Markie 2005). 'Nondoxastic' is opposed to Dretske's (1993, 1995) term 'doxastic' as it occurs in the context of Dretske's distinction between a phenomenal (to wit, nonconceptual) and a doxastic (to wit, conceptual) sense of "see." All subdoxastic content is nondoxastic, in that it does not involve concepts and thus it is not propositionally articulated. On the other hand, there is nondoxastic content that is not subdoxastic, since it can be the object of awareness, namely the phenomenal content of experience.

6. With the exception of the nonconceptual content of sensation, which as I said in the terminological note above, it is not representational.

7. This paves the way for a Fregean account of NCC (Tye 2006), since a Fregean could argue that the concepts that enter into the specification or individuation of that content by means of conceptual modes of presentation need not be concepts that the subject of the experience possesses.

8. I think that this view of Stalnaker's can be read independently of his earlier view (1998) that all contents, whether they be the contents of beliefs or of perceptions, should be understood in terms of sets of possible worlds, in which case all contents are nonconceptual. That does not mean, of course, that Stalnaker thinks that propositional attitudes and perceptions are the same, only that any differences they have should be determined in terms extrinsic to the type of contents involved.

9. The thesis that veridical experiences and hallucinatory experiences have different nonconceptual contents even though they can have the same phenomenal character contradicts Tye's (1995, 2000) strong intentionalism, according to which

the phenomenal character of perceptual states *is* the nonconceptual representational content of the perceptual states. Tye (2007) acknowledges this tension and tries to develop an account of weak representationalism, according to which phenomenal character *supervenes* on nonconceptual representational content, which avoids this problem. Tye (2007, p. 609) ends up by sketching a form of "second-order" intentionalism in the way of functionalism's account of mental states.

10. McDowell (1984, p. 103; 1986, p. 165) argues that the inner contents are not contents at all, only bearers of content or vehicles of content.

11. I think that Campbell may be taken to hold the same view about the nature of nonconceptual content when he writes (2002, p. 69) that, although one cannot intentionally attend to Fs without having the concept for *F*, one can attend to *an F* without having that concept. The distinction between a conceptual attending *to F* and a nonconceptual attending to *an F* could signal the distinction between seeing a token-object *F* and perceiving an object-type *F*. Notice also that where Campbell speaks of "attending without having a concept" I have substituted "perceiving."

12. Although Tye uses expressions like "it seems to me there is a red surface before me," I think it goes without saying that this is *un facon de parler*, and Tye does not assume that the perceiver need describe, linguistically or in thought, her experience using the concept "red."

13. Noa (2003) does not address the issue of the nonconceptual as opposed to conceptual character of perceptual content. His account applies to either perception (nonconceptual) or observation (conceptual).

14. This way Noa accounts for cases in which we experience a round object, which, however, from our perspective seems elliptical. Thus, we experience that the plate is round and that it looks elliptical from here. I suspect, though I will not pursue it here, that Noa is after what Smith (2003) captures by saying that although sensations (seeing an elliptical shape) are inherent into perceptual experience they are not the objects of awareness of this experience. The object of awareness is the round table. What allows us to perceive its shape is the fact that we can move around it (Smith's second nonconceptual phenomenon that characterizes intentional perception as opposed to mere nonintentional sensation). Noa (2003) also draws attention to the role of motion on the part of the perceiver that allows her to keep track not only of how things are but also of her changing relation to how things are.

15. Bermudez (2007, p. 70, note 4) offers a nice account of why Evans's notion of nonconceptual content is meant to apply to personal level contents in addition to sub-personal-level contents.

16. The reader may have noticed that I adopt a thesis similar to Fodor's (1998) "semantic externalism," only in this case the causal links establish the nature of the nonconceptual content and not the meaning of concepts.

17. Vision (1998, pp. 425–426) argues that McDowell falls victim to this same confusion, in that he considers the conceptual/nonconceptual content distinction to be a matter internal to the subject and to whether she possesses the relevant concepts and not a distinction about kinds of contents. McDowell thinks that perceiving requires perceptual awareness, which McDowell construes as access awareness since for McDowell perceiving involves inherently concepts. From this, one can easily locate the root of McDowell's confusion that leads him to think of the conceptual/nonconceptual distinction in terms of the conceptual arsenal of the perceiver.

18. Although this commits me to representationalism, my account is neutral with respect to the kind of representationalism—that is, whether it is strong or weak representationalism (Tye 2002b and forthcoming).

19. Peacocke (2001, p. 257) also distinguishes between ways that determine which object is perceived from those which do not. The determination of what object is perceived amounts to the individuation of an object and its indexing by the perceptual system. Thus, these ways may correspond to the mode of presentation of information in the relevant perceptual states that are responsible for the segmentation of a visual scene. This time, Peacocke is correct.

20. Block (1996, 2005a, 2007) also distinguishes between phenomenal and access awareness.

21. Actually, things (as always) are more complicated. There is a distinction between propositional seeing (seeing that p is the case), objectual seeing (seeing x), and predicative seeing (seeing X to be F or seeing X as being F). The issues about these forms of seeing are largely irrelevant to our theme and thus I will restrict my discussion to the distinction between conceptual and nonconceptual seeing.

22. Thus, the content of a perceptual state includes a mode of presentation, but in contrast with Frege's theory this is not a mode of presentation in thought (because a mode in thought involves concepts) but a mode of presentation in perception.

23. Evans (1983, pp. 227–228) makes a similar point when he claims that the conceptualization of nonconceptual content produces a cognitive state "whose content is systematically dependent upon the content of the informational state." Evans's informational state corresponds to our perceptual state.

24. BonJour (2003, pp. 17–18) insists that the fact that a belief describes an experience correctly in a non-accidental way does not suffice to justify the belief. If it did, then there would be no difference between his internalist account and externalism. Justification also requires that "the character of the experience in virtue of which the description is correct is cognitively given or presented to the person via the act of immediate acquaintance or direct apprehension, and is thereby cognitively accessible."

Chapter 5

1. The degree of solidity of objects (that is, the degree to which solids are not deformable) probably is not directly retrievable from a scene (Glover 2003). Its computation may involve comparison with objects stored in memory. In that sense, it may rely on previously acquired knowledge, and thus it may require a top-down flow of information from higher cognitive centers. Thus, it may not be part of the nonconceptual content of experience, although rigidity is certainly part of the nonconceptual content of experience.

2. Clark (1999, p. 346) defines affordances as "the possibilities for use, intervention and action which the physical world offers a given agent and are determined by the 'fit' between the agent's physical structure, capacities and skills and the action-related properties of the environment itself."

3. One notes that the set of entities that fill Peacocke's scenarios is similar to the set of fundamental "entities," which provide the elementary representational space in Langacker's grammar.

4. In his *Critique of Pure Reason*, Kant calls the faculty by which we apply the conceptual element to the causal effects from the external world on our sense organs "spontaneity."

5. This view brings immediately to mind Descartes' (1984) conception that error is involved in perception only if the perceiver attempts to interpret the content of her experience, and thus goes beyond what is immediately given to his senses; a given about which she has absolute certainty.

6. Though McDowell (1994) holds that perception is from the very beginning conceptual, he does not claim that perception is a form of belief; perception and perceptual beliefs are separate.

7. One should include among the motives behind the rejection of the "Myth of the Given" Sellars's (1956) rejection of foundationalist epistemologies that sought a firm basis on which to ground knowledge in the pure content of our experiential states.

8. Sensory qualities are the ways the sensible qualities of objects, namely their perceptible properties, appear to the perceiver in perception. For a discussion, see Smith 2002, pp. 51–52.

9. For the shift in the term, see note 8.

10. Another problem with Vision's account, at least from the perspective of this book, is that he does not clarify what he means by "the output of perception." Does he consider, for instance, the 3D shape, or the affordances, of an object as constituents of this output?

11. This is similar to Smith's (2003) contention that the phenomenal properties of experience are not properly speaking the objects of awareness of a perceptual experience, though they are inherent features of it; objects and their properties are the objects of awareness of perceptual experience. In Tye's example, one is aware of the blue ocean, not of "blueness."

12. The demand that properties such as "being an acute pain" or "being a blue seeing experience" be reduced to, or be explained in terms of, brain states—as opposed to the demand that the phenomenal properties "acuteness," or "blueness," should be reduced to, or be explained in terms of, brain states—constitutes physicalism's solution to the problem of how phenomenal properties or qualia are related to brain states (Kim 1998).

Chapter 6

1. I discussed deictic pointers at length in chapter 3.

2. Furthermore, we know that the concepts are learned through our interaction with the environment (which includes other people as well). Thus, concepts are grounded in these interactions. But this means that demonstrative concepts, such as "that round shape," must be grounded eventually in our preconceptual interactions with the environment.

3. As Pylyshyn (2003, p. 213) remarks, though there certainly are properties that cause index assignments and allow object tracking, it is plausible that the list of these properties is heterogeneous and they may differ from case to case.

4. This conventional usage of an indexical type is what Kaplan (1989) calls the "character," as opposed to "content" of that type, and Perry (1977), the "role" of the type. The character of an indexical corresponds to its linguistic meaning, that is, the grammatical convention that determines its usage in the language. Occasionally the character is also referred to as the linguistic mode of presentation of the indexical (Recanati 1997). The linguistic meaning is constant; it is a function from contexts of utterance to contents. The content of the type is not repeatable from context to context, as the character; it corresponds to what a particular tokening of the type expresses (and that is why it is the semantically relevant part of the token). Evans (1990, p. 72) calls the "character" of a type a "semantical convention." Devitt (1996, p. 222) calls the conventional way the demonstrative functions in context "the property of referring to a specified object under the general demonstrative mode." This property is distinguished from the property of "referring to a specific object by a specified demonstrative." Devitt takes this last mode of reference to narrow down the mode ascribed by the general demonstrative mode, which is determined by convention, to one particular demonstrative mode.

5. The reason is that a definite description could have a different denotation in another possible world. The definite description "the president of the USA in 1970," to use Kripke's example, refers to Nixon, but it could refer to Humphrey, had the latter won the 1968 presidential election. A demonstrative or a name, in contrast, designates the same object in every possible world where the object exists, hence the term "rigid designator."

6. For a discussion of some problems related to Burge's analysis of beliefs and an extended analysis of perception as a *de re* relationship with the world, see pp. 85–89 of Smith 2002.

7. The term "narrow content" is intended to denote the purely subjective or psychological aspect of a thought, the sense of the thought or the mode of presentation of the object the thought is about in the thought, the part of the thought which "is in the head," as opposed to the term "wide content" that includes the object that the thought is about. There is a debate as to what is the semantic content of a thought, and it is roughly about whether that content should be analyzed along two dimensions, an objective truth-conditional, the wide content, and a subjective psychological dimension, the narrow content, (internalism) or whether there is only one dimension, the wide one, and there is really no narrow content (externalism).

8. Since I want to avoid discussing issues such as the disjunctive or not nature of perception, or whether perceptual demonstratives are object involving and in what sense, I restrict my self to examining successful perceptions and exclude cases of hallucinations, although not cases of illusions, in which case perceptual content simply misrepresents the objects of perception. The restricted scope of my inquiry allows me to claim that perceptual senses are object involving, in the sense discussed in the text.

9. The characteristics of the object-files that index objects, which derive from the fact that these files contain nonconceptual information, to wit, that they have a limited spatio-temporal existence, last for a very short period of time, are not retained across fixations, and are erased when new information enters the retina resemble those assigned to object-files by Recanati (1997, pp. 126–127). Recanati writes that at a given moment the object-file or buffer of an object contains information about the object that is acquired through the fundamental epistemic relation that underwrites the mode of acquaintance with the object. The file exists only for so long as the viewer is in position to gather nondescriptive *de re* information from the object by means of the fundamental epistemic relation. Finally, the object-file is unstable, because its content is available only so long as the viewer is in the fundamental epistemic relation with the object.

10. Of course, by being provided such information, one might attend to the relevant part of the scene and individuate the same objects. But, and this is also Campbell's

point, it is one's perceptual system that will perform object segmentation, not the information itself.

11. I think that Devitt (1996, p. 228) also is close to such a solution, which is certainly compatible with his theory, when he discusses Field's (1973) notion of partial reference. He claims there that confusions regarding referents arise when sometimes one creates two files where one should have created only one.

12. I say "standard modern accounts" because it is not at all clear what Frege actually thought of concepts and their references and sense. Frege saw concepts as functions, as essentially unsaturated (as in "x is a Greek"), that produce a truth value if an argument is fed in, i.e. an object, not an object-word. He took the view that a concept is the reference of a concept word like "Greek," but this concept is not an object, since it is a function. What is now called the "extension" of a concept is Frege's "value range" (*Wertverlauf*)—this is not the reference of the concept word in Frege. What the sense of concept words should be, is fairly obscure, on his account. So, though it is clearly true that Frege saw reference as a relation between a symbol and an object, he did not apply this view to concepts because there is no object here, just the function itself—that function is the reference of the concept word for him. I would prefer to use "concept" for the sense of the concept word and reference for the extension.

13. Thus, Vision (1998, p. 426) is wrong to accept this requirement as plausible. It is not.

14. Thus, the object-centered segmentation processes provide the additional binding mechanism, over the initial binding of features into a bundle of features, that Bermudez (2003, p. 73) deems necessary for the perception of objects *qua* objects: "One way of describing the distinction between a body and a bundle of properties would be to say that this featural binding problem is not the only binding problem. A solution to the featural binding problem will still give us a bundle of features. It would not be enough to underwrite our experience of a world of objects. Something more needs to be added. A further binding problem needs to be solved."

15. "The meaning of a term is a concept, which determines reference, in the sense that it provides a criterion of belonging to the extension" (Putnam 1993, p. 150).

16. Wiggins tries to extend the Fregean framework to include in the Fregean account of "sense" of a term the referent of the term itself. He attempts, thus, to make Fregean sense "reality invoking." Wiggins (1993, p. 198) aims to render compatible Putnam's theory of reference and its rejection of purely descriptive accounts of reference fixing with this extended Fregean framework, by including in the latter the flow of the world into the word. According to this extended account, names without bearers would have had no sense for Frege. Evans (1993) shares the same interpretation of Frege's and argues that it would be wrong to attribute to Frege the thesis that the sense of a singular term is existence-independent. McDowell (1993, p. 118),

however, argues that for Frege, names without bearers could have a sense in exactly the same way as a name with a bearer.

17. This is, as a matter of course, another version of Bickhard's critique of encodingism.

18. See Kaplan 1979, 1989; Salmon 1981.

19. The theories of direct reference are incompatible with the theory presented here, insofar as they deny the role of the mode of presentation of a demonstrative in the way the demonstrative functions in language. Putnam's theory of direct reference differs from the theories we targeted in that discussion. It is "direct" in that it grounds natural kind terms and singular words in the world without the intervention of conceptual content (avoiding thus the problems of the descriptive theories of reference). Still, Putnam claims that the world determines in part the referent of, say, a singular word. As our discussion in the main text shows, the mode of presentation of a singular word plays an indispensable part in establishing the causal chains that ground the term in the world and fix its referent. Contrast this with the other theories of direct reference, according to which only the world determines such a referent.

20. As Kripke himself remarks (1980, p. 95), this initial baptism cannot explain how other people refer when using the same word. For that one needs to take into consideration other people in the community and the way they use the term, the history of how one acquainted himself with the name etc. Hence, in the case of singular terms, the reference can be fixed in various ways; "in an initial baptism it is typically fixed by an ostentation or a description. Otherwise, the reference is usually determined by a chain, passing the name from link to link" (Kripke 1980, p. 135). As Devitt (1996, p. 164) claims the initial baptism or grounding may run through many people by means of "reference borrowing" in communication. The link of reference borrowings creates the causal network that grounds a token of a singular term.

21. See Campbell's (1999) "indexical causality."

22. What Frege calls a "recognition judgment."

23. Thus, Vision's (1998, pp. 414–415) answer to Geach's (1957) attack against the doctrine of abstractionism is correct. Geach argues that according to that doctrine, a concept is acquired by a process of singling out in attention some one feature given in direct experience and abstracting this feature from other features. Geach rejects it on the ground that this doctrine presupposes that one actively chooses among or abstracts from an arbitrary selection of features and how could this be done outside a conceptual framework. Therefore, concepts cannot be learned that way. McDowell uses this to reject the notion of a nonconceptual experience, since such a notion requires abstractionism; for if perception is not modulated by a conceptual framework that determines which features among those present in a scene are to be selected, how does perception selects its features? Vision's answer is that

no such arbitrary selection need be involved in perception, since our perceptual system is attuned only to certain packages of reality and does not choose which package to select.

Chapter 7

1. All references to Fodor 1984 are from the version reprinted in *Readings in Philosophy and Cognitive Science*, ed. A. Goldman (MIT Press, 1993).

2. All references to Churchland 1988 are from the version reprinted in Churchland 1989.

3. These "object recognition" units are not necessarily semantic, since we may recognize an object that we had seen before, even though we have no idea of its name, of what it does and how it functions—that is, even if we have no semantic and lexical information about it. Thus, Humphreys and Bruce (1989) introduced a distinction between the "perceptual classification" and "semantic classification" and "naming." These processes are independent of one another.

Chapter 8

1. According to externalism, a belief is justified if the believer has formed that belief on the basis of a reliable belief formation process, which may be, and usually is, outside the cognitive grasp of the believer; a belief is justified if "it comes from an epistemically, truth-conducively reliable process or faculty or intellectual virtue" (Sosa 2003, p. 109); perception and memory are characteristic examples of such intellectual virtues. This means that one can know that X is the case without having access to the reasons or processes that justify one's belief that X is the case; it suffices for a belief to be justified that this belief be produced in a causal reliable way by some process of belief formation. One can know (for instance) that X is the case if, supposing that X is an empirical fact, one is in an appropriate causal relation with the corresponding world state without being aware that one is in such a relation.

2. I use the adjective 'correct' rather than 'true' for perceptual states because I consider them to be nonpropositional; 'true' usually applies to propositional structures.

3. Many accounts that invoke success in negotiating the environment to argue for the truth of beliefs rely on some form of biological/evolutionary/teleological account of representation and truth that is highly problematic. However, my account relies on a causal theory of perception that extracts bottom-up information from the environment. I rely on success in action to argue for the correctness of perceptual representations from within the framework of a success semantics that purports to establish the correctness of NCC from successful action when combined with a causal theory of perception. The reliance on successful interaction ('successful' being a normative term) introduces the "normative" parameter.

4. Bermudez (2003, pp. 66–67) sketches an account of how 'satisfaction' could be defined in a way that avoids the circularity of defining desires using the contents of beliefs.

5. A belief has the form "X believes that O is F." The sentence "O is F," which is the complement clause of "that," has a linguistic meaning, its primary intension or character or linguistic mode of presentation, that maps world states as contexts of utterance of the sentence to the semantic content of the sentence or its secondary intension. The secondary intension or content is a function from world states as circumstances of evaluation to the extension of the sentence (its truth value). The semantic content or intension of a sentence, in the neo-Fregean framework that I espouse, is a semi-single proposition consisting of a structured pair whose first member is itself a structured pair consisting of the referent of O and its sense or mode of presentation in the cognitive or perceptual system of the person uttering the sentence (this sense is sometimes called the psychological mode of presentation), and the second member is F. To say that success semantics does not fix the intension of the clause of the belief it means that success semantics does not allow one to determine either the referent or its psychological mode of presentation.

6. "To expect a distinctive physical mechanism behind every genuinely distinct mental state is one thing; to expect a distinctive mechanism for every purported distinction that can be phrased in traditional mentalistic language is another. The question whether the foreigner really believes A or believes rather B, is a question whose very significance I would put into doubt. This is what I am getting at in arguing the indeterminacy of translation." (Quine 1970, pp. 180–181)

7. I do not mean to preclude the role of development and learning in the formation of the visual circuits. I have addressed this elsewhere (Raftopoulos 1997), so here I will just state my main point. Development and learning, and specifically neural maturation and the interaction with the environment, play an important role in the formation of brain circuits through the processes of pruning and constructivism, whereby synapses are eliminated and new synapses are built to form the brain circuits.

8. These regularities may not be true laws of nature. They describe the behavior of objects in an idealized and abstract model of reality. From the perspective of evolution and survival, it is sufficient that the regularities allow successful interaction with the world, even though they cannot describe the real behavior of objects in the real world, or they do it in an approximate way. A classical example is Newton's theory of gravity, a regularity that holds true in a model of reality. It allows us to predict motions and even send objects to the moon, but it does that not because it is a true law of nature but because it allows calculations the results of which deviate from the values predicted from the true, so to speak, theory (Einstein's theory of relativity), within a margin of error such that it allows successful planning.

9. I use the word 'entity' to show that the representation of objecthood does not require the application of the sortal concept 'object'.

10. It follows that when one forms a *de re* belief one stands in "an appropriate nonconceptual, contextual relations to objects the belief is about" (Burge 1977, p. 346). This allows one to be in a position to make *de re* judgments or form *de re* beliefs about the world.

11. Even though in the example discussed perceptual processing takes place along the dorsal visual pathway, and thus awareness of the information processed in perception is not relevant for whether perceptual states correctly represent the environment, awareness eventually emerges as the information is processed along the perceptual system, albeit in another visual stream (the ventral stream). Thus, it is only natural to ask whether the aware information correctly presents the world as being such and such. In addition to that, awareness of content is very important for the causal relation between that content and the ensuing perceptual beliefs. In fact, it may be plausible to assume that the perceptual content that plays a direct role in causing perceptual beliefs is the content that is formed along the ventral pathway (the visual pathway that is dedicated to representing and knowing the world). Now, since the debate between constructivism and realism concerns, among other things, the issue of whether or how we are even aware of things and events in the world and of their being in our awareness the way they actually are, one must ensure that one establishes the truth of perceptual contents that play, beyond any doubt, an active role in causing perceptual beliefs, that is, perceptual contents along the ventral system. Thus, one is bound to establish that some of the ventral representational contents correctly present the world as being such and such. I have attempted to establish that in Raftopoulos 2008.

References

Ahhisar, M., and Horchstein, S. 1993. Attentional control of early perceptual learning. *Proceedings of the National Academy of Sciences (USA)* 90: 5718–5722.

Aine, C. J., Supek, S., and George, J. S. 1995. Temporal dynamics of visual-evoked neuromagnetic sources: Effects of stimulus parameters and selective attention. *International Journal of Neuroscience* 80: 79–104.

Aloimonos, Y., Bandyopadhyay, A., and Weiss, I. 1988. Active vision. *International Journal of Computer Vision* 1 (4): 333–356.

Altmann, G. T., and Steedman, M. 1988. Interaction with context during human sentence processing. *Cognition* 30: 191–238.

Amassian, V. E., Cracco, R. Q, Maccabee, P. J., Cracco, J. B., Rudell, A., and Eberle, L. 1989. Suppression of visual perception by magnetic coil stimulation of human occipital cortex. *Electroencephalography and Clinical Neurophysiology* 74: 458–462.

Antonini, A., Strycker, M. P., and Chapman, B. 1995. Development and plasticity of cortical columns and their thalamic inputs. In *Maturational Windows and Adult Cortical Plasticity*, ed. B. Julesz and I. Kovacs. Addison-Wesley.

Attneave, F. 1971. Multistability in perception. *Scientific American* 225: 63–71.

Bach, K. 1987. *Thought and Reference*. Clarendon.

Baddeley, A. 1995. Working memory. In *The Cognitive Neurosciences*, ed. M. Gazzaniga. MIT Press.

Ballard, D. H., Hayhoe, M. M., Pook, P. K., and Rajesh, R. P. 1997. Deictic codes for the embodiment of cognition. *Behavioral and Brain Sciences* 20: 723–767.

Barsallou, L. 1999. Perceptual symbol systems. *Behavioral and Brain Sciences* 22: 577–660.

Bates, E., Thal, D., and Janowsky, J. 1992. Early language development and its neural correlates. In *Handbook of Neuropsychology*, volume 7: *Child Neuropsychology*, ed. I. Rapin and S. Segalowitz. Elsevier.

Bates, E., Thal, D., Aram, D., Eisele, J., Nass, R., and Trauner, D. 1997. From first words to grammar in children with focal brain injury. *Developmental Neuropsychology* 13 (3): 275–343.

Baylis, G. C. 1994. Visual attention and objects: Two-object cost with equal convexity. *Journal of Experimental Psychology: Human Perception and Performance* 20: 208–212.

Bechtel, W. 2002. Aligning multiple research techniques in cognitive neuroscience: Why is it important? *Philosophy of Science* 69: S48–S58.

Bechtel, W., and Mundale, J. 1999. Multiple realizability revisited: Linking cognitive and neural states. *Philosophy of Science* 66 (2): 175–208.

Bechtel, W., and Stufflebeam, R. S. 2001. Epistemic issues in procuring evidence about the brain: The importance of research instruments and techniques. In *Philosophy and the Neuroscience: A Reader*, ed. W. Bechtel et al. Blackwell.

Bermudez, J. L. 1995. Nonconceptual content: from perceptual experience to subpersonal computational states. *Mind and Language* 10 (4): 333–369.

Bermudez, J. L. 2003. *Thinking without Words*. Oxford University Press.

Bermudez, J. L. 2007. What is at stake in the debate about nonconceptual content? *Philosophical Perspectives* 21, Philosophy of Mind: 55–72.

Bichot, N. P., Schall, J. D., and Thompson, K. G. 1996. Visual feature selectivity in frontal eye fields induced by experience in mature macaques. *Nature* 381: 697–699.

Bickhard, M. H. 1993. Representational content in humans and machines'. *Journal of Experimental and Theoretical Artificial Intelligence* 5: 285–333.

Bickhard, M. H. 1996. Troubles with computationalism. In *The Philosophy of Psychology*, ed. W. O'Donohue and R. F. Kitchener. Sage.

Bickhard, M. H. 1998. Constraints on the architecture of mind. *New Ideas in Psychology* 16: 97–105.

Bickhard, M. H. 2000. Dynamic representing and representational dynamics. In *Cognitive Dynamics: Conceptual and Representational Change in Humans and Machines*, ed. E. Dietrich and A. Markman. Erlbaum.

Biederman, I. 1987. Recognition by components: A theory of human image understanding. *Psychological Review* 94: 115–147.

Biederman, J., Mezzanotte, R. J., and Rabinowitz, J. C. 1982. Scene perception: detecting and judging objects undergoing relational violations. *Cognitive Psychology* 14: 143–177.

Block, N. 1995. On a confusion about a function of consciousness. *Behavioral and Brain Sciences* 18: 227–247.

Block, N. 1996. How can we find the neural correlate of consciousness. *Trends in Neuroscience* 19: 456–459.

Block. N. 2005a. Two neural correlates of consciousness. *Trends in Cognitive Sciences* 9 (2): 46–53.

Block. N. 2005b. The merely verbal problem of consciousness. *Trends in Cognitive Sciences* 9 (3): 270.

Block, N. 2007. Consciousness, accessibility, and the mesh between psychology and neuroscience. *Brain and Behavioral Sciences* 30: 481–548.

[See Brockmole below.]Bogen, J. 2002. Epistemological custard pies from functional brain image. *Philosophy of Science* 69: S59–S71.

BonJour, L. 2003. A Version of internalist foundationalism. In L. BonJour and E. Sosa, *Epistemic Justification: Internalism vs. Externalism, Foundations vs. Virtues.* Blackwell.

Boyce, S. J., and Pollatsek, A. 1992. An exploration of the effects of scene context on object identification. In *Eye Movements and Visual Cognition: Scene Perception and Reading*, ed. K. Rayner. Springer-Verlag.

Boyce, S. J., Pollatsek, A., and Rayner K. 1989. Effects of background information on object identification. *Journal of Experimental Psychology: Human Perception and Performance* 15: 556–566.

Braitenberg, V. 1984. *Vehicles: Experiments in Synthetic Psychology.* MIT Press.

Brandom, R. B. 1996. *Making It Explicit: Reasoning, Representing, and Discursive Commitment.* Harvard University Press.

Brewer, B. 1999. *Perception and Reason.* Oxford University Press.

Brockmole, J. R., and Henderson, J. M. 2005. Prioritization of new objects in real-world scenes: Evidence from eye movements. *Journal of Experimental Psychology: Human Perception and Performance* 31 (5): 857–868.

Brockmole, J. R., Castelhano, M. S., and Henderson, J. M. 2006. Contextual cueing in naturalistic scenes: Global and local contexts. *Journal of Experimental Psychology: Learning, Memory, and Cognition* 32 (4): 699–706.

Brooks, Rodney, A. 1991. Intelligence without reason. *Artificial Intelligence* 47: 139–159.

Brown, H. I. 1987. *Observation and Objectivity.* Oxford University Press.

Bruce, V., and Green P. R. 1993. *Visual Perception: Physiology, Psychology and Ecology*, second edition. Erlbaum.

Burge, T. 1977. Belief de re. *Journal of Philosophy* 74: 338–362.

Campbell, J. 1997. Sense, reference and selective attention. *Proceedings of the Aristotelian Society, Supplementary Volume* 71: 55–74.

Campbell, J. 1999. The role of physical objects in spatial thinking. In *Spatial Representation: Problems in Philosophy and Psychology*, ed. N. Eilan, R. McCarthy, and B. Brewer. Oxford University Press.

Campbell, J. 2002. *Reference and Consciousness*. Clarendon.

Campbell, J. 2005. Information processing, phenomenal consciousness and Molyneux's question. In *Thought, Reference and Experience: Themes from the Philosophy of Gareth Evans*, ed. J. Bermudez. Oxford University Press.

Campion, J., and Latto, R. 1985. Apperceptive agnosia due to carbon poisoning: An interpretation based on critical band masking from disseminated lesions. *Behavioural Brain Research* 15: 227–240.

Carey, S. 1995. Continuity and discontinuity in cognitive development. In *An Invitation to Cognitive Science*, volume 3: *Thinking*, ed. E. Smith and D. Osherson. MIT Press.

Carey, S., and Xu, F. 2001. Infant's knowledge of objects: Beyond object files and object tracking. *Cognition* 80: 179–213.

Castiello, U., Paulgnan, Y., and Jeannerod, M. 1991. Temporal dissociation of motor responses and subjective awareness: A study in normal subjects. *Brain* 114: 2639–2655.

Cavanagh, P. 1988. Pathways in early vision. In *Computational Processes in Human Vision: An Interdisciplinary Perspective*, ed. Z. Pylyshyn. Ablex.

Cave, K., and Wolfe, J. 1994. Modeling the role of parallel processing in visual search. *Cognitive Psychology* 22: 225–271.

Chambers, D., and Reisberg, D. 1992. What an image depicts depends on what an image means. *Cognitive Psychology* 24: 145–174.

Changeux, J-P., and Dehaene, S. 1989. Neuronal models of cognitive functions. *Cognition* 33: 63–109.

Chelazzi, L., Miller, E., Duncan, J., and Desimone, R. 1993. A neural basis for visual search in inferior temporal cortex. *Nature* 363: 345–347.

Chun, M. M., and Jiang, Y. 1998. Contextual cueing: Implicit learning and memory of visual context guises spatial attention. *Cognitive Psychology* 36: 28–71.

Chun, M. M., and Jiang, Y. 2003. Implicit, long-term spatial contextual memory. *Journal of Experimental Psychology: Learning, Memory, and Cognition* 29 (2): 224–234.

Churchland, P. M. 1988. Perceptual plasticity and theoretical neutrality: A reply to Jerry Fodor. *Philosophy of Science* 55: 167–187. Reprinted in P. Churchland, *A Neurocomputational Perspective: The Nature of Mind and the Structure of Science* (MIT Press, 1989).

Clark, A. 1991. *Microcognition: Philosophy, Cognitive Science, and Parallel Distributed Processing.* MIT Press.

Clark, A. 1993. *Associative Engines: Connectionism, Concepts, and Representational Change.* MIT Press.

Clark, A. 1999. An embodied cognitive science? *Trends in Cognitive Sciences* 3 (9): 345–351.

Clark, V., and Hillyard, S. A. 1996. Spatial selective attention affects early extrastriate but not striate components of the visual evoked potentials. *Journal of Cognitive Neuroscience* 8 (5): 387–402.

Connor, C. E., Preddie, D. C., Gallant, J. L., and Van Essen D. C. 1997. Spatial attention effects in macaque area V4. *Journal of Neuroscience* 17: 3201–3214.

Crain, S., and Steedman, M. 1985. On not being led up the garden path: The use of context by the psychological syntax parser. In *Natural Language Parsing: Psychological, Computational, and Theoretical Perspectives*, ed. D. Dowty, L. Karttunen, and A. Zwicky. Cambridge University Press

Crane, T. 1992. The Nonconceptual content of experience. In *The Contents of Experience: Essays on Perception*, ed. T. Crane. Cambridge University Press.

Cussins, A. 1990. The connectionist construction of concepts. In *The Philosophy of Artificial Intelligence*, ed. M. Boden. Oxford University Press.

Cynader, M., and Chernenko, G. 1976. Abolition of direction selectivity in the visual cortex of the cat. *Science* 193: 504–5.

Czigler, I., and Balazs, L. 1998. Object-related attention: An event-related potential study. *Brain and Cognition* 38: 113–124.

Damasio, H, Grabowski, T. J., Damasio, A., Tranel, D., Boles-Ponto, L., Watkins, G. L., and Hichwa, R. D. 1993. Visual recall with eyes closed and covered activates early visual cortices [Abstract]. *Society for Neuroscience Abstracts* 19: 1603.

Davidson, D. 1984. *Inquiries into Truth and Interpretation.* Oxford University Press.

Deco, G., Pollatos, O., and Zihl, J. 2002. The time course of selective visual attention: theory and experiments. *Vision Research* 42: 2925–2945.

Dehaene, S., Kerszberg, M., and Changeux, J. P. 1998. A neuronal model of global workspace in effortful cognitive tasks. *Proceedings of the National Academy of Sciences (USA)* 95: 14529–14534.

Dehaene, S., Naccashe, L., Le Clec'H, G., Koechlin, E., Mueller, M., Dehaene-Lambertz, G., van de Moortele, P.-F., and Le Bihan, D. 1998. Imaging unconscious semantic priming. *Nature* 395: 597–600.

Dehaene, S., Sergent, C., and Changeux, J. P. 2003. A neuronal network model linking subjective reports and objective physiological data during conscious perception. *Proceedings of the National Academy of Sciences (USA)* 100 (14): 8520–8525.

Dehaene, S., and Changeux, J-P. 2005. Ongoing spontaneous activity controls access to consciousness: A neuronal model for inattentional blindness. *PLoS Biology* (http://biology.plosjournals.org).

Dennett, D. 1978. *Brainstorms*. Bradford Books.

Dennett, D. 1987. *The Intentional Stance*. MIT Press.

Dennett, D. 1993. *Consciousness Explained*. Penguin

De Renzi, E., Scotti, G., and Spinnler, H. 1969. Perceptual and associative disorders of visual recognition. *Neurology* 19: 634–642.

Descartes, R. 1984. *Meditations on First Philosophy*. In *The Philosophical Writings of Descartes*, volume 2, ed. J. Cottingham, R. Stoothoff, and D. Murdoch. Cambridge University Press.

Desimone, R. 1999. Visual attention mediated by biased competition in extrastriate visual cortex. In *Attention, Space and Action: Studies in Cognitive Neuroscience*, ed. G. Humphreys, J. Duncan, and A. Treisman. Oxford University Press.

Desimone, R., and Duncan, J. 1995. Neural mechanisms of selective visual attention. *Annual Review of Neurosciences* 18: 193–222.

De Valois, R. L., Yund, E. W., and Hepler, N. 1982. The orientation and direction selectivity of cells in macaque visual cortex. *Vision Research* 22: 531–544.

Devitt, M. 1991. *Realism and Truth*. Blackwell.

Devitt, M. 1996. *Coming to Our Senses: A Naturalistic Program for Semantic Localism*. Cambridge University Press.

DiRusso, F., Martinez, A., and Hillyard, S. A. 2003. Source analysis of event-related cortical activity during visuo-spatial attention. *Cerebral Cortex* 13: 486–499.

Dodwell, P. C. 1992. Perspectives and transformations. *Canadian Journal of Psychology* 46: 510–538.

Dokic, J., and Pacherie, E. 2001. Shades and concepts. *Analysis* 61 (3): 193–202.

Dretske, F. 1981. *Knowledge and the Flow of Information*. MIT Press.

Dretske, F. 1993. Conscious experience. *Mind* 102 (406): 263–283.

Dretske, F. 1995. *Naturalizing the Mind*. MIT Press.

Driver, J., and Baylis, G. S. 1996. Eye-assignment and figure-ground segregation in short- term visual matching. *Cognitive Psychology* 31: 248–306.

Driver, J., David, G., Russell, C., Turatto M., and Freeman, E. 2001. Segmentation, attention and phenomenal visual objects. *Cognition* 80: 61–95.

Duhem, P. 1914. *The Aim and Structure of Physical Theory*, second edition. Atheneum.

Dummett, M. 1973. *Frege: Philosophy of Language*. Duckworth.

Duncan, J., and Humphreys, G. W. 1989. Visual search and stimulus similarity. *Psychological Review* 96: 433–458.

Duncan, J., and Humphreys, G. W. 1992. Beyond the surface search: Visual search and attentional engagement. *Journal of Experimental Psychology: Human Perception and Performance* 18: 578–588.

Duncan, J., and Nimmo-Smith, I. 1996. Objects and attributes in divided attention: surface and boundary systems. *Perception and Psychophysics* 54: 425–430.

Ebbesson, S. O. E. 1988. Ontogenetic parcellation: Dual processes. *Behavioral and Brain Sciences* 11: 548–549.

Eckstein, M. 1998. The lower visual search efficiency for conjunctions is due to noise and not serial attentional processing. *Psychological Science* 9: 111–118.

Edelman, G. M. 1987. *Neural Darwinism*. Basic Books.

Edelman, G. M. 1992. *Bright Air, Brilliant Fire: On the Matter of Mind*. Basic Books.

Edelman, S. 1999. *Representation and Recognition in Vision*. MIT Press.

Egeth, H. E., Virzi, R. A., and Garbart, H. 1984. Searching for conjunctively defined targets. *Journal of Experimental Psychology* 10: 32–39.

Egeth, H. E., and Yantis, S. 1997. Visual attention: control, representation, and time course. *Annual Review of Psychology* 48: 269–297.

Ellis, J. 2007. Content externalism and phenomenal character: A new worry about privileged access. *Synthese* 159: 47–60.

Elman, J. L., Bates, E. A., Johnson, M. H., Karmiloff-Smith, A., Parisi, D., and Plunkett, K. 1996. *Rethinking Innateness: A Connectionist Perspective on Development*. MIT Press.

Enns, J. T., and Rensink, R. A. 1991. Preattentive recovery of three-dimensional orientation from line drawings. *Psychological Review* 98: 335–351.

Estany A. 2001. Theory-ladenness in the light of cognitive psychology. *Philosophy of Science* 68 (2): 213–217.

Evans, G. 1982. *The Varieties of Reference*. Oxford University Press.

Evans, G. 1985. Molyneux's question. In G. Evans, *Collected Papers*. Oxford University Press.

Evans, G. 1990. Understanding demonstratives. In *Demonstratives*, ed. P. Yourgrau. Oxford University Press.

Evans, G. 1993. The causal theory of names. In *Meaning and Reference*, ed. A. Moore. Oxford University Press.

Evans, M. A., Shedden, J. M., Hevenor, S. J., and Hahn, M. C. 2000. The effect of variability of unattended information on global and local processing: Evidence from lateralization at early stages of processing. *Neurophysiologia* 38: 225–239.

Farah, M. J. 1984. The Neurological basis of mental imagery: A component analysis. In *Visual Cognition*, ed. S. Pinker. MIT Press.

Feldman, J. A. 1985. Four frames suffice: A provisional model of vision and space. *Behavioral and Brain Sciences* 8: 265–289.

Felleman, D. J., Xiao, Y., and McClendon, E. 1997. Modular organization of occipital-temporal pathways: cortical connections between visual area 4 and visual area 2 and posterior inferotemporal ventral area in macaque monkeys. *Journal of Neuroscience* 17: 3185–3200.

Fernandez-Duque, D., and Thornton, I. M. 2000. Change detection without awareness: Do explicit reports underestimate the representation of change in the visual system? *Visual Cognition* 7: 324–244.

Fernandez-Duque, D., Grossi, G., Thornton, I. M., and Neville, H. J. 2003. Representation of change: separate electrophysiological markers of attention, awareness, and implicit processing. *Journal of Cognitive Neuroscience* 15 (4): 491–507.

Ferster, D. 1981. A comparison of binocular depth mechanisms in areas 17 and 18 of the cat visual cortex. *Journal of Physiology* 311: 623–655.

Ferstl, E. C. 1994. The construction-integration model: A framework for studying context effects in sentence processing. In *Proceedings of the Sixteenth Annual Conference of the Cognitive Science Society*. Erlbaum.

Ferrante, D., Gerbino, D., and Rock, I. 1997. The right angle. In *Indirect Perception*, ed. I. Rock. MIT Press.

Feyerabend, P. 1962. Explanation, reduction, and empiricism. In *Scientific Explanation, Space, and Time*, ed. H. Feigl and G. Maxwell. University of Minnesota Press.

Field, H. 1973. Theory change and the indeterminacy of reference. *Journal of Philosophy* 70: 462–481.

Findlay, J. M., and Gilchrist, I. D. 2003. *Active Vision: The Psychology of Looking and Seeing*. Oxford University Press.

Flombaum, J. I., Kundey, S. M., Santos, L. R., and Scholl, B. J. 2004. Dynamic object individuation in rhesus macaques: A study of the tunnel effect. *Psychological Science* 15 (12): 795–800.

Fodor, J. 1975. *The Language of Thought*. MIT Press.

Fodor, J. 1983. *The Modularity of Mind*. MIT Press.

Fodor, J. 1984. Observation reconsidered. *Philosophy of Science* 51: 23–43. Reprinted in *Readings in Philosophy and Cognitive Science*, ed. A. Goldman (MIT Press, 1993).

Fodor, J. 1986. The modularity of mind. In *Meaning and Cognitive Structure*, ed. Z. Pylyshyn and W. Demopoulos. Ablex.

Fodor, J. 1988. A Reply to Churchland's perceptual plasticity and theoretical neutrality. *Philosophy of Science* 55: 188–198. Reprinted in *Readings in Philosophy and Cognitive Science*, ed. A. Goldman (MIT Press).

Fodor, J. 1994. *The Elm and the Expert*. MIT Press.

Fodor, J. 1998. *Concepts*. Oxford University Press.

Fodor, J., and Pylyshyn, Z. 1981. How direct is visual perception? Some reflections on Gibson's "ecological approach." *Cognition* 9: 139–196.

Folk, C. L., Remington, R. W., and Johnston, J. C. 1992. Involuntary covert orienting is contingent on attentional control settings. *Journal of Experimental Psychology: Human Perception and Performance* 20: 203–207.

Forster, K. I. 1979. Levels of processing and the structure of the language processor. In *Sentence Processing: Psycholinguistic Studies Presented to Merrill Garrett*, ed. W. Cooper and E. Walker. Erlbaum.

Franconeri, S. L., Hollingworth, A., and Simons, D. J. 2005. Do new objects capture attention? *Psychological Science* 16 (4): 275–281.

Franklin, A. 1986. *The Neglect of Experiment*. Cambridge University Press.

Frege, G. 1962 (1892). Begriff und gegenstand. In *Funktion, Begriff, Bedeutung*, ed. G. Patzig. Vandenhoek and Ruprecht.

Freiwald, W. A., and Kanwisher, N. G. 2004. Visual elective attention: Evidence from brain imaging and neurophysiology. In *The Cognitive neurosciences III*, third edition, ed. M. Gazzaniga. MIT Press.

Garcia-Carpintero, M. 2000. A presuppositional account of reference fixing. *Journal of Philosophy* 30 (3): 109–147.

Geach, P. 1957. *Mental Acts*. Routledge and Kegan Paul.

Gelman, R. 1990. First principles organize attention to and learning about relevant data: Number and the animate-inanimate distinction as examples. *Cognitive Science* 14: 79–106.

Gibson, J. J. 1979. *The Ecological Approach to Visual Perception*. Houghton Mifflin.

Gilbert, C., and Wiesel, T. N. 1989. Columnar specificity of intrinsic horizontal and cortical-cortical connections in cat visual cortex. *Journal of Neuroscience* 9: 2432–2442.

Gilbert, C., Minami, I., Kapadia M., and Westheimer, G. 2000. Interactions between attention, context and learning in primary visual cortex. *Vision Research* 40: 1217–1226.

Gilchrist, I. D., Humphreys, G. W., Neumann, H., and Riddoch, M. 1997. Luminance and edge information in grouping: A study using visual search. *Journal of Experimental Psychology: Human Perception and Performance* 23: 464–480.

Girelli, M., and Luck, S. J. 1997. Are the same attentional mechanisms used to detect visual search targets defined by color, orientation, and motion? *Journal of Cognitive Neurosciences* 9 (2): 238–253.

Glover S. 2004. Separate visual representations in the planning and control of action. *Behavioral and Brain Sciences* 27 (1): 3–79.

Goldstone, R., and Barsalou, L. 1998. Reuniting perception and conception. *Cognition* 65: 231–262.

Goodale, M. A., and Milner, D. A. 1992. Separate visual pathways for perception and action. *Trends in Neuroscience* 15: 20–25.

Goodale, M. A., and Milner, D. A. 2004. *Sight Unseen*. Oxford University Press.

Gooding, D. 1990. *Experiment and the Making of Meaning*. Kluwer.

Gooding, D., Pinch T., and Schaffer, S., eds. 1989. *The Uses of Experiment*. Cambridge University Press.

Greenough, W. T., Black, J. E., and Wallace, C. S. 1993. Experience and brain development. In *Brain Development and Cognition: A Reader*, ed. M. Johnson. Blackwell.

Gregory, R. 1974. *Concepts and Mechanisms of Perception*. Scribner.

Haenny, P. E., and Schiller, P. H. 1998. State dependent activity in monkey visual cortex. I. Single cells activity in V1 and V4 on visual tasks. *Experimental Brain Research* 69: 225–244.

Han, S., Liu, W., Yund, E. W., and Woods, D. L. 2000. Interactions between spatial attention and global/local feature selection: An ERP study. *Neuroreport* 11: 2753–2758.

Hanson, N. R. 1958. *Patterns of Discovery*. Cambridge University Press.

Hardcastle, V. G., and Stewart, M. C. 2002. What do brain data really show? *Philosophy of Science* 69, S72–S82.

Harnad, S. 1990. The symbol grounding problem. *Physica D* 42: 335–346.

Haugeland, J. 1998. *Having Thought*. Harvard University Press.

Heck, R. Jr. 2000. Nonconceptual content and the "space of reasons." *Philosophical Review* 109 (4): 483–523.

Heeger, D. J., and Ress, D. 2004. Neuronal correlates of visual attention and perception. In *The Cognitive Neurosciences III*, third edition, ed. M. Gazzaniga. MIT Press.

Heinze, H. J., Mangun, G. R., Burchert, W., Hinrichs, H., Scholtz, M., Muntel, T. F., Gosel, A., Schreg, S., Johannes, S., Hundeshagen, H., Gazzaniga, M. S., and Hillyard, S. A. 1994. Combined spatial and temporal imaging of brain activity during visual selective attention in humans. *Nature* 372: 543–546.

Heinze, H. J., Hinrichs, H., Scholz, M., Burchert, W., and Mangun, G. R. 1998. Neural mechanisms of global and local processing: A combined PET and ERP study. *Journal of Cognitive Neuroscience* 10: 485–498.

Henderson. J. M., and Hollingworth, A. 1999. High-level scene perception. *Annual Review of Psychology* 243 (1): 1–18.

Henderson. J. M., and Hollingworth, A. 2003. Global transsaccadic change blindness during scene perception. *Psychological Science* 14 (5): 493–497.

Hildreth, E. C., and Ulmann S. 1989. The computational study of vision. In *Foundations of Cognitive Science*, ed. M. Posner. MIT Press.

Hillyard, S. A., Teder-Salejarvi, W. A., and Munte, T. F. 1998. Temporal dynamics of early perceptual processing. *Current Opinion in Neurobiology* 8: 202–210.

Hochstein, S., and Ahissar, M. 2002. View from the top: Hierarchies and reverse hierarchies in the visual system. *Neuron* 36: 791–804.

Hollingworth, A. 2005. Memory for object position in natural scenes. *Visual Cognition* 12 (6): 1003–1016.

Hollingworth, A. 2006. Visual memory for natural scenes: Evidence from change detection and visual search. *Visual Cognition* 14 (4–8): 781–807.

Hollingworth, A., and Henderson. J. M. 1998. Does consistent scene context facilitate object perception? *Experimental Psychology: General* 127: 398–415.

Hollingworth, A., and Henderson. J. M. 2002. Accurate visual memory for previously attended objects in natural scenes. *Journal of Experimental Psychology: Human Perception and Performance* 28 (1): 113–136.

Hollingworth, A., and Henderson. J. M. 2004. Sustained change blindness to incremental scene rotation: A dissociation between explicit change detection and visual memory. *Perception and Psychophysics* 66 (5): 800–807.

Hollingworth, A., Williams, C., and Henderson. J. M. 2001. To see and remember: Visually specific information is retained in memory from previously attended objects in natural scenes. *Psychonomic Bulletin and Review* 8 (4): 761–768.

Hopf, J. M., and Mangun, G. R. 2000. Shifting visual attention in space: An electrophysiological analysis using high spatial resolution mapping. *Clinical Neurophysiology* 111: 1241–1257.

Hopfinger, J. B., Luck, S. J., and Hillyard, S. A. 2004. Selective attention: Electrophysiological and neuromagnetic studies. In *The Cognitive Neurosciences III*, third edition, ed. M. Gazzaniga. MIT Press.

Hubel, D. H., and Wiesel, T. N. 1968. Receptive fields and functional architecture of monkey striate cortex. *Journal of Physiology* 195: 215–243.

Humphreys, G. W. 1999. Neural representation of objects in space: A dual coding account. In *Attention, Space and Action: Studies in Cognitive Neuroscience*, ed. G. Humphreys, J. Duncan, and A. Treisman. Oxford University Press.

Humphreys, G. W., and Riddoch, M. J. 1984. Routes to object constancy: Implications from neurological impairments of object constancy. *Quarterly Journal of Experimental Psychology* 36A: 385–415.

Humphreys, G. W., and Riddoch, M. J. 1985. Authors' correction to "Routes to object constancy." *Quarterly Journal of Experimental Psychology* 37A: 493–495.

Hupé, J. M., James, A. C., Payne, B. R., Lomber, S. G., Girard, P., and Bullier, J. 1998. Cortical feedback improves discrimination between figure and background by V1, V2 and V3 neurons. *Nature* 394: 784–787.

Irwin, D. E. 1991. Information integration across saccadic eye movements. *Cognitive Psychology* 23: 420–456.

Irwin, D. E. 1992. Memory for position and identity across eye movements. *Journal of Experimental Psychology: Learning, Memory, and Cognition* 18: 307–317.

Irwin, D. E., and Andrews, R. 1996. Integration and accumulation of information across saccadic eye movements. In *Attention and Performance XVI: Information Integration in Perception and Communication*, ed. T. Inui and J. McLelland. MIT Press.

Jackendoff, R. 1989. *Consciousness and the Computational Mind*. MIT Press.

Jacobs, R. A., Jordan, M. I., and Barto, A. G. 1991. Task decomposition through competition in a modular connectionist architecture: The what and where vision tasks. *Cognitive Science* 15: 219–250.

Jacob, P., and Jeannerod, M. 2003. *Ways of Seeing: The Scope and Limits of Visual Cognition*. Oxford University Press.

Jiang, Y., Song, J.-H., and Rigas, A. 2005. High capacity spatial contextual memory. *Psychonomic Bulletin* 12 (3): 524–529.

Johnson, M. 1996. *The Body in the Mind*. University of Chicago Press.

Johnson, M. 1997. *Developmental Cognitive Neuroscience*. Blackwell.

Johnson, M., and Morton, J. 1991. *Biology and Development: The Case of Face Recognition*. Blackwell.

Johnson, M., and Karmiloff-Smith A. 1992. Can neural selectionism be applied to cognitive development and its disorders? *New Ideas in Psychology* 10: 35–46.

Johnston, A. 1992. Object constancy in face processing: Intermediate representations and object forms. *Irish Journal of Psychology* 13: 425–438.

Jonides, J. 1980. Toward a model of the mind's eye. *Canadian Journal of Psychology* 34: 103–112.

Jonides, J. 1983. Further toward a model of the mind's eye movement. *Bulletin of the Psychonomic Society* 21: 247–250.

Joseph, J. S., Chun, M. M., and Nakayama, K. 1997. Attentional requirements in a "preattentive" feature search task. *Nature* 387: 805–807.

Kahneman, D., and Treisman, A. 1984. Changing views of attention and automaticity. In *Varieties of Attention*, ed. R. Parasuraman. Erlbaum.

Kahneman, D., Treisman, A., and Gibbs, B. 1992. The reviewing of object files: Object specific integration of information. *Cognitive Psychology* 24: 175–219.

Kanwisher, N. 2001. Neural events and perceptual awareness. *Cognition* 79: 89–113.

Kanwisher, N., and Driver, J. 1992. Objects, attributes, and visual attention: Which, what, and where. *Current Directions in Psychological Science* 1: 26–31.

Kapadia, M. K., Westheimer, G., and Gilbert, C. D. 1999. Dynamics of spatial summation in primary visual cortex of alert monkeys. *Proceedings of the National Academy of Sciences USA* 96: 12073–12078.

Kaplan, D. 1989. Demonstratives. In *Themes from Kaplan*, ed. J. Almog, J. Perry, and H. Wettstein. Oxford University Press.

Karmiloff-Smith, A. 1992. *Beyond Modularity: A Developmental Perspective on Cognitive Science*. MIT Press.

Karni, A., and Sagi, D. 1995. A memory system in the adult visual cortex. In *Maturational Windows and Adult Cortical Plasticity*, ed. B. Julesz and I. Kovacs. Addison-Wesley.

Kastner, S., and Ungerleider, L. G. 2000. Mechanisms of visual attention in the human cortex. *Annual Review of Neuroscience* 23: 315–341.

Kastner, S., Pinsk, M. A., De Weerd, P., Desimone, R., and Ungerleider, L. 1999. Increased activity in human visual cortex during directed attention in the absence of visual stimulation. *Neuron* 22: 751–761.

Katz, J. 1994. Names without bearers. *Philosophical Review* 103: 1–39.

Katz, E., Victor, J. D., and Purpura, K. 1995. Dynamic changes in cortical response following removal and restoration of nearby visual inputs. In *Maturational Windows and Adult Cortical Plasticity*, ed. B. Julesz and I. Kovacs. Addison-Wesley.

Kaufman, D. A. 2002. Reality and common sense: Reflections on realism and anti-realism from a "common sense naturalist" perspective. *Philosophical Investigations* 25 (4): 331–361.

Kawabata, N. 1986. Attention and depth perception. *Perception* 15: 563–572.

Kellman, P. J. 1984. Perception of three -dimensional form by human infants. *Perception and Psychophysics* 36: 353–8.

Kellman, P. J., and Spelke, E. S. 1983. Perception of partly occluded objects in infancy. *Cognitive Psychology* 15: 483–524.

Kellman, P. J., Spelke, E. S., and Short, K. 1986. Infant perception of object unity from translatory motion in depth and vertical translation. *Child Development* 57: 72–86.

Kelly, S. D. 2001. Demonstrative concepts and experience. *Philosophical Review* 110 (3): 397–420.

Killackey, H. P. 1990. Neocortical expansion: An attempt toward relating phylogeny and ontogeny. *Journal of Cognitive Neuroscience* 2: 1–17.

Kim. J. 1998. *Philosophy of Mind*. Westview.

Kitcher, P. 2001. Real realism: The Galilean strategy. *Philosophical Review* 110 (2): 151–199.

Koch, C., and Poggio, T. 1987. Biophysics of computational systems: Neurons synapses, and membranes. In *Synaptic Function*, ed. G. Edelman, W. Gall, and W. Cowan. Wiley.

Koch, C. 2004. *The Quest for Consciousness: A Neurobiological Approach*. Roberts.

Koivisto, M., and Revonsuo, A. 2004. Preconscious analysis of global structure: Evidence from masked priming. *Visual Cognition* 11 (1): 105–127.

Kolb, B. 1993. Brain development, plasticity, and behavior. In *Brain Development and Cognition: A Reader*, ed. M. Johnson. Blackwell.

Kosslyn, S. M. 1988. Aspects of cognitive neuroscience of mental imagery. *Science* 240: 1621–1626.

Kosslyn, S, M., Alpert, N. M., Thompson, W., L., Malikovic, V., Weise, S. B., Chabris, C. F., Hamilton, S. E., Rauch, S. L., and Buonnano, F. S. 1993. Visual mental imagery activates topographically organized visual cortex. *Journal of Cognitive Neuroscience* 5: 263–287.

Kripke, S. A. 1980. *Naming and Necessity*. Harvard University Press.

Kuhn, T. S. 1962. *The Structure of Scientific Revolutions*. University of Chicago Press.

LaBerge, D. 1995. *Attentional Processing: The Brain's Art of Mindfulness*. Oxford University Press.

LaBerge, D. 2000. Networks of attention. In *The New Cognitive Neurosciences*, second edition, ed. M. Gazzaniga. MIT Press.

Ladavas, E., Paladini, R., and Cubelli, R. 1993. Implicit associative priming in a patient with left visual neglect. *Neuropsychologia* 31: 1307–1320.

Lakoff, G. 1997. *Women, Fire, and Other Dangerous Things*. University of Chicago Press.

Lamme, V. A. F. 1995. The neurophysiology of figure-ground segregation in primary visual cortex. *Journal of Neuroscience* 15: 1605–1615.

Lamme, V. A. F. 2000. Neural mechanisms of visual awareness: A linking proposition. *Brain and Mind* 1: 385–406.

Lamme, V. A. F. 2003. Why visual attention and awareness are different. *Trends in Cognitive Sciences* 7 (1): 12–18.

Lamme, V. A. F. 2005. Independent neural definitions of visual awareness and attention. In *The Cognitive Penetrability of Perception: An Interdisciplinary Approach*, ed. A. Raftopoulos. Nova.

Lamme, V. A. F., and Roelfsema, P. R. 2000. The distinct modes of vision offered by feedforward and recurrent processing. *Trends in Neuroscience* 23: 571–579.

Lamme, V. A. F., and Spekreijse, H. 2000. Contextual modulation in primary visual cortex and scene perception. In *The New Cognitive Neurosciences,* second edition, ed. M. Gazzaniga. MIT Press.

Lamme, V. A. F., Rodriguez, V., and Spekreijse, H. 1999. Separate processing dynamics for texture elements, boundaries and surfaces in primary visual cortex. *Cerebral Cortex* 9: 406–413.

Lamme, V. A. F, Supér, H., Landman, R., Roelfsema, P. R., and Spekreijse, H. 2000. The role of primary visual cortex (V1) in visual awareness. *Vision Research* 40: 1507–1521.

Langacker, R. 1987. *Foundations of Cognitive Grammar, volume* 1. Stanford University Press.

Lavie, N., and Driver, J. 1996. On the spatial extent of attention in object-based visual selection. *Perception and Psychophysics* 58: 1238–1251.

Lawson, R., Humphreys, G. W., and Watson, D. G. 1994. Object recognition under sequential viewing conditions: Evidence for viewpoint-specific recognition procedures. *Perception* 23: 595–614.

Leopold, D. A., and Logothetis, N. K. 1996. Activity changes in early visual cortex reflect monkeys' percepts during binocular rivalry. *Nature* 379: 549–554.

Leslie, A. M., Xu, F., Tremoulet, P., and Scholl, B. J. 1998. Indexing and the object concept: Developing "What" and "Where" systems. *Trends in Cognitive Science* 2 (1): 10–18.

Leyton, M. 1992. *Symmetry, Causality, Mind*. MIT Press.

Livingstone, M. S., and Hubel, D. H. 1987. Psychophysical evidence for separate channels for the perception of form, color, movement, and depth. *Journal of Neuroscience* 7: 3416–3468.

Loar, B. 1976. The semantics of singular terms. *Philosophical Studies* 30: 353–377.

Logothetis, N. K., and Schall, J. D. 1989. Neuronal correlates of subjective visual perception. *Science* 245: 761–764.

Lowe, E. J. 1992. Experience and its objects. In *The Contents of Experience: Essays on Perception*, ed. T. Crane. Cambridge University Press.

Luck, S. J. 1995. Multiple mechanisms of visual-spatial attention: Recent evidence from human electrophysiology. *Behavioral and Brain Research* 71: 113–123.

Luck, S. J., and Hillyard, S. A. 2000. The operation of selective attention at multiple stages of processing: Evidence from human and monkey electrophysiology. In *The New Cognitive Neurosciences*, second edition, ed. M. Gazzaniga. MIT Press.

Luck, S. J., Chelazzi, L., Hillyard, S. A., and Desimone, R. 1997. Neural mechanisms of spatial selective attention in areas V1, V2, and V4 of macaque visual cortex. *Journal of Neurophysiology* 77: 24–42.

Mack, A., and Rock, I. 2000. *Inattentional Blindness*. MIT Press.

Magnuson, S. 1970. Reversibility of perspective in normal and stabilized viewing. *Scandinavian Journal of Psychology* 11: 153–156.

Maljkovic, V., and Nakayama, K. 1994. Priming of pop-out. I. Role of features. *Memory and Cognition* 22: 657–672.

Maljkovic, V., and Nakayama, K. 1996. Priming of pop-out. II. Role of position. *Perception and Psychophysics* 58: 977–991.

Mangun, G. R., and Hilyard, S. A. 1995. Electrophysiological studies of visual selective attention in humans. In *The Neurobiology of Higher Cognitive Function*, ed. M. Rugg and M. Coles. Oxford University Press.

Mangun, G. R., Amish,i J. P., Hopfinger, J. B., and Handy, C. T. 2000. The Temporal dynamics and functional architecture of attentional processes in human extrastriate cortex. In *The New Cognitive Neurosciences*, second edition, ed. M. Gazzaniga. MIT Press.

Markie, P. J. 2005. Nondoxastic perceptual evidence. *Philosophy and Phenomenological Research* 68 (3): 530–554.

Marr, D. 1982. *Vision: A Computational Investigation into Human Representation and Processing of Visual Information*. Freeman.

Marr, D., and Ullman, S. 1981. Directional sensitivity and its use in early visual processing. *Proceedings of the Royal Society of London B* 211: 151–180.

Martin, M. G. F. 1992. Perception, concepts, and memory. *Philosophical Review* 101 (4): 645–663.

Martin, M. G. F. 2002. The transparency of experience. *Mind and Language* 17 (4): 376–425.

Martinez, A. F., DiRusso, F., Annlo-Vento, L., Sereno, M. I., Buxton, R. B., and Hillyard, S. A. 2001. Putting spatial attention on the map: Timing and localization of stimulus selection processes in striate and extrastriate visual areas. *Vision Research* 41: 1437–1457.Mayfew, J. F. W., and Frisby, J. P. 1981. Psychophysical and computational studies towards a theory of human stereopsis. *Artificial Intelligence* 17: 349–385.

McDowell, J. 1984. De re senses. In *Frege: Tradition and Influence*, ed. W. Crispin. Blackwell.

McDowell, J. 1986. Singular thought and inner space. In *Subject, Thought, and Context*, ed. P. Pettit and J. McDowell. Clarendon.

McDowell, J. 1993. On the sense and reference of proper names. In *Meaning and Reference*, ed. A. Moore. Oxford University Press.

McDowell, J. 1994. *Mind and World.* Harvard University Press.

McLeod, Peter, Driver, J., and Crisp, J. 1988. Visual search for a conjunction of movement and form is parallel. *Nature* 332: 154–155.

McLeod, Peter, Driver, J., Dienes, Z., and Crisp, J. 1991. Filtering by movement in visual search. *Journal of Experimental Psychology: Human Perception and Performance* 17: 55–64.

Merikle, P. M., and Joordens, S. 1997. Parallels between perception without attention and perception without awareness. *Consciousness and Cognition* 6: 219–236.

Merikle, P. M., Smilek, D., and Eastwood, J. D. 2001. Perception without awareness: Perspectives from cognitive psychology. *Cognition* 79: 115–134.

Merzenich, M. M., and Jenkins, W. M. 1995. Cortical plasticity, learning, and learning dysfunction. In *Maturational Windows and Adult Cortical Plasticity*, ed. B. Julesz and I. Kovacs. Addison-Wesley.

Miller, E. K., and Cohen, J. D. 2001. An integrative theory of prefrontal cortex function. *Annual Review of Neuroscience* 24: 167–202.

Millikan, R. 1999. Content and vehicle. In *Spatial Representation: Problems in Philosophy and Psychology*, ed. N. Eilan, R. McCarthy, and B. Brewer. Oxford University Press.

Mills, D. L. S., Coffey-Corina, S. A., and Neville, H. J. 1993. Language acquisition and cerebral specialization in 20-month-old infants. *Journal of Cognitive Neuroscience* 5 (3): 317–334.

Mitroff, S. R., Simons, D. J., and Levin, D. T. 2004. Nothing compares 2 views: Change blindness can occur despite preserved access to the changed information. *Perceptual Psychophysics* 66 (8): 1268–1281.

Moore, C. M, and Egeth, H. 1998. Perception without attention: evidence of grouping under conditions of inattention. *Journal of Experimental Psychology: Human Perception and Performance* 23: 339–352.

Mounts, J. R. W., and Tomaselli, R. G. 2005. Competition for representation is mediated by relative attentional salience. *Acta Psychologica* 118: 261–275.

Moutoussis, K., and Zeki, S. 1997. Functional segregation and temporal hierarchy of the visual perceptive systems. *Proceedings of the Royal Society of London* 264: 1407–1414.

Moutoussis, K., and Zeki, S. 2002. The relationship between cortical activation and perception investigated with invisible stimuli. *Proceedings of the National Academy of Sciences* 99 (14): 9527–9532.

Nakayama, K., and Silverman, G. 1986. Attention, pattern recognition, and pop-out visual search. In *The Attentive Brain*, ed. R. Parasuraman. MIT Press.

Nakayama, K. H., Zijiang, J., and Shimojo, S. 1995. Visual surface representation: A critical link between low-level and higher-level vision. In *Visual Cognition*. second edition, ed. S. Kosslyn and D. Osherson. MIT Press.

Navon, D. 1977. Forest before trees: The precedence of global features in visual perception. *Cognitive Psychology* 9: 353–383.

Needham, A., and Baillargeon, R. 2000. Infants' use of featural and experiential information in segregating and individuating objects: A Reply to Xu, Carey, and Welch 1999. *Cognition* 74: 255–284.

Neisser, U. 1976. *Cognition and Reality*. Freeman.

Neisser, U., and Becklen, R. 1975. Selective looking: Attending to visually specified events. *Cognitive Psychology* 7: 480–494.

Nersessian, N. 1984. *Faraday to Einstein: Constructing Meaning in Scientific Theories*. Kluwer.

Newcombe, F., and Ratcliff, G. 1977. Agnosia: A disorder of object recognition. In *Les Syndromes de Disconnection Calleuse chez l'Homme*, ed. F. Michel and B. Scot. Colloque International de Lyon.

Niedeggen, M., Wichmann, P., and Stoerig, P. 2001. Change blindness and time to consciousness. *European Journal of Neuroscience* 14: 1719–1726.

Niederer, J., Maimon, G., and Finlay, B. 1995. Failure to reroute or compress thalamocortical projections after prenatal posterior cortical lesions. *Society for Neuroscience Abstracts* 21.

Nielsen, K. R. K., and Poggio, T. 1984. Vertical image registration in stereopsis. *Vision Research* 24: 1133–1140.

Noa, A. 2003. Causation and perception: The puzzle unravelled. *Analysis* 63 (2): 93–100.

Nobre, A. C., Truett, A., and McCarthy, G. 1994. Word recognition in the human inferior temporal lobe. *Nature* 372: 260–263.

Norman, J. 2002. Two visual systems and two theories of perception: An attempt to reconcile the constructivist and ecological approaches. *Behavioral and Brain Sciences* 25: 73–144.

O'Craven, K. M., Downing, P., and N. Kanwisher 1999. FMRI evidence for objects as the units of attentional selection. *Nature* 401: 584–587.

O'Leary, D. D. M. 1993. Do cortical areas emerge from a protocortex? In *Brain Development and Cognition: A Reader*, ed. M. Johnson. Blackwell.

Olson, C. R., and Gettner, S. N. 1996. Brain representation of object-centered space. *Current Opinion in Neurobiology* 6: 165–170.

Oram, M. W, and Perret, D. I. 1992. The time course of neural responses discriminating between different views of the head and face. *Journal of Neurophysiology* 68: 70–84.

O'Regan, J. K. 1992. Solving the real mysteries of visual perception: The world as an outside memory. *Canadian Journal of Psychology* 46: 461–488.

O'Regan, J. K., and Noë, A. 2001. A sensorimotor account of vision and visual consciousness. *Behavioral and Brain Sciences* 24: 939–1031.

O'Reilly, R. O., and Johnson, M. H. 1994. Object recognition and sensitive periods: A computational analysis of visual Imprinting. *Neural Computation* 6: 357–389.

Palmer, S. E. 1983. The psychology of perceptual organization: A transformational approach. In *Human and Machine Vision*, ed. J. Beck, B. Hope, and A. Rosenfeld. Academic Press.

Palmer, S. E. 1992. Modern theories of gestalt perception. In *Understanding Vision*, ed. G. Humphreys. Blackwell.

Palmer, J., Verghese, P., and Pavel, M. 2000. The psychophysics of visual search. *Vision Research* 40: 1227–1268.

Paquet, L., and Merikle, P. M. 1998. Global processing in attended and non attended objects. *Journal of Experimental Psychology: Human Perception and Performance* 14: 89–100.

Peacocke, C. 1992. *A Study of Concepts*. MIT Press.

Peacocke, C. 1994. Nonconceptual content: Kinds, rationales and relations. *Mind and Language* 9 (4): 419–429.

Peacocke, C. 1998. Nonconceptual content defended. *Philosophy and Phenomenological Research* 58 (2): 381–388.

Peacocke, C. 2001. Does perception have a nonconceptual content? *Journal of Philosophy* 98 (5): 239–269.

Peatfield, M. D., and Marslen-Wilson, W. 1995. Pragmatic effects in zero anaphor resolution: Implications for modularity. In *Proceedings of the Seventeenth Annual Conference of the Cognitive Science Society*, ed. J. Moore and J. Lehman. Erlbaum.

Perret, D. I., Harries, M. H., Benson, P. J., Chitty, A. J., and Mistlin, A. J. 1990. Retrieval of structure from rigid and biological motion: an analysis of the visual responses of neurones in the macaque temporal cortex. In *AI and the Eye*, ed. A. Blake and T. Troscianko. Wiley.

Perrett, D. I., Oram, M. W., Hietanen, J. K., and Benson, P. J. 1994. Issues of representation in object vision. In *The Neuropsychology of Higher Vision: Collated Tutorial Essays*, ed. M. Farah and G. Ratcliff. Erlbaum.

Perry, J. 1977. Frege on demonstratives. *Philosophical Review* 86: 474–497.

Perry, J. 1990. Individuals in informational and intentional content. In *Information, Semantics and Epistemology*, ed. E. Villanueva. Blackwell.

Perry, J. 2001. *Knowledge, Possibility, and Consciousness*. MIT Press.

Peterson, M. A. 1994. Object recognition processes can and do operate before figure-ground organization. *Current Directions in Psychological Science* 3: 105–111.

Peterson, M. A., and Gibson, B. S. 1991. Directing spatial attention within an object: Altering the functional equivalence of shape descriptions. *Journal of Experimental Psychology: Human Perception and Performance* 17: 170–182.

Peterson, M. A., and Gibson, B. S. 1993. Shape recognition contributions to figure ground organization in three-dimensional displays. *Cognitive Psychology* 25: 383–429.

Peterson, M. A., and Gibson B. S. 1994. Object recognition contributions to figure-ground organization: operations and outlines and subjective contours. *Psychological Science* 5: 253–259.

Peterson, M. A., and Hochberg, J. 1983. Opposed set-measurements procedure: A quantitative analysis of the role of local cues and intention in form perception. *Journal of Experimental Psychology: Human Perception and Performance* 9: 183–193.

Petitot, J. 1995) Morphodynamics and attractor syntax: Constituency in visual perception and cognitive grammar. In *Mind as Motion: Explorations in the Dynamics of Cognition*, ed. R. Port and T. Van Gelder. MIT Press.

Poggio, G. F. 1984. Processing of stereoscopic information in primate visual cortex. In *Dynamic Aspects of Neocortical Function*, ed. G. Edelman, W. Cowan, and W. Gall. Wiley.

Poggio, G. F., and Talbot, W. H. 1981. Mechanisms of static and dynamic stereopsis in foveal cortex of the rhesus monkey. Journal *of Physiology* 315: 469–492.

Polat, U., and Shagi, D. 1995. Plasticity and interactions in early vision. In *Maturational Windows and Adult Cortical Plasticity*, ed. B. Julesz and I. Kovacs. Addison-Wesley.

Posner, M. I. 1980. Orienting of attention. *Quarterly Journal of Experimental Psychology.* 32: 3–25.

Posner, M. I., and Carr, T. H. 1992. Lexical access and the brain: Anatomical constraints on cognitive models of word recognition. *American Journal of Psychology* 105: 1–26.

Posner, M. I., and Petersen, S. E. 1990. The Attention system of the human brain. *Annual Review of Neuroscience* 13: 25–42.

Posner, M. I., and Raichle, M. E. 1994. *Images of Mind*. Scientific American.

Posner, M. I., and Rothbart, M. K. 1992: Attentional mechanisms and conscious experience. In *The Neuropsychology of Consciousness*, ed. A. Milner and M. Rugg. Academic Press.

Potter, M. C. 1993. Very short term conceptual memory. *Memory and Cognition* 21 (2): 151–161.

Price, C., Mummery, C. J., Moore, C. J., Frackowiak, R. S. J., and Friston, K. J. 1999. Delineating necessary and sufficient neural systems with functional imaging studies of neuropsychological patients. *Journal of Cognitive Neuroscience* 11 (4): 371–382.

Psillos, S. 1999, *Scientific Realism: How Science Tracks Truth*. Routledge.

Putnam, H. 1975. The meaning of meaning. In *Mind, Language and Reality: Philosophical papers. Vol. 2*. Cambridge University Press.

Putnam, H. 1980: Models and reality. *Journal of Symbolic Logic* 45: 464–482.

Putnam, H. 1981. *Reason, Truth and History*. Cambridge University Press.

Putnam, H. 1983. Reference and truth. In *Realism and Reason: Philosophical Papers, volume 3*. Cambridge University Press.

Putnam, H. 1991. *Representation and Reality*. MIT Press.

Pylyshyn, Z. 1979. The rate of mental rotation of images: a test of a holistic analogue hypothesis. *Memory and Cognition*: 19–28.

Pylyshyn, Z. 1989. The role of location indexes in spatial perception. A sketch of the *FINST* spatial-index model. *Cognition* 32: 65–97.

Pylyshyn, Z. 1994. Some primitive mechanisms of spatial attention. *Cognition* 50: 363–384.

Pylyshyn, Z. 1999. Is vision continuous with cognition? *Behavioral and Brain Sciences* 22: 341–365.

Pylyshyn, Z. 2001. Visual indexes, preconceptual objects, and situated vision. *Cognition* 80: 127–158.

Pylyshyn, Z. 2003. *Seeing and Visualizing: It's Not What You Think*. MIT Press.

Pylyshyn, Z. 2007. *Things and Places: How the Mind Connects with the World*. MIT Press.Pylyshyn, Z., and Storm, R. W. 1988. Tracking multiple independent targets: Evidence for a parallel tracking mechanism. *Spatial Vision* 3: 178–197.

Quartz, S. R., and Sejnowski, T. J. 1997. The neural basis of cognitive development: A constructivist manifesto. *Behavioral and Brain Sciences* 20: 537–556.

Quine, W. V. O. 1960. *Word and Object*. MIT Press.

Quine, W. V. O. 1970. On the reasons for indeterminacy of translation. *Journal of Philosophy* 67: 178–183.Quine, W. V. O 1995. *From Stimulus to Science*. Harvard University Press.

Ramachandran, V. S. 1985. The neurobiology of perception. *Perception* 14: 97–103.

Raftopoulos, A. 1997. Resource limitations in early infancy and its role in successful learning: A connectionist approach. *Human Development* 40 (5): 293–319.

Raftopoulos, A. 2001a. Is perception informationally encapsulated? The issue of the theory-ladenness of perception. *Cognitive Science* 25: 423–451.

Raftopoulos, A. 2001b. Reentrant pathways and the theory-ladenness of observation. *Philosophy of Science* 68: 187–200.

Raftopoulos, A. 2004. Two types of object representations in the brain, one nondescriptive process of reference fixing. *Behavioral and Brain Science* 27 (1): 47–48.

Raftopoulos, A. 2006. Defending realism on the proper ground. *Philosophical Psychology* 19 (1): 1–31.

Raftopoulos, A. 2008. Perceptual systems and realism. *Synthese* 164 (1): 61–91.

Raftopoulos, A., and Muller, V. 2006a. The phenomenal content of experience. *Mind and Language* 27 (2): 187–219.

Raftopoulos, A., and Muller, V. 2006b. Deictic codes, object files, and demonstrative reference. *Philosophical and Phenomenological Research* 72 (2).

Rainer, G., Assad, W. F., and Miller, E. K. 1998. Selective representation of relevant information by neurons in the primate prefrontal cortex. *Nature* 393: 575–579.

Rakic, P. 1988. Specification of cerebral cortical areas. *Science* 241: 170–176.

Ramachandran, V. S. 1985. The neurobiology of perception. *Perception* 14: 97–103.

Recanati, F. 1997. *Direct Reference: From Language to Thought*. Blackwell.

Rensink, R. A. 2000a. The dynamic representation of scenes. *Visual Cognition* 7: 17–42.

Rensink, R. A. 2000b. Seeing, sensing, and scrutinizing. *Vision Research* 40: 1469–1487.

Rensink, R. A. 2002. Change detection. *Annual Review of Psychology* 33: 245.

Rensink, R. A., O'Reagan, J. K., and Clark, J. J. 1997. To see or not to see: The need for attention to perceive changes in scenes. *Psychological Science* 8: 368–373.

Rensink, R. A., O'Reagan, J. K., and Clark, J. J. 2000. On the failure to detect changes in scenes across brief interruptions. *Visual Cognition* 7: 127–145.

Revonsuo, A. 1999. Binding and the phenomenal unity of consciousness. *Consciousness and Cognition* 8: 173–185.

Reynolds, J. H., Chelazzi, L., and Desimone, R. 2000. Attention increases sensitivity in V4 neurons. *Neuron* 26: 703–714.

Reynolds, J. H., and Desimone, R. 2001. Neural mechanisms of attentional selection. In *Visual Attention and Cortical Circuits*, ed. J. Braun, C. Koch, and J. Davis. MIT Press.

Richard, M. 1983. Direct reference and ascriptions of belief. *Journal of Philosophical Logic* 12: 425–452.

Roelfsema, P. R. 2005. Elemental operations in vision. *Trends in Cognitive sciences* 9 (5): 226–233.

Roelfsema, P. R., Lamme, V. A. F., and Spekreijse, H. 1998. Object-based attention in the primary visual cortex of the macaque monkey. *Nature* 395: 376–381.

Roelfsema, P. R., Lamme, V. A. F., and Spekreijse, H. 2000. The implementation of visual routines. *Vision Research* 40: 1385–1411.

Rolls, E., and Tovee, M. 1995. Sparseness of the neuronal representation of stimuli in the primate temporal visual cortex. *Journal of Neurophysiology* 73: 713–726.

Rousselet, G., Fabre-Thorpe, M., and Thorpe, S. 2002. Parallel processing in high-level visual scene categorization. *Nature Neuroscience* 5: 629–630.

Salmon, N. 1981. *Reference and Essence*. Princeton University Press.

Schall, J. D., and Bichot, N. P. 1998. Neural correlates of visual and motor decision processes. *Current Opinions in Neurobiology* 76: 2841–2852.

Schall, J. D., and Hanes, D. P. 1993. Neural basis of saccade target selection in frontal eye field during visual search. *Nature* 366: 467–459.

Scholl, B. J. 2001. Objects and attention: The state of the art. *Cognition* 80: 1–46.

Scholl, B. J., and Leslie, A. M. 1999. Explaining the infant's object concept: Beyond the perception/cognition dichotomy. In *What Is Cognitive Science?* ed. E. Lepore and Z. Pylyshyn. Blackwell.

Scholl, B., Pylyshyn, Z., and Feldman, J. 2001. What is a visual object? Evidence from multiple-object tracking. *Cognition* 80: 159–177.

Sedivy, S. 2004a. Wittgenstein's diagnosis of empiricism's third dogma: Why perception is not an amalgam of sensation and conceptualization. *Philosophical Investigations* 27 (1): 1–33.

Sedivy, S. 2004b. Minds: Contents without vehicles. *Philosophical Psychology* 17 (2): 149–180.

Sellars, W. 1956. Empiricism and the philosophy of mind. In *Minnesota Studies in the Philosophy of Science*, volume 1, ed. H. Feigl and M. Scriven. University of Minnesota Press.

Sellars, W. 1963. *Science, Perception, and Reality*. Routledge and Kegan Paul.

Sergent, C., Baillet, S., and Dehaene, S. 2005. Timing of the brain events underlying access to consciousness during the attentional blink. *Nature: Neuroscience* 8: 1391–1400.

Shepard, R. N., and Cooper, L. A, eds. 1982. *Mental Images and Their transformations*. MIT Press.

Shipp, S. 2004. The brain circuitry of attention. *Trends in Cognitive Sciences* 8 (5): 223–230.

Shoemaker, S. 2002. Introspection and phenomenal character. In *Philosophy of Mind*, ed. D. Chalmers. Oxford University Press.

Shrager, J. 1990. Commonsense perception and the psychology of theory formation. In *Computational Models of Scientific Discovery and Theory Formation*, ed. J. Shrager and P. Langley. Morgan Kaufmann.

Shrager, J., and Johnson, M. H. 1995. Waves of growth in the development of cortical function: A computational model. In *Maturational Windows and Adult Cortical Plasticity*, ed. B. Julesz and I. Kovacs. Addison-Wesley.

Simons, D. J., and D. T. Levin 1997. Change blindness. *Trends in Cognitive Sciences* 1 (7): 261–267.

Simons, D. J., and Rensink, R. A. 2004. Change blindness: Past, present, and future. *Trends in Cognitive Sciences* 9 (1): 16–20.

Smith, A. D. 2002. *The Problem of Perception*. Harvard University Press.

Smith, P. L., and Ratcliff, R. 2004. Psychology and neurobiology of simple decisions. *Trends in Neurosciences* 27 (3): 161–168.

Snowdon, P. 1992. How to interpret direct perception. In *The Contents of Experience: Essays on Perception*, ed. T. Crane. Cambridge University Press.

Soames, S. 2005. *Reference and Description*. Princeton University Press.

Sosa, E. 2003. Beyond internal foundations to external virtues. In L. BonJour and E. Sosa, *Epistemic Justification: Internalism vs. Externalism, Foundations vs. Virtues*. Blackwell.

Spekreijse, H. 2000. Pre-attentive and attentive mechanisms in vision: Perceptual organization and dysfunction. *Vision Research* 40: 1179–1182.

Spelke, E. S. 1988. Object perception. In *Readings in Philosophy and Cognitive Science*, ed. A. Goldman. MIT Press.

Spelke, E. S. 1990. Principles of object perception. *Cognitive Science* 14: 29–56.

Spelke, E. S., Hofsten, C. V., and Kestenbaum, R. 1989. Object perception in infancy: interaction of spatial and Kinetic information for objects boundaries. *Development Psychology* 25: 185–96.

Spelke, E. S., Kestenbaum, R., Simons, Daniel J., and Wein, D. 1995. Spatio-temporal continuity, smoothness of motion and object identity in infancy. *British Journal of Developmental Psychology* 13: 113–142.

Spivey, M. 2007. *The Continuity of Mind*. Oxford University Press.

Stalnaker, R. 1984. *Inquiry*. Cambridge University Press.

Stalnaker, R. 2003. What might nonconceptual content be? In *Essays on Nonconceptual Content*, ed. Y. Gunther. MIT Press.

Stich, S. P. 1985. Could man be an irrational animal? *Synthese* 64: 115–135.

Stiles, J. 1995. Plasticity and development. Evidence from children with early occurring focal brain injury. In *Maturational Windows and Adult Cortical Plasticity*, ed. B. Julesz and I. Kovacs. Addison-Wesley.

Strawson, P. F. 1959. *Individuals*. Methuen.

Super, H., Spekreijse, H., and Lamme, V. A. F. 2001a. Two distinct modes of sensory processing in monkey primary visual cortex (V1). *Nature Neuroscience* 4: 304–310.

Super, H., Spekreijse, H., and Lamme, V. A. F. 2001b. A neural correlate of working memory in the monkey primary cortex. *Science* 293: 120–124.

Super, H., van der Togt, C., Spekreijse, H., and Lamme, V. A. 2003. Internal state of monkey primary visual cortex (V1) predicts figure-ground perception. *Journal of Neuroscience* 23: 3407–3414.

Sur, M., Pallas, S. L., and Roe, A. W. 1990. Cross-modal plasticity in cortical development: Differentiation and specification of sensory neocortex. *Trends in Neuroscience* 13: 227–233.

Taddei-Ferretti, C., Musio, C., Santillo, S., Colucci, R. F., and Cotugno, A. 1996. The top-down contributions of will to the modulation of bottom-up inputs in the reversible perception phenomenon. In *Brain Processes, Theories and Models*, ed. R. Moreno-Diaz and J. Mira-Mira. MIT Press.

Taylor, A. M., and Warrington, E. K. 1971. Visual agnosia: A single case report. *Cortex* 7: 152–161.

Thatcher, R. W. 1992. Cyclic cortical reorganization during early childhood. *Brain and Cognition* 20: 24–50.

Thelen, E., and Smith, L. 1994. *A Dynamic System Approach to the Development of Cognition and Action*. MIT Press.

Thompson, K. G., and Schall, J. D. 1999. The detection of signals by macaque frontal eye field during masking. *Nature Neuroscience* 2: 283–288.

Thompson, K. G., and Schall, J. D. 2000. Antecedents and correlates of visual detection and awareness in macaque prefrontal cortex. *Vision Research* 40: 1523–1538.

Thornton, I. M, and Fernandez-Duque, D. 1999. Representing the "what" and "where" of undetected change. *Abstracts of the Psychonomic Society* 4: 1.

Thorpe, S., Fize, D., and Kutas, M. 1996. Speed of processing in the human visual system. *Nature* 381: 520–522.

Tovee, M. J. 1994. How fast is the speed of thought? *Current Biology* 4: 1125–1127.

Trehub, A. 1994. What does calibration solve? *Behavioral and Brain Sciences* 17: 279–280.

Treisman, A. 1988. Features and objects. *Quarterly Journal of Experimental Psychology* 40: 201–237.

Treisman, A. 1993. The Perception of features and objects. In *Attention: Selection, Awareness and Control*, ed. A. Baddeley and L. Weiskrantz. Oxford University Press.

Treisman, A. 1996. The binding problem. *Current Opinions in Neurobiology* 6: 171–178.

Treisman, A. 2004. Psychological issues in selective attention. In *The Cognitive Neurosciences III*, third edition, ed. M. Gazzaniga. MIT Press.

Treisman, A., and Gelade, G. A feature integration theory of attention. *Cognitive Psychology* 12: 97–136.

Treisman, A., and Kanwisher, N. G. 1998. Perceiving visually presented objects: Recognition, awareness, and modularity. *Current Opinions in Neurobiology* 8: 218–226.

Tremoulet, P., Leslie, A. M., and Hall, D. G. 2000. Infant individuation and identification of objects. *Cognitive Development* 15: 499–522.

Treue, S., and Maunsell, J. H. R. 1996. Attentional modulation of visual motion processing in cortical areas MT and MST. *Nature* 382: 539–541.

Tsotsos, J. K., Culhane, S. M., Wai, W. Yan K., Davis, N., and Vuflo, F. 1995. Modeling visual attention via selective tuning. *Artificial Intelligence* 78: 507–545.

Tye, M. 1995. *Ten Problems of Consciousness*. MIT Press.

Tye, M. 2000. *Consciousness, Color, and Content*. MIT Press.

Tye, M. 2002a. Visual qualia and visual content revisited. In *Philosophy of Mind*, ed. D. Chalmers. Oxford University Press.

Tye, M. 2002b. Representationalism and the transparency of experience. *Nous* 36 (1): 137–151.

Tye, M. 2006. Nonconceptual content, richness and fineness of grain. In *Perceptual Experience*, ed. T. Gendler and J. Hawthorne. Oxford University Press.

Uller, C., Carey, S., Fenner, G. H., and Klatt, L. 1999. What representations underlie infant numerical knowledge? *Cognitive Development* 14: 1–36.

Ulmann, S. 1979. *The Interpretation of Visual Motion*. MIT Press.

Ulmann, A., and Richards, W., eds. 1990. *Image Understanding*. Ablex.

Ungerleider, L., and Haxby, J. 1994. "What" and "where" in the human brain. *Current Opinion in Neurobiology* 4: 157–165.

Ungerleider, L., and Mishkin, M. 1984. Two cortical visual systems. In *Analysis of Visual Behavior*, ed. D. Ingle, M. Goodale, and R. Mansfield. MIT Press.

Usher, M., and Niebur, E. 1996. Modeling the temporal dynamics of IT neurons in visual search: A mechanism for top-down selective attention. *Journal of Cognitive Neuroscience* 8 (4): 311–327.

Van Essen, D. C. 1985. Functional organization of primate visual cortex. In *Cerebral Cortex*, volume 3: *Visual Cortex*, ed. A. Peters and E. Jones. Plenum.

Vecera, P. 2000. Toward a biased competition account of object-based segmentation and attention. *Brain and Mind* 1: 353–384.

Vecera, P., and Farah, J. 1994. Does visual attention select objects or locations? *Journal of Experimental Psychology: General* 123: 146–160.

Vecera, P., and Farah, J. 1997. Is visual image segmentation a bottom-up or an interactive process? *Perception and Psychophysics* 59: 1280–1296.

Vecera, P., and O'Reilly, R. C. 2000. Graded effects in hierarchical figure-ground organization: Reply to Peterson 1999. *Journal of Experimental Psychology: Human Perception and Performance* 26: 1221–1231.

Vision, G. 1997. *Problems of Vision*. Oxford University Press.

Vision, G. 1998. Perceptual content. *Philosophy* 73: 395–427.

Von Hofsten, C., and Spelke, E. S. 1985. Object perception and object-directed reaching in infancy. *Journal of Experimental Psychology: General* 114: 198–212.

Wallach, H., and O'Connell, D. N. 1953. The kinetic depth effect. *Journal of Experimental Psychology* 45: 205–217.

Walsh, V., and Cowey, A. 1998. Magnetic stimulation studies of visual cognition. *Trends in Cognitive Sciences* 2 (3): 103–111.

Warrington, E. K. 1975. The selective impairment of semantic memory. *Quarterly Journal of Experimental Psychology* 27: 635–657.

Warrington, E. K. 1982. Neuropsychological studies in object recognition. *Philosophical Transactions of the Royal Society B* 298: 15–33.

Warrington, E. K., and Taylor, A. M. 1978. Two categorical stages of object recognition. *Perception* 7: 695–705.

Watt, R. J., and Morgan, M. J. 1983. The recognition and representation of edge blur; Evidence for spatial primitives in human vision. *Vision Research* 23 (12): 1465–1477.

Webster, M. J., Behavalier, J., and Ungerleider, L. G. 1995. Development and plasticity of visual memory circuits. In *Maturational Windows and Adult Cortical Plasticity*, ed. B. Julesz and I. Kovacs. Addison-Wesley.

Wiggins, D. 1993. Putnam's doctrine of natural kind words and Frege's doctrine of sense, reference, and extension: Can they cohere? In *Meaning and Reference*, ed. A. Moore. Oxford University Press.

Wittgenstein, L. 1958. *Philosophical Investigations*. Macmillan.

Wolfe, J. M. 1994. Guided search 2.0: A revised model of visual search. *Psychonomic Bulletin and Review* 1: 202–238.

Wolfe, J. M. 1998. What can 1 million trials tell us about visual search? *Psychological Science* 9: 33–39.

Wolfe, J. M. 1999. Inattentional amnesia. In *Fleeting Memories*, ed. V. Coltheart. MIT Press.

Wolfe, J. M., Klempen, N., and Dahlen, K. 2000. Postattentive vision. *Journal of Experimental Psychology: Human Perception and Performance* 26: 693–716.

Wolfe, J. M., Oliva, C., Horowitz, T. S., Butcher, S. J., and Bompas, A. 2002. Segmentation of objects from background in visual search tasks. *Vision Research* 42: 2985–3004.

Wynn, K. 1992. Addition and subtraction by human infants. *Nature* 358: 749–750.

Xu, F., and Carey, S. 1996. Infant's metaphysics: The case of numerical identity. *Cognitive Psychology* 30: 11–153.

Yantis, S. 1995. Perceived continuity of occluded visual objects. *Psychological Science* 6: 182–186.

Yeo. R. M., Yonebayashi, Y., and Allman, J. M. 1995. Perceptual memory of cognitively defined contours: A rapid, robust and long-lasting form of memory. In *Maturational Windows and Adult Cortical Plasticity*, ed. B. Julesz and I. Kovacs. Addison-Wesley.

Zeki, S. M. 1978. Uniformity and diversity of structure and function in rhesus monkey prestriate visual cortex. *Journal of Physiology* 277: 273–290.

Zeki, S. 1981. The mapping of visual function in the cerebral cortex. In *Brain Mechanisms of Sensation*, ed. Y. Katsuki, R. Norgren, and S. Masayasu. Wiley.

Zeki, S. 1993. *A Vision of the Brain*. Blackwell.

Ziegler, J. C., Mireille, B., Arthur, M., and Nazir, T. A. 1997. Word, pseudoword, and nonword processing: A multitask comparison using event-related brain potentials. *Journal of Cognitive Neuroscience* 9 (6): 758–775.

Zipser, K., Lamme, V. A. F., and Schiller, P. H. 1996. Contextual modulation in primary visual cortex. *Journal of Neuroscience* 16: 7376–7389.

Index